Maths Matters 7

Series Editor
Mona Jhunjhunwala

Collins

Maths Matters 7

Series Editor
Mona Jhunjhunwala

Published by Collins Learning
A division of HarperCollins*Publishers* India Private Limited
HarperCollins *Publishers*
A-75, Sector 57, Noida, Uttar Pradesh 201301, India
1 London Bridge Street, London SE1 9GF, United Kingdom
2 Bloor Street East, Toronto, Ontario M4W 1A8, Canada
Lvl 13, 201 Elizabeth Street (PO Box A565, NSW, 1235), Sydney NSW 2000, Australia
195 Broadway, New York, NY 10007, USA

Browse the complete Collins catalogue at **www.collins.in**

First published in 2017

Reprint: 10 9 8 7 6 5 4 3 2

ISBN: 978-93-5264-338-7

Content developed by **ExcelSoft Technologies Pvt. Ltd.**

Artwork by **Mukesh Technologies Pvt. Ltd.**

Layout by **Archetype**

Printed and bound by Saurabh Printers Pvt. Ltd.

Acknowledgements

Cover: shuoshu, iStockphoto

Title Page: shuoshu, iStockphoto

Inside: Page 7: Ani_Ka; 74: GeorgeManga; **112:** lolon; **135:** SireAnko; **219:** shaunl, P_Wei, Whiteway, MapensStudio, yukipon, ymgerman, teenah02, Aleksangel, deomis, omergenc, AlexKalina, putu_leong, timoph, eriksvoboda, neyro2008, Weenee; **223:** anzlyldrm; **247:** GoodGnom; **261:** robuart

Preface

Maths Matters is a series of eight books for Classes 1 to 8. The middle school series is based on the **new syllabus** prescribed by the **Council for the Indian School Certificate Examinations**. In line with the new syllabus, a thematic and structured approach has been followed and all the new topics suggested in the syllabus have been included.

In this updated edition, strong emphasis is placed to develop the ability of investigation, analysis and problem solving. The approach followed in the books would facilitate hands on experiences and enable children to link mathematics with day-to-day life experiences. Following the guidelines laid down in the syllabus, these books aim to enable students to see mathematics as something to talk about, to communicate, to discuss among themselves, to work together on. Sufficient number of solved examples, exercises and mental maths questions are provided to ensure a holistic grasp of the mathematical thought process.

Some Key Features

Why This Theme Matters points out real-life applications of the theme

Let's Get Started to revise the concepts learnt earlier

Hints and Tips for better conceptual understanding

Try These to test student's understanding of the topic covered

Note brings the focus to certain important points

Remember to highlight key points of the concept discussed

Exercise to revise the topics just learnt

Revision Exercise for a well-integrated review of the concepts covered in a chapter

For the Curious Mind to encourage students to think beyond the textual knowledge

Theme Worksheet, after each theme, to reinforce practice with fun exercise

Skill-based Worksheet, after each theme, to develop analytical and problem solving skills

Mental Maths to sharpen the calculation skills and logical reasoning

Project to extend the concept learnt to real–life applications

We would like to take this opportunity to thank all the teachers who reviewed the books and provided their valuable feedback which helped in improving the quality of the content.

Any suggestions or constructive criticism from the users are welcome. We shall try to incorporate those in the future editions.

Authors

Key Features

Why This Theme Matters

Points out real-life applications of the theme

> **Why this Theme Matters**
>
> We are surrounded by numbers. Numb integral part of our life. Also, there is n numbers; they just go on forever. You write them all down!

Mental Maths

To hone the calculation skills and logical reasoning.

> **Mental Maths**
>
> **Chapter 1**
> 1. How many hundreds mak
> 2. How many zeros are ther
> 3. What is the product of th
> 4. What is the difference o
> 5. What is the sum of 2

Try These!

To test student's understanding of the concept

> **Try These!**
>
> 3 × 2 = ____
> 5 × 2 = ____
> 7 × 2 = ____
> 9 × 2 = ____

Note

To bring the focus to certain important points

> **Note**
>
> Bigger objects may not necessarily be heavier than smaller objects. A lock is heavier than a pencil box

Hints and Tips

To provide hints and tips for better understanding of the concept

> **Hints and Tips**
>
> Distinguish between the terms Cost Price and Actual Cost. Always remember that if overhead expenses are mentioned in the question, then Actual cost = CP + Overhead expenses.

Remember

To highlight key points of the concept discussed

> **Remember**
>
> When we subtract 0 from a number, the value of the number remains the same; it does not decrease.
>
> 12345 – 0 = 12345
> 56789 – 0 = 56789

Exercises

To revise the concepts just learnt

> **Exercise 9.2**
>
> 1. A lamp costs ₹835 and a book costs ₹ cost?
>
> | | H | T | O |
> |---|---|---|---|
> | Lamp costs | | | |
> | Book costs | | | |
>
> Thus, both the things cost ₹ ____.
>
> 2. Ram has ₹750. Shyam has ₹525. How have than Shyam?
>
> Ram has ₹ ____.
> Shyam has ₹ ____.
> Thus, Ram has ₹ ____ mo

Revision Exercise

At the end of each chapter for a comprehensive review of the concepts

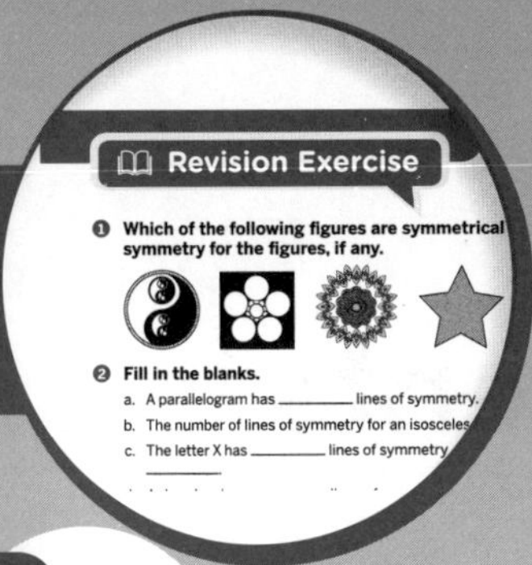

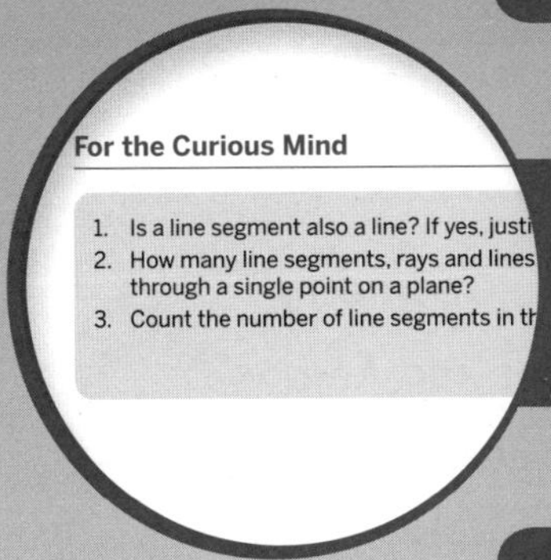

For the Curious Mind

To encourage students to think beyond the textual knowledge

Theme Worksheet

To reinforce practice with fun exercise

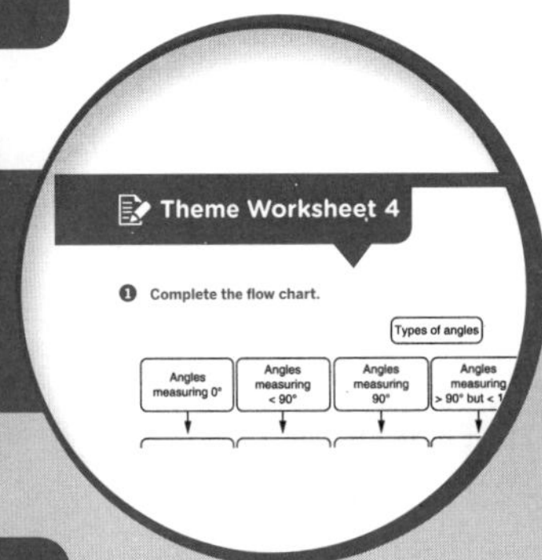

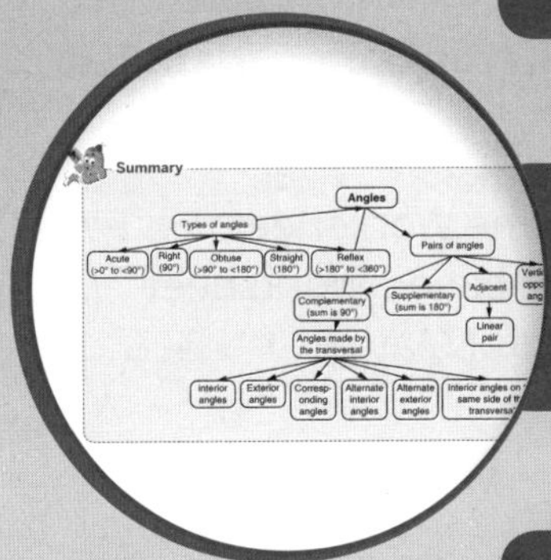

Summary

To provide the gist of the chapter for quick revision

Skill-based Worksheet

To develop analytical and problem solving skills

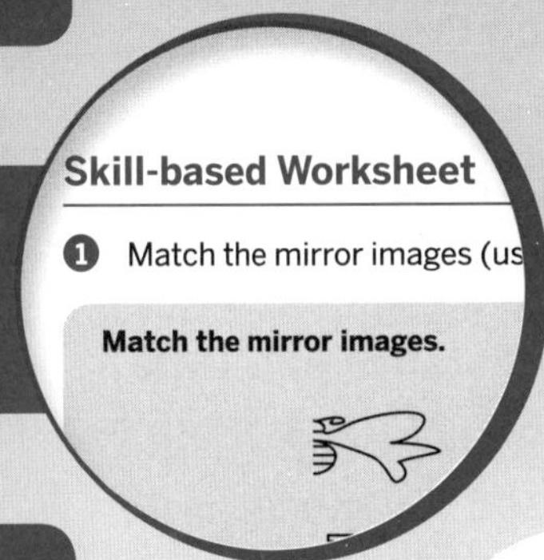

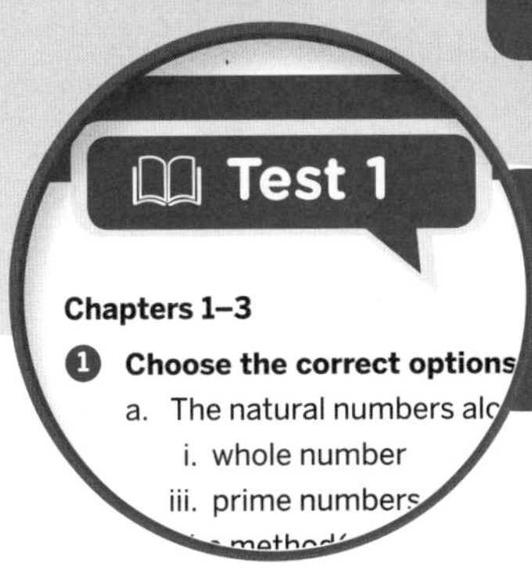

Test Paper

To provide more practice after every few chapters

Collins DigiSuite is an innovative digital solution for teachers. It contains four modules delivering classroom content that can be used to effectively integrate the teaching and evaluation tools with the coursebooks.

The **E-book** includes animations, interactive exercises and worksheets. The E-book reader also includes interactive teaching tools like pen tool, text highlighter, page zoom, search and bookmark.

The **Test Generator** is a question bank with a variety of questions for effective evaluation. It is an easy-to-use assessment tool for the teachers to create test papers and worksheets.

The **Teacher's Resource** consists of lesson plans, answer keys and teaching techniques for the teachers.

This module has a PDF of the **Collins dictionary** appropriate for each level with all the words and definitions one needs.

Contents

Number System

Chapters Covered

1. **Integers**
2. **Rational numbers**
3. **Fractions**
4. **Exponents**
5. **Sets**

Why this Theme Matters

We use numerals 0, 1, 2, 3, 5, 6, 7, 8, and 9 to write numbers. We know numbers are used for counting. But there is much more to numbers. We use them for measuring, labelling, ordering and for coding. Numbers are an integral part of our everyday life. The modern computers use codes of ones and zeros.

The Indian Connection -The Indian mathematician Aryabhata I has the honour of being the first to develop the decimal-based place value system.

Numbers over the centuries have been extended to include, 0, negative numbers, rational numbers and real numbers.

THEME 1

Integers

1

What I shall learn

- To perform basic operations on integers
- To infer the properties of integers
- To solve word problems on integers

Let's Get Started

In our earlier classes, we have learned about numbers less than zero. Such numbers are called **negative numbers** and are denoted as −1, −2, −3, ... Negative numbers are the opposites of positive numbers (1, 2, 3, ...). These numbers help us to distinguish above sea level from below sea level, hot temperature from cold temperature, profit from loss, etc.

Integers

Whole numbers and negative numbers are together known as **integers**. The set of integers is denoted by I or Z.

Integers, Z = {..., −3, −2, −1, 0, 1, 2, 3, ...}

Representation of Integers on the Number Line

Observe the following pattern of numbers.

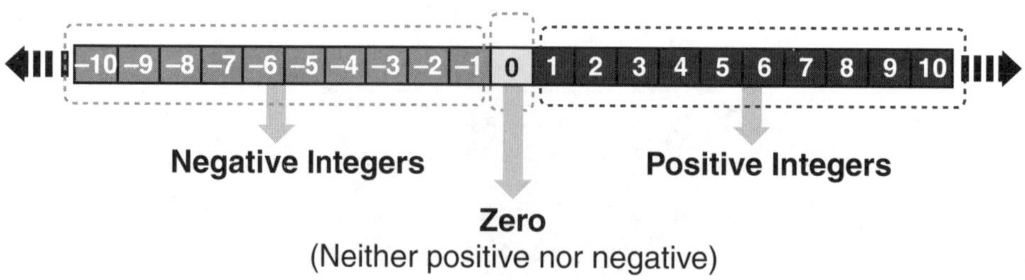

The values of the numbers increase as we move to the right and decrease as we move to the left.

If we represent the above pattern of numbers on a line with equal distances between them, we get the number line representing integers.

Absolute Value of Integers

The absolute value of an integer is the numerical value of the integer regardless of its sign. The symbol for absolute value is two vertical bars on either side of the number.

For example, the absolute value of 5 is 5, that is, $|5| = 5$. Similarly, the absolute value of −5 is also 5, that is, $|-5| = 5$.

Comparison of Integers

1. The positive integers are always greater than the negative integers and zero.
2. The negative integers are always less than the positive integers and zero.
3. For comparing positive integers, the integer with the larger absolute value is greater.
4. For comparing negative integers, the integer with the smaller absolute value is greater.

Examples:

a. $-2 > -4$ because $|-2|$ is smaller than $|-4|$.

b. $-1000 < -10$ because $|-10|$ is smaller than $|-1000|$.

Operations on Integers

Addition of Integers

1. If two numbers have the same sign, we first add them without the sign and then put their sign.

Examples:

a. $+210 + 76 = +286$

b. $-208 + (-28) = -208 - 28 = -236$

2. If two numbers have different signs, we first find the difference between the bigger number and the smaller number (without the signs) and then put the sign of the bigger number.

Examples:

a. $-25 + 10 = -15$

b. $-3210 + 3220 = +10$

3. If there is a '+' sign outside a bracket and we remove the bracket, all the signs inside the bracket remain the same.

Examples:

a. $15 + (+6)$
$= 15 + 6 = 21$

b. $15 + (-6)$
$= 15 - 6 = 9$

4. If there is a '−' sign outside the bracket and we remove the bracket, all the signs inside the bracket change.

Examples: a. $34 - (+8)$ $= 34 - 8 = 26$

b. $34 - (-8)$ $= 34 + 8 = 42$

When adding/subtracting many numbers:

1. Write all the numbers with the '+' sign first.
2. Then, write all the numbers with the '–' sign.
3. Add the positive numbers separately.
4. Add the negative numbers separately.
5. Finally, subtract the 2 numbers with different signs.

Example 1: Simplify the expression $(-80) + (+40) + (-30) + (+60)$.

$-80 + 40 - 30 + 60$

$= 40 + 60 - 80 - 30$

$= 100 - 110$

$= -10$

Subtraction of Integers

We have already learned about the addition of integers. Now, let us learn about subtraction of integers.

For any two integers a and b, $a - b = a + (-b)$.

Example 2: Subtract (–3) from 2.

First, identify the integer that is to be subtracted. In this case, –3 is to be subtracted from 2, that is, we have to find $2 - (-3)$.

$\therefore 2 - (-3) = 2 + 3 = 5$

Example 3: Subtract 15 from 7.

$7 - 15 = -8$

Example 4: Subtract (–22) from (–66).

$-66 - (-22) = -66 + 22 = -44$

Example 5: Subtract (–567) from (–715).

$-715 - (-567)$

$= -715 + 567$

$= -148$

Example 6: Simplify the expression $(-16) - (+17) - (-34)$.

$(-16) - (+17) - (-34)$

$-16 - 17 + 34$

$= -33 + 34 = +1$

Exercise 1.1

1 Write each group of integers in the ascending order.

a. –6, –51, 6, 0, –3, 8, –1

b. –263, +632, –623, +236, –633, +266

2 Write each group of integers in the descending order.

a. 0, –1, –5, –113, –13, 1, –2

b. +157, +517, –511, –517, +511, –571

3 **Find all the integers that lie between each of the two integers. Also represent them on the number line.**

a. −1, 3 b. 7, 6 c. −6, −2 d. −2, −7

4 **Simplify the following expressions.**

a. (−7) + (−14) + 8 + 17 b. (−20) + (+24) + (−15) + (18)

c. 90 + (−38) + (−10) + (−27) d. 25 + (−25) + (−20) + (+17) + (−1)

5 **Simplify the following expressions.**

a. (−8) − (7) − (+4) b. (−17) + 47 − 12 − 7

c. (−10) + (−13) + (−31) d. 90 − (−100) − (42)

Multiplication of Integers

We know that the multiplication of whole numbers is repeated addition.

For example,

$$4 \times 6 = 4 + 4 + 4 + 4 + 4 + 4 = 24$$

Now let us learn how two multiply two integers.

Case 1: **Multiplication of two positive integers**

Observe the following table.

Example	Sign of the First Number	Sign of the Second Number	Sign of the Product
(5) x (3) = 15	+	+	+
(2) x (9) = 18	+	+	+
(6) x (4) = 24	+	+	+

- What do you observe?
- Is the product of two positive numbers positive?

The product of two positive integers is always a positive integer.

For any two positive integers *a* and *b* we can say $a \times b = ab$, where *ab* is always positive.

Case 2: **Multiplication of a positive and a negative integer**

Complete the following table. A few examples have been done for you.

Example	Sign of the First Number	Sign of the Second Number	Sign of the Product
(3) × (−4) = −12	+	−	−
(−4) × 6 = −24	−	+	−
12 × (−8) = −96			

What is the product of a positive and a negative number?

The product of a positive and a negative integer is always a negative integer.

For any two positive integers a and b, we can say $a \times (-b) = (-a) \times b = -(a \times b)$.

Case 3: Multiplication of two negative integers

Observe the pattern carefully and complete the following table.

Example	Sign of the First Number	Sign of the Second Number	Sign of the Product
$(-4) \times (-4) = 16$	−	−	+
$(-5) \times (-6) = 30$	−	−	+
$(-11) \times (-8) =$			

The product of two negative integers is a positive integer.

For any two positive integers a and b, $(-a) \times (-b) = a \times b$.

Example 7: What will be the sign of the product in the following multiplication problems?

(a) $-9 \times +8$ (b) -5×-7

The sign of the product will be as follows:

(a) Negative (−) (b) Positive (+)

Examples 8: Solve $(+7) \times (+31)$.

$(+7) \times (+31) = 217$

Examples 9: Solve $(-14) \times (-23)$.

$(-14) \times (-23) = 322$

Examples 10: Solve $(+710) \times (-16)$.

$(+710) \times (-16) = -11360$

Exercise 1.2

1. **Find the products of the following.**
   - a. 3 by 6
   - b. (−5) by 2
   - c. (−1) by (−4)
   - d. (−9) by (6)
   - e. 7 by (−4)
   - f. 81 by (−2)
   - g. $(-24) \times 0 \times (-8)$
   - h. $(-21) \times (-10) \times (+9)$
   - i. $(-2) \times (-4) \times (-6) \times (+10)$
   - j. $(-1) \times (-3) \times (-5) \times (-7)$

Division of Integers

In previous classes, we have learned about division of whole numbers.

You know that **division is the inverse operation of multiplication.** Now, let us extend the same for integers.

Observe the example and write the corresponding division statements for the multiplication statements in the following table.

Multiplication Statement	Corresponding Division Statements	
(First number × Second number = Product)	Statement 1 (Product ÷ First number)	Statement 2 (Product ÷ Second number)
$(3) \times (-4) = -12$	$-12 \div 3 = (-4)$	$-12 \div (-4) = 3$
$(-5) \times (-7) = 35$		
$(-2) \times (8) = -16$		
$(7) \times (4) = 28$		
$(-9) \times (-3) = 27$		

Observe the following.

$a \div (-b)$	$(-a) \div (b)$	$-(a \div b)$
$12 \div (-4) = -3$	$(-12) \div 4 = -3$	$-(12 \div 4) = -3$
$18 \div (-9) = -2$	$(-18) \div 9 = -2$	$-(18 \div 9) = -2$
$25 \div (-5) = -5$	$(-25) \div 5 = -5$	$-(25 \div 5) = -5$

Is $a \div (-b) = (-a) \div b = -(a \div b)$ true for any integers a and b?

Therefore, division of a positive and a negative integer results in a negative integer.

$(-a) \div (-b)$	$a \div b$
$(-12) \div (-4) = 3$	$12 \div 4 = 3$
$(-18) \div (-9) = 2$	$18 \div 9 = 2$
$(-25) \div (-5) = 5$	$25 \div 5 = 5$

Is $(-a) \div (-b) = a \div b$ true for any integers a and b?

Therefore, division of two negative integers results in a positive integer.

Example 11: Divide the following.

a. 198 by 6

$$198 \div 6 = \frac{198}{6} = 33$$

b. (−432) by 8

$$(-432) \div 8 = \frac{-432}{8} = -54$$

c. (−732) by (−12)

$$(-732) \div (-12) = \frac{-732}{-12} = 61$$

d. 891 by (−11)

$$891 \div (-11) = \frac{891}{-11} = -81$$

Exercise 1.3

1 **Carry out the following divisions.**

a. 8 by (−2)	b. (−4) by 2	c. (−9) by (−9)
d. (−6) by 3	e. 8 by (−4)	f. 62 by (−2)
g. (−81) by 9	h. (−99) by (−9)	i. (+544) ÷ (+8)
j. (−306) ÷ (+9)	k. (−102) ÷ (−17)	l. (+112) ÷ (−16)

Properties of Integers

We have learned about different properties of different operations for whole numbers.

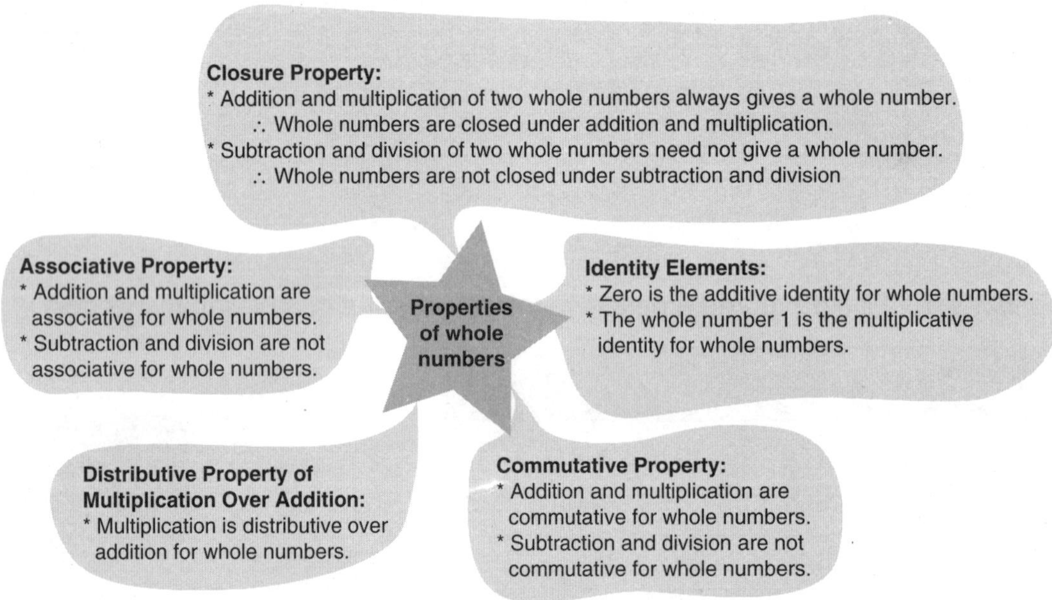

Now, let us check whether these properties hold for integers or not.

Closure Property

Under addition: Observe the following examples.

(−8) + 2 = (−6) 15 + (−10) = 5 7 + 3 = 10 −25 + (−20) = −45

Is the addition of two integers an integer?

Are integers closed under addition?

In general, for any two integers *a* and *b*, *a* + *b* is also an integer.

We observe that integers are closed under addition.

Under subtraction: Now, evaluate the following problems. One has been done for you.

$10 - 5 = 5$ | $7 - 20 = (\ \ )$ | $-50 - (-20) = (\ \ )$ | $10 - (-3) = (\ \ )$

Is the subtraction of two integers an integer?

Are integers closed under subtraction?

In general, for any two integers *a* and *b*, $a - b$ is also an integer.

We observe that integers are closed under subtraction.

Under multiplication: Complete the multiplication problems below. One has been done for you.

$10 \times 5 = 50$ | $(-3) \times (-18) = (\ \ )$ | $10 \times (-8) = (\ \ )$ | $(-13) \times 19 = (\ \ )$

Is the product of two integers an integer?

Are integers closed under multiplication?

In general, $a \times b$ is also an integer for all integers *a* and *b*.

We observe that integers are closed under multiplication.

Under division: Again, let us check the closure property for division of two integers. Complete the following division table. One has been done for you.

$56 \div 8 = 7$	$4 \div 24 = (\ \ )$
$(-42) \div (-12) =$	$(-36) \div 6 = (\ \ )$
$(-4) \div (-16) = (\ \ )$	$(-600) \div (-50) = (\ \ )$

In general, for any two integers *a* and *b*, where *b* is not zero, $a \div b$ need not be an integer.

Is the division of two integers an integer?

Are integers closed under division?

We observe that integers are not closed under division.

Do it yourself

Complete the following table by putting ✓ or ✗.

Numbers	**Closed Under**			
	Addition	Subtraction	Multiplication	Division
Integers				

Commutative Property

Under addition: Take any two integers and write them under columns *a* and *b*. Then, find *a* + *b* and *b* + *a*.

a	*b*	*a* + *b*	*b* + *a*	Is *a* + *b* = *b* + *a*? (Yes/No)
+7	−10	−3	−3	Yes
−5	+8			
+2	+4			
−2	−7			

Is addition commutative for integers?

We can observe that two integers can be added in any order. Therefore, addition is commutative for integers. It is called the **commutative property of addition**.

In general, for any two integers *a* and *b*, $a + b = b + a$.

Under subtraction: Take any two integers and write them under columns *a* and *b*. Then, find the value of $a - b$ and $b - a$. Also, check whether $a - b = b - a$. One has been done for you.

a	*b*	*a* − *b*	*b* − *a*	Is *a* − *b* = *b* − *a*? (Yes/No)
+7	−10	17	−17	No
−5	+8			
+2	+4			
−2	−7			

Is subtraction commutative for integers?

In general, for any two distinct integers *a* and *b*, $a - b \neq b - a$.

We observe that integers are not commutative under subtraction.

Under multiplication: Now, let us check the commutative property for the product of two integers. For the given integers *a* and *b*, find the values of $a \times b$ and $b \times a$. Also, check whether $a \times b = b \times a$. Complete the following table. One has been done for you.

a	*b*	*a* × *b*	*b* × *a*	Is *a* × *b* = *b* × *a*? (Yes/No)
+7	−10	−70	−70	Yes
5	2			
−3	8			
12	−4			

Is multiplication commutative for Integers?

In general, for any two integers *a* and *b*, $a \times b = b \times a$.

We observe that integers are commutative under multiplication.

Under division: For the given non-zero integers a and b, find $a \div b$ and $b \div a$. Also, check whether $a \div b$ and $b \div a$ are equal. Enter the answers in the following table. One has been done for you.

a	b	a ÷ b	b ÷ a	Is a ÷ b = b ÷ a? (Yes/No)
−4	2	−2	$-\frac{1}{2}$	
−3	−3			
8	−9			
−4	−6			

Are all the values in the columns $a \div b$ and $b \div a$ integers? Observe the last column.

Is division commutative for integers?

We observe that integers are not commutative under division.

In general, for any two distinct integers a and b, $a \div b \neq b \div a$.

Do it Yourself

Complete the following table by putting ✓ or ✗.

Numbers	Commutative Under			
	Addition	Subtraction	Multiplication	Division
Integers				

Associative Property

Under addition: Observe the following examples.

Example 12: Consider three negative integers, say −4, −2 and −7. Then, find whether $(-4) + [(-2) + (-7)] = [(-4) + (-2)] + (-7)$.

Now, let us verify by actual addition.

$$(-4) + [(-2) + (-7)] = [(-4) + (-2)] + (-7)$$
$$(-4) + [-9] = [-6] + (-7)$$
$$-13 = -13$$

Therefore, addition of integers is associative.

In general, for any integers a, b and c, we can say that $a + (b + c) = (a + b) + c$.

Under subtraction: Consider any three integers, for example, 6, 5 and 2.

$6 - (5 - 2) = 6 - 3 = 3$

$(6 - 5) - 2 = 1 - 2 = -1$

Therefore, we can observe that $6 - (5 - 2) \neq (6 - 5) - 2$. That is, subtraction of integers is not associative.

In general, for any three distinct integers a, b and c, $a - (b - c) \neq (a - b) - c$.

Under multiplication: Take any three integers and write them under columns *a*, *b* and *c*. Then, find the value of $(a \times b)$, $(a \times b) \times c$, $(b \times c)$ and $a \times (b \times c)$ and write them in the given table. Also, check whether $a \times (b \times c) = (a \times b) \times c$. One has been done for you.

a	b	c	(b × c)	a × (b × c)	(a × b)	(a × b) × c	Is a × (b × c) = (a × b) × c? (Yes/No)
+7	–10	–6	60	420	–70	420	Yes

You can observe that, the product of the three integers is the same irrespective of the order. Therefore, multiplication is associative for integers.

In general, for any three integers a, b and c, $a \times (b \times c) = (a \times b) \times c$.

Under division: Observe the following example.

Consider any three integers, say, 16, 8 and 2, we have:

$16 \div (8 \div 2) = 16 \div 4 = 4$ and $(16 \div 8) \div 2 = 2 \div 2 = 1$

$\therefore 16 \div (8 \div 2) \neq (16 \div 8) \div 2$

From the above example, we observe that integers are not associative under division.

In general, for any three distinct non-zero integers a, b and c, $a \div (b \div c) \neq (a \div b) \div c$.

Do it Yourself

Complete the following table by putting ✓ or ✗.

Numbers	Associative Under			
	Addition	Subtraction	Multiplication	Division
Integers				

Special Properties of Zero and 1

Under addition:

1. **Property of 1 or Successor of an integer**

   Addition of 1 to any integer gives its successor.

   Examples: $4 + 1 = 5$, $-3 + 1 = -2$

Hence, 5 is the successor of 4 and −2 is the successor of −3.

In general, for any integer a, $a + 1$ is called the successor of a.

2. **Additive Identity**

Complete the following.

16 + ( ) = 16; 0 + ( ) = 19; −5 + ( ) = −5

You can observe that when you add zero to any integer, you get the same integer.

The **additive identity** for integers is that number which when added to any integer gives the same integer. Hence, 0 is the additive identity.

In general, for any integer a, $a + 0 = 0 + a = a$.

3. **Additive Inverse**

The **additive inverse** of an integer is that number which when added to its opposite gives the result as zero.

Therefore, an integer and its opposite are called **additive inverse** of each other.

Example: 5 + (−5) = 0 = (−5) + 5

Hence, 5 and −5 are additive inverse of each other.

In general, for any integer a, $-a$ is its opposite (or vice-versa) such that $a + (-a) = 0 = (-a) + a$

Under subtraction:

1. **Property of 1 or Predecessor of an integer**

Subtraction of 1 from any integer gives its predecessor.

Example: 8 − 1 = 7; (−2) − 1 = (−3)

Hence, 7 is predecessor of 8 and (−3) is predecessor of (−2).

In general, for any integer a, $a - 1$ is called the predecessor of a.

2. **Property of Zero**

Subtraction of 0 from any integer gives the same integer.

Example: 9 − 0 = 9; (−3) − 0 = (−3)

In general, for any integer a, $a - 0 = a$.

Under multiplication:

Look at the integer multiplication table below:

×	−5	−4	−3	−2	−1	0	1	2	3	4	5
−5	25	20	15	10	5	0	−5	−10	−15	−20	−25
−4	20	16	12	8	4	0	−4	−8	−12	−16	−20
−3	15	12	9	6	3	0	−3	−6	−9	−12	−15
−2	10	8	6	4	2	0	−2	−4	−6	−8	−10
−1	5	4	3	2	1	0	−1	−2	−3	−4	−5
0	0	0	0	0	0	0	0	0	0	0	0
1	−5	−4	−3	−2	−1	0	1	2	3	4	5
2	−10	−8	−6	−4	−2	0	2	4	6	8	10
3	−15	−12	−9	−6	−3	0	3	6	9	12	15
4	−20	−16	−12	−8	−4	0	4	8	12	16	20
5	−25	−20	−15	−10	−5	0	5	10	15	20	25

Observe the coloured row and column.

$0 \times 0 = (\quad)$

$-100 \times 0 = (\quad)$

1. **Property of Zero**

The product of any integer with zero is zero.

In general, for any integer *a*, $a \times 0 = 0 \times a = 0$

$(-3) \times 1 = (\quad)$

$(-5) \times 4 = (\quad)$

2. **Multiplicative Identity**

Now, what is the product of any integer say *a* and 1?
What is the product of 1 and *a*?

The answer is *a*.

Therefore, 1 is the **multiplicative identity** for integers.

The **multiplicative identity** for integers is that number which when multiplied by any integer gives the same integer.

In general, for any integer *a*, $a \times 1 = 1 \times a = a$.

3. **Multiplicative Inverse**

The product of any non-zero integer and its reciprocal gives the result as 1.

Example: For any integer, say 5, its reciprocal is $\frac{1}{5}$.
Therefore, $5 \times \frac{1}{5} = 1$ (Multiplicative Identity).

Hence, 5 and $\frac{1}{5}$ are multiplicative inverse of each other.

In general, if *a* is any non-zero integer, then $a \times \frac{1}{a} = \frac{1}{a} \times a = 1$.

Under division:

1. **Property of 1**

Division by 1 gives the same integer as the quotient.

Examples: $5 \div 1 = 5$, $(-15) \div 1 = (-15)$.

In general, if a is any integer, then $a \div 1 = a$.

2. **Property of Zero**

When zero is divided by any non-zero integer, the result is always zero.

Examples: $0 \div 5 = 0$; $0 \div (-7) = 0$

In general, if a is any non-zero integer, then $0 \div a = 0$.

Solved Examples

Example 13: Verify $[7 \times (-5)] \times 6 = 7 \times [(-5) \times 6]$.

Consider LHS $= [7 \times (-5)] \times 6 = (-35) \times 6 = -210$

RHS $= 7 \times [(-5) \times 6] = 7 \times (-30) = -210$

$\therefore$ LHS = RHS

$\therefore [7 \times (-5)] \times 6 = 7 \times [(-5) \times 6]$

Hence, verified.

Exercise 1.4

1 Fill in the blanks.

a. (−9) + (______) = (5) + (______)

b. (______) + 25 = 0

c. 12 − (______) = 24

d. (______) + (−15) = (______) + (−3)

e. (−54) − (−21) = − (______)

f. (−255) ÷ ______ is not defined

g. (−21) ÷ ______ = −21

h. ______ ÷ (−98) = 0

2 Evaluate the following.

a. $(-1) \times (-2) \times (-3) \times (-4) \times (-5)$

b. $(-1) \times (-5) \times (-4) \times (-6)$

c. $-245 + 90 + (-140)$

d. $(-9) \times 5 \times (-1) \times 1$

3 Subtract the sum of −1878 and 878 from 2000.

4 What will be the value of a if $a \times (-2) = (-30)$?

5 The product of two integers is −51. If one integer is −17, find the other.

Distributive Law

Distributive law of multiplication over addition.

Multiplication of integers is distributive over addition.

For any integers a, b and c, we have $a \times (b + c) = (a \times b) + (a \times c)$.

Example 14: Use distributive property of multiplication of integers and simplify the following. $18 \times [7 + (-3)]$.

According to the distributive property, we have $a \times (b + c) = (a \times b) + (a \times c)$.

$$18 \times [7 + (-3)] = (18 \times 7) + (18 \times -3) = 126 + (-54) = 126 - 54 = 72$$

Therefore, $18 \times [7 + (-3)] = 72$.

Distributive law of multiplication over subtraction

Multiplication of integers is distributive over subtraction.

For any integers a, b and c, we have $a \times (b - c) = (a \times b) - (a \times c)$.

Example 15: Use distributive property of multiplication of integers and evaluate

$(-21) \times [(-4) - (-6)]$.

According to distributive property, we have, $a \times (b - c) = (a \times b) - (a \times c)$.

$$(-21) \times [(-4) - (-6)] = (-21 \times -4) - (-21 \times -6) = 84 - 126 = -42$$

Therefore, $(-21) \times [(-4) - (-6)] = -42$.

Exercise 1.5

1 Verify the distributive property of multiplication of integers over addition and subtraction for the values of a, b and c given in the table.

a	b	c
−2	5	−3
7	−9	−11
−24	−12	−5

2 Evaluate the following.

(a) $12 \div [(13) + (-13)]$

(b) $[(56) \div (-2)] \div (-4)$

(c) $[(-100) + (60)] \div [(29) - (9)]$

(d) $(-6) \div [(36) \div (-12)]$

3 Complete the puzzle.

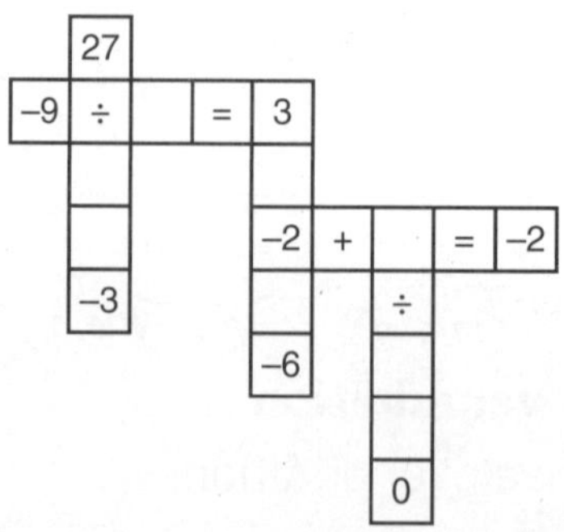

Word Problems

We have learnt different operations on integers and their properties. Let us solve some problems on them.

Example 16: Mithra has attempted civil services preliminary exam in which every correct answer is assigned +2 marks and for every 3 incorrect answers 2 marks will be reduced. No negative marking for questions that are not attempted. Out of 180 questions if she has answered 130 correct, 45 wrong and left 20 un-attempted what is her score?

Number of questions answered correctly = 130

Marks assigned for each correct answer = 2

Total marks scored for correct answers = 130 × 2 = 260

Number of questions answered incorrectly = 45

For every 3 incorrect answers 2 marks are deducted.

Therefore, for 45 incorrect answers the marks that are deducted is $\left(\frac{45}{3}\times 2\right) = 15 \times 2 = 30$

Hence, the total score of Mithra in the civil services preliminary exam is 260 – 30 = 230.

Example 17: A submarine has reached 5200 ft below the sea level. If it rises at a rate of 15 ft per minute, what is the position of the submarine after 2 hours?

Depth of the submarine = –5200 ft (5200 ft below the sea level)

Rate at which the submarine is rising = 15 ft per minute = 15 ft × 60 per hour = 900 ft per hour

Distance travelled by the submarine in 2 hours = 2 × 900 ft = 1800 ft.

The position of the submarine after 2 hours = –5200 ft + 1800 ft = –3400 ft.

Therefore, the submarine is at a depth of 3400 ft below the sea level after 2 hours.

Example 18: Sharan has taken a loan of amount ₹2,00,000 from 4 different banks. If he has taken the same amount from all the banks what is the loan amount in each bank?

Total loan amount = ₹2,00,000

Loan amount in each bank = ₹2,00,000 ÷ 4 = ₹50,000

Example 19: At 5 a.m., the temperature in Country A was –4°C. At 11 a.m., the temperature was 3°C.

a. By how many degrees did the temperature rise?

b. The temperature in Country B was 2°C lower than that in Country A at 5 a.m. What was the temperature in Country B at 5 a.m.?

a. Temperature at 5 a.m. in Country A = −4°C
Temperature at 11 a.m. = 3°C
Therefore, rise in temperature = 3°C − (−4°C) = 3°C + 4°C = 7°C
So, the temperature rose by 7°C.

b. Temperature at 5 a.m. in Country B = −4°C − 2°C = −4°C + (−2°C) = −6°C
So, the temperature in Country B at 5 a.m. was −6°C.

Example 20: The temperature in a fridge is −4°C. When the electricity supply gets turned off, the temperature rises by 3°C every hour. What is the temperature in the fridge 3 hours after the electricity is turned off?

Initial temperature = −4°C.

After 3 hours, the temperature in the fridge = −4 + 3 + 3 + 3 = −4 + 9 = 5°C

Exercise 1.6

Solve the following word problems.

1. The statement of account of a savings account of Ms. Ananya is as follows. Fill in the blank spaces.

Ms. Ananya,
6th cross, 3rd Main,
MR Nagar,
Bangalore.

Account No: xxxxxxxxx3075

From: 1/06/2018 To: 5/06/2018 Statement of account

Date	Narration	Withdrawal amt.	Deposit Amt.	Closing Balance
01/06/2018	Salary Credited		10,000.00	10,000.00
02/06/2018	Monthly EMI	2500.00		
03/06/2018	NEFT Cr.		3,500.00	
04/06/2018	ATM Withdrawl	5,000.00		
05/06/2018	Monthly Interest Credit		120.00	

What is the balance amount as on 05 June 2018?

2. The highest record in long jump at a particular place is 9 m. If Mr. X has recorded 7 m in long jump, by how much is he short to reach the record?

3. In a competitive exam consisting of 100 questions, each correct answer gets 2 marks and each wrong answer gets −1 mark. If a student has written 70 correct answers and 30 wrong answers, what is his/her score?

4. A submarine has gone 4000 ft deep into the sea. If it rises at a rate of 30 ft per minute what is its position after 45 minutes?

Summary

1. Whole numbers and negative numbers are together known as integers. $Z = W \cup Z^-$
2. The absolute value of an integer is the numerical value of the integer regardless of its sign.
3. For integers, zero is the additive identity and 1 is the multiplicative identity.
4. Two distinct numbers are said be additive inverse of each other if their sum is 0.
5. a. Distributivity under multiplication over addition $a \times (b + c) = (a \times b) + (a \times c)$

   b. Distributivity under multiplication over subtraction $a \times (b - c) = (a \times b) - (a \times c)$
6. For any integer a, $a \div 1 = a$ and $a \div a = 1$ $(a \neq 0)$; $a \div 0$ is not defined but $0 \div a = 0$ for $a \neq 0$.

For the Curious Mind

A frog fell into a 20-metre deep well. Each day, it managed to climb up 3 metres, but the same night, it would slip back 2 metres. How many days did it take to get out of the well?

Revision Exercise

1 **State whether the following statements are true or false.**

a. The smallest integer is not defined.

b. The smallest positive integer is 1.

c. Zero is both a non-negative and a non-positive integer.

d. −6 is on the right side of −3 on a number line.

e. 1 is the additive identity element.

2 **Match the following.**

i. $a + (-a) = (-a) + a = 0$	a. Closure property
ii. $a \times b = b \times a$	b. Commutative property
iii. $a \times 1 = 1 \times a = a$	c. Associative property
iv. $a + (b + c) = (a + b) + c$	d. Existence of identity
v. $a \times (b + c) = (a \times b) + (a \times c)$	e. Existence of inverse
	f. Distributive property

3 **Write all the integers between each of the given pairs in ascending order.**

a. −5 and 1 b. 3 and −3 c. −1 and −9

4 **Simplify the following expressions.**

a. (−1100) + (+232) b. −405 + (−150) c. 48 + (−10) + (−19) + (−9)

5 **Simplify the following expressions.**

a. 720 − (256) b. 852 − (−951) c. (−25) − (−75) − (+29) − (+14)

6 **Simplify the following expressions.**

a. 1969×-11 b. $-6 \times -18 \times -10$ c. $-7 \times 15 \times 0 \times -5$

7 **Divide the following.**

a. 1331 by −11 b. −3888 by −18 c. 0 by 357 d. −1728 by 1728

8 A certain type of liquid freezes at −16°C. The frozen liquid is heated by 5°C every 30 minutes. Find the temperature of the liquid after two hours of heating?

9 **Verify the following.**

a. $[(-15) + (+7)] + (+8) = (-15) + [(+7) + (+8)]$

b. $(-15) \times (+7) = (+7) \times (-15)$

c. $[(+3) + (-4)] \times (-5) = [(+3) \times (-5)] + [(-4) \times (-5)]$

d. $[(-21) \times (-16)] + [(-21) \times (-4)] = (-21) \times [(-16) + (-4)]$

10 **Complete the following statements and state the property used.**

a. 31 + _____ = 31 b. −17 × _____ = −17

c. _____ $\times 1 = 16$

d. $59 + [25 + (-18)] = [$_____ $+$ _____$] + (-18)$

e. $(-12) +$ _____ $= 0$

f. $65 +$ _____ $= 0$

g. $145 \times$ _____ $= (-37) \times 145$

h. $(-36) + 112 =$ _____ $+ (-36)$

11 **State whether the following statements are true or false. Give reasons.**

a. $(-21) + 13 = 13 + (-21)$

b. $5100 \times 1024 = 1024 \times 5100$

c. $34 - (9 - 15) = (34 - 9) - 15$

d. $28 \times (31 \times 11) = (28 \times 31) \times 11$

e. $56 - 32 = 32 - 56$

f. $81 \div (-8) = (-8) \div 81$

12 **In a test, (+4) marks are given for every correct answer and (−2) marks are given for every incorrect answer. Answer the following.**

a. Amrita scored 30 marks. If she got 10 correct answers, how many questions did she answer incorrectly?

b. Babu answered all the questions in a test and scored (−14) marks through 4 correct answers. How many incorrect answers did Babu give?

13 **A page from Karan's bank passbook shows the following entries for the month of March.**

Date	Narration	Withdrawal	Deposit
03/03/2015	Salary for the month		₹17,500
05/03/2015	House expenditure	₹12,000	
10/03/2015	Cheque deposited		₹1700
20/03/2015	Cash from ATM	₹6000	

Find Karan's bank balance as on 20/03/2015.

14 **Complete the given diagram in each of the following.**

a. The three numbers on each line add up to a total of −5.

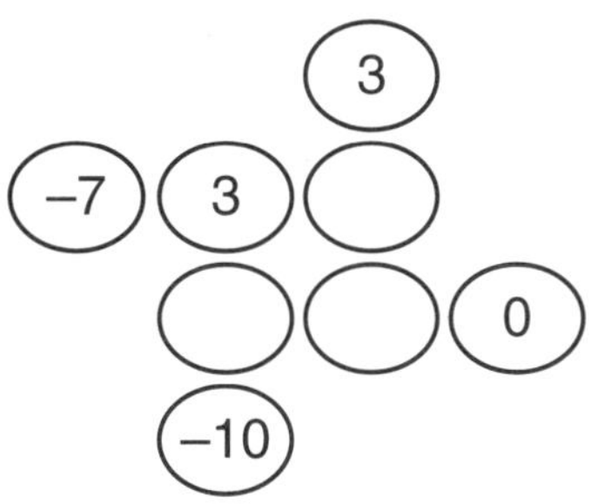

b. The sum of the numbers in a line is equal to zero.

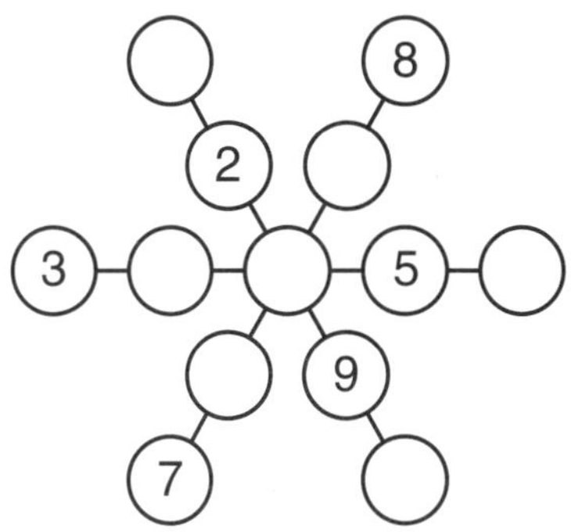

THEME 1

Rational Numbers

2

What I shall learn

- To define rational numbers and to represent them on a number line
- To compare, add, subtract, multiply and divide rational numbers
- To represent rational numbers as decimals
- To solve word problems on rational numbers and decimal fractions

Let's Get Started

Observe the following examples:

1. $8 - 8 = (0)$	2. $(-9) + 4 = (-5)$
3. $15 - 11 = (4)$	4. $42 + (-12) = (30)$
5. $3 - 9 = (-6)$	6. Find x if $3x + 7 = 0$, $x = \left(\frac{-7}{3}\right)$
7. $\frac{1}{8} - \frac{1}{6} = \left(-\frac{1}{24}\right)$	8. Find x if $2x + 3 = 8$ $x = \left(\frac{5}{2}\right)$
9. $\frac{3}{7} - \frac{1}{4} = \left(\frac{5}{28}\right)$	10. $(-23) - (-13) = (-10)$
11. $(-7) + (7) = (0)$	12. $(6) - (4) = (2)$

- The numbers 2, 4, 30 can be placed in natural numbers, whole numbers and integers group.
- The numbers –10, –6, –5, 0, 2, 4, 30 can only be placed in the integers group.

Natural Numbers	Whole Numbers	Integers	Others
2, 4, 30	0, 2, 4, 30	–10, –6, –5, 0, 2, 4, 30	$-\frac{1}{24}, -\frac{7}{3}, \frac{5}{28}, \frac{5}{2}$

Look at the numbers that are in **Others group**. What type of numbers are these? Are these fractions?

Observe that these numbers cannot be placed either in the group of integers or whole numbers or natural numbers. Among the four answers in the others group, $\frac{5}{2}$ and $\frac{5}{28}$ are fractions but the other two are not fractions because they have negative sign. These numbers form a new group of numbers known as **rational numbers**.

A rational number is defined as a number that can be expressed in the form $\frac{p}{q}$, where p and q are integers and $q \neq 0$. The integer p is called the numerator and the integer q is called the denominator.

For example, the number $-\frac{1}{24}$ is a rational number. Here, $p = -1$ and $q = 24$. The numbers $\frac{3}{4}$, $\frac{7}{1}$, $\frac{0}{1}$ and $\frac{5}{2}$ are also rational numbers because they are also in the form $\frac{p}{q}$, where $q \neq 0$. In the above examples, 3, 7, 0 and 5 are the numerators and 4, 1, 1 and 2 are the denominators.

Interesting Fact

Look at the diagrammatic representation that shows the relationship between natural numbers, whole numbers, integers and rational numbers. The group of rational numbers contains natural numbers, whole numbers and integers.

(a) All natural numbers are whole numbers.

(b) All whole numbers are integers.

(c) All integers are rational numbers.

Relation between natural numbers, whole numbers, integers and rational numbers

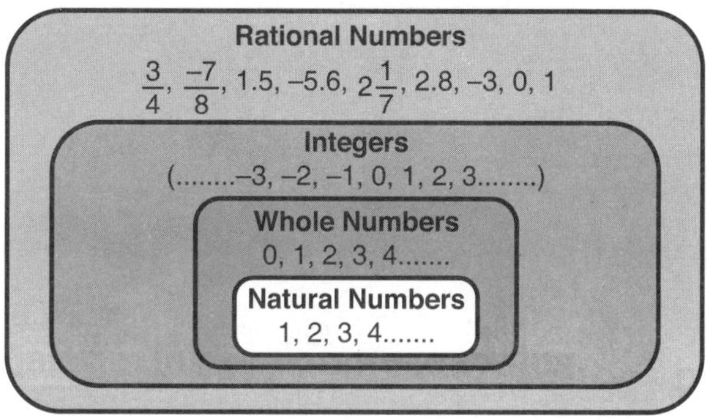

Positive and Negative Rational Numbers

To find whether a given rational number is positive or negative, we need to write it in such a way that its denominator is positive. Then, if the numerator of the given rational number is positive, then rational number will be positive and if the numerator is negative, then rational number will be negative.

Example 1: Consider the rational numbers $\frac{1}{2}, \frac{2}{3}, \frac{5}{7}$. The denominators of these rational numbers are positive; now, observe the numerators. Since all the numerators are positive, the given rational numbers are positive.

Example 2: Consider the rational numbers $\frac{-2}{3}, \frac{-3}{7}, \frac{-11}{15}$. Observe that the denominators of these rational numbers are positive; now observe that the numerators are having negative signs. Hence, the given rational numbers are negative.

Example 3: Consider rational numbers $\frac{20}{-6}, \frac{5}{-8}, \frac{7}{-10}$. Observe that the denominators are having negative signs and they can be written as negative numerators and positive denominators, that is, $\frac{-20}{6}, \frac{-5}{8}, \frac{-7}{10}$. Hence, the given rational numbers are negative.

Example 4: Consider rational numbers $\frac{-2}{-9}, \frac{-7}{-15}, \frac{-3}{-16}$. Observe that both numerators and denominators are having negative signs and they can be written as positive numerators and positive denominators, that is, $\frac{2}{9}, \frac{7}{15}, \frac{3}{16}$. Hence, the given rational numbers are positive.

$$\frac{-2}{-9} = \frac{-2 \times -1}{-9 \times -1} = \frac{2}{9}$$

If *p* and *q* are positive integers, then, $\frac{p}{q}$ and $\frac{-p}{-q}$ are positive rational numbers, and $\frac{-p}{q}$ and $\frac{p}{-q}$ are negative rational numbers.

Representation of Rational Numbers on a Number Line

You have learned to represent integers on a number line. Look at the following figure. You can observe that every positive integer lies to the right of 0 and every negative integer lies on the left of 0.

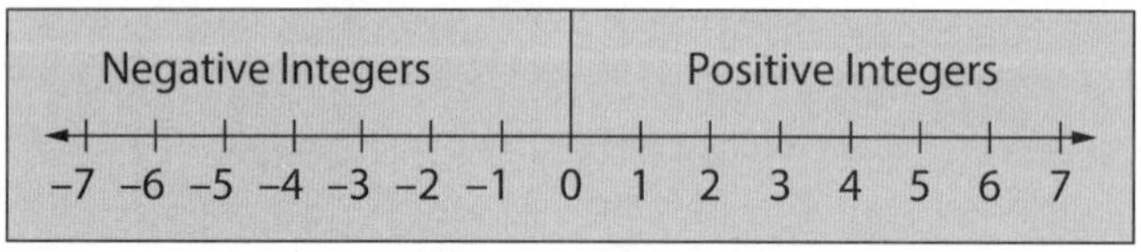

Example 5: Represent $-\frac{1}{2}$ on the number line.

Draw a number line. Let the distance between two consecutive numbers be 1 unit.

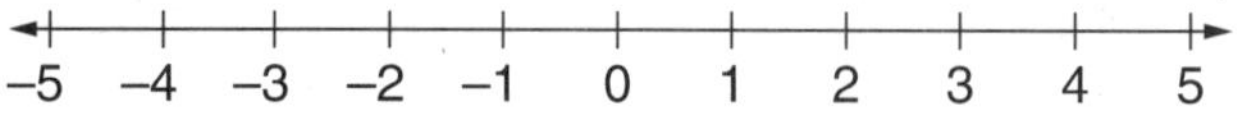

Now, divide each unit into two equal parts. That is,

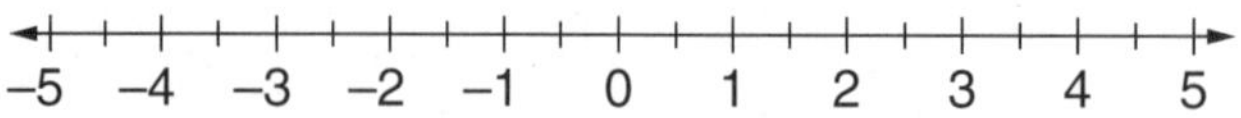

Since $-\frac{1}{2}$ is a negative rational number, show $-\frac{1}{2}$ to the left of zero on the given number line.

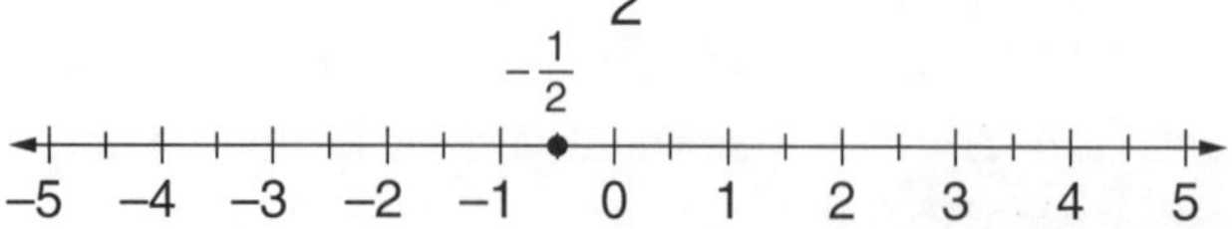

A unit on the number line is divided into *n* equal parts where *n* is the value of the denominator.

Example 6: Represent $\frac{5}{3}$ on the number line.

Draw a number line. Let the distance between two consecutive numbers be 1 unit.

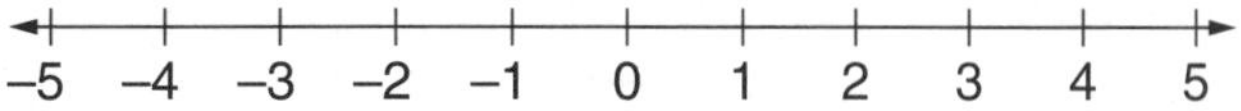

Now, divide each unit into three equal parts. That is,

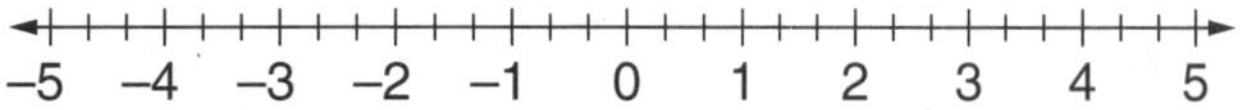

Since $\frac{5}{3}$ is a positive rational number, show $\frac{5}{3}$ to the right of 0 on the given number line.

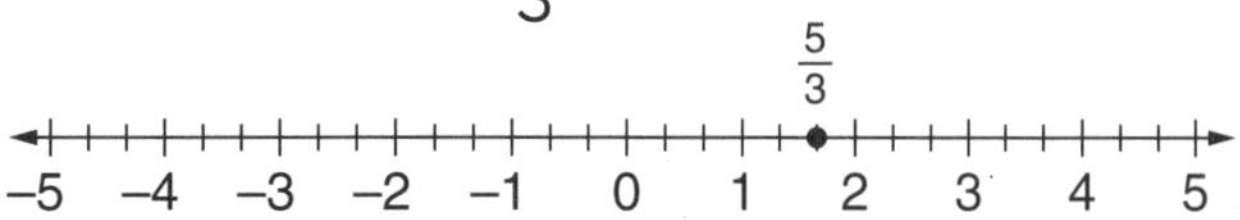

Absolute Value of Rational Numbers

Absolute value of a rational number is the number itself without regard to its sign. Absolute value is the distance of a number from zero on the number line.

The absolute value of a number is always positive.

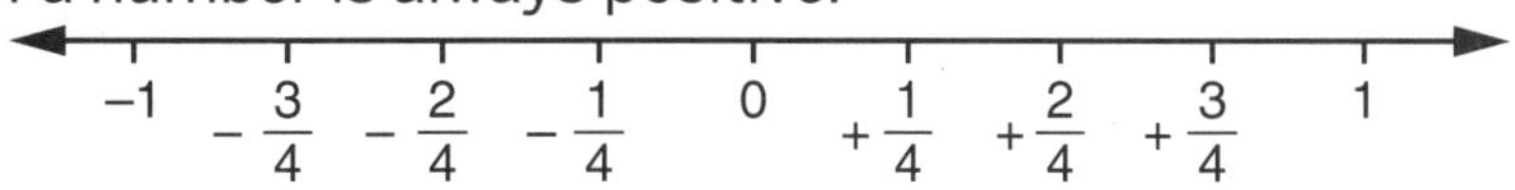

In the shown number line, both $+\frac{3}{4}$ and $-\frac{3}{4}$ are at a distance of $\frac{3}{4}$ units from 0 on either sides.

Absolute value of $+\frac{3}{4} = \frac{3}{4}$

Absolute value of $-\frac{3}{4} = \frac{3}{4}$

Remember

Absolute value of zero is zero.

The symbol used to represent the absolute value is two vertical lines. If $\frac{p}{q}$ is a rational number, then its absolute value is represented as $\left|\frac{p}{q}\right|$.

Example 7: Write the absolute values of

(a) $-\frac{15}{4}$ b) $\frac{26}{7}$ c) $-\frac{4}{16}$.

(a) Absolute value of $-\frac{15}{4} = \left|-\frac{15}{4}\right| = \frac{15}{4}$ (b) Absolute value of $\frac{26}{7} = \left|\frac{26}{7}\right| = \frac{26}{7}$

(c) Absolute value of $-\frac{4}{16} = \left|-\frac{4}{16}\right| = \left|-\frac{1}{4}\right| = \frac{1}{4}$

Equivalent Rational Numbers

You know that $\frac{1}{2}, \frac{2}{4}, \frac{3}{6}, \frac{4}{8}$ and $\frac{5}{10}$ represent the same fraction. They are said to be equivalent fractions. Equivalent fractions are obtained by multiplying or dividing the numerator and the denominator by the same number.

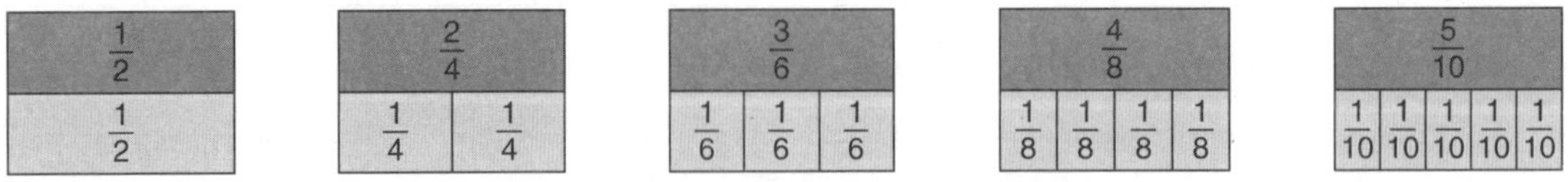

The same rule applies for rational numbers also.

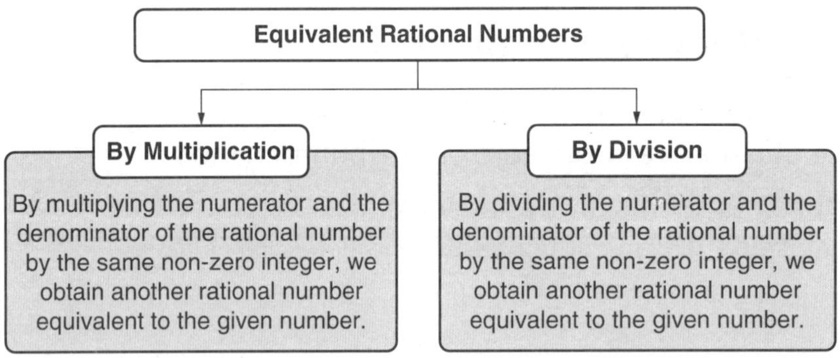

Solved Examples

Example 8: Find two rational numbers equivalent to the rational number $\frac{-5}{6}$.

We have, $\frac{-5}{6} = \frac{(-5) \times 2}{6 \times 2} = \frac{-10}{12}; \frac{-5}{6} = \frac{(-5) \times 3}{6 \times 3} = \frac{-15}{18}$

$\therefore \frac{-5}{6} = \frac{-10}{12} = \frac{-15}{18}$

Thus, two rational numbers equivalent to $\frac{-5}{6}$ are $\frac{-10}{12}$ and $\frac{-15}{18}$.

Example 9: Express $\frac{-3}{4}$ as a rational number with denominator 20.

The denominator of $\frac{-3}{4}$ is 4.

Multiply its numerator and denominator by 5.

$\therefore \frac{-3}{4} = \frac{-3 \times 5}{4 \times 5} = \frac{-15}{20}$ Hence, $\frac{-3}{4} = \frac{-15}{20}$

By which number should we multiply 4 to get 20?
Let us divide the number by 4.
That is, $20 \div 4 = 5$

Example 10: Express $\frac{-2}{3}$ as a rational number with numerator **−**12.

The numerator of $\frac{-2}{3}$ is −2.

Multiply its numerator and denominator by 6.

By which number should we multiply 2 to get 12?
Let us divide the number 12 by 2.
That is, 12 ÷ 2 = 6

$\therefore \frac{-2}{3} = \frac{-2 \times 6}{3 \times 6} = \frac{-12}{18}$ Hence, $\frac{-2}{3} = \frac{-12}{18}$

Rational Numbers in Standard Form

A rational number $\frac{p}{q}$ is said to be in the standard form if its denominator q is a positive integer, and the numerator p and the denominator q have no common factor other than 1.

Method to convert a rational number to its standard form

To reduce a rational number to its standard form, divide its numerator and denominator by their highest common factor (HCF). To find the standard form of a rational number with a negative integer as the denominator, divide it by their HCF with a minus sign.

Solved Examples

Example 11: Express $\frac{16}{56}$ in the standard form.

The HCF of 16 and 56 is 8.

Divide the numerator and the denominator by +8.

$\therefore \frac{16}{56} = \frac{16 \div 8}{56 \div 8} = \frac{2}{7}$

Hence, $\frac{16}{56} = \frac{2}{7}$, which is in the standard form.

Example 12: Express $\frac{3}{-15}$ in the standard form.

The HCF of 3 and 15 is 3.

Divide the numerator and the denominator by HCF (−3).

$\therefore \frac{3}{-15} = \frac{3 \div (-3)}{-15 \div (-3)} = \frac{-1}{5}$

Hence, $\frac{3}{-15} = \frac{-1}{5}$, which is in the standard form.

To test if two rational numbers are equivalent, you need to find the cross product of the numerator of one rational number with the denominator of the other rational number. If the cross products are equal, the rational numbers are equivalent.

Let $\frac{p}{q}$ and $\frac{r}{s}$ be any two rational numbers. By cross product, if $ps = rq$, then the given rational numbers are equivalent.

Example 13: Show that $\frac{-7}{13}$ and $\frac{14}{-26}$ are equivalent rational numbers.

We have, $(-7) \times (-26) = 182$ and $13 \times 14 = 182 \Rightarrow (-7) \times (-26) = 13 \times 14 \Rightarrow \frac{-7}{13} = \frac{14}{-26}$

Hence, $\frac{-7}{13}$ and $\frac{14}{-26}$ are equivalent.

Example 14: Find *a* such that $\frac{-56}{63}$ and $\frac{a}{-9}$ are equivalent rational numbers.

It is given that $\frac{-56}{63} = \frac{a}{-9}$.

$\Rightarrow a \times 63 = (-9) \times (-56) \Rightarrow 63a = 504 \Rightarrow a = \frac{504}{63} = 8$

Hence, $a = 8$.

Exercise 2.1

1 Write down the numerator and the denominator of the following rational numbers.

a. $\frac{1}{5}$ b. $\frac{-11}{13}$ c. $\frac{-14}{-15}$ d. $\frac{7}{-8}$ e. 5

2 State whether the following statements are true (T) or false (F).

a. All fractions are not rational numbers.

b. All integers are rational numbers.

c. All rational numbers are fractions.

d. 0 is not a rational number.

e. 56 is a rational number.

3 Write the following as rational numbers.

a. −18 b. 29 c. −101 d. 315 e. −1234

4 Represent each of the following rational numbers on a number line.

a. $-\frac{5}{9}$ b. $-\frac{4}{7}$ c. $\frac{9}{4}$ d. $\frac{3}{5}$

5 Write the absolute values of the following:

a. $-\frac{29}{3}$ b. $\frac{35}{17}$ c. $-\frac{25}{20}$ d. $-\frac{4}{5}$

6 Express $\frac{5}{-8}$ as a rational number with:

a. − 56 as its denominator b. 40 as its numerator c. 50 as its numerator

7 **Fill in the blanks.**

a. $\frac{[\ ]}{6} = \frac{40}{60}$ b. $\frac{2}{3} = \frac{[\ ]}{21}$ c. $\frac{[\ ]}{8} = \frac{18}{24}$ d. $\frac{6}{8} = \frac{[\ ]}{56}$

8 **Find four rational numbers equivalent to each of the following.**

a. $\frac{4}{9}$ b. $\frac{-3}{5}$ c. $\frac{8}{-11}$ d. $\frac{7}{-9}$

9 **Write each of the following rational numbers in its standard form.**

a. $\frac{2}{-14}$ b. $\frac{-10}{-8}$ c. $\frac{32}{28}$ d. $\frac{-16}{20}$ e. $\frac{-24}{80}$ f. $\frac{28}{63}$

10 **Check if the following rational numbers are equal.**

a. $\frac{-8}{5}$ and $\frac{56}{-35}$ b. $\frac{-12}{7}$ and $\frac{32}{21}$ c. $\frac{-7}{3}$ and $\frac{84}{-36}$

11 **Find a such that:** a. $\frac{25}{125} = \frac{100}{a}$ b. $\frac{a}{84} = \frac{204}{504}$

Comparison of Rational Numbers

Before we compare rational numbers, let us recall some facts about comparison of fractions and integers.

Comparison of Fractions	Comparison of Integers
1. If two fractions have the same denominator, then the fraction with the greater numerator is greater. 2. If two fractions have the same numerator, then the fraction with the smaller denominator is greater. 3. If two fractions are given with different denominators, then we take LCM of the denominators and express each fraction with this LCM as the denominator. The fraction with the greater numerator is greater.	1. A positive integer is always greater than a negative integer. For example, $5 > -1$ 2. Every positive integer is greater than 0. For example, $+2 > 0$ 3. Every negative integer is less than 0. For example, $-1 < 0$

The rules for comparison of rational numbers are also similar. Now, let us learn to compare two rational numbers.

Solved Examples

Example 15: Among the two rational numbers $\frac{-3}{5}$ and $\frac{2}{5}$, which is greater?

We have, $\frac{-3}{5}$ and $\frac{2}{5}$

We know that a positive rational is always greater than the negative rational number.

$$\therefore \frac{2}{5} > \frac{-3}{5}$$

Example 16: Among the two rational numbers $\frac{-3}{10}$ and $\frac{7}{-10}$, which is greater?

First, let us write each of the given numbers with a positive denominator.

One number $= \frac{-3}{10}$; other number $= \frac{7}{-10} = \frac{7 \times (-1)}{-10 \times (-1)} = \frac{-7}{10}$

Since, $-3 > -7$, $\frac{-3}{10} > \frac{-7}{10}$. Hence, $\frac{-3}{10} > \frac{7}{-10}$.

Example 17: Arrange the rational numbers in descending order: $\frac{-1}{2}, \frac{-1}{3}, \frac{-1}{4}, \frac{-2}{-5}$

Observe that all the rational numbers except $\frac{-2}{-5}$ are negative.

$$\therefore \frac{-2}{-5} = \frac{-2 \times (-1)}{-5 \times (-1)} = \frac{2}{5}$$

Since $\frac{2}{5}$ is positive, it is bigger than the other numbers.

Let us now compare $\frac{-1}{2}, \frac{-1}{3}$ and $\frac{-1}{4}$.

The LCM of the denominators 2, 3 and 4 is 12.

$\frac{-1}{2} = \frac{-1 \times 6}{2 \times 6} = \frac{-6}{12}$; $\frac{-1}{3} = \frac{-1 \times 4}{3 \times 4} = \frac{-4}{12}$; $\frac{-1}{4} = \frac{-1 \times 3}{4 \times 3} = \frac{-3}{12}$

Comparing numerators, we get $-6 < -4 < -3$.

Hence, $\frac{-1}{2} < \frac{-1}{3} < \frac{-1}{4}$

Therefore, the rational numbers can be arranged in descending order as:

$\frac{2}{5} > \frac{-1}{4} > \frac{-1}{3} > \frac{-1}{2}$.

Exercise 2.2

1 Compare each pair of the fractions given below and put appropriate symbols (< or >) in the brackets given.

a. $\frac{5}{9}$ [ ] $\frac{-4}{9}$ b. $\frac{-4}{7}$ [ ] $\frac{5}{-7}$ c. $\frac{-3}{7}$ [ ] 0 d. $\frac{5}{9}$ [ ] $\frac{-4}{5}$ e. -8 [ ] $\frac{-11}{2}$

2 Arrange the following rational numbers in the ascending order.

a. $\frac{2}{3}, \frac{4}{5}, \frac{3}{7}$ b. $\frac{3}{5}, \frac{-7}{10}, \frac{-11}{12}, \frac{-13}{-30}$ c. $\frac{2}{3}, \frac{4}{7}, \frac{-8}{3}, \frac{6}{-9}$

d. $\frac{-8}{9}, \frac{5}{-2}, \frac{5}{-6}, \frac{-5}{3}$ e. $\frac{-2}{3}, \frac{-7}{18}, \frac{-5}{12}, \frac{-4}{9}$ f. $4, 9, \frac{2}{3}, \frac{7}{2}$

3 Arrange the following rational numbers in the descending order.

a. $\frac{4}{9}, \frac{-4}{3}, \frac{-7}{-12}, \frac{-11}{24}$ b. $\frac{3}{4}, \frac{5}{-8}, \frac{3}{-16}, \frac{-5}{-8}$ c. $\frac{4}{7}, \frac{-7}{8}, \frac{2}{9}, \frac{-13}{14}$

d. $\frac{-3}{-5}, \frac{-8}{15}, \frac{7}{-10}, \frac{17}{30}$ e. $\frac{-7}{-6}, \frac{1}{2}, \frac{2}{5}, \frac{-3}{-4}$

Rational Numbers Between Two Rational Numbers

Observe the following number line. What are the integers between –5 and 5?

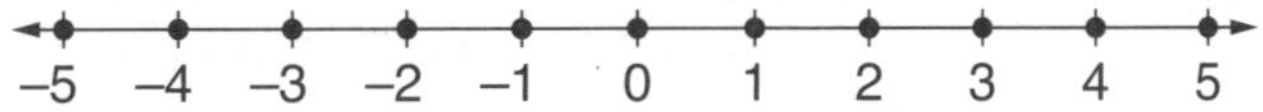

Is it possible to find integers between –4 and –3? No. Hence, we can conclude that there are no integers between two successive integers and that the number of integers between any two integers is finite.

Let's see whether there any rational numbers between two consecutive integers with the help of the following examples.

Example 18: Let us find the rational numbers between 4 and 3.

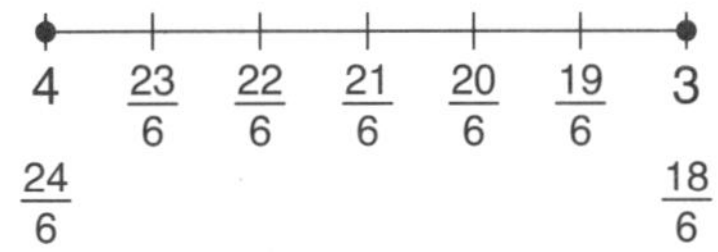

If the distance between 4 and 3 is divided into six equal parts and 4 is written as $\frac{24}{6}$ and 3 as $\frac{18}{6}$, then each $\frac{1}{6}$ th part between these two numbers represents a rational number. Starting from the left,

we have, $\frac{23}{6} > \frac{22}{6} > \frac{21}{6} > \frac{20}{6} > \frac{19}{6}$.

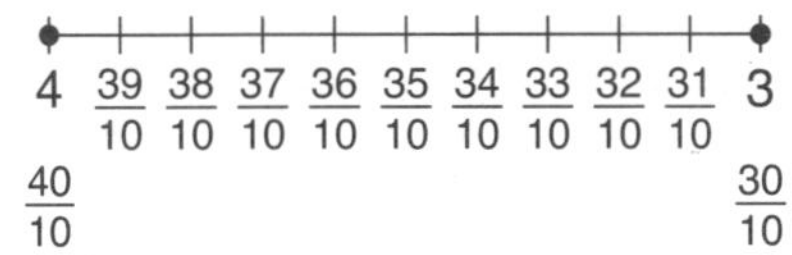

If the same distance is divided into ten equal parts, then the rational numbers obtained are:

$$\frac{39}{10} > \frac{38}{10} > \frac{37}{10} > \frac{36}{10} > \frac{35}{10} > \frac{34}{10} > \frac{33}{10} > \frac{32}{10} > \frac{31}{10}$$

Thus, depending upon the number of parts into which the distance between any two numbers is divided, we can find any number of rational numbers between any two rational numbers.

Example 19: List four rational numbers between $\frac{1}{3}$ and $\frac{3}{4}$.

The LCM of 3 and 4 is 12.

$$\therefore \frac{1}{3} = \frac{1}{3} \times \frac{4}{4} = \frac{4}{12} \text{ and } \frac{3}{4} = \frac{3}{4} \times \frac{3}{3} = \frac{9}{12}$$

Clearly, $\frac{5}{12} < \frac{6}{12} < \frac{7}{12} < \frac{8}{12} \Rightarrow \frac{5}{12} < \frac{1}{2} < \frac{7}{12} < \frac{2}{3}$

Therefore, four rational numbers between $\frac{1}{3}$ and $\frac{3}{4}$ are $\frac{5}{12}, \frac{1}{2}, \frac{7}{12}$ and $\frac{2}{3}$.

Exercise 2.3

1. List five rational numbers between –2 and 2.
2. List six rational numbers between $\frac{-3}{11}$ and $\frac{8}{11}$.
3. List three rational numbers between $\frac{1}{3}$ and $\frac{1}{7}$.
4. List any ten rational numbers between $\frac{4}{5}$ and $\frac{2}{7}$.

Operations on Rational Numbers

Addition of Rational Numbers

Addition of rational numbers is similar to the addition of fractions. However, before addition of rational numbers, we need to convert the negative rational numbers into rational numbers with positive denominators. For the purpose of addition, we divide rational numbers into two groups, namely, rational numbers with same denominators and rational numbers with different denominators.

Case 1: Addition of rational numbers with same denominators

To add two rational numbers with same denominators, we add their numerators by keeping the denominator same and writing the answer in the simplest form.

Example 20: Add $\frac{7}{-13}$ and $\frac{12}{13}$.

$$\frac{7}{-13} = \frac{7 \times (-1)}{-13 \times -1} = \frac{-7}{13}$$

$$\therefore \frac{7}{-13} + \frac{12}{13} = \frac{-7}{13} + \frac{12}{13} = \frac{(-7) + 12}{13} = \frac{5}{13}$$

Case 2: Addition of rational numbers with different denominators

To add rational numbers with different denominators, we follow the method we had followed for the addition of fractions.

(a) Find the LCM of the denominators and write each rational number with their LCM as the common denominator.

(b) Add the rational numbers and simplify.

Example 21: Add $\frac{5}{6}$ and $\frac{-3}{7}$.

The LCM of 6 and 7 is 42.

Now, $\frac{5}{6} = \frac{5}{6} \times \frac{7}{7} = \frac{35}{42}$ and $\frac{-3}{7} = \frac{-3}{7} \times \frac{6}{6} = \frac{-18}{42}$

$$\therefore \frac{5}{6} + \frac{-3}{7} = \frac{35}{42} + \frac{-18}{42} = \frac{35 + (-18)}{42} = \frac{17}{42}$$

Additive Inverse of Rational Numbers

We know, $\left(\frac{5}{10}\right) + \left(\frac{-5}{10}\right) = \frac{5-5}{10} = 0$

Thus, adding $\frac{5}{10}$ to $-\frac{5}{10}$ gives 0. When the sum of two rational numbers is 0, we say that each of them is the additive inverse of the other. In this case, $-\frac{5}{10}$ is the additive inverse of $\frac{5}{10}$ and $\frac{5}{10}$ is the additive inverse of $-\frac{5}{10}$.

Conclusion: The additive inverse of a number p is that number which when added to p gives zero. $(-p)$ is the additive inverse of p since $p + (-p) = 0$.

Example 22: Find the additive inverse of: (a) $\frac{3}{5}$ (b) $\frac{-9}{17}$ (c) $\frac{10}{-13}$ (d) $\frac{-7}{-9}$

We have,

(a) The additive inverse of $\frac{3}{5}$ is $-\frac{3}{5}$. (b) The additive inverse of $\frac{-9}{17}$ is $\frac{9}{17}$.

(c) The additive inverse of $\frac{10}{-13}$ is $\frac{10}{13}$ since $\frac{10}{-13} = \frac{10 \times (-1)}{-13 \times (-1)} = \frac{-10}{13}$.

(d) The additive inverse of $\frac{-7}{-9}$ is $\frac{-7}{9}$ since $\frac{-7}{-9} = \frac{-7 \times (-1)}{-9 \times (-1)} = \frac{7}{9}$.

Subtraction of Rational Numbers

We know that subtraction is the inverse process of addition. Hence, we can say that subtracting a rational number means adding its additive inverse.

Steps

If m and n are two rational numbers, then to subtract n from m $(m - n)$:

↓

Find the opposite or additive inverse of n.

↓

Add the opposite of n to m.

↓

Find the LCM of denominators and write the result in standard form.

Example 23: Subtract $\frac{7}{3}$ from $\frac{1}{6}$.

We have,

$$\frac{1}{6} - \frac{7}{3} = \frac{1}{6} + \left(-\frac{7}{3}\right) \quad [\because \text{Additive inverse of } \tfrac{7}{3} \text{ is } \left(-\tfrac{7}{3}\right).]$$

$$= \frac{1 + (-14)}{6} \quad [\text{ The LCM of 6 and 3 is 6.}]$$

$$= -\frac{13}{6}$$

Example 24: What should be added to $\left(-\frac{5}{9}\right)$ to get $\frac{1}{8}$?

The sum of two numbers $= \frac{1}{8}$. Let the required number be a.

Then, $\left(-\frac{5}{9}\right) + a = \frac{1}{8}$

$\Rightarrow a = \frac{1}{8} - \left(-\frac{5}{9}\right) \Rightarrow a = \frac{1}{8} + \frac{5}{9} = \frac{9 + 40}{72} = \frac{49}{72}$ $\therefore$ The required number is $\frac{49}{72}$.

Example 25: What should be subtracted from $\left(-\frac{2}{7}\right)$ to get $\frac{13}{14}$?

Let the required number be a.

Then, $\left(-\frac{2}{7}\right) - a = \frac{13}{14} \Rightarrow \left(-\frac{2}{7}\right) = \frac{13}{14} + a$

$\Rightarrow a = \left(-\frac{2}{7}\right) - \frac{13}{14} = \left(-\frac{2}{7}\right) + \left(\frac{-13}{14}\right) = \frac{-4 + (-13)}{14} = \frac{-17}{14}$ $\therefore$ The required number is $\frac{-17}{14}$.

Multiplication of Rational Numbers

The product of two given fractions is a fraction whose numerator is the product of the numerators of the given fractions and whose denominator is the product of the denominators of the given fractions.

This is true even for the rational numbers. That is,

$$\text{Product of two rational numbers} = \frac{\text{Product of their numerators}}{\text{Product of their denominators}}$$

Solved Examples

Example 26: Find the product of $\left(-\frac{6}{7}\right)$ and $\frac{4}{9}$.

We have, $\left(-\frac{6}{7}\right) \times \frac{4}{9}$

$= \frac{-6 \times 4}{7 \times 9} = \frac{-24}{63} = -\frac{8}{21}$

Example 27: Simplify $\frac{9}{-17} \times \frac{-44}{21}$.

We have, $\frac{9}{-17} = \frac{9 \times (-1)}{-17 \times (-1)} = \frac{-9}{17}$

$\therefore \frac{9}{-17} \times \frac{-44}{21} = \frac{-9}{17} \times \frac{-44}{21}$

$= \frac{(-9) \times (-44)}{17 \times 21} = \frac{396}{357} = \frac{132}{119}$

Hence, $\frac{9}{-17} \times \frac{-44}{21} = \frac{132}{119}$

Reciprocal or Multiplicative Inverse of a Rational Number

A rational number $\frac{1}{p}$ is called the reciprocal or multiplicative inverse of a non-zero rational number p such that $p \times \frac{1}{p} = \frac{1}{p} \times p = 1$.

Observe that the reciprocal of 1 is 1 and the reciprocal of –1 is –1. Therefore, we can say that 1 and – 1 are the only rational numbers which are their own reciprocals. Also, the rational number 0 has no reciprocal or multiplicative inverse.

Example 28: Find the reciprocal of: (a) –7 (b) $\frac{4}{5}$ (c) $\frac{-2}{3}$

(a) The reciprocal of –7 is $\frac{1}{-7} = \frac{-1}{7}$. (b) The reciprocal of $\frac{4}{5}$ is $\frac{5}{4}$.

(c) The reciprocal of $\frac{-2}{3}$ is $\frac{3}{-2} = \frac{-3}{2}$.

Division of Rational Numbers

You know that division is the inverse operation of multiplication.

Therefore, we can say that if $a \times b = c$, then $c \div b = a$ and $c \div a = b$. This fact is also true for rational numbers.

To divide $\frac{p}{q}$ by $\frac{r}{s}$ $(\neq 0)$

Step 1: Find the reciprocal of $\frac{r}{s}$, i.e., $\frac{s}{r}$.

Step 2: Multiply $\frac{p}{q}$ by $\frac{s}{r}$, i.e., $\frac{p}{q} \times \frac{s}{r}$.

Step 3: Write the product $\frac{p}{q} \times \frac{s}{r}$ in the standard form.

Example 29: Simplify $\frac{1}{5} \div \left(\frac{-2}{15}\right)$.

We have,

$$\frac{1}{5} \div \left(\frac{-2}{15}\right) = \frac{1}{5} \times \left(\frac{15}{-2}\right) = \frac{1}{5} \times \left(\frac{15 \times -1}{-2 \times -1}\right)$$

$$= \frac{1}{5} \times \left(\frac{-15}{2}\right) = \frac{1 \times -15}{5 \times 2}$$

$$= \frac{-15}{10} = \frac{-3}{2}$$

$$\therefore \frac{1}{5} \div \left(\frac{-2}{15}\right) = \frac{-3}{2}$$

Example 30: Simplify $\frac{-1}{4} \div \frac{-3}{8}$.

We have,

$$\frac{-1}{4} \div \frac{-3}{8} = \frac{-1}{4} \div \frac{8}{-3} \times \frac{-1}{4} \times \left(\frac{8 \times -1}{-3 \times -1}\right)$$

$$= \frac{-1}{4} \times \left(\frac{-8}{3}\right) = \frac{(-1) \times -8}{4 \times 3}$$

$$= \frac{8}{12} = \frac{2}{3}$$

$$\therefore \frac{-1}{4} \div \frac{-3}{8} = \frac{2}{3}$$

Exercise 2.4

1 Find the sum of the following.

a. $\frac{5}{6}$ and $\frac{-1}{6}$ b. $\frac{9}{17}$ and $\frac{-5}{17}$ c. $\frac{-17}{15}$ and $\frac{-1}{15}$

d. $\frac{5}{6}$ and $\frac{7}{9}$ e. $\frac{5}{8}$ and $\frac{-7}{2}$ f. $\frac{7}{-18}$ and $\frac{8}{27}$

2 Subtract the following.

a. $\frac{-7}{9}$ from $\frac{4}{6}$ b. $\frac{3}{4}$ from $\frac{5}{6}$ c. $\frac{1}{4}$ from $\frac{-3}{8}$

d. $\frac{-4}{13}$ from $\left(\frac{-5}{26}\right)$ e. $\frac{13}{15} - \frac{12}{25}$ f. $\frac{-3}{-8}$ from $\left(\frac{-2}{7}\right)$

3 Simplify the following.

a. $\frac{7}{11} \times \frac{5}{4}$ b. $\frac{-2}{9} \times \frac{5}{11}$ c. $\frac{25}{-9} \times \frac{3}{-10}$

d. $\frac{16}{-21} \times \frac{14}{5}$ e. $\frac{-12}{5} \times \frac{10}{-3}$ f. $\frac{5}{-18} \times \frac{-9}{20}$

4 Simplify the following.

a. $5 \div \frac{-5}{7}$ b. $\frac{-16}{35} \div \frac{-15}{14}$ c. $\frac{-12}{7} \div 18$

d. $\frac{4}{9} \div \frac{-5}{12}$ e. $\frac{-3}{4} \div -6$ f. $\frac{2}{3} \div \frac{-7}{12}$

Rational Numbers as Decimals

Rational numbers can be converted into decimals as every fraction has a decimal representation.

Rational numbers can be **Terminating Decimals** or **Non-Terminating Decimals**.

Terminating Decimals	Non-Terminating decimals
Decimals which have finite number of digits after the decimal point.	Decimals which have infinite number of digits after the decimal point.
Examples : $\frac{4}{5}=0.8$; $\frac{7}{8}=0.875$; $\frac{3}{5}=0.6$	Examples: $\frac{17}{7}=2.4285...$; $\frac{5}{3}=1.6666...$

In some non-terminating decimals, a digit or block of digits repeats itself in decimal part. Such decimals are called **Recurring Decimals**. The repeating digits or block of digits are represented with a bar over them.

Examples:

$\frac{1}{3}=0.3333...=0.\bar{3}$; $\frac{8}{3}=2.6666...=2.\bar{6}$; $\frac{6}{11}=0.545454...=0.\overline{54}$

Rules to find terminating or non-terminating decimals:

- Rational numbers whose denominator is a power of 2 (2, 4, 8, 16 ...) are terminating decimals. **Examples:** $\frac{1}{2}=0.5$; $\frac{29}{4}=7.25$; $\frac{3}{8}=0.375$

- Rational numbers whose denominator is a power of 5 (5, 25, 125, 625...) are terminating decimals. **Examples:** $\frac{1}{5}=0.2$; $\frac{136}{25}=5.44$; $\frac{99}{125}=0.792$

- Rational numbers whose denominator is a product of powers of 2 and 5 are terminating decimals. **Examples:** $\frac{1}{4\times25}=\frac{1}{100}=0.01$; $\frac{76}{2\times125}=\frac{76}{250}=0.304$; $\frac{2978}{16\times5}=\frac{2978}{80}=37.225$

- Rational numbers apart from the above three cases are non-terminating decimals.

  Examples: $\frac{1}{15}=0.\bar{6}$; $\frac{289}{49}=5.89795...$; $\frac{1024}{14}=73.14285...$

Example 31: Check whether the given rational numbers are terminating or non-terminating decimals.

(a) $\frac{456}{25}$ (b) $\frac{1892}{26}$ (c) $\frac{9003}{8}$ (d) $\frac{12390}{50}$ (e) $\frac{998}{36}$

(a) The denominator 25 is power of 5. So, it is a terminating decimal.

(b) The denominator 26 is not a power of 2 or 5. So, it is a non-terminating decimal.

(c) The denominator 8 is a power of 2. So, it is a terminating decimal.

(d) The denominator 50 (2 x 25) is a product of powers of 2 and 5. So, it is a terminating decimal.

(e) The denominator 36 is not a power of 2 or 5. So, it is a non-terminating decimal.

Conversion of Recurring Decimals into Rational Numbers:

Follow the steps given below for converting recurring decimals into rational numbers:

Step 1: Write the given recurring decimal as a decimal by removing the bar from the repeating digits and writing the repeating digit at least twice.

Step 2: Let the decimal be equal to '*x*'.

Step 3: Find the number of repeating digits in the decimal.

- If 1 digit is repeating, then multiply both sides by 10.
- If 2 digits are repeating, then multiply both sides by 100.
- If 3 digits are repeating, then multiply both sides by 1000.

Step 4: Subtract the result obtained in step 2 and step 3.

Step 5: Divide both sides of the equation by coefficient of *x*.

Step 6: Write the resultant rational number in simplest form.

Example 32: Convert the given recurring decimals into rational numbers.

(a) $0.\overline{4}$ (b) $0.\overline{987}$ (c) $0.45\overline{3}$

(a) Let $x = 0.4444$ -----------> (1)

As the repeating digit is only one number, multiply the equation by 10.

$10x = 4.444$ -----------> (2)

Subtracting (1) from (2), we get

$10x - x = 4.444 - 0.444$

$9x = 4$

Dividing by 9, we get $x = \frac{4}{9}$

(b) Let $x = 0.987987$ -----------> (1)

As the repeating digits are three numbers, multiply the equation by 1000.

$1000x = 987.987$ -----------> (2)

Subtracting (1) from (2), we get

$999x = 987$

Dividing by 999, we get $x = \frac{987}{999}$

(c) Let $x = 0.45333$ -----------> (1)

As the repeating digits is only one number, multiply the equation by 10.

$10x = 4.5333$ -----------> (2)

Subtracting (1) from (2), we get

$9x = 4.08$

Dividing by 9, we get $x = \frac{4.08}{9} = \frac{408}{900}$

Word Problems

Example 33: Rahul went to purchase a book from a bookshop which is $\frac{3}{5}$ km far from his house towards north. When Rahul was coming back home from the bookshop, he got a call from his friend who asked him where he was then. At that point, he was $\frac{2}{5}$ km from the shop, towards south. How far is Rahul from his house?

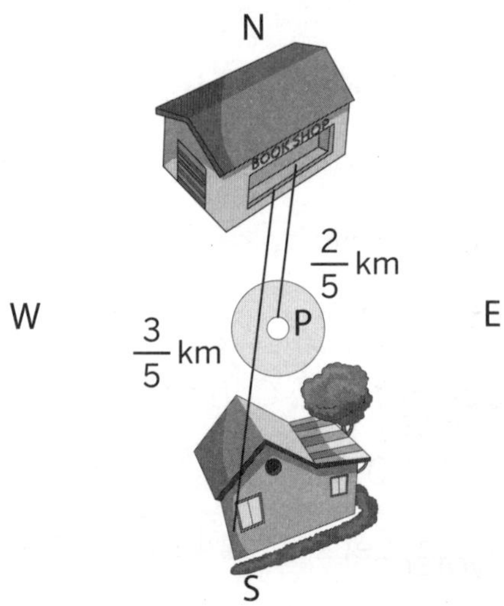

The distance from house to point P = Distance from house to shop – distance travelled from shop to point P

$$= \frac{3}{5} - \frac{2}{5} = \frac{3-2}{5} = \frac{1}{5} \text{ km}$$

Hence, he is $\frac{1}{5}$ km away from his house towards south.

Example 34: The sum of two rational numbers is $-\frac{1}{35}$. If one of the numbers is $-\frac{3}{5}$, then find the other number.

Given that the sum of two rational numbers is $-\frac{1}{35}$. Let the other number be a.

Then, $-\frac{3}{5} + a = -\frac{1}{35} \Rightarrow a = -\frac{1}{35} - \left(-\frac{3}{5}\right)$

$\Rightarrow a = \frac{-1}{35} + \frac{3}{5} = \frac{-1 + 21}{35} = \frac{20}{35} = \frac{4}{7}$

$\therefore$ The required number is $\frac{4}{7}$.

Example 35: From a water tank, $12\frac{1}{2}$ litres of water is used per day, find the amount of water used in $4\frac{1}{4}$ days.

Amount of water used per day = $12\frac{1}{2}$ litres

Amount of water used in $4\frac{1}{4}$ days = $12\frac{1}{2} \times 4\frac{1}{4} = \frac{25}{2} \times \frac{17}{4} = \frac{25 \times 17}{2 \times 4} = \frac{425}{8} = 53\frac{1}{8}$.

Hence, $53\frac{1}{8}$ litres of water is used in $4\frac{1}{4}$ days.

Example 36: How many 0.5 kg packages can be made with $24\frac{1}{2}$ kg of coffee beans?

Total amount = $24\frac{1}{2}$ kg; Weight of each pack = 0.5 kg = $\frac{1}{2}$ kg.

Number of packets that can be packed = $24\frac{1}{2}$ kg $\div \frac{1}{2}$ kg = $\frac{49}{2} \div \frac{1}{2} = \frac{49}{2} \times 2 = 49$

$\therefore$ Number of 0.5 kg packets that can be packed is 49.

Example 37: Jyotsna wanted to lose her weight and started following a diet and exercise plan. The change in her weight for 4 weeks is given below. What is her weight at the end of 4th week if her weight before the diet plan was $\frac{755}{10}$?

Week	Week 1	Week 2	Week 3	Week 4
Loss in weight (kg)	$\frac{27}{10}$	$\frac{22}{10}$	$\frac{13}{10}$	$\frac{8}{10}$

Jyotsna's weight before the diet plan = $\frac{755}{10}$ kg

Jyotsna's weight after week 1 = $\left(\frac{755}{10} - \frac{27}{10}\right)$ kg = $\frac{755 - 27}{10}$ kg = $\frac{728}{10}$ kg

Jyotsna's weight after week 2 = $\left(\frac{728}{10} - \frac{22}{10}\right)$ kg = $\frac{728 - 22}{10}$ kg = $\frac{706}{10}$ kg

Jyotsna's weight after week 3 = $\left(\frac{706}{10} - \frac{13}{10}\right)$ kg = $\frac{706 - 13}{10}$ kg = $\frac{693}{10}$ kg

Jyotsna's weight after week 4 = $\left(\frac{693}{10} - \frac{8}{10}\right)$ kg = $\frac{693 - 8}{10}$ kg = $\frac{685}{10}$ kg

Therefore, Jyotsna's weight at the end of the 4th week is $\frac{685}{10}$ kg.

Exercise 2.5

1 Check whether the given rational numbers are terminating or non-terminating decimals.

a. $\frac{125}{4}$ b. $\frac{1025}{86}$ c. $\frac{5296}{20}$ d. $\frac{6575}{125}$ e. $\frac{99}{98}$ f. $\frac{125}{4}$

2 Convert the following recurring decimals into rational numbers.

a. $0.\overline{7}$ b. $0.\overline{89}$ c. $0.\overline{567}$ d. $0.24\overline{3}$

3 Two persons A and B planned to reach a point on the beach. They started from the same point P but took two different routes, PCQ and PDQ, respectively as shown in the picture. Find the distance travelled by each person and find who has travelled more distance.

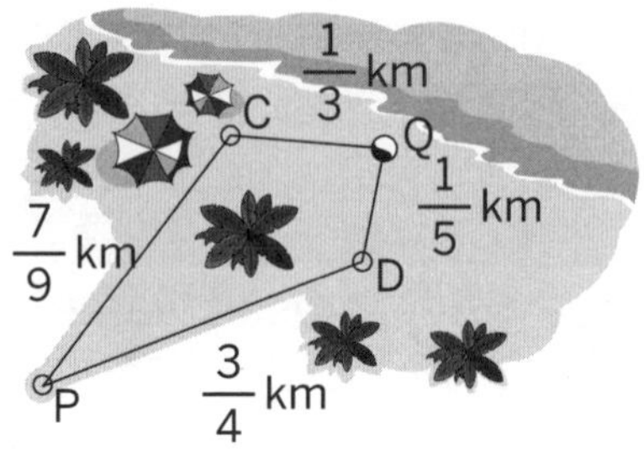

4 The shopkeeper has $75\frac{3}{4}$ kg of sugar. If he sold $\frac{1}{4}$ of it, find the amount of sugar sold.

5 A bottle of medicine contains $1\frac{1}{2}$ litres. Each dose of medicine is $\frac{3}{14}$ litres. How many doses are there in the bottle?

6 What is the difference in the water level in the two cans, A and B, if can A is $\frac{2}{3}$ full and can B is $\frac{4}{5}$ full?

Summary

1. Rational numbers are numbers that are expressed in the form of $\frac{p}{q}$, where p and q are integers and $q \neq 0$.
2. All integers and fractions are rational numbers.
3. A rational number can be represented on a number line.
4. Equivalent rational numbers are obtained by multiplying or dividing the numerator and the denominator by a non-zero integer.
5. A rational number $\frac{p}{q}$ is said to be in the standard form if its denominator q is a positive integer and p and q have no common factor other than 1.
5. The additive inverse of a number p is that number which when added to p gives zero. $-p$ is the additive inverse of p since $p + (-p) = 0$ and vice versa.
6. A rational number $\frac{1}{p}$ is called the reciprocal or multiplicative inverse of a non-zero rational number p such that $p \times \frac{1}{p} = \frac{1}{p} \times p = 1$.
8. Rational numbers can be terminating decimals or non-terminating decimals.
9. Terminating decimals are decimals which have finite number of digits after the decimal point.
10. Non-terminating decimals are decimals which have infinite number of digits after the decimal point.

Revision Exercise

1 **Express the following numbers in the form of $\frac{p}{q}$.**

a. 5 b. −7 c. 2.79 d. 0.8

2 **Draw a number line and mark the following rational numbers on it. Write those rational numbers in the form of $\frac{p}{q}$.**

a. Any three rational numbers between +2 and +3

b. Any two rational numbers between −1 and 0

c. Any two rational numbers between 0 and +1

d. Any four rational numbers between +1 and +2

3 **Classify the following into positive and negative rational numbers.**

a. $\frac{4}{-5}$ b. $\frac{-4}{-5}$ c. $\frac{-9}{4}$ d. $\frac{-9}{13}$

e. $\frac{4}{5}$ f. $\frac{9}{13}$ g. $\frac{9}{-13}$ h. $\frac{-9}{-13}$

4 **Fill in the blanks.**

a. The number of rational numbers between any two rational numbers is ________.

b. An equivalent rational number of $\frac{-3}{7}$ is ________.

c. The rational number $\frac{-5}{6}$ is situated between the integers ________ and ________.

d. The sum of $\frac{-11}{13}$ and $\frac{11}{13}$ is ________.

e. The product of $\frac{-3}{8}$ and − 5 is ________.

f. $\frac{6}{-5} \div \frac{-6}{5} =$ ________

5 **State whether the following statements are true (T) or false (F).**

a. $\frac{0}{5}$ is a rational number.b. The standard form of $-\frac{24}{80}$ is $-\frac{12}{40}$.

c. $-\frac{10}{4}$ lies between the rational numbers −3 and −2.

d. The product of a rational number and its reciprocal is zero.

e. The additive inverse of $-\frac{3}{8}$ is $\frac{8}{3}$.

f. The sum of a number and its additive inverse is 1.

6 **Write three equivalent rational numbers for the following.**

a. $-\frac{3}{4}$ b. $\frac{7}{8}$ c. $-\frac{1}{7}$

7 **Write the standard form of the following.**

a. $-\dfrac{24}{15}$ b. $-\dfrac{24}{80}$ c. $-\dfrac{105}{207}$

8 **Compare each pair of fractions given and put the appropriate symbol (< or >) in the bracket.**

a. $\dfrac{12}{25}\,[\ \ ]\,\dfrac{-32}{52}$ b. $\dfrac{-17}{21}\,[\ \ ]\,\dfrac{-19}{26}$ c. $\dfrac{-17}{21}\,[\ \ ]\,\dfrac{-1}{21}$

9 **Simplify the following.**

a. $\dfrac{-8}{7}+\left(\dfrac{-5}{4}\right)$ b. $\dfrac{-8}{13}-\dfrac{8}{13}$ c. $\dfrac{5}{7}-\dfrac{1}{3}$ d. $-\dfrac{5}{3}+\dfrac{3}{11}$

e. $-\dfrac{15}{7}-\left(\dfrac{-1}{8}\right)$

10 **Simplify the following.**

a. $\dfrac{-3}{8}\times\dfrac{7}{5}$ b. $\dfrac{-18}{6}\times\dfrac{-1}{9}$ c. $\dfrac{11}{13}\times\dfrac{2}{-9}$ d. $-4\div\dfrac{3}{8}$

11 **Convert the following recurring decimals into rational numbers.**

a. $0.\overline{4}$ b. $0.\overline{12}$ c. $0.\overline{777}$ d. $0.13\overline{2}$

12 **Solve the following word problems.**

a. If the temperatures of two places, P and Q, having a cold climate, are $-9\dfrac{7}{13}^{\circ}$C and $-9\dfrac{5}{11}^{\circ}$C, then which of the two places is colder?

b. The height of a building is $19\dfrac{3}{5}$ feet.
The height of a tree near the building is $11\dfrac{5}{7}$ feet. What is the difference in the heights of the building and the tree?

c. If the cost of 1 litre petrol is ₹ $73\dfrac{3}{4}$, find the cost of $2\dfrac{1}{2}$ litres petrol.

d. Raghu has purchased $5\dfrac{1}{4}$ m of cloth. He wants to distribute $\dfrac{3}{4}$ m of cloth to each of his friends. Find the number of friends to whom he can distribute the cloth?

e. Suraj is playing a computer video game. His score in different rounds is given below. What is his final score?

Rounds	Round 1	Round 2	Round 3	Round 4	Round 5
Score (points)	Wins $12\frac{1}{2}$	Wins $\frac{155}{10}$	Loses $\frac{15}{2}$	Loses $\frac{19}{2}$	Wins $\frac{225}{10}$

THEME 1

Fractions

3

What I shall learn

- To understand fraction as an operator
- To multiply and divide fractions
- To multiply and divide decimal fractions

Let's Get Started

Fractions are in the form $\frac{p}{q}$ $(q \neq 0)$, where the digit above the horizontal line (p) is called the **numerator** and the digit below the horizontal line (q) is called the **denominator**.

Types of Fractions

Types of fractions	Explanation	Examples
1. Proper fraction	Fraction where the numerator is less than the denominator	$\frac{3}{4}, \frac{2}{5}, \frac{1}{2}, \frac{7}{8}, \frac{6}{11}$
2. Improper fraction	Fraction where the numerator is greater than or equal to the denominator	$\frac{3}{2}, \frac{6}{5}, \frac{11}{7}, \frac{5}{3}, \frac{10}{9}$
3. Mixed fraction	Combination of a whole number and a proper fraction	$1\frac{3}{4}, 1\frac{1}{2}, 2\frac{1}{5}, 5\frac{1}{3}, 3\frac{9}{10}$
4. Like fractions	Fractions having the same denominator	$\frac{3}{4}, \frac{4}{4}, \frac{1}{4}, \frac{7}{4}, \frac{2}{4}$
5. Unlike fractions	Fractions having different denominators	$\frac{3}{5}, \frac{4}{7}, \frac{12}{15}, \frac{7}{9}, \frac{8}{11}$
6. Unit fraction	Fractions that have 1 as numerator	$\frac{1}{5}, \frac{1}{4}, \frac{1}{10}, \frac{1}{8}, \frac{1}{7}$
7. Simple fraction	Fractions in which numerators and denominators are whole numbers	$\frac{3}{8}, \frac{2}{5}, \frac{8}{11}, \frac{7}{3}, \frac{4}{9}$
8. Complex fraction	Fractions in which the numerator or the denominator or both are fractions	$\frac{\frac{1}{2}}{5}, \frac{6}{\frac{3}{10}}, \frac{\frac{1}{2}}{\frac{1}{3}}, \frac{\frac{3}{10}}{15}, \frac{25}{\frac{5}{6}}$
9. Decimal fraction	Fraction where denominator is 10 or higher power of 10	$\frac{7}{100}, \frac{50}{100}$

Fraction as an Operator

Each shaded portion in the given figures represents $\frac{1}{4}$ of 1.

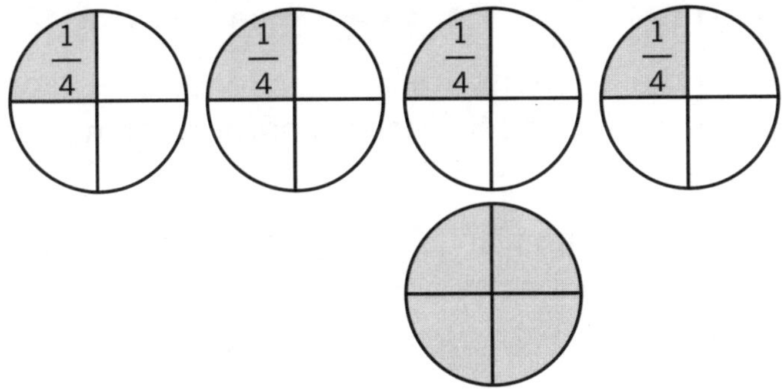

So, the shaded portions together will represent $\frac{1}{4}$ of 4.

Combine the four shaded $\frac{1}{4}$ parts.

It represents 1.

Therefore, $\frac{1}{4}$ of 4 is 1.

It can also be written as $\frac{1}{4}$ of $4 = \frac{1}{4} \times 4 = 1$.

Example 1: Find $\frac{3}{6}$ of 9.

$\frac{3}{6}$ of $9 = \frac{3}{6} \times 9 = \frac{3 \times 9}{6} = \frac{27}{6}$

$= \frac{9}{2} = 4\frac{1}{2}$

Example 2: Find $\frac{4}{12}$ of 20.

$\frac{4}{12}$ of $20 = \frac{4}{12} \times 20 = \frac{4 \times 20}{12}$

$= \frac{80}{12} = \frac{20}{3} = 6\frac{2}{3}$

Example 3: A vendor bought 60 mangoes from the market. He sold $\frac{3}{5}$ of them in the morning. Find the number of mangoes sold by the vendor in the morning.

The number of mangoes sold by the vendor $= \frac{3}{5}$ of $60 = \frac{3}{5} \times 60 = \frac{3}{\cancel{5}} \times \cancel{60}^{12} = 36$

The vendor sold 36 mangoes in the morning.

Example 4: There are 45 students in a class. If $\frac{7}{9}$ of them likes to play outdoor games, find the number of students who like to play outdoor games.

$\frac{7}{9}$ of 45 likes to play outdoor games $= \frac{7}{9} \times 45 = \frac{7}{\cancel{9}} \times \cancel{45}^{5} = 35$.

Thus, 35 students like to play outdoor games.

Exercise 3.1

1. **Find the following.**

   a. $\frac{3}{5}$ of 5 b. $\frac{2}{3}$ of 6 c. $\frac{3}{12}$ of 8 d. $\frac{12}{24}$ of 21 e. $2\frac{4}{5}$ of 21

2. Rama arranged 15 roses in a vase, out of which $\frac{3}{5}$ are red. Find the number of red flowers arranged in the vase.
3. Meena had a pocket money of ₹500. She spends $\frac{3}{10}$ of it to buy books. Find the amount spent on books.
4. Raju spends $\frac{1}{3}$ of the day in the school. Find the number of hours spent in school.

Basic Operations on Fractions

We have already learned about the basic operations on fractions. Let us revise them.

Addition and Subtraction of Fractions

- If the fractions are like fractions, we add or subtract the numerators depending upon the question and the denominator remains the same. We express the answer in its simplest form.
- If the given fractions are not like fractions, then convert the given fractions into like fractions before adding or subtracting.
- If the given fractions are mixed fractions, then convert them into improper fractions before adding or subtracting.

Example 5: Find the sum of $\frac{3}{10}$ and $\frac{9}{10}$.

We have, $\frac{3}{10}+\frac{9}{10}=\frac{12}{10}=1\frac{2}{10}=1\frac{1}{5}$

Example 6: Find the difference between $2\frac{5}{6}$ and $1\frac{1}{4}$.

$$2\frac{5}{6}-1\frac{1}{4}=\frac{17}{6}-\frac{5}{4}=\frac{17\times2-5\times3}{12}=\frac{34-15}{12}=\frac{19}{12}=1\frac{7}{12}$$

Multiplication and Division of Fractions

The product of fractions is the product of the numerators of the given fractions as the numerator and the product of the denominators of the given fractions as the denominator. If the given fractions are mixed fractions, then convert the same into improper fractions before multiplying.

Example 7: Find the product of $\frac{4}{5}$ and $\frac{3}{8}$.

We have, $\frac{\cancel{4}}{5}\times\frac{3}{\cancel{8}_2}=\frac{3}{10}$

Example 8: Find the product of $1\frac{1}{2}$ and $2\frac{1}{3}$.

We have, $1\frac{1}{2}\times2\frac{1}{3}=\frac{\cancel{3}}{2}\times\frac{7}{\cancel{3}}=\frac{7}{2}=3\frac{1}{2}$

- To divide a whole number by a fraction, multiply the whole number by the reciprocal of the given fraction.
- To divide a fraction by another fraction, multiply the fraction by the reciprocal of the other.

Example 9: Divide 21 by $\frac{7}{5}$.

We have, $\frac{21}{1}\div\frac{7}{5}=\frac{\cancel{21}^3}{1}\times\frac{5}{\cancel{7}}=15$

Example 10: Divide $2\frac{1}{3}$ by $3\frac{3}{6}$.

We have, $2\frac{1}{3}\div3\frac{3}{6}=\frac{7}{3}\div\frac{21}{6}=\frac{\cancel{7}}{\cancel{3}}\times\frac{\cancel{6}^2}{\cancel{21}_3}=\frac{2}{3}$

The fractions in which the denominators are 10, 100, 1000 and so on are known as decimal fractions. Decimal fractions are multiplied and divided in the same way as fractions are.

Example 11: Multiply $\frac{4}{100}$ and $\frac{25}{10}$

We have,

$$\frac{4}{100}\times\frac{25}{10} = \frac{\cancel{4}}{_{25}\cancel{100}}\times\frac{\cancel{25}}{10} = \frac{1}{10}$$

Example 12: Divide $\frac{3}{1000}$ by $\frac{41}{10}$

We have,

$$\frac{3}{1000} \div \frac{41}{10} = \frac{3}{1000}\times\frac{10}{41}$$

$$= \frac{3}{\cancel{1000}_{100}}\times\frac{\cancel{10}}{41} = \frac{3}{4100}$$

Exercise 3.2

1 Find the sum of the following fractions.

a. $2\frac{3}{5}$ and $1\frac{1}{5}$ b. $\frac{7}{12}$ and $\frac{9}{16}$ c. $1\frac{4}{15}$ and $1\frac{3}{20}$ d. $3\frac{1}{3}$ and $4\frac{1}{4}$

2 Find the difference between each of the following pairs of fractions.

a. $4\frac{3}{7}$ and $2\frac{4}{7}$ b. $\frac{1}{2}$ and $\frac{3}{8}$ c. $2\frac{3}{10}$ and $1\frac{7}{15}$ d. 10 and $6\frac{3}{8}$

3 Find the product of the following.

a. $\frac{4}{8}$ and 18 b. 3 and $3\frac{1}{5}$ c $2\frac{5}{15}$ and $\frac{5}{10}$ d. $\frac{6}{10}$ and $1\frac{2}{100}$

4 Divide the following fractions.

a. 45 by $\frac{5}{9}$ b. $\frac{5}{20}$ by $\frac{12}{5}$ c. $1\frac{6}{15}$ by $\frac{7}{30}$ d. $\frac{18}{10}$ and $\frac{9}{10}$

Real Life Application of Fractions

Example 13: Shamita read $\frac{13}{35}$ of a book on first day, $\frac{3}{7}$ of the book on second day and finished the rest of the book on third day. Find the part of the book she read on the third day.

Part of the book read on 3rd day = Whole book – Parts of the book read on 1st and 2nd days.

$$= 1-\left(\frac{13}{35}+\frac{3}{7}\right) = 1-\left(\frac{13+15}{35}\right) = 1-\frac{28}{35} = \frac{35-28}{35} = \frac{7}{35} = \frac{1}{5}$$

Therefore, Shamita read $\frac{1}{5}$ part of the book on 3rd day.

Example 14: Nishant has a rectangular plot which has $5\frac{5}{11}$ m as its breadth and $2\frac{1}{3}$ times of its breadth as its length. Find the length of the boundary.

Breadth of the plot = $5\frac{5}{11}$ m

Length of the plot = $2\frac{1}{3}$ times of $5\frac{5}{11}$ m

$$= 2\frac{1}{3} \times 5\frac{5}{11} = \frac{7}{\cancel{3}} \times \frac{\cancel{60}^{20}}{11} = \frac{140}{11} = 12\frac{8}{11} \text{ m}$$

Perimeter of the plot = 2 (Length + Breadth)

$$= 2\left(5\frac{5}{11} + 12\frac{8}{11}\right) = 2\left(\frac{60}{11} + \frac{140}{11}\right) = 2\left(\frac{200}{11}\right)$$

$$= 2 \times \frac{200}{11} = \frac{400}{11} = 36\frac{4}{11} \text{ m}$$

Therefore, the boundary measures $36\frac{4}{11}$ m.

Example 15: $\frac{5}{6}$ of a class of 30 students are wearing blue t-shirts today. How many students are wearing blue T-shirts?

Number of students wearing blue T-shirts = $\frac{5}{\cancel{6}_1}$ of $\cancel{30}^5 = 25$

Therefore, 25 students are wearing blue T-shirts today.

Example 16: Ani has $12\frac{1}{2}$ kg of grains to distribute. If he gives $2\frac{1}{2}$ kg to each of his friends, how many friends get a share?

Number of friends who get shares = $12\frac{1}{2} \div 2\frac{1}{2} = \frac{25}{2} \div \frac{5}{2} = \frac{25}{2} \times \frac{2}{5} = 5$

Therefore, 5 friends get shares of grains.

Exercise 3.3

1. A merchant buys a $100\frac{1}{2}$ kg sack of wheat. If he sells $7\frac{1}{2}$ kg, $9\frac{1}{2}$ kg, $5\frac{1}{5}$ kg and $25\frac{1}{5}$ kg of wheat to different customers on different days, then how many kg of wheat does he sell? How many kg of wheat is left in the sack?
2. If the cost of 1 litre milk is ₹35.50, find the cost of $15\frac{1}{2}$ litres of milk.

3. Raju was given 24 problems as homework. He could solve $\frac{3}{4}$ of them correctly. Find the number of problems he could not solve correctly.

4. If a cable measuring $11\frac{1}{5}$ m is cut into equal pieces measuring $1\frac{2}{5}$ m each, then find the number of small cable pieces.

5. Each box of clothes some children collected for a clothing drive weighs $\frac{3}{4}$ kg. How many kg would $15\frac{1}{2}$ of these boxes weigh?

6. If we divide $15\frac{1}{2}$ kg of sweets among 6 members, how many sweets will each one get?

Summary

1. Fractions are added or subtracted only if they are like fractions. Unlike fractions are converted into like fractions before adding or subtracting.
2. Like fractions or unlike fractions can be multiplied or divided.

Revision Exercise

1 **Solve the following.**

a. $\frac{1}{3}$ of 12 b. $\frac{1}{12}$ of 60 c. $\frac{2}{3}$ of 12 d. $\frac{1}{3}$ of $\frac{1}{3}$

e. $\frac{10}{100} \times \frac{3}{100}$ f. $\frac{51}{10} \times \frac{2}{10}$ g. $\frac{8}{100} \div \frac{4}{10}$ h. $\frac{1}{10} \div \frac{1}{10}$

2 The perimeter of an isosceles triangle is $8\frac{10}{28}$ cm. If its unequal side measures $3\frac{2}{4}$ cm, find the measure of its equal sides.

3 A fruit seller buys 297 fruits, of which $\frac{2}{3}$ are apples. $\frac{3}{11}$ of the apples were rotten. If he sells each apple at ₹6.20, how much money does he receive?

4 A bridge was constructed in 3 phases. $\frac{2}{9}$ of the bridge was completed during the 2nd phase and $\frac{1}{3}$ during the 3rd phase. Find the part completed during the 1st phase.

5 A truck helper earns ₹3745 per month. The truck driver earns $2\frac{5}{7}$ more than the helper. Find the truck driver's earnings.

6 If the width and the length of a rectangle are $2\frac{1}{2}$ m and $3\frac{1}{2}$ m respectively, what is the area of the rectangle?

7 Akshay organised a trip and invited $\frac{1}{3}$ of his classmates. If $\frac{1}{4}$ of the classmates invited were boys, find how many girls were invited if the total strength of the class was 72.

8 John found 18 toys under his bed. If $\frac{1}{3}$ of the toys were toy cars, how many toy cars did he find under the bed?

9 Anita reads $1\frac{1}{3}$ of a book in one hour. What part of the book will she read in $5\frac{1}{2}$ hours?

10 In a students' hostel, each student is given $\frac{2}{3}$ litre milk. Among how many children can $20\frac{2}{3}$ litres of milk be distributed?

11 How many halves are there in six-fourth?

For the Curious Mind

1. 54 passengers were travelling in the lower deck of a double-decker bus and $1\frac{2}{3}$ times the people travelling in the lower deck were sitting in the upper deck of the same bus. Find the number of passengers travelling in the upper deck of the bus and the total passengers in the bus.
2. Rahul read $\frac{1}{6}$ of a book on the first day, $\frac{2}{9}$ on the second day, and $\frac{5}{12}$ on the third day, but he still had 35 pages to finish the book. Find the total number of pages of the book and number of pages read by Rahul on each day.

THEME 1

Exponents

4

What I shall learn

- To understand the laws of exponents
- To solve problems using the laws of exponents

Let's Get Started

We use the exponential form to represent repeated multiplication of a number. In the exponential form, the number written at the bottom is known as the **base** and the number of times it is multiplied is known as the **power** or **exponent**. For example, 7^9 is read as 'seven raised to the power of 9'. Here, 7 is the base and 9 is the exponent.

Examples: $216 = 6 \times 6 \times 6$ is represented in the exponential form as 6^3.

$5^4 = 5 \times 5 \times 5 \times 5 = 625$

In general, $\boldsymbol{a \times a \times a \times a \times a \times a \times \ldots}$ **(*n* times)** $\boldsymbol{= a^n}$. Here, a is the base and n is the index or exponent. The plural of 'index' is 'indices'.

Now, let us understand the different laws of exponents.

Laws of Exponents

Laws of exponents are the set of rules that help us to simplify the exponential form of expressions.

Law 1: $\boldsymbol{a^m \times a^n = a^{m+n}}$.

Thus, to multiply the exponents with the same base, add the powers and retain the base.

Example 1: a. $2^4 \times 2^3$

$2^4 \times 2^3 = 2^{4+3} = 2^7$

b. $15^6 \times 15^7$

$15^6 \times 15^7 = 15^{6+7} = 15^{13}$

Law 2: For $m > n$, $\boldsymbol{a^m \div a^n = a^{m-n}}$, that is, $\boldsymbol{\frac{a^m}{a^n} = a^{m-n}}$.

Thus, to divide exponents with the same base, subtract the powers and retain the base.

Example 2: a. $3^5 \div 3^2 = 3^{5-2} = 3^3$

b. $\frac{24^9}{24^4} = 24^{9-4} = 24^5$

Law 3: $\boldsymbol{(a^m)^n = a^{m \times n}}$.

Thus, when an exponent is raised to a power, retain the base and multiply the powers.

Example 3: Simplify the following expressions.

a. $(8^4)^5$

Using the law of exponents,

$(8^4)^5 = 8^{4\times5} = 8^{20}$

b. $(6^3)^8$

Using the law of exponents,

$(6^3)^8 = 6^{3\times8} = 6^{24}$

Additional Rules

1. $\boldsymbol{(ab)^n = a^n b^n}$.
   That is, when a product of two numbers is raised to a power, the answer is the product of each number raised to that particular power. For example, $(4 \times 5)^3 = 4^3 \times 5^3$.

2. $\boldsymbol{\left(\frac{a}{b}\right)^n = \frac{a^n}{b^n}}$.
   That is, when a fraction is raised to a power, we raise both the numerator and the denominator of the fraction to the given power. For example, $\left(\frac{3}{5}\right)^4 = \frac{3^4}{5^4}$.

3. Any non-zero number raised to the power 0 is 1. That is, $\boldsymbol{a^0 = 1}$, where $a \neq 0$.
   For example, $5^0 = 1$; $2^0 = 1$; $7^0 = 1$ and $8^0 = 1$.

4. Any number raised to the power 1 is the number itself. That is, $\boldsymbol{a^1 = a}$.
   For example, $5^1 = 5; 452^1 = 452$ and $1000^1 = 1000$.

Simplifying the Exponential Form of Expressions

Example 4: Simplify the following expression.

$$\left(2^4\right)^3 - \frac{4^4 \times 18^4}{81 \times 12^3}$$

Applying $(a^m)^n = a^{m\times n}$, $a^m \times a^n = a^{m+n}$ and $a^m \div a^n = a^{m-n}$,

$\left(2^4\right)^3 = 2^{4\times3} = 2^{12}$

$4^4 = (2\times2)^4 = 2^4 \times 2^4 = 2^8$

$18^4 = (3\times3\times2)^4 = 3^4 \times 3^4 \times 2^4 = 3^8 \times 2^4$

$81 = 3^4$ and $12^3 = (3\times2\times2)^3 = 3^3 \times 2^3 \times 2^3 = 3^3 \times 2^6$

$$\left(2^4\right)^3 - \frac{4^4 \times 18^4}{81 \times 12^3} = 2^{12} - \frac{2^8 \times 3^8 \times 2^4}{3^4 \times 3^3 \times 2^6} = 2^{12} - \frac{3^8 \times 2^{8+4}}{3^{4+3} \times 2^6} = 2^{12} - \frac{3^8 \times 2^{12}}{3^7 \times 2^6}$$

$= 2^{12} - 3^{8-7} \times 2^{12-6} = 2^{12} - 3 \times 2^6 = 2^{12} - (3 \times 64)$

$= 4096 - (3 \times 64) = 4096 - 192 = 3904$

$$\therefore \left(2^4\right)^3 - \frac{4^4 \times 18^4}{81 \times 12^3} = 3904$$

Example 5: Find the value of $(3)^3 \times 2^3$.

We have, $(3)^3 \times 2^3 = (3 \times 2)^3$ (Since $a^n b^n = (ab)^n$)

$= (6)^3 = 6^3 = 216$

Note

1. $(5 + 3)^2$ is not equal to $5^2 + 3^2$.
   But $(5 \times 3)^2 = 5^2 \times 3^2$.
2. $a^m \times a^m = (a^m)^2 = a^{2m}$
   or
   $a^m \times a^m = a^{m+m} = a^{2m}$

Exercise 4.1

1 Compute the following using the suitable laws of exponents.

a. $(5)^0$ b. $5^{12} \times 5^9$ c. $(9)^5$

d. $(2)^8 \div (2)^5$ e. $(5^3)^9$ f. $(6^5)^2$

2 Simplify the following using the suitable laws of exponents.

a. $3^0 \times 3^1$ b. $15^5 \div 5^3$ c. $(-2)^{12} \times (-2^2)^5 \times (-2^3)^9$

d. $\left(\frac{6}{3}\right)^3 \times \left(\frac{9}{4}\right)^3$ e. $\frac{42^3 \times 30^3}{64 \times 729 \times 35^3}$

Application of Laws of Exponents

Example 6: A microscope's objective lens can magnify an object 10^3 times, and its eyepiece can magnify the object 10^2 times. Find the maximum magnification of the microscope.

Magnification of objective lens = 10^3 times.

Magnification of eyepiece = 10^2 times.

Maximum magnification of the microscope = $a^m \times a^n = a^{m+n}$

$= 10^3 \times 10^2 = 10^{3+2} = 10^5$

Example 7: In a factory, the capacity of juice produced per day is 7^8 litres. If each small container can hold 7^2 litres of juice, how many such containers are required to hold the juice produced?

Capacity of juice produced per day = 7^8 litres

Capacity of each container = 7^2 litres

Number of containers required = $\frac{7^8}{7^2} = 7^6$

Example 8: The number of chocolates with each student in a class is 5^2. If the class had same number of students as the number of chocolates with each student, then what is the total number of chocolates with the students in the class?

Number of chocolates with each student = 5^2

Number of students in the class = 5^2

Total number of chocolates = $(5^2)^2 = 5^4$

Exercise 4.2

1. In a factory, there are 9^3 boilers, which each having the capacity of 9^5 tons. Find the total capacity of the boilers in the factory.
2. Find the volume of the washing machine if it's washing dimension is 2^6 by 3^4 by 2^3.
3. Mohit can type 10^3 words per hour. Find the number of words he can type in 10^4 hours.
4. The transportation industry transported 6^9 tonnes of coal. Each ship used for transportation could carry 6^2 tonnes of coal. If 6^2 number of ships were used for transportation, how many trips were made by these ships for transporting such huge amount of coal?

Summary

1. **Laws of Exponents:**
   - $a^m \times a^n = a^{m+n}$
   - $a^m \times b^m = (ab)^m$
   - $(a^m)^n = a^{mn}$
   - $\dfrac{a^m}{a^n} = a^{m-n}\ (m > n)$
   - $\dfrac{a^m}{b^m} = \left(\dfrac{a}{b}\right)^m$
   - $a^0 = 1$
2. Repeated multiplication of a number is expressed in the exponential form and it is read as number 'raised to the power'.

Revision Exercise

1 Fill in the blanks.

a. The exponential form of $5 \times 5 \times 5 \times 5 \times 5 \times 2 \times 2 \times 2 \times 2 \times 2 \times 2 \times 3 \times 3 \times 3$ is _______.

b. The value of $15^2 - 5^2$ is _______.

c. The product of 2^2 and 2^3 is _______.

d. The exponential form of 1000000 is _______.

2 Simplify the following expressions using the suitable laws of exponents.

a. $12^5 \div 6^4$

b. $(3)^4 \times (3^2)^0 \times (3^3)^1$

c. $(4)^2 \times (2)^2$

d. $\left(\frac{12}{10}\right)^3 \times \left(\frac{30}{45}\right)^3$

e. $\frac{49 \times 45^3}{729 \times 35^2}$

3 A sweet vendor prepared 10^2 amount of sweets for a function. If the order was given to same number of sweet vendors as the number of sweets prepared by each vendor, find the total number of sweets prepared for the function.

4 There were 3^5 mangoes distributed among 3^4 children. How many mangoes did each child get?

5 There were 4^6 books in the library. If 2^4 books have been lent, how many books are left in the library?

For the Curious Mind

1. The distance between the earth and moon is about 4×10^5 km. Express this value in metres.
2. How will you express this in the exponent form: on a social media 1 person informs 10 other people, these 10 people inform another 10 people and so on?

THEME 1

5 Sets

What I shall learn

- To understand the cardinal number of a set
- To learn different representations of sets
- To identify different types of sets

Let's Get Started

In the previous class, we have learned that a **set** is a well-defined collection of objects. 'Well-defined' means that there is a definite criteria to determine whether an object belongs to the given set or not.

Examples:

a. Collection of tigers in India

b. Collection of prime numbers less than 20, that is, P = {2, 3, 5, 7, 11, 13, 17, 19}.

Elements of a Set

The objects in the set are called **elements** or **members** of the set. We put the elements of a set within curly braces { } and usually denote a set by a capital letter.

Example 1: Write the set of all the composite numbers from 1 to 20.

The set of composite numbers from 1 to 20 includes 4, 6, 8, 9, 10, 12, 14, 15, 16, 18 and 20.

Let this set be called C.

$\therefore$ C = {4, 6, 8, 9, 10, 12, 14, 15, 16, 18, 20}

Here, 18 is an element of set C, that is, 18 belongs to set C and it is written as $18 \in C$. But 13 is not an element of this set, so it is written as $13 \notin C$.

Example 2: Write the elements of the following set.

A = {*x* | *x* is a factor of 26}

A = {1, 2, 13, 26}

Therefore, the elements of set A are 1, 2, 13 and 26.

Representation of Sets

There are two ways of representing the same set.

Roster Form

The method in which we list the elements of a given set is called the **roster form** or the **listing method**.

Consider the collection of all the months in a year. Let us call this set A.

We represent this set in the roster form as:

A = {January, February, March, April, May, June, July, August, September, October, November, December}

Example 3: Represent the following sets in roster form.

a. The collection of all the factors of 56

Let A be the required set.

$\therefore$ A = {1, 2, 4, 7, 8, 14, 28, 56}

b. The set of the first ten English consonants

Let X be the required set.

$\therefore$ X = $\{b, c, d, f, g, h, j, k, l, m\}$

Set-builder Form

The method in which we list the property or properties satisfied by the elements of the set is known as the **set-builder form** or the **rule method**.

Again consider the collection of all the months in a year. Let us call it set B now.

We represent this set in set-builder form as:

B = $\{x \mid x$ is a month in a year$\}$

Example 4: Represent S as the collection of all the integers between −10 and −20 in the set-builder form.

S = $\{x \mid x$ is an integer, $-20 < x < -10\}$

The same set can be expressed in the roster form as:

S = {−19, −18, −17, −16, −15, −14, −13, −12, −11}

Cardinal Number of a Set

Cardinal number of a set A is the number of distinct elements in the set. It is denoted as n(A).

Consider the following examples.

a. Set X = $\{a, b, c, d, e\}$ has 5 distinct elements.

b. Set Y = {1, 1, 2, 2, 2, 3, 4, 4, 5, 6} has 6 distinct elements although there are 10 elements in the set.

Example 5: Write the cardinal number of Set E = { }.

Set E = { } has no element. Therefore, the cardinal number of set E is 0. It is denoted as n(E) = 0.

Note

The cardinal number of a singleton set is 1.

Exercise 5.1

1 **State whether each of the following collections make up a set. Justify your answer.**

a. Collection of all the letters in your name

b. Collection of all integers

c. Collection of tall students in your class

d. Collection of polygons having four sides

e. Collection of sweet mangoes in a basket

2 **Express the following sets in roster form.**

a. Set of all whole numbers between 0 and 15

b. Set of all 3-digit even numbers less than 120

c. Set of all the multiples of 7 less than 100

d. Set of the first 5 odd numbers divisible by 13

e. Set of all the consonants in the word 'Bharat'

3 **Represent the following sets in set-builder form.**

a. A = {5, 10, 15, 20, 25, 30}   b. P = {2, 3, 5, 7, 11}

c. S = {M, A, T, H, E, M, A, T, I, C, S}   d. F = {a, e, i, o, u}

e. N = {January, February, March, April, May, June}

4 **Write the cardinal number of the following sets.**

a. A = {F, O, U, N, D, A, T, I, O, N}   b. B = {89, 52, 98, 89, 56, 56, 52, 87, 78, 78, 96}

c. C = $\{x \mid x + 2 = -5\}$ d. D = $\{x \mid x$ is a prime factor of 568$\}$

e. E = $\{x \mid x$ is a 2-digit prime number$\}$ f. F = $\{x \mid x$ is a multiple of 3 less than 15$\}$

Types of Sets

Let us recall the different types of sets.

Equivalent Sets

If the number of elements in two sets is equal, then they are called equivalent sets.

Consider the sets A = $\{p, q, r, s, t\}$ and B = {15, 30, 45, 60, 75}.

Sets A and B have equal number of elements and so, they are equivalent sets.

Thus, set A $\leftrightarrow$ set B if $n(A) = n(B)$.

Example 6: Are the two sets A = {2, 4, 6, 8, 10, 12, 14, 16, 18} and B = {1, 3, 5, 7, 9, 11, 13, 15} equivalent sets?

Here, $n(A) = 9$ and $n(B) = 8$. $\therefore n(A) \neq n(B)$

Therefore, the given sets are not equivalent sets.

Equal Sets

Two sets are said to be equal if they have the same elements.

Example 7: State whether the following pairs of sets are equal sets.

a. A = {2} and B = {1}

As sets A and B do not contain the same elements, they are not equal sets.

b. A = {2, 4, 6, 8} and B = {8, 6, 4, 2}

Here, sets A and B contain the same elements. Therefore, they are equal sets.

Finite Sets

If a set contains only a finite number of elements, then it is called a finite set.

Example 8: State whether the following sets are finite sets.

a. The set of all the prime factors of 425

Let A be the required set. Here, A = {5, 17} and n(A) = 2. Therefore, set A is a finite set.

b. The set of all the multiples of 8

Let B be the required set. Here, B = {8, 16, 24, 32, 40, 48, ...} and n(B) is infinite. Therefore, set B is not a finite set.

Infinite Sets

If the number of elements of a set cannot be counted, then it is an infinite set.

Example 9: State whether the following sets are infinite sets.

a. Set of all the factors of 200

It is a finite set as the number of factors of 200 is countable.

b. Set A = {−1, −2, −3, −4, ...}

It is an infinite set as the counting does not stop.

Singleton Sets

A set that contains only one element is known as a singleton set.

Example 10: State whether the following sets are singleton sets.

a. Set of even prime numbers

It is a singleton set as it contains only one element, that is, 2.

b. Set of odd composite numbers

It is not a singleton set as there are many odd composite numbers.

Empty Set

A set that contains no elements is known as an empty set.

Example 11: State whether the following sets are empty sets.

a. Set of all integers between −2 and −6

Here, set A = {−3, −4, −5} and n(A) = 3. Therefore, set A is not an empty set.

b. Set of the prime factors of 1

Here, $n(\text{B}) = \{\ \}$. Therefore, set B is an empty set.

Example 12: Classify the following into different types of sets.

Sets	Types of Set
A = {11, 13, 17, 19} and B = {2, 4, 6, 8}	Equivalent sets
C = { }	Empty set
D = Set of all even prime numbers	Singleton set
P = {*m*, *n*, *o*, *p*, *q*} and Q = {*o*, *p*, *m*, *q*, *n*}	Equal sets
R = Set of all the multiples of 25	Infinite set
S = Set of all the factors of 456	Finite set
A = {1, 2, 2, 1} and B = {1, 2}	Equal sets

Think and Discuss

Is a singleton set finite?

Exercise 5.2

1 Identify the equivalent sets among the following pairs of sets.

a. $\text{E} = \{x \mid x \text{ is a prime factor of } 25\}$ and $\text{F} = \{x \mid x \text{ is a multiple of } 5, x < 45\}$

b. C = {m, n, o, p} and D = {d, e, f, g}

c. A = {101, 103, 105, 107, 109} and B = {100, 102, 104, 106, 108}

d. $\text{G} = \{x \mid x \text{ is a letter in the word CULTURE}\}$ and $\text{H} = \{x \mid x \text{ is a letter in the word NATURE}\}$

e. X = {4, 8, 12, 16, 20} and Y = {8, 16, 20, 4, 12}

2 Identify the equal sets among the following pairs of sets.

a. C = {−1, −2, −3, −3, −2} and D = {−2, −3, −1, −2, −3, −1, −1}

b. G = {1, 2, 3, 4, 5, 6, 7, 8, 9} and H = {0, 1, 2, 3, 4, 5, 6, 7, 8}

c. $\text{E} = \{x \mid x \text{ is an odd number}, 15 < x < 25\}$ and $\text{F} = \{x \mid x \text{ is an even number}, 16 < x < 26\}$

d. Set of the first 10 positive integers and set of the first 10 natural numbers

e. $\text{A} = \{x \mid x \text{ is a prime number}, 2 < x < 6\}$ and B = {3, 5}

3 Classify the following as singleton and empty sets.

a. The set of all negative whole numbers

b. The set of even prime number(s)

c. A = {s}

d. $\text{B} = \{x \mid x \text{ is a month having 32 days}\}$

e. $\text{C} = \{x \mid x \text{ is a natural number}, 100 < x < 101\}$

4 Classify the following as finite or infinite sets.

a. The set of all the factors of 1000

b. The set of all the multiples of 15

c. The set of all the integers between –100 and 100
d. The collection of all the radii in a circle
e. The set of all the districts in India

5 **Match the following.**

Example	Type of Set
a. Set of all the multiples of 3	i. Finite set
b. Set of people working in a company	ii. Equal sets
c. Set of the first 5 whole numbers and the set of the first 5 natural numbers	iii. Infinite set
d. $A = \{x \mid x \in N, 9 < x < 10\}$	iv. Equivalent sets
e. C = Set of composite numbers between 0 and 6	v. Singleton set
f. $A = \{x \mid x$ is an even prime number$\}$ and $B = \{2\}$	vi. Empty set

Some More Types of Sets

Disjoint Sets

Two sets having no element in common are known as disjoint sets.

Example 13: State whether the following pairs of sets are disjoint sets.

a. $A = \{2, 4, 6, 8, 10\}$ and $B = \{3, 6, 9, 12, 15\}$

Here, sets A and B have a common element, namely, 6. Therefore, sets A and B are not disjoint sets.

b. $C = \{x \mid x$ is an odd natural number, $x < 10\}$ and $D = \{x \mid x$ is an even natural number, $x < 10\}$

Here, $C = \{1, 3, 5, 7, 9\}$ and $D = \{2, 4, 6, 8\}$. Sets C and D have no element in common. Therefore, they are disjoint sets.

Overlapping Sets

Two sets having at least one element in common are known as overlapping sets or intersecting sets.

Example 14: State whether the following pairs of sets are overlapping sets.

a. $A = \{1, 2, 3, 4, 5\}$ and $B = \{0, 1, 2, 3, 4\}$

Here, sets A and B are overlapping sets because they have 4 common elements.

b. A = Set of letters in the word MATHS and B = Set of letters in the word GEO

Here, sets A and B have no common elements. Therefore, they are not overlapping sets.

Universal Set

The set that contains all the elements of the sets under consideration is known as the universal set. It is denoted using the symbol U or ξ.

For example, let N be the set of all natural numbers, E be the set of all even natural numbers and O be the set of all odd natural numbers. Then, N will be a universal set as it contains both odd and even natural numbers.

That is, O = {1, 3, 5, 7, 9, ...} and E = {2, 4, 6, 8, 10, ...}

Therefore, N = {1, 2, 3, 4, 5, 6, 7, 8, 9, 10, ...} is a universal set.

Example 15: Write a universal set for the following sets.

a. A = {1, 3, 5, 7}, B = {2, 4, 6, 8} and C = {9, 10, 11, 12, 13, 14, 15}

∴ U = {1, 2, 3, 4, 5, 6, 7, 8, 9, 10, 11, 12, 13, 14, 15}

b. A = {a, d, f, e, c} and B = {a, e, f, b, g, h, i}

∴ U = {a, b, c, d, e, f, g, h, i}

Exercise 5.3

1 Identify overlapping and disjoint sets in the following pairs of sets.

a. A = {..., −50, −40, −30, −20, −10, 0} and B = {10, 20, 30, 40, 50, ...}

b. X = {x | x is a whole number, $x < 50$} and Y = {x | x is an integer, $x > -10$}

c. P = {Set of the first 10 prime numbers} and Q = {Set of the first 10 even numbers}

d. M = {x | x is a letter in the word MOON} and N = {x | x is a letter in the word EARTH}

e. Set of the first 5 multiples of 5 and set of the first 6 multiples of 6

2 Write a universal set for each of the following groups of sets.

a. A = {*a*, *c*, *f*, *g*, *h*} and B = {*b*, *d*, *e*, *i*, *j*}

b. A = {−1, −4, −6, −8, −9, −10} and B = {−2, −3, −5, −7}

c. A = {2, 4, 6, 8} and B = {10, 12, 14, 16, 18}

d. A = {2, 3, 5, 7, 11} and B = {13, 17, 19, 23, 31}

e. X = Factors of 8, Y = Factors of 10 and Z = Factors of 15

Summary

1. A set is a well-defined collection of objects.
2. Roster form and set-builder form are the two ways of representing sets.
3. The number of distinct elements of a set A is called the cardinal number of A.
4. There are different types of sets, namely, equivalent sets, equal sets, finite sets, infinite sets, singleton sets and empty sets.

Revision Exercise

1 **If P = {x | x is letter in the word OCEAN}, Q = {4, 16, 64, 256}, R = {3, 6, 9, 12, 15} and S = {x | x is a letter in the word INDIAN}, then write the sets to which each of the following belongs.**

a. 12 b. A c. 64 d. E

2 **Identify the method that has been used to represent the following sets. Also, find the cardinal number for each set.**

a. C = {7, 14, 21, 28, 35, 42, 49}
b. D = {x | x is an even prime number}

3 **Identify whether the given sets are finite, infinite, singleton or empty sets.**

a. A = {x | x is neither a prime nor a composite number}
b. B = {x | x is a multiple of 15}
c. C = {1, 2, 5, 10, 25, 50}
d. D = {x | x is a whole number between 50 and 51}
e. E = {x | x is a 3-digit number}
f. F = {5, 55, 555, 5555, ...}
g. G = {0}
h. H = {x | x is a negative integer between −5 and −6}

4 **Write the universal set for each of the following.**

a. A = {a, e, i, o, u}, B = {$b, c, d, f, g, h, j, k, l, m, n, p, q, r, s, t, v, w, x, y, z$}
b. G = {0, 2, 4, 6, 8}, R = {1, 3, 5, 7, 9}

Theme Worksheet 1

1 **Write a number in each circle so that the number in each box is equal to the sum of the two numbers in circles on either side of it.**

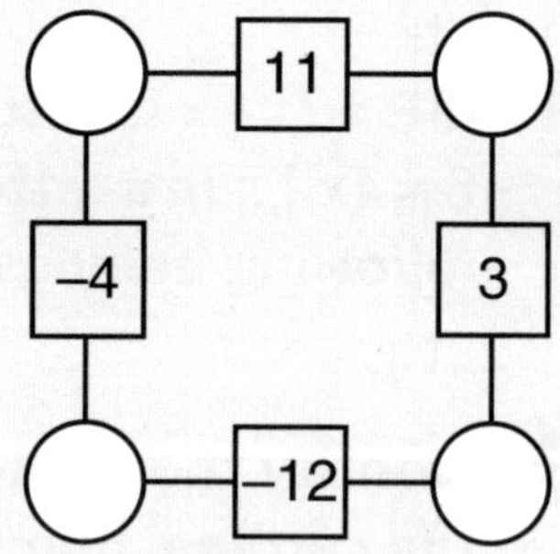

2 **In the arrangement, each number in the outer ring of a circle is the product of the number in the inner ring and the number in the center circle. Fill the vacant spaces correctly.**

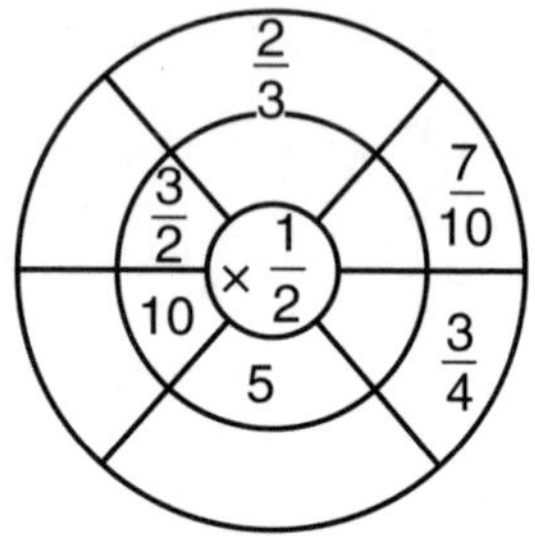

3 **Complete the following table using different properties of whole numbers.**

5 + 3 = 8	3 + 5 = 8	Commutative property under addition
(9 + 3) + 5 = 17	9 + (___ + 5) = ___	______
2 (5 − 2) = 6	(2 × 5) − (___ × 2) = ___	______
12 × (3 × 5) = ___	______	Associative property under multiplication
52 × 1 = ___	1 × 52 = ___	______

4 **Write the cardinal number for the following sets.**

a. First five multiples of 10

b. Factors of 48

5 **Solve the following riddles**

a. I am an exponential number

My base is an even prime number and the power is the even composite number between 9 and 11.

What number am I?

Solution: ____________

b. I am an exponential number

My base is an odd prime number between 10 and 20 and it is 3 less than the power. I have a power which is the second multiple of 10

What number am I?

Solution: ____________

Skill-based Worksheet - Solving Daily Life Problems

1. The temperature on a particular day of a city is as follows. In the morning it was 5°C, and then it went down to –7°C by 11 a.m. It continued at that temperature for 4 hours and then increased by 5°C. What is the temperature of the city at 4 p.m.?

2. The highest temperature recorded in India was 50.6° C in Rajasthan and the coldest temperature recorded was –45°C in Kashmir? What is the difference in these temperatures?

3. A dolphin is at 45 m below sea level. If it is going down at the rate of 10 m per second, at what depth will it be after 5 seconds?

4. Nihal had ₹250. He spent $\frac{2}{5}$ of the amount to buy a book. What is the amount remaining with him?

5. The table given below shows the schedule at a holiday camp. How much time has been allotted for each activity, if the total time spent at the camp was 20 hours?

Activity	Pitching Tents	Rafting	Playing Games & rest	Trekking
Time Spent	$\frac{1}{10}$	$\frac{1}{10}$	$\frac{3}{5}$	$\frac{1}{5}$
Time Spent in hours				

6. The 8 brothers together own half of their fathers land. If they divide it equally among themselves, how much of the land will each get?

7. There are 2^3 shelves in a stand. If each shelf has 2^3 books on them, how many books are there totally in the stand?

8. Students have gathered in the auditorium for the morning Assembly. The students standing on the right side are from classes 1-5. The students standing on the left side are from classes 6-10. Write the universal set for the classes present in the auditorium.

Mental Maths

Chapter 1 - Integers

Find the value of the following.

1. $-100 \times (-50)$
2. $77 \times (-7)$
3. $-5 \times 5 \times (-10) \times 2 \times (-1)$
4. $-9999 \div 11$
5. $(-844) \div (-4)$
6. $-625 \div 25$

Chapter 2 - Rational Numbers

Find the value of the following.

1. $5 - 1\frac{1}{4}$
2. $\frac{2}{5} \times 100$
3. $\frac{12}{24} + \frac{36}{48}$
4. $\frac{3}{8}$ of $\frac{1}{3}$
5. $12 \div \frac{1}{2}$
6. $\frac{15}{16} \div \frac{9}{16}$

Chapter 3 - Fractions

Find the value of the following.

1. $\frac{1}{4}$ of 36
2. $\frac{2}{3}$ of $\frac{1}{6}$
3. $15 \times \frac{2}{30}$
4. $26 \div \frac{13}{2}$
5. $\frac{6}{10} \div \frac{12}{10}$
6. $\frac{17}{13} \div 13$

Chapter 4 - Exponents

Find the value of the following.

1. $2^5 \times 10^2$
2. $3^2 \times 3^2$
3. $(12)^0$
4. $5^5 \div 5^3$
5. $4 \times 11^2 \div 2^2 \times 3$
6. $10^4 \div 10$

Chapter 5 - Sets

1. Find four elements of the set S = {x I x is a fraction between 1 and 2}
2. What are the elements of the set B = {x I x is a colour in the rainbow}?
3. Express this set in the set builder form: G = {Blue, Green, Yellow}
4. What is the cardinal number of the set: T = {x I x is an ocean on the earth}?
5. Write the universal set for these sets: D = {50, 60, 80, 90}, E = {10, 20, 30, 40, 70, 100}
6. Write the universal set for these sets: W = {x I x is a two digit number whose sum of the digits is 10}, X = {20, 30, 40, 50}

Ratio and Proportion

Chapters Covered

6. **Ratio and Proportion**
7. **Percentage**
8. **Profit and loss**
9. **Simple interest**
10. **Speed, distance and time**

Why this Theme Matters

Percentage

You must have seen certain hoardings with "Upto 50% off" written on it. Percentage is usually seen on hoardings, banners, pamphlets, digital display screen, television, internet etc.

Percentage plays an important role in various sectors. Observe the following statements belonging to different fields where percentage is used.

Banking sector: The interest for home loan is 10% per annum.

Insurance sector: The premium amount is 5% every year compared to the returns.

Manufacturing sector: The value of the machinery is depreciated by 10%.

Real estate sector: The value of the apartment is appreciated by 20%.

Education sector: The rise in the examination fee is 5% compared to last year.

Sales sector: Gold prices have gone up by 10%.

Economy sector: GDP of India has risen by 1%.

Environment protection sector: Pollution level has raised by 3%.

Certain factors such as commission, profit, loss, discount, sales, returns, results, income, salary, consumption, resources etc are usually expressed as percentage.

We will study about percentage and its applications under this theme.

THEME 2

Ratio and Proportion

6

Ratio

The ordered comparison of two similar quantities by division is called **ratio**. We denote ratio using the symbol ':'.

Thus, the fraction $\frac{a}{b}$ is also written as the ratio $a : b$.

In general, the ratio of two quantities a and b is written as $\boldsymbol{a : b}$ and we read it as 'a is to b'. The two quantities a and b are called the **terms** of the ratio. The first quantity a is called the **first term or antecedent** and the second quantity b is called the **second term or consequent**.

Two quantities can be compared only if they are in the same unit.

Note that the ratio 2 : 1 is different from 1 : 2. Hence, **the order of ratio is important when we compare two quantities.**

$a : b$

First term or Antecedent — Second term or Consequent

The **inverse ratio** of $a : b$ is $b : a$ and $a : b \neq b : a$ (where $a \neq 0$ and $b \neq 0$) unless $a = b$.

What I shall learn

- To understand the concept of ratios
- To understand the concepts of proportion
- To solve problems using unitary method

Remember

Ratio compares one quantity with another of the same kind. It is a pure number. It does not have a unit.

Note

- Ratio of 5 cm to 7 m is not 5 : 7. First, 7 m has to be converted and written as 700 cm. Then, the ratio will be 5 : 700 = 1 : 140.
- The ratio of 55 km and 76 kg cannot be found as their units are different and cannot be made same.

Example 1: Vani requires 45 minutes to finish her homework, whereas Rani requires 1 hour. What is the ratio of the time required by Vani to the time required by Rani for doing their homework?

Time required by Vani = 45 minutes

Time required by Rani = 1 hour = 60 minutes

Ratio of the time required by Vani to the time required by Rani = $45 : 60 = \frac{45}{60} = \frac{3}{4} = 3 : 4$

$\therefore$ Required ratio = 3 : 4

Example 2: If the ratios of the three interior angles of a triangle is 1 : 3 : 5, then find the measure of each angle of the triangle.

Method 1

Sum of the terms in the ratio = 1 + 3 + 5 = 9

Sum of three interior angles of a triangle = 180°

Thus, the three angles of the triangle are:

$\frac{1}{\cancel{9}} \times \overset{20}{\cancel{180}}° = 20°$; $\frac{3}{\cancel{9}} \times \overset{20}{\cancel{180}}° = 60°$ and $\frac{5}{\cancel{9}} \times \overset{20}{\cancel{180}}° = 100°$

Note

Algebraic method: When two or more unknown quantities are expressed in the ratio $a : b : c$, they can be expressed algebraically as ax, bx and cx.

Method 2

Let the three interior angles be x, $3x$ and $5x$.

Sum of the three interior angles of a triangle = 180°

That is, $x + 3x + 5x = 180° \Rightarrow 9x = 180° \Rightarrow x = 20°$

Thus, the three angles of the triangle are $x = 20°$, $3x = 3 \times 20° = 60°$ and $5x = 5 \times 20° = 100°$.

Properties of Ratio

Since ratios can be expressed as fractions, all the properties that hold true for fractions also hold true for ratios.

Simplest Form: A ratio is said to be in its simplest form if its terms do not have any common factor other than 1.

Equivalent Ratios: Like equivalent fractions, two ratios are said to be equivalent if their values are same in their simplest form.

To convert a given ratio into its simplest form, find the HCF of its antecedent and consequent, and divide both the terms of the ratio by the HCF.

Example 3: Write the ratio 85 : 136 in its simplest form.

The HCF of 85 and 136 is 17. Divide both the terms of the ratio by the HCF.

$$85 : 136 = \frac{85}{17} : \frac{136}{17} = 5 : 8$$

To Convert a Fractional Ratio into a Whole Number Ratio

If the antecedent or the consequent or both the terms of a ratio are fractions, then find the LCM of the denominators of the fractions and multiply both the terms of the ratio by this LCM. This will convert the fractional terms into whole numbers.

Example 4: Simplify each of the following ratios.

a. $3\frac{3}{4} : 6\frac{2}{3}$

$3\frac{3}{4} : 6\frac{2}{3} = \frac{15}{4} : \frac{20}{3}$

The LCM of 4 and 3 is 12.

$\frac{15}{4} : \frac{20}{3} = \frac{15}{4} \times 12 : \frac{20}{3} \times 12$

$= 15 \times 3 : 20 \times 4 = 45 : 80$

The HCF of 45 and 80 is 5.

$45 : 80 = \frac{45}{5} : \frac{80}{5} = 9 : 16$

$\therefore 3\frac{3}{4} : 6\frac{2}{3} = 9 : 16$

b. $\frac{3}{4} : \frac{5}{6} : \frac{7}{5}$

The LCM of 4, 6 and 5 is 60.

$\frac{3}{4} : \frac{5}{6} : \frac{7}{5} = \frac{3}{4} \times 60 : \frac{5}{6} \times 60 : \frac{7}{5} \times 60$

$= 3 \times 15 : 5 \times 10 : 7 \times 12$

$= 45 : 50 : 84$

Note

When we multiply/divide each term of a ratio by the same number, the ratio remains unchanged.

Example 5: A milkman has two milk cans. The ratio of water to milk in cans 1 and 2 are 7 : 9 and 8 : 11 respectively. Which can contains more water?

Ratio of water to milk in can 1 = 7 : 9

Ratio of water to milk in can 2 = 8 : 11

We must compare the ratios by making their consequents equal.

The LCM of the consequents 9 and 11 is 99.

Ratio of water to milk in can 1 = $7 : 9 = 7 \times 11 : 9 \times 11 = 77 : 99$

Ratio of water to milk in can 2 = $8 : 11 = 8 \times 9 : 11 \times 9 = 72 : 99$

$\therefore (77 : 99) > (72 : 99)$

Thus, there is more water in can 1 than in can 2.

Ratio as Percentage

A ratio can be expressed as percentage and vice-versa.

In order to convert a ratio into a percentage, multiply the ratio by 100 and write the answer using the percentage symbol (%).

Example: $1{:}2 = \frac{1}{2} = \frac{1}{2} \times 100\% = 50\%$

Similarly, to convert a percentage into a ratio, divide the given number by 100 and write it as a ratio.

Example: $25\% = \frac{25}{100} = \frac{1}{4} = 1 : 4$

Exercise 6.1

1. **Look at the tile patterns. What is the ratio of the shaded tiles to the non-shaded tiles in each case?**

   a. 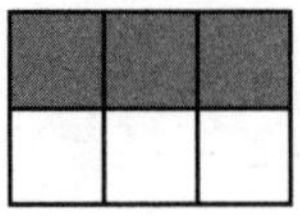
   b. 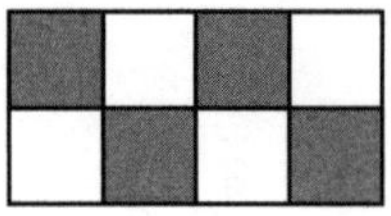
   c. 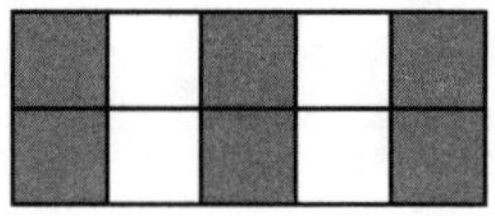
   d. 

2. **Express the following ratios in their simplest form.**

   a. 33 : 45 b. 120 : 65 c. 240 : 140 d. 2625 : 6250

3. **In each of the following, find the ratio of the first quantity to the second quantity in its simplest form.**

   a. ₹4, ₹2.50 b. 7 days, 7 weeks c. 2 h, 45 min d. 2 kℓ, 750 ℓ

4. **Rewrite the following ratios with their terms as natural numbers.**

   a. $\frac{1}{3} : \frac{1}{4}$ b. 10.5 : 17.5 c. $3\frac{3}{4} : 6\frac{2}{3}$ d. $4\frac{1}{4} : 2\frac{1}{3}$

5. **Shade the following tiles to make patterns showing the given ratios.**

   a. One black tile to every two white tiles
   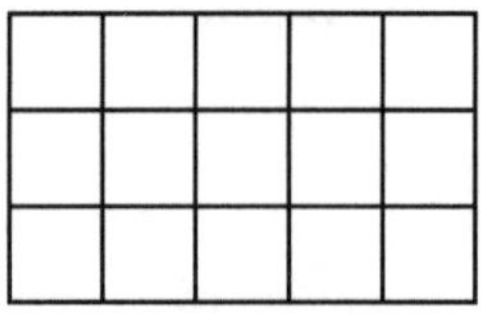
   b. 2 white tiles to every 3 black tiles
   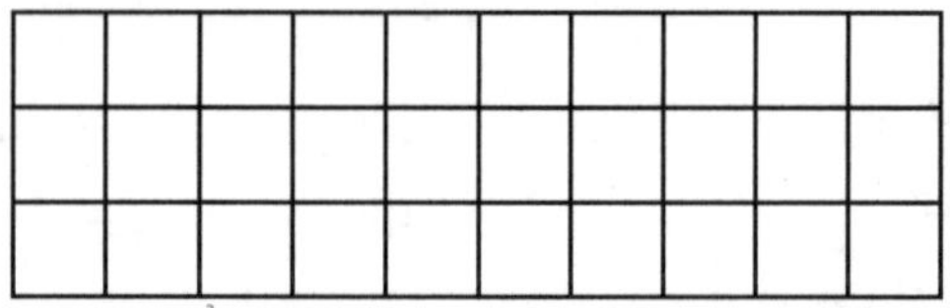

6. **In a group of 25 children, 15 are girls and 10 are boys. Find the following ratios and also express them as fractions.**

   a. The number of girls to the total number of children
   b. The total number of children to the number of boys
   c. The number of boys to the number of girls

7. In a bag of 30 mugs, two out of every three mugs are blue in colour. Find the number of blue mugs.

8. In a set of 40 books, three out of every five books are science books. Find the number of science books.

9. In Jasmine's birthday party, the ratio of children to adults is 4 : 1. If there are 24 children at the party, how many adults are there?

Proportion

When two ratios are equal, then the four numbers forming the two ratios in order are said to be in proportion. Thus, four numbers *a*, *b*, *c* and *d* are said to be in proportion if $a : b = c : d$. We write it as $a : b :: c : d$ and read it as '*a* is to *b* is as *c* is to *d*'.

Here, *a*, *b*, *c*, *d* are known as the first, second, third and fourth terms respectively of the given proportion.

The first and the fourth terms are called the **extremes**. The second and the third terms are called the **middle terms or means**.

Middle terms

$a : b :: c : d$

Extremes

Consider the proportion 4 : 12 = 100 : 300. Here, 4 and 300 are the extremes, and 12 and 100 are the means.

Product of extremes = $4 \times 300 = 1200$

Product of means = $12 \times 100 = 1200$

$\therefore$ Product of extremes = Product of means

If four numbers are in proportion, then the product of the extremes is equal to the product of the means. That is, if $a : b = c : d \Rightarrow \frac{a}{b} \times \frac{c}{d}$ Cross multiplying, we get $ad = bc$.

Note

Some other proportions of $a : b = c : d$

Alternendo	$a : c = b : d$
Componendo	$\frac{a+b}{b} = \frac{c+d}{d}$
Dividendo	$\frac{a-b}{b} = \frac{c-d}{d}$
Componendo and Dividendo	$\frac{a+b}{a-b} = \frac{c+d}{c-d}$

Also, check whether 12 : 4 = 300 : 100 is in proportion or not.

Yes, they are in proportion and this is called **invertendo** of 4 : 12 = 100 : 300.

If $a : b = c : d$, then its invertendo is $b : a = d : c$.

Now, consider the ratios 4 : 7 and 100 : 200.

Product of extremes = $4 \times 200 = 800$; Product of means = $7 \times 100 = 700$

Product of extremes $\neq$ Product of means

Here, $4 : 7 \neq 100 : 200$

Therefore, 4, 7, 100 and 200 are not in proportion.

If four numbers are not in proportion, then the product of extremes is not equal to the product of means.

Example 6: Find the missing quantity of the proportion 25 : 30 = 60 : ____.

Let the missing number be x.

It is given that, 25, 30, 60 and x are in proportion.

Then, product of extremes = product of means

$\Rightarrow 25 \times x = 30 \times 60 \Rightarrow 25x = 1800 \Rightarrow x = 72$

Therefore, the missing number of the proportion is 72.

Example 7: If A : B = 2 : 3 and B : C = 9 : 5, then find A : B : C.

B is the common term in both the ratios, but the values of B in both the ratios are not equal. So, we make them equal by finding their LCM.

The LCM of 3 and 9 is 9.

$A : B = 2 : 3 = 2 \times 3 : 3 \times 3 = 6 : 9$

A : B = 6 : 9 and B : C = 9 : 5

∴ A : B : C = 6 : 9 : 5

Example 8: Divide ₹6,81,540 among three sisters, Sameera, Sabeena and Shabana, such that Sameera gets twice that of what Sabeena gets and Sabeena gets three times that of what Shabana gets.

According to the problem,

Ratio of Sameera's amount to Sabeena's amount = 2 : 1

Ratio of Sabeena's amount to Shabana's amount = 3 : 1

Note that Sabeena's amount is common in both the ratios.

So, multiply the ratio of Sameera's amount to Sabeena's amount by 3, to make it the same.

Then, ratio of Sameera to Sabeena = $2 : 1 = 2 \times 3 : 1 \times 3 = 6 : 3$

∴ Ratio of the amounts of the three sisters = 6 : 3 : 1

Sum of the terms of the ratios = 6 + 3 + 1 = 10

Sameera's amount = $\frac{6}{10} \times 681540$ = ₹408924

Sabeena's amount = $\frac{3}{10} \times 681540$ = ₹204462

Shabana's amount = $\frac{1}{10} \times 681540$ = ₹68154

Exercise 6.2

1. **Which of the following sets of numbers taken in the given order are in proportion?**

   a. 5, 10, 16, 8 b. 16, 18, 8, 9 c. 24, 30, 10, 15 d. 7, 8, 28, 32

2. **Fill in the blanks with the missing numbers in the following proportions.**

   a. 9 : 12 = ____ : 48 b. 18 : 25 = 90 : ____

   c. ____ : 9 = 9 : 27 d. $5\frac{1}{2}$: ____ = $10\frac{1}{2} : 5\frac{1}{4}$

3. If P : Q is 6 : 5 and Q : R = 4 : 1, then find P : Q : R.

4. Divide ₹10,750 among X, Y and Z in such a way that X : Y = 5 : 4 and Y : Z = 3 : 4.

5. **Find the value of x in the following proportions.**

   a. $11 : x :: 4 : 8$ b. $5 : 12 :: 10 : x$ c. $7 : 5 :: 14 : x$ d. $12 : 21 :: x : 35$

6. Find the fourth proportional of 3, 8 and 12.

Unitary Method

Look at the following statements.

Statement 1: A car travels 120 km with 10 litres of petrol. What is its mileage?

Statement 2: A hostel needs 30 litres of oil per month to cook for 120 students. If the number of students increases to 200, how much oil is required?

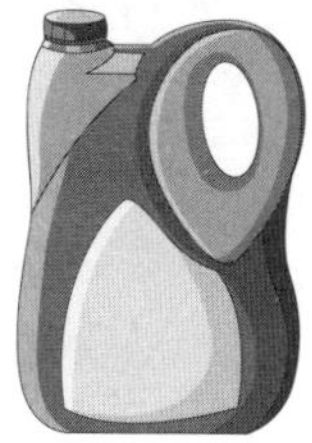

We have to find the value of one unit and then we have to find the value of the required number of units. This method is known as **unitary method**. Let us now look at the above examples again to get a clear idea of the unitary method.

Number of km travelled in 10 litres = 120 km

Number of km travelled in 1 litre = 120 ÷ 10

= 12 km per litre

Therefore, mileage of the car is 12 km per litre.

Oil needed for 120 students = 30 litres

Oil needed for one student = 30 litres ÷ 120

$= \frac{1}{4}$ litre

Therefore, oil needed for 200 students =

$\frac{1}{\cancel{4}_1} \times \cancel{200}^{50} = 50$ litres

Hence, 50 litres of oil is needed for 200 students.

Exercise 6.3

Solve the following word problems.

1. 5 workers in a handicraft workshop produce 15 things per day. What is the output per worker?
2. A car travels 80 km in 4 hours. Find the distance covered by the car in one hour.
3. There are 6 members in a family and they together earn ₹60,000 per month. How much does each member contribute towards the family if each of them earns equal amount?
4. A motor used to run a tube well makes 3720 rotations per minute. How many rotations does it make in a second? (Hint: Divide the number of rotation per minute by the number of seconds in 1 minute.)
5. Royal basmati rice is available in 25 kg and 15 kg packs. The 25 kg pack costs ₹700. What will be the cost of the 15 kg pack?
6. 12 farmers harvest a crop in a field in 20 hours. How many farmers will be required to harvest the same crop in 15 hours?

Summary

1. The ratio of two quantities *a* and *b* is written as $a : b$ and read as '*a* is to *b*'. The two quantities *a* and *b* are called the terms of the ratio. The first quantity *a* is called the first term or the antecedent and the second quantity *b* is called the second term or the consequent.
2. Four quantities *a*, *b*, *c* and *d* are said to be in proportion if $a : b = c : d$. We write it as $a : b :: c : d$ and read it as '*a* is to *b* is as *c* is to *d*'. Here, *a*, *b*, *c* and *d* are respectively the first, second, third and fourth terms of the given proportion. The first and the fourth terms are called the extremes. The second and the third terms are called the middle terms or means.
3. The method in which we first find the value of one unit and then the value of the required number of units is known as the unitary method.

For the Curious Mind

1. In a cricket match, Sachin scores 2 times the runs scored by Ganguly and Ganguly scores 4 times the runs scored by Dravid. Find the ratio of the runs scored by all the three players in the lowest terms.
2. What is the least number that should be added to each of the numbers 4, 7, 14, and 22 so that the terms in a proportion?

Revision Exercise

1 Fill in the blanks.

a. The ordered comparison of two similar quantities by division is called __________.

b. The inverse ratio of $p : q$ is __________.

c. If $a : b = c : d$, then a, b, c and d are said to be in __________.

d. If p, q, r and s are in proportion, then ps = __________.

2 State whether the following are true or false.

a. The ratio of an hour to 15 minutes is 1 : 15.

b. The ratio of 4 days to a week is 4 : 7.

c. The ratio of 1 gram to 1 kg is 1 : 1.

d. The ratio of 100 m to 1 km is 1 : 10.

3 Find the value of *x* in each case.

a. $3 : 7 = 9 : x$ b. $x : 16 = 63 : 112$ c. $15 : 22\frac{1}{2} = x : 9$ d. $3\frac{1}{5} : x = 7\frac{1}{2} : 12\frac{1}{2}$

4 The given quantities in each case are not in proportion. Change the order of the numbers so that they are in proportion.

a. 8, 7, 21, 24 b. 30, 45, 24, 36 c. 13, 11, 33, 39 d. 5, 10, 16, 8

5 The cost of repairing a road of length 2 km 125 m is estimated at ₹30,60,000. Out of the length of the road, 1 km 375 m belongs to the municipality and the remaining to the Road and Building Department. How much amount each has to bear to repair the part of the road under their control if the expenses have to be shared in the ratio 11 : 17?

6 The ratio of income to expenditure of Leena and Veena are 3 : 2 and 4 : 3 respectively. Both Leena and Veena earn ₹35,000 each per month. Find whose expenditure is more.

7 If L : M = 5 : 12 and M : N = 8 : 7, find L : M : N.

8 If A : B = $\frac{3}{5} : \frac{5}{7}$ and B : C = = $\frac{3}{4} : \frac{2}{5}$, find A : B : C.

9 The perimeter of a triangle is 3.15 m and the sides of the triangle are in the ratio 10 : 17 : 8. Find the lengths of the sides.

10 Three people contributed towards an investment in the ratio 4 : 5 : 6. If they have invested a total of ₹7,87,500, then find the amount contributed by each person.

11 The length and breadth of a rectangle are in the ratio 5 : 3. If the perimeter of the rectangle is 880 cm, then find the length and breadth of the rectangle.

12 The ratio of orange squash to sugar in two bottles A and B is 15 : 7 and 17 : 8 respectively. Which juice is sweeter?

13 The weight of 56 books is 8 kg. What is the weight of 152 such books? How many such books will weigh 5 kg? (Hint: First find the weight of 1 book and then multiply it with the required number of books. Secondly, find the number of books that weigh 1 kg and then multiply it with the required weight of the books.)

14 76 persons can complete a job in 42 days. In how many days will 56 persons complete the same job?

THEME 2

Percentage

7

What I shall learn

- To understand and apply the concept of percentage
- To relate fractions, decimals and ratios to percentage

Let's Get Started

The word 'per cent' is derived from the Latin word *per centum* meaning 'per hundred'.

The symbol for percentage is % and is read as 'per cent'.

Percentage is the numerator of a fraction with the denominator being 100. So, the term 'per cent' is another name of hundredths.

$3\% = \frac{3}{100}$, $17\% = \frac{17}{100}$, $63\% = \frac{63}{100}$

Conversions

Percentage Into Fraction

To convert a percentage into a fraction, divide the percentage numeral by 100 or multiply by $\frac{1}{100}$ and remove the % sign.

Example 1: Convert 75% into a fraction.

$$75\% = \frac{75}{100} = \frac{75 \div 25}{100 \div 25} = \frac{3}{4}$$

After conversion, express the fraction in its simplest form.

Example 2: Convert $6\frac{2}{3}\%$ into a fraction.

$$6\frac{2}{3}\% = \frac{20}{3}\% = \frac{20}{3} \times \frac{1}{100} = \frac{1}{15}$$

Example 3: Convert 207.5% into a fraction.

$$207.5\% = \frac{207.5}{100} = \frac{2075}{1000} = \frac{83}{40} = 2\frac{3}{40}$$

Fraction Into Percentage

To convert a fraction into a percentage, change it to a fraction of hundredths and put % sign. Or, multiply the fraction by 100%.

Example 4: Convert $\frac{2}{5}$ into a percentage.

Change the denominator, i.e., 5 of the fraction $\frac{2}{5}$ to 100 by multiplying the numerator and denominator by 20.

$$\frac{2}{5} = \frac{2 \times 20}{5 \times 20} = \frac{40}{100} = 40\%$$

or $\frac{2}{5} \times 100\% = 2 \times 20\% = 40\%$

Example 5: Express 29 out of 40 as a percentage.

$$\frac{29}{40} = \frac{29}{40} \times 100\% = \frac{29}{2} \times 5\% = \frac{145}{2}\%$$

$$= 72\frac{1}{2}\%$$

Example 6: Convert $1\frac{3}{7}$ into a percentage.

$$1\frac{3}{7} = \frac{10}{7} = \frac{10}{7} \times 100\% = \frac{1000}{7}\%$$

$$= 142\frac{6}{7}\%$$

Percentage Into Decimal

To convert a percentage into a decimal, express it as a fraction of hundredths, remove the % sign and then convert it to a decimal. Or, divide the percentage by 100 and remove the % sign.

Note

The number of zeros in the denominator is the same as the number of digits after the decimal point in the given decimal number and vice versa.

Example 7: Convert 84% into a decimal.

Divide the percentage by 100.

$$84\% = \frac{84}{100} = 0.84 \qquad \therefore 84\% = 0.84$$

Example 8: Convert 0.07% into a decimal.

$$0.07\% = \frac{0.07}{100} = 0.0007$$

Example 9: Convert 1025% into a decimal.

$$1025\% = \frac{1025}{100} = 10.25$$

Decimal Into Percentage

To convert a decimal into a percentage, express it as a fraction of hundredths and then convert it to a percentage. Or, multiply the decimal by 100%.

Example 10: Convert 0.05 into a percentage.

$$0.05 = \frac{5}{100}$$

Multiply the fraction by 100%.

$$\frac{5}{100} \times 100\% = 5\% \text{ or } 0.05 = 0.05 \times 100\% = 5\%$$

Example 11: Convert 0.7 into a percentage.

$$0.7 = 0.7 \times 100\% = 70\%$$

Example 12: Convert 2.236 into a percentage.

$$2.236 = 2.236 \times 100\% = 223.6\%$$

Percentage Into Ratio

To convert a percentage into a ratio, divide the percentage numeral by 100 or multiply it by $\frac{1}{100}$ and write the fraction as a ratio.

Example 13: Convert $86\frac{2}{5}$ % into a ratio.

$$86\frac{2}{5}\% = \frac{432}{5}\% = \frac{432}{5} \times \frac{1}{100} = \frac{108}{125}$$

$$= 108 : 125$$

Example 14: Convert 6.25% into a ratio.

$$6.25\% = \frac{6.25}{100} = \frac{625}{10000} = \frac{1}{16} = 1 : 16$$

Ratio Into Percentage

To convert a ratio into a percentage, first change the given ratio into a fraction and then multiply it by 100%.

Example 15: Convert 7 : 8 into a percentage.

$$7 : 8 = \frac{7}{8} = \frac{7}{8} \times 100\% = \frac{7}{2} \times 25\% = \frac{175}{2}\%$$

$$= 87\frac{1}{2}\%$$

Example 16: Convert 4 : 3 into a percentage.

$$4 : 3 = \frac{4}{3} = \frac{4}{3} \times 100\% = \frac{400}{3}\%$$

$$= 133\frac{1}{3}\%$$

Exercise 7.1

1. **Express the following percentage as fractions.**
   a. 2% b. 175% c. 4.25% d. $3\frac{1}{8}\%$
2. **Express the following fractions as percentage.**
   a. $\frac{1}{12}$ b. $\frac{29}{50}$ c. $\frac{51}{10}$ d. $6\frac{1}{4}$
3. **Express the following percentage as decimals.**
   a. 1% b. 75% c. $3\frac{1}{8}\%$ d. 12.5%
4. **Express the following decimals as percentage.**
   a. 0.21 b. 0.02 c. 1.2 d. 0.125
5. **Express the following percentage as ratios.**
   a. 3% b. 48% c. $8\frac{1}{3}\%$ d. 7.5%
6. **Express the following ratios as percentage.**
   a. 3:10 b. 13:60 c. 3:4 d. 8:5

Expressing One Quantity as a Percentage of Another Quantity

Convert both the quantities into the same unit, divide the first quantity by the second quantity and multiply by 100%.

Example 17: Mahesh got 60 marks out of 75 marks. Find his marks in percentage.

First quantity = 60; Second quantity = 75

Marks in percentage = $\frac{60}{75} \times 100\% = 80\%$

Finding Percentage of a Given Quantity

Convert the percentage into a fraction and then multiply the fraction by the given quantity.

Example 18: Find $35\frac{1}{3}\%$ of 150.

$35\frac{1}{3}\%$ of 150 = $\frac{106}{3}\%$ of 150

$= \frac{106}{3} \times \frac{1}{100} \times 150 = 53$

Example 19: $\frac{3}{5}\%$ of a number is 15,000. Find the number.

Let the required number be x.

$\frac{3}{5}\%$ of $x = 15000$

$\frac{3}{5} \times \frac{1}{100} \times x = 15000$

$x = 15000 \times 100 \times \frac{5}{3} = 25,00,000$

Example 20: There are two gift vouchers:
(a) 75% of ₹4200
(b) 35% of ₹8800.
Which one will you select?

75% of 4200 = $\frac{75}{100} \times 4200 = 75 \times 42$
= ₹3150

35% of 8800 = $\frac{35}{100} \times 8800 = 35 \times 88$
= ₹3080

75% of ₹4200 gift voucher is worthier than 35% of ₹8800. So, we select the first gift voucher.

Increase or Decrease of Measures in Percentage

$$\text{Increase per cent} = \left[\frac{\text{New value} - \text{Old value}}{\text{Old value}} \times 100\right]\% = \left[\frac{\text{Increase in value}}{\text{Old value}} \times 100\right]\%$$

$$\text{Decrease per cent} = \left[\frac{\text{Old value} - \text{New value}}{\text{Old value}} \times 100\right]\% = \left[\frac{\text{Decrease in value}}{\text{Old value}} \times 100\right]\%$$

Example 21: The price of petrol decreases from ₹75 to ₹72. What is the percentage of decrease in the price of petrol?

Old value = ₹75; New value = ₹72

$$\text{Decrease per cent} = \left[\frac{\text{Old value} - \text{New value}}{\text{Old value}} \times 100\right]\% = \frac{(75-72) \times 100\%}{75} = \frac{3 \times 100\%}{75} = 4\%$$

Example 22: Sanju's salary has been increased by 14%. Last year, he got ₹42,500 per month. What is his salary per month this year?

Method 1

Sanju's salary per month last year = ₹42,500

Percentage of increase in the salary = 14%

Increase in salary = 14% of 42500

$= \frac{14}{100} \times 42500 = 5950$

Therefore, Sanju's salary per month this year

= 42500 + 5950 = ₹48,450

Method 2

If there is 14% increase, 100 will become 114.

Ratio of increased value to original value

= 114 : 100

Therefore, the increased value of ₹42,500 in this ratio $= 42500 \times \frac{114}{100}$ = ₹48,450

If there is an increase of x% in a quantity, then its value increases to $(100 + x)$% over the original value. So, to get the increased value, multiply the given quantity with $\frac{100 + x}{100}$.

Similarly, if there is a decrease of x% in a quantity, then its value decreases to $(100 - x)$% over the original value. To get the decreased value, multiply the given quantity with $\frac{100 - x}{100}$.

Exercise 7.2

1. **What per cent of the first quantity is the second quantity in each of the following?**

   a. ₹2,000; ₹4 b. ₹2.80; ₹0.56 c. 3.5 ℓ; 630 mℓ d. $7\frac{1}{3}$ kg; $5\frac{1}{2}$ kg

2. **Find the following.**

   a. 15% of ₹80 b. 6.5% of 1,400 c. $8\frac{1}{3}$% of 4 dozens d. 30% of 1 ℓ 20 mℓ

3. **Increase the value of each quantity by the given percentage and write the answer.**

   a. 500 by 3.4% b. ₹125 by 125% c. ₹2,400 by $16\frac{2}{3}$% d. 11.20 m by 25%

4. **Decrease the value of each quantity by the given percentage and write the answer.**

   a. 50 by 12.5% b. ₹25,000 by 50% c. ₹15.40 by 15% d. 15 kg by $16\frac{2}{3}$%

5. $13\frac{1}{3}$% of an amount is ₹520. What is $3\frac{12}{13}$% of the same amount?

Uses of Percentage

Percentage is widely used in real life for calculating profit or loss, discount, interest, dividend/commission, tax and so on. Recall that when the selling price (SP) is greater than the cost price (CP), there is a profit. When the selling price is lesser than the cost price, there is a loss. It is more meaningful if we express profit and loss in terms of percentage.

Revision Exercise

1. **Express each of following as per cents.**

   a. $\frac{7}{18}$ b. $1\frac{3}{4}$ c. 1.08 d. 0.025

2. $6\frac{1}{4}$% of a number is 0.25. Find the number.

3. 72% of a volume is 36 litres. What is 25% of this volume?

4. Naveen spends ₹22,490 and saves $13\frac{1}{2}$% of his income. What is Naveen's monthly income?

5. In an online test, one is required to get 36% of the maximum marks in order to pass. A student got 80 marks and was declared as failed by 28 marks. Find the maximum marks of the online test.

6. Santoshi Singh earns ₹36,000 per month. She spends $8\frac{1}{3}$% on house rent, $33\frac{2}{3}$% on food and the remaining on shopping. Find the amount she spends on each of these items.

7. The cost of a bus last year was ₹6.72 lakhs. Now, the cost of the same bus is ₹7.28 lakhs. What is the percentage of increase?

8. The cost of a two wheeler is ₹52,000. Its cost decreases by 5% every year due to its usage. What will be the cost after 2 years?

9. The salary of Seema was first increased by 10% but the next year it was decreased by 10%. If her salary before the increase was ₹50,000, what was the change in her salary? Also, find the increase or decrease percentage.

For the Curious Mind

In School A, 68 students appeared for a public exam, out of which 51 students passed. In School B, 40 students appeared and 32 of them passed. Which school's performance can be called better and why?

THEME 2

Profit and Loss 8

Let's Get Started

Cost price is the price at which the goods are purchased from the wholesaler or producer. It is written as **CP**.

Overhead expenses are the expenses incurred during buying and selling. These include transportation, packing, rent, labour, fuel and are added to the cost price.

Thus, actual or total cost is the sum of the cost price and the overhead expenses put together.

What I shall learn

- To find profit or profit percentage and loss or loss percentage
- To solve problems on profit and loss

Marked price is the price at which goods are available in the shop or market. It is written as **MP**.

Selling price is the price at which the shopkeeper sells the goods to the consumer or customer. Selling price may be different from the marked price. Selling price is written as **SP**.

Profit is earned when the selling price is more than the cost price.

Profit = SP – CP

Loss is incurred when the selling price is less than the cost price.

Loss = CP – SP

Example 1: Rohan bought 10 kg mushrooms from the market at ₹45 per kg. He spent ₹100 on fuel for transportation and ₹50 on packing. Then, he sold all mushrooms at ₹64 per kg. Find the profit or loss incurred during the sale.

CP of the mushrooms = 10 × ₹45 = ₹450

Overhead expenses = Cost of fuel + Cost of packaging

= ₹100 + ₹50 = ₹150

∴ Actual cost price of 10 kg mushrooms = ₹450 + ₹150 = ₹600

Total SP of 10 kg mushrooms

= SP of 10 kg mushrooms at ₹64 per kg

= 64 × 10 = ₹640

Hints and Tips

Always remember that if overhead expenses are mentioned in the question, then total CP = CP + Overhead expenses.

Here, the total selling price is more than the actual cost.

Therefore, Rohan made a profit of ₹640 – ₹600 = ₹40.

Example 2: A fruit seller bought 100 apples at ₹6 each. He spent ₹250 on transportation and storage. He sold all the apples for ₹800. Find the profit or loss incurred by the fruit seller.

Cost of 100 apples = ₹100 × 6 = ₹600

Overhead expenses = ₹250

∴ Total CP of the apples = ₹600 + ₹250 = ₹850

Total SP of the apples = ₹800

Here, the total SP is less than the total CP. Therefore, the fruit seller incurred a loss of ₹850 – ₹800 = ₹50.

Exercise 8.1

1. A shopkeeper buys 25 pencils at ₹65. He sells them at ₹3.50 each. Find the profit or loss incurred by the shopkeeper.
2. A pen drive bought for ₹210 is sold for ₹250. Find the profit/loss.
3. Find the CP of a cell phone, if on selling it for ₹8200 a gain of ₹540 is made.
4. Find the SP of a cricket bat which is bought for ₹990 and sold at a loss of ₹77.
5. Chocolates are bought at 3 for ₹30 and sold at 2 for ₹24. Find
   i. Profit/Loss made on selling 1 chocolate.
   ii. Profit/Loss made on selling 6 similar chocolates.

Profit % or Loss %

Profit % or loss % is calculated on the actual cost price for every ₹100.

$$\text{Profit } \% = \frac{\text{Profit}}{\text{CP}} \times 100$$

$$\text{Loss}\% = \frac{\text{Loss}}{\text{CP}} \times 100$$

Example 3: Mahesh bought a radio for ₹500. Find the SP and profit percent if he gains ₹45.

CP of the radio = ₹500

Profit = ₹45

SP = CP + Profit = ₹500 + ₹45 = ₹545

$$\text{Profit}\% = \frac{\text{Profit}}{\text{CP}} \times 100 = \frac{45}{500} \times 100 = \frac{\overset{9}{\cancel{45}}}{\cancel{500}} \times \cancel{100} = 9\%$$

Therefore, Mahesh earned 9% profit.

Example 4: Krishna bought a chair for ₹480 and sold it for ₹540. Find his gain or loss per cent.

CP of the chair = ₹480

SP of the chair = ₹540

$\therefore$ Profit = ₹540 − ₹480 = ₹60 as SP > CP

$$\text{Profit\%} = \frac{\text{Profit}}{\text{CP}} \times 100 = \frac{60}{480} \times 100 = \frac{\cancel{60}}{_8\cancel{480}} \times 100 = \frac{100}{8} = 12.5\%$$

Therefore, the profit percentage earned by Krishna was 12.5%.

Exercise 8.2

1. What is the profit percentage if a calculator worth ₹150 is being sold at ₹186?
2. What is the profit or loss per cent earned when a dozen bananas worth ₹48 are sold at ₹3.80 each?
3. Sushmita bought a dress for ₹600 and sold it for ₹690. Find the profit percentage.
4. Find the loss percentage if Pratyush incurred a loss of ₹310 when he sold cosmetics for ₹1550.

Calculating Profit/Loss When Profit/Loss Percentage is Given

The amount of profit or loss is calculated on the total cost price. If the percentage of profit or loss is known to us, we can calculate the selling price by adding the profit or by deducting the loss from the cost price.

Profit or loss = Total cost price × % of profit or loss

Example 5: A calculator was bought for ₹300. It was sold at a profit of 8% after inserting a new battery worth ₹50. Find the price at which the calculator was sold.

CP of the calculator = ₹300

Overhead charges = ₹50

$\therefore$ Total CP = ₹300 + ₹50 = ₹350

Profit = Total cost price × profit%

$$= 350 \times \frac{8}{100} = ₹28$$

$\therefore$ SP of the calculator = CP + Profit = ₹350 + ₹28 = ₹378

Example 6: Darshana bought an oil painting from an art gallery for ₹45,000 and spent ₹2100 on framing and packing it. She sold it at a profit of 12%. Find the selling price of the oil painting.

CP of the oil painting = ₹45,000

Overhead charges = ₹2100

Actual CP = ₹45000 + ₹2100 = ₹47100

$$\text{Profit} = \frac{12}{100} \times 47100 = ₹5652$$

SP of the oil painting = ₹47100 + ₹5652 = ₹52752

Therefore, the SP of the oil painting is ₹52,752.

Example 7: A shopkeeper buys sugar worth ₹1200 and flour worth ₹1800. Find the selling price and the total profit earned or the loss incurred by the shopkeeper if he sells the sugar at 5% profit and the flour at 2% loss.

CP of the sugar = ₹1200

Profit percentage on sugar = 5%

$$\text{Profit} = 1200 \times \frac{5}{100} = ₹60$$

∴ SP of the sugar = ₹1200 + ₹60 = ₹1260

CP of the flour = ₹1800

Loss percentage on flour = 2%

$$\text{Loss} = 1800 \times \frac{2}{100} = ₹36$$

∴ SP of the flour = ₹1800 − ₹36 = ₹1764

The CP of both the sugar and the flour = ₹1200 + ₹1800 = ₹3000

The SP of both the sugar and the flour = ₹1260 + ₹1764 = ₹3024

SP > CP

∴ Profit = ₹3024 − ₹3000 = ₹24

Therefore, the shopkeeper made a profit of ₹24.

Exercise 8.3

1. **Find the selling price in each of the following.**
   a. Cost price = ₹750, profit = 10%
   b. Cost price = ₹600, loss = 9%
   c. Cost price = ₹1000, loss = 2%
   d. Cost price = ₹350, overhead expenses = ₹50, profit = 15%
2. Find the selling price of a television set that was bought for ₹15,000 and sold at a profit of 12%.
3. Find the selling price of a car worth ₹5,00,000 if it was sold at a loss of 6% or at a profit of 6%.

Summary

- Cost price is the price at which a shopkeeper purchases goods from the wholesaler or producer. Overhead expenses are the expenses incurred during buying and selling. They include transportation, packing, rent, labour, fuel, etc. Total CP is cost price and overhead expenses put together.
- Marked price is the price at which goods are available in the shop or market.
- Selling price is the price at which a shopkeeper sells goods to the consumer or customer. It may be different from the marked price due to discounts and bargaining during sale.
- Profit is earned when the selling price is more than the cost price.
- Loss is incurred when the selling price is less than the cost price.
- Percentage of profit or loss is calculated on the cost price for every ₹100.

For the Curious Mind

A mechanic bought an old cycle for ₹500 and spent ₹750 on extra fittings and other spares. He expected ₹1500 but sold it for ₹1400. Find the expected profit percentage and actual profit percentage.

Revision Exercise

1. **Find the selling price in each case and complete the table.**

Cost Price (₹)	Overhead Expenses (₹)	Profit (₹)	Loss (₹)	Selling Price (₹)
85	25	–	10	
150	35	15	–	
300	25	–	15	
800	125	20	–	

2. **Find the profit or loss percentage and complete the table.**

Cost Price (₹)	Overhead Expenses (₹)	Selling Price (₹)	Profit %	Loss %
45	15	72		
165	0	176		
585	40	575		
5320	80	5238		

3. **State whether the following statements are true or false.**

   a. Marked price usually includes cost price, overhead expenses and profit of the seller.

   b. Selling price is different from marked price due to the discounts, offers and bargaining done during the sale.

   c. Profit is earned when the selling price is less than the cost price.

4. **Solve the following.**

   a. Find the profit or loss percentage when Parankush sells goods worth ₹1800 at ₹1440.

   b. Find the selling price of a computer that was bought for ₹35,000 and sold at a profit of 9%.

   c. A vegetable vendor bought vegetables worth ₹2000 and spent ₹400 on transportation and storage. Find the percentage of profit or loss if the vegetables are sold at ₹2520.

   d. If the cost price of 25 articles is equal to the selling price of 10 articles, then what is the percentage of profit or loss incurred by the merchant?

THEME 2

Simple Interest 9

What I shall learn

- To understand the concept of simple interest
- To apply the concept of simple interest in real life

Let's Get Started

I borrowed money from the bank to buy a house. The sum of money borrowed or loaned is known as the principal. For using this money borrowed from the bank and for keeping it for some time, I have to pay some extra money to the bank. This is the charge on the borrowed money and is known as the interest. Thus, at the expiry of the time for which the loan was taken, I have to pay to the bank the sum borrowed, that is, the principal, as well as the charge on the borrowed money, that is, the interest. This money that is the sum of the principal and the interest is known as the amount.

Remember

- The amount of money one borrows for his needs or one lends to others is called the **principal**. It is denoted by 'P'.
- The period for which the money is borrowed or given is known as the **time period**. It is denoted by 'T'.
- The rate at which the lender charges the borrower is known as the **rate of interest**. It is denoted by 'R'.
- Rate is calculated per unit of money and per unit of time. The rate of interest per ₹100 per annum is called **rate per cent**.
- The extra money that is repaid to the lender in addition to the money borrowed is called the **interest**. It is denoted by 'I'.
- The **amount** that is to be repaid is equal to the sum of the principal and the interest. It is denoted by 'A'.

  Amount = Principal + Interest

Simple Interest

Let us see how to calculate interest. Consider the following example.
A farmer borrows ₹3,00,000 at 15% for three years from a cooperative society bank.
Here, the rate is 15% per annum. That is, interest on ₹100 for 1 year = ₹15
Given below is the table that shows the amount after each year.

Time	Principal	Rate of interest	Interest	Amount for two years
For 1st year	₹3,00,000	15%	$\frac{15 \times 300000}{100} = 45000$	300000 + 45000 = 345000
For 2nd year	₹3,00,000	15%	$\frac{15 \times 300000}{100} = 45000$	300000 + 45000 + 45000 = 390000

Here, you can see that we calculated the simple interest by multiplying the principal P, the rate $\frac{R}{100}$ and the time period T. Thus, we can use the formula:

$$SI = \frac{P \times R \times T}{100} = \frac{PRT}{100}$$

where, SI = Simple interest, P = Principal/Sum borrowed, R = Rate per annum and T = Time (in years) (Note: Both time and rate are taken either yearly or monthly.)

Therefore, when the interest is calculated on the same principal throughout the period, it is called **simple interest**.

Amount = Principal + Interest

$$\text{Amount (A)} = P + \frac{P \times R \times T}{100} = P\left(1 + \frac{R \times T}{100}\right)$$

Note

Whenever time is given in days, we divide it by 365 to convert it into years. For calculating the time between two given dates, only one of those two days is counted.

Also, we get $SI = \frac{PRT}{100} \Rightarrow 100\ SI = PRT$

1. $P = \frac{100 \times SI}{RT}$ 2. $R = \frac{100 \times SI}{PT}$ 3. $T = \frac{100 \times SI}{PR}$

Example 1: Suresh deposited ₹10,200 for 3 years at a rate of 8% per annum. Find the interest and amount that Suresh got.

Principal (P) = ₹10,200 Rate of interest (R) = 8% Time (T) = 3 years

$SI = \frac{PRT}{100} = \frac{10200 \times 8 \times 3}{100} = ₹2448$

Amount = Principal + Interest = 10200 + 2448 = ₹12,648

Therefore, Suresh got an interest of ₹2448 and an amount of ₹12,648.

Example 2: In how much time will the sum of ₹6500 amount to ₹7670 at 6% rate of interest?

Amount = ₹7670; Principal = ₹6500; Rate of interest = 6%

Interest = Amount – Principal = 7670 – 6500 = ₹1170

$$T = \frac{100 \times SI}{PR} = \frac{100 \times 1170}{6500 \times 6} = 3 \text{ years}$$

So, ₹6500 will amount to ₹7670 in 3 years.

Example 3: Prashant deposited ₹27,500 in a bank. After 2 years, it became ₹35,750. What is the rate of interest given by the bank?

Amount = ₹35,750; Principal = ₹27,500; Time = 2 years

Interest = Amount – Principal = 35750 – 27500 = ₹8250

$$R = \frac{100 \times SI}{PT} = \frac{100 \times 8250}{27500 \times 2} = \frac{100 \times 8250}{27500 \times 2} = 15\%$$

Therefore, the rate of interest given by the bank is 15%.

Example 4: A money lender was paid back ₹2250, which included the principal and the interest, after a period of 2 years at an interest rate of 12.5% per annum. Find the sum lent by him.

Amount = ₹2250; Time = 2 years; Rate of interest = 12.5%

$$A = P\left(1 + \frac{T \times R}{100}\right) \Rightarrow 2250 = P\left(1 + \frac{2 \times 12.5}{100}\right)$$

$$\Rightarrow 2250 = P\left(1 + \frac{25}{100}\right) \Rightarrow 2250 = P\left(\frac{125}{100}\right) \Rightarrow P\left(\frac{5}{4}\right) = 2250 \Rightarrow P = 2250 \times \frac{4}{5} \Rightarrow P = 1800$$

Therefore, the sum lent by him was ₹1800.

Example 5: In how much time will the interest on ₹1,20,000 at 5% be equal to the interest on ₹80,000 at 7.5% in 2 years?

First, we find the interest on the principal of ₹80,000 at 7.5% in 2 years.

$$SI = \frac{PRT}{100} = \frac{80000 \times 7.5 \times 2}{100} = ₹12{,}000$$

This interest is the same as on the principal of ₹1,20,000 at 5%.

$$\text{Now, } T = \frac{100 \times SI}{PR} = \frac{100 \times 12000}{120000 \times 5} = 2 \text{ years}$$

Therefore, the time in which the interest on both the investments will be same is 2 years.

Example 6: In how many years will a certain sum get doubled and tripled at the rate of $16\frac{2}{3}\%$ per annum?

Rate of interest (R) = $16\frac{2}{3}\% = \frac{50}{3}\%$

Let the principal be x.

If the amount gets doubled, then A = 2x.

$$A = P\left(1+\frac{T\times R}{100}\right) \Rightarrow 2x = x\left(1+\frac{T\times 50}{100\times 3}\right) \Rightarrow 2 = 1+\frac{50T}{300} \Rightarrow 2-1=\frac{T}{6} \Rightarrow T=6$$

Therefore, the amount will get doubled at $16\frac{2}{3}$% in 6 years.

If the amount gets tripled, then A = 3x.

$$A = P\left(1+\frac{T\times R}{100}\right) \Rightarrow 3x = x\left(1+\frac{T\times 50}{100\times 3}\right) \Rightarrow 3 = 1+\frac{50T}{300} \Rightarrow 3-1=\frac{T}{6} \Rightarrow T=6\times 2=12$$

Therefore, the amount will get tripled at $16\frac{2}{3}$% in 12 years.

Exercise 9.1

1. **Find the interest using the following information.**
   a. Principal = ₹480, Rate of interest = $5\frac{1}{4}$%, Time = $1\frac{1}{4}$ years
   b. Principal = ₹2224, Rate of interest = 6.25%, Time = 2 years 3 months
2. **Find the sum borrowed using the following information.**
   a. Interest = ₹455, Rate of interest = $2\frac{1}{3}$%, Time = 3 years
   b. Interest = ₹675, Rate of interest = 12%, Time = 36 months
3. **Find the rate of interest for the following.**
   a. Principal = ₹1000, Interest = ₹210, Time = $3\frac{1}{2}$ years
   b. Principal = ₹30,000, Interest = ₹2310, Time = 2.2 years
4. **Find the time period for the following.**
   a. Principal = ₹1800, Rate = 10% p.a., Interest = ₹420
   b. Principal = ₹1080, Rate = $3\frac{1}{3}$% p.a., Interest = ₹90
5. Saima borrowed some money at 15% rate of interest and cleared the debt at the end of 2 years by paying ₹92,400. Find the sum borrowed.

Summary

1. Amount = Principal + Interest
2. If the interest is calculated on the same principal throughout the loan period, then it is called simple interest. It is calculated by the formula SI = $\frac{P\times R\times T}{100}$
3. Amount for simple interest is calculated by the formula: A = $P\left(1+\frac{T\times R}{100}\right)$

Revision Exercise

1. Mahesh borrowed ₹14,000 at 4.5% rate of interest per annum for 4 years. Find the interest and the amount to be paid at the end of the fourth year.
2. Find the time period to get an interest of ₹160 on the principal of ₹3200 at rate of interest of 2% per annum.
3. If Tanu pays an interest of ₹15,000 for two years on a sum of ₹75,000, find the rate of interest.
4. In how many years will the interest on ₹3600 at 10% be equal to the interest on ₹1800 at 12.5% in 4 years?
5. Yamini took an amount of ₹50,000 at 15% from a merchant association. She lent the amount to three of her colleagues as follows.

   First colleague: ₹10,000 at 18% per annum

   Second colleague: ₹15,000 at 24% per annum

   Third colleague: ₹25,000 at 27% per annum

   After 2 years, she collects the amount from all three friends and clears the loan. How much did she gain/lose?
6. Anwar took a house loan of ₹1,00,000 from a bank at the rate of 24% per annum. Being unable to repay the debt, he sold the house after 2 years for ₹1,80,000. How much did he gain/lose?
7. A sum of ₹45,000 amounts to ₹49,500 in 2 years. In how much time will the sum of ₹82,000 amount to ₹94,300 at the same rate?
8. **In a post office scheme, certain amount doubles the principal in 6 years. In what time will the amount become:**

   a. $1\frac{1}{2}$ times the principal

   b. 3 times the principal
9. **A person borrowed an amount of ₹5,00,000 from a bank at the rate of 18% per annum. He lent this amount to two of his friends as follows:**

   a. ₹3,00,000 to a friend at the rate of 24% per year

   b. ₹2,00,000 to another friend at the rate of 12% per year

   He collected the amount after 2 years and paid back the due amount to the bank. What was his gain or loss?

For the Curious Mind

A person deposited ₹15,000 in a mutual fund that gives an interest of 12% per annum. The interest is calculated every year and added to the principal. How much does he get after 3 years? Is this simple interest? Justify.

THEME 2

Speed, Distance and Time

10

Speed

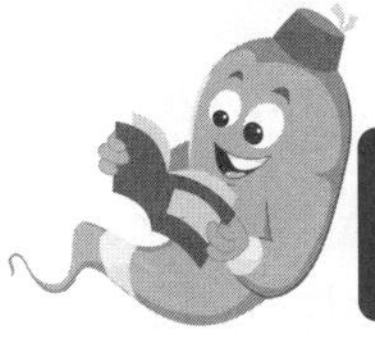

What I shall learn

- To learn conversion of units of time
- To understand the concept of speed, average speed and relative speed

Recall that the distance covered by an object in unit time is called its **speed**.

Speed is calculated as the ratio of the distance covered by an object to the time taken by the object to cover that distance.

$\text{Speed} = \dfrac{\text{Distance covered}}{\text{Time taken}}$ $\text{Time taken} = \dfrac{\text{Distance covered}}{\text{Speed}}$

Distance covered = Speed × Time taken

An object has a **uniform speed** if it travels equal distances in equal intervals of time, otherwise it is said to have a **variable speed**.

For example, a bicycle is said to have a uniform speed, say 10 km/h if it travels 10 km every hour.

Suppose the bicycle travels 8 km in the first hour, 10 km in the second hour, 12 km in the third hour and so on. Then, the bicycle is said to be moving with a variable speed as the speed is changing every hour.

Average Speed

The speed of an object does not always remain the same over the entire stretch of distance covered. It may vary during the period. Thus, we find the average speed of the object for the whole journey using the formula:

$$\text{Average speed} = \frac{\text{Total distance covered}}{\text{Total time taken}}$$

If a certain distance is covered at u km/h and the same distance is also covered at v km/h, then the average speed during the whole journey is $\left(\dfrac{2uv}{u+v}\right)$ km/h.

$$\text{We know, } 18 \text{ km/h} = 5 \text{ m/s} \quad \text{So, } 1 \text{ km/h} = \frac{5}{18} \text{ m/s or } 1 \text{ m/s} = \frac{18}{5} \text{ km/h}$$

Example 1: A cheetah can cover a distance at 96.48 km/h. Find the speed of the cheetah in metres per second.

Speed = 96.48 km/h

$96.48 \text{ km/h} = \left(96.48 \times \dfrac{5}{18}\right) \text{ m/s} = 26.8 \text{ m/s}$

Therefore, the speed of the cheetah in metres per second = 26.8 m/s

Example 2: A moped covers a distance of 550 metres in 1 min, whereas a bike covers a distance of 33 km in 45 min. Between the moped and the bike, which can travel faster and by how much?

1 min = 60 s

$$\text{Speed of moped} = \frac{\text{Distance covered}}{\text{Time taken}} = \frac{550}{60}\text{ m/s} = \frac{55}{6}\times\frac{18}{5}\text{ km/h} = 11\times 3 = 33\text{ km/h}$$

$$45\text{ min} = \frac{45}{60}\text{ h} = \frac{3}{4}\text{ h; Speed of bike} = \frac{33}{\frac{3}{4}}\text{ km/h} = 33\times\frac{4}{3} = 11\times 4 = 44\text{ km/h}$$

Therefore, the bike can travel faster than the moped by (44 – 33) km/h = 11 km/h

Example 3: An aeroplane travels distances of 250 km, 120 km and 50 km at 500 km/h, 400 km/h and 250 km/h respectively. Find the average speed.

Total distance covered = 250 km + 120 km + 50 km = 420 km

$$\text{Total time taken} = \left(\frac{250}{500}+\frac{120}{400}+\frac{50}{250}\right)\text{ h} = \left(\frac{500+300+200}{1000}\right)\text{ h} = 1\text{ h}$$

$$\text{Average Speed} = \frac{\text{Total distance covered}}{\text{Total time taken}} = \frac{420}{1} = 420\text{ km/h}$$

Example 4: Ram walks from his house to the school at 2.5 km/h and arrives 12 min late. The next day he walks at 4 km/h and reaches the school 15 min before time. Find the distance from his house to the school.

Let the distance between school and house be 1 km.

$$\text{Time taken to travel at a speed of 2.5 km/h} = \frac{1}{2.5}\text{ h} = \frac{10}{25}\text{ h} = \frac{2}{5}\text{ h}$$

$$\text{Time taken to travel at a speed of 4 km/h} = \frac{1}{4}\text{ h}$$

$$\text{Difference in these timings} = \left(\frac{2}{5}-\frac{1}{4}\right)\text{ h} = \frac{3}{20}\text{ h} = \frac{3}{20}\times 60\text{ min} = 9\text{ min}$$

Actual difference in timings = 15 – (–12) = 15 + 12 = 27 min

Distance travelled when the difference in timings is 9 min = 1 km

$$\text{Distance travelled when the difference in timings is 27 min} = \frac{1}{9}\times 27 = 3\text{ km}$$

Problem Related to Crossing a Platform

Hints and Tips

While crossing a lamp post, we do not include the length of the lamp post.

When a train crosses a standing man, the distance it covers is equal to the length of the train.

In crossing the platform, the train has to cover a distance equal to the sum of the lengths of the train and the platform.

Example 5: A train crosses a standing man in 8 s and a 200 m long platform in 24 s. Find the length and the speed of the train.

Let the length of the train be x m.

Time taken to cross the man = 8 s

Speed of the train = $\frac{x}{8}$ m/s ... (1)

Thus, distance covered in passing the platform = $(x + 200)$ m

Time taken to cross the length of the train and the length of the platform = 24 s

Speed of the train = $\frac{x+200}{24}$ m/s ... (2)

From (1) and (2), we get

$$\frac{x}{8}=\frac{x+200}{24} \Rightarrow \frac{x}{1}=\frac{x+200}{3} \Rightarrow 3x = x+200 \Rightarrow 2x = 200 \Rightarrow x = 100$$

Therefore, the length of the train = 100 m

Speed of the train = $\frac{100}{8}$ m/s = $\frac{25}{2}$ m/s = $12\frac{1}{2}$ m/s

Exercise 10.1

1. A boy covers a distance of 4.32 km in 4 min 48 s. Find the speed of the boy.
2. Jaya rides at 48 km/h. How much distance does she cover in 25 min?
3. Rashmi goes to school at 4 km/h in 2 h 30 min. How much time will she take to cover the same distance if she cycles at 12 km/h?
4. Two race cars travel in a race at 90 km/h and 120 km/h respectively. If the second car takes 30 min less than the first car, find the distance covered to complete the race.
5. A tour bus covers 250 km in the first five hours, 128 km in the next two hours and 216 km in the next three hours. Find its average speed for the whole journey.
6. A woman goes uphill with an average speed of 25 km/h and downhill with an average speed of 35 km/h. Find the average speed of the total journey.
7. Tanuj walks from his house at 5 km/h and reaches office 10 min late. If his speed had been 6 km/h, he would have reached 15 min early. Find the distance of his office from his house.
8. A bus runs at 40 km/h to reach its destination but arrives 11 min late. If it runs at 50 km/h, it will be 5 min late. Find the correct time in which the bus will not be late in reaching its destination.
9. A train 180 m long is running with a speed of 54 km/h. In what time will it pass (a) an electric pole and (b) a tunnel that is 540 m long?

10. A train crosses a telegraph post and a bridge 125 m long in 15 s and 30 s respectively. Find the length and the speed of the train.
11. Find the time taken by a 150m long train to cross a railway platform 200 m long at the speed of 90 km/h.
12. A 160 m long train passes a railway platform in 18 sec. How long will it take to pass another platform 100 m long?

Relative Speed

Relative speed of two objects moving in the opposite directions is equal to the sum of their speeds. That is, if two objects move in the opposite directions at respective speeds of x km/h and y km/h, then their relative speed = $(x + y)$ km/h.

Suppose two objects start together from the same place, both at a speed of 12 km/h, in the same direction. They keep travelling together in the same direction. That is, there is no difference in the distance covered by them.

Let us suppose A and B are travelling in the same direction from the same point. In 1 hour, A travels 4 km less than B. After 1 hour, B is 4 km ahead of A or A is 4 km behind B. The distance between them after 2 hours will be 8 km. So, the relative speed of any two objects moving in the same direction is the difference between their speeds = $\frac{4 \text{ km}}{1 \text{ h}}$ = 4 km/h.

Relative speed of two objects moving in the same direction is equal to the difference of their speeds. That is, if two objects move in the same direction at respective speeds of x km/h and y km/h, then their relative speed = $(x - y)$ km/h.

Therefore, the time taken by one object to overtake the other = $\frac{\text{Distance between them}}{\text{Relative speed}}$

Example 6: A train 90 m long travelling at 22.5 km/h passes a man walking at 4.5 km/h. Find the time taken by the train to pass the man if they are moving

a. in the opposite directions.

b. in the same direction.

Length of the train = 90 m

Speed of the train = 22.5 km/h = $22.5 \times \frac{5}{18}$ m/s = 6.25 m/s

Speed of the man = 4.5 km/h = $4.5 \times \frac{5}{18}$ m/s = 1.25 m/s

a. If they are moving in the opposite directions, then the relative speed is 6.25 + 1.25 = 8.5 m/s.

$$\text{Time taken} = \frac{\text{Distance between them}}{\text{Relative speed}} = \frac{90}{8.5} =$$

$$= 11 \text{ s (approximately)}$$

b. If they are moving in the same direction, then the relative speed is 6.25 – 1.25 = 5 m/s.

$$\text{Time taken} = \frac{\text{Distance between them}}{\text{Relative speed}} = \frac{90}{5} = 18 \text{ s}$$

Example 7: Two trains of lengths 250 m and 200 m long cross each other in 20 s when they move in the opposite direction and 3 min when they move in the same direction. Find their speeds.

Lengths of the two trains are 250 m and 200 m.

Total distance covered by the two trains to cross each other = 250 + 200 = 450 m

Let us suppose the speeds of the two trains are u m/s and v m/s respectively.

If the two trains are moving in the opposite direction, relative speed will be $(u + v)$ m/s.

Time taken to cross each other is 20 s.

$$\text{Relative speed} = \frac{\text{Distance between them}}{\text{Time taken}}$$

$$\Rightarrow u+v = \frac{450}{20} \Rightarrow u+v = 22.5 \qquad ...(1)$$

If the two trains are moving in the same direction, then the relative speed will be $(u - v)$ m/s.

Time taken to cross each other = 3 min = 180 s

$$\text{Relative speed} = \frac{\text{Distance between them}}{\text{Time taken}}$$

$$\Rightarrow u-v = \frac{450}{180} \Rightarrow u-v = 2.5 \Rightarrow u = 2.5+v \qquad ...(2)$$

Note

If one train passes another train in the same direction or in the opposite direction, the distance covered is equal to the sum of the lengths of both the trains.

Substituting (2) in eq. (1),

we get $(2.5 + v) + v = 22.5 \Rightarrow 2v = 22.5 - 2.5 \Rightarrow 2v = 20 \Rightarrow v = 10$

$u = 2.5 + v = 2.5 + 10 = 12.5$

The speeds of the two trains are 10 m/s and 12.5 m/s respectively.

Problems on Upstream and Downstream

Example 8: The speed of a boat in still water is 9.5 km/h and the speed of the current is 2.5 km/h. Find the time taken to row 84 km upstream and then the same distance downstream.

Distance covered = 84 km

Speed of the boat in still water = 9.5 km/h

Speed of the current = 2.5 km/h

Speed of the boat upstream = 9.5 – 2.5 = 7 km/h

Time taken = $\frac{\text{Distance between them}}{\text{Relative speed}} = \frac{84}{7} = 12\text{ h}$

Time taken to row upstream is 12 h.

Speed of the boat downstream = 9.5 + 2.5 = 12 km/h

Time taken = $\frac{\text{Distance between them}}{\text{Relative speed}} = \frac{84}{12} = 7\text{ h}$

Time taken to row downstream is 7 hours.

Note

If the speed of a boat in still water is x km/h and the speed of the stream is y km/h, then
speed of the boat downstream = $(x + y)$ km/h and
speed of the boat upstream = $(x - y)$ km/h

Therefore, the total time taken to row upstream and downstreamis is 12 h + 7 h = 19 h.

Example 9: A stream flows at the rate of 5 km/h. A boat rows downstream 3 times the distance rowed by it upstream in equal time. Find the speed of the boat in still water.

Speed of the stream = 5 km/h

Let the speed of the boat in still water be u km/h.

Speed of the boat upstream = $(u - 5)$ km/h

Speed of the boat downstream = $(u + 5)$ km/h

Let the distance rowed upstream be x km.

According to the question, the distance rowed downstream will be $3x$ km.

Time taken to row upstream = $\frac{x}{u-5}$ h

Time taken to row downstream = $\frac{3x}{u+5}$ h

According to the problem,

$$\frac{x}{u-5} = \frac{3x}{u+5} \Rightarrow \frac{1}{u-5} = \frac{3}{u+5} \Rightarrow u+5 = 3(u-5) \Rightarrow u+5 = 3u-15$$

$$\Rightarrow u - 3u = -5 - 15 \Rightarrow -2u = -20 \Rightarrow u = 10$$

Therefore, the speed of the boat in still water is 10 km/h.

Exercise 10.2

1. Two people start from the same place, in the same direction at speeds 8 km/h and 6 km/h respectively. Find the distance between them after 12 min.
2. Two trains 195 m and 180 m in length are running on parallel lines, one at 90 km/h and the other at 12.5 m/s. In what time will they cross each other
   a. when they are running in the same direction?
   b. when they are running in the opposite directions?
3. Two trains 137 m and 163 m long run on parallel tracks in the same direction. The speed of the first train is 48 km/h and the second train crosses the first train in 3 min. Find the time taken by them to cross each other in the opposite directions.

4. A train 120 m long travelling at 45 km/h, overtakes another train travelling in the same direction at 36 km/h and passes it in 80 s. Find the length of the second train.
5. The speed of a boat in still water is 9 km/h and the speed of the stream is 2 km/h. Find the time taken by the boat to go 35 km upstream.
6. A stream is flowing at 2 km/h. A boat is rowed downstream for a distance of 34.5 km in 3 h. Find the speed of the boat in the still water.
7. The rate of current in a river is 3 km/h. A boat with a speed of 10 km/h in still water is rowed upstream for 13 h. Find the distance rowed and the time taken to row downstream.

Summary

1. If two objects move in the opposite directions at respective speeds of x km/h and y km/h, then their relative speed = $(x + y)$ km/h.
2. If two objects move in the same direction at respective speeds of x km/h and y km/h, then their relative speed = $(x - y)$ km/h.

Revision Exercise

1. Satish walks at 5 km/h. How much time does he take to cover 625 m?
2. A school bus, running at 45 km/h, takes 4 h to pick the children for school. At what speed must it run in order to pick the children in 3 h?
3. In a cycle race, a man rides his first 50 km at 25 km/h, the next 40 km at 20 km/h and then 90 km at 15 km/h. Find his average speed for the whole journey.
4. A student walks from his house to school at a speed of 3 km/h and arrives at the school 20 min late. When he walks at 4 km/h, he reaches school 15 minutes before time. Find the distance between the house and the school.
5. Find the length and the speed of a train if it crosses a standing man in 6 s and a platform 200 m long in 16 s.
6. The distance between an old town and a new town is 36 km. Waseem and Bhaskar start simultaneously from the old town and the new town respectively at speeds of 8 km/h and 4 km/h. Find when and where they meet each other.
7. The speed of a boat in still water is 8 km/h and the speed of the stream is 2.5 km/h. Find the time taken by the boat to go 63 km downstream.
8. The speed of a boat in still water in 7 km/h. Find the speed of the current when the boat is rowed upstream for a distance of 22 km in 4 h.

Theme Worksheet 2

Solve the following riddles.

1. I begin with 'u'.
   I need to be same if two quantities have to be compared.
   I can be converted from one form to another.
   Solution: ______________

2. I begin with 'd'.
   I am a method of comparing two quantities.
   I am used to find ratios.
   Solution: ______________

3. I begin with 'p'.
   I am also called as variation.
   I have two quantities depending on each other.
   Solution: ______________

4. I end with 'y'.
   I will find the value of one unit.
   I can find the value of required number of units.
   Solution: ______________

5. I start with 's'.
   I am the representative value of the given distance traveled by time taken.
   I always represent the values in units of distance/ units of time.
   Solution: ______________

6. I start with 'c'.
   I am a fixed number.
   I am the ratio of two quantities, when they vary directly.
   Solution: ______________

7. I end with 'e'.
   I am derived from Latin word.
   I mean per every hundred.
   Solution: ______________

8. I end with 's'.
   I mean money lost while product is sold.
   I am always calculated using cost price and selling price
   Solution: ______________

9. I begin with 'o'.
   I include transportation, packing, rent, labour, fuel and any little extra expenses.
   I am included to the cost price
   Solution: ______________

10. I start with 's'.
    I have two words.
    I am calculated only on the principal throughout the period.
    Solution: ______________

Skill-based Worksheet - Solving Daily Life Problems

1. Ravi bought mouse and keyboards in the ratio 5: 3. If he has bought 40 mouse devices then find the number of keyboards bought by him.

2. The cost of 50 monitors is 50,000. Find the cost of 25 monitors.

3. Sanjana's profit increased to 15% from last year. Her last year's profit was ₹1,00,000. Find the profit of this year.

4. Company A offered ₹15,000 as salary per month with 10% increase every year and company B offered ₹20,000 as salary per month with 8% increase every year. Which is the better offer if the person is willing to work for 2 years?

5. Rahul bought 25 photo frames from the market at ₹25 per frame. He spent ₹100 on transportation and ₹50 on packing. Then, he sold all the frames at ₹35. Find the profit earned by him.

6. Anitha bought 125 pencils at ₹3 per pencil. She spent ₹200 on packing. Then, she sold all the pencils at ₹5. Find the profit earned by her.

7. Tarun took a loan of ₹20,000 at a rate of 2% interest for a period of 2 years. Find the amount paid at the end of 2 years.

8. Nikitha borrowed ₹12,000 at a rate of 2% interest for a period of 4 years. Find the amount paid at the end of 4 years.

9. A bus travels distances of 240 km, 120 km and 80 km at 50 km/h, 40 km/h and 25 km/h respectively. Find the average speed.

10. A train crosses a standing man in 10 s and a 300 m long platform in 30 s. Find the length and the speed of the train.

Mental Maths

Chapter 6 - Ratio and Proportion

1. Between the two ratios 2 : 5 and 3 : 7, which is the greater one.
2. Are the ratios 20 cm : 1 m and ₹40 to ₹200 in proportion?
3. Are the ratios 3 : 18 and 5 : 30 in proportion?
4. Find the cost of 20 purses if the cost of 10 purses is ₹150.
5. Find the cost of 15 mobile pouches if the cost of 3 mobile pouches is ₹36.

Chapter 7 - Percentage

1. Express $\frac{11}{2}$ as a percentage.
2. What percent of 2 kg is 400 g?
3. Find the total amount if 15% of it is ₹45.
4. Find the amount which is 12% less than ₹1200.
5. If 1,500 is increased to 3,000, what is the percentage of increase?

Chapter 8 - Profit and Loss

1. A salesman buys an article for ₹120 and sells it for ₹150. Find the profit or loss.
2. Aruna sold a watch for ₹1250 at a profit of ₹350. Find the CP of the watch.
3. Find the loss percentage if the CP of the handbag is ₹2,000 and the SP is ₹1,600.
4. Find the profit percentage if the CP of the shoes is ₹3,000 and the profit is ₹900.
5. Find the SP of the article if the cost price is ₹5,000 and the profit percentage is 20%.

Chapter 9 - Simple Interest

1. Find the SI if the principal is ₹20,000 at a rate of 5% per annum for a period of 2 years.
2. Find the rate of interest for the principal of ₹50,000 for a period of 3 years if the SI is ₹3,000.
3. Find the time period required to repay the loan of ₹5,000 at the rate of 2% per annum with SI being ₹1,000.
4. Find the amount repaid at the end of 2 years if the principal is ₹25,000 at a rate of 20% per annum.
5. Find the amount repaid at the end of 5 years if the principal is ₹7,000 at a rate of 15% per annum.

Chapter 10 - Speed, Distance and Time

1. Find the speed of the car if the distance travelled is 500 km in 5 hours.
2. Find the speed of the train if the distance travelled by the train is 250 km in 2 hours.
3. Find the distance travelled by a two-wheeler if the time taken is 3 hours and the speed is 72 km/h.
4. Find the distance travelled by a motor boat if the speed is 45 km/h and the time taken is 4 hours.
5. Find the time taken by a cyclist to cover a distance of 80 km if the speed is 10 km/h.

Algebra

Chapters Covered

11. **Operations on Algebraic Expressions**
12. **Linear Equations and Inequations**

Why this Theme Matters

Algebra is an integral part of our lives. Linear equations play a major role in solving many problems in our day-to-day-life. Look at the following examples:

- The bill amount to be paid when we buy items in the supermarket is linearly related to the number of items we buy and the price of each item.
- Distance covered by the car in x hours given that the speed of the car is y km/h is xy km.
- A mobile company has the following post paid plans for the 2G data usage.

Plans	Monthly Rental (₹)	Free Usage (GB)	Rate for Post Free Usage (₹)
Plan 1	199	1.5	10 paisa/kb
Plan 2	299	3	10 paisa/kb
Plan 3	499	5	10 paisa/kb

The monthly bill for each plan can be expressed as a linear expression. For example, for plan 2, the bill is given by $299 + 0.1x$, where x is the number of kilobytes of data used after the free usage.

We come across many situations where the inequalities are involved. A few are listed below.

- The speed limit in the school zone is 30 km/h. This means that the speed of our vehicle should be less than or equal to 30 km/h.
- Discounts at shopping malls: Avail discount up to 50% with a minimum purchase for ₹5000. This means that we can get a discount only when we purchase items of worth greater than or equal to ₹5000.

This theme helps us to solve many such real life problems using linear equations and inequations.

THEME 3

Operations on Algebraic Expressions

11

Let's Get Started

We use algebraic expressions to solve many day-to-day life problems by making use of variables and constants.

Algebraic expression is a combination of variables and constants that are connected by mathematical operators (+, −, × and ÷).

A **variable** (literal) in an algebraic expression is the letter used to represent a certain quantity. A variable can take any value.

A **constant** in an algebraic expression is the number whose value is fixed.

Consider the following situation.

Arvind has 10 biscuits more than what Arun has.
The algebraic expression representing this situation is $x + 10$, where x is the number of biscuits Arun has. In this expression x is the variable and 10 is the constant.

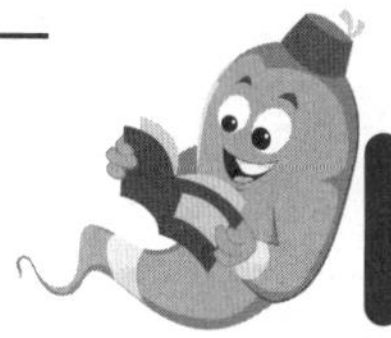

What I shall learn

- To identify terms related to algebra like constants, variable, terms, factors and coefficient of terms, like and unlike terms, degree etc.
- To generate algebraic expressions involving one or two variables/unknowns
- To add and subtract algebraic expressions

Know Your Mathematician – Aryabhata

Aryabhata is an Indian mathematician born in 476 AD at Patliputra (Patna). He was the first Indian mathematician to use algebraic expressions. His famous work is *Aryabhatiya*, which covers various problems of arithmetic, algebra, trigonometry, number theory and astronomy.

Terms in Algebraic Expressions

A **term** in an algebraic expression is a variable or a constant or combination of variable(s) and constant. For example, in the algebraic expression $5t + 12$, $5t$ and 12 are two terms.

Terms that are products of variables and constants are known as **variable terms**. Terms that consist of only constants are known as **constant terms**. In the above expression, $5t$ is the variable term, which is the product of 5 and t, and 12 is the constant term.

Some more examples of terms are $16y^2$, $2xy$, $-3xy^2$, a^3b^2c, $\frac{2h}{6}$.

Consider the expression $5k^2 + 3kx$. Here, $5k^2$ and $3kx$ are two different terms. The term $5k^2$ is the product of 5, k and k. So, 5, k and k are known as the **factors** of the term $5k^2$.

Similarly, 3, k and x are the factors of the term $3kx$.

Hence, a term is the product of its factors.

Remember

The terms in an algebraic expression are separated either by + or – and not by × or ÷.

For example, $2t \times 3y$ and $\frac{8x}{y}$ are single terms.

Example 1: List all the terms and identify the factors of each term in the following algebraic expressions.

a. $6x^2y + 3x^3 + 15xy$ b. $9ab + 2abc$

Algebraic expression	Term	Factors
$6x^2y + 3x^3 + 15xy$	$6x^2y$	3, 2, x, x, y
	$3x^3$	3, x, x, x
	$15xy$	5, 3, x, y
$9ab + 2abc$	$9ab$	3, 3, a, b
	$2abc$	2, a, b, c

Each factor in a term is called the **coefficient** of the product of the other factors in the term. If the factor is a constant, it is known as the **numerical coefficient** and if it is a variable, it is called the **literal coefficient** of the constant.

Example 2:

a. In $5t$, 5 is the numerical coefficient of t and t is the literal coefficient of 5.

b. In $14ab$, 14 is the numerical coefficient of ab, a is the variable coefficient of $14b$ and b is the variable coefficient of $14a$.

Think and Discuss

What is the difference between constant and numerical coefficient?

Can a letter represent a coefficient?

Example 3: Write the numerical coefficient as well as coefficient of the variable t in each term of the algebraic expression $2kt - 4k^2t + 12t$.

Algebraic expression	Term	Coefficient of t	Numerical coefficient
$2kt - 4k^2t + 12t$	$2kt$	$2k$	2
	$-4k^2t$	$-4k^2$	−4
	$12t$	12	12

Degree of Algebraic Expressions

Degree of a polynomial refers to the highest power of the variable in any of the terms of a polynomial.

Degree of $5x$ is 1. Degree of $5x + 4$ is 1. Degree of $5xy + x$ is 2.

A polynomial of degree 0 is called a constant. Examples: $-5, \frac{1}{2}$.

Like and Unlike Terms in Algebraic Expressions

Observe the following sets of terms.

Group A	Group A	Group B	Group B
Same variables raised to the same power are like terms	$5ab, 17ab, 54ab$ $2x^2y, -31x^2y, 6x^2y$ $9p^3q^2, -2p^3q^2, 27p^3q^2$	$3ab, -7a^2b, 4ab^2$ $x^3y, -xy, 5yx^2$ $6p^3q^2, -9k^3l^2, 27a^3b^2$	Different variables or same variables raised to the different powers are called unlike terms
	Like terms	**Unlike terms**	

Remember

Generally speaking, monomials, binomials and trinomials also fall under the category of polynomials as the word 'polynomials' is used as a general term. To be a polynomial, the power of the variables cannot be negative or fractional. Hence, $\sqrt{x} + 2$ and $x^{-1} + 2y$ are not polynomials.

Types of Algebraic Expressions

An algebraic expression with one term is called a **monomial**. For example, 7, y, $5x$ and $6xy$.

An algebraic expression with two terms is called a **binomial**. For example, $4x + 6$ and $-6y + z$.

An algebraic expression with three terms is called a **trinomial**. For example, $4x^2 + 5x + 6$ and $5ab^2 + 6a + 3$.

An algebraic expression is called a **polynomial** if the power of the variables is not negative or fractional.

Exercise 11.1

1 Find the factors for each term in the following algebraic expressions.

a. $36x^2y + 28xy + 10$ b. $2x^5 - 6x^3 + 28x^2 + x + 9$ c. $5abc + 25a^2bc$

❷ **Identify all the terms and the numerical coefficients of each term in the following algebraic expressions.**

Algebraic expression	Variable term	Numerical coefficient of variable term	Constant term
$45x + 32y - 6$			
$3t^3 + 2t^2 + 10$			
$\frac{h}{4} + 7h + 21$			

❸ **Find the degree of the following monomials.**

a. $12x^2yz$ b. $9ab$ c. $16h^3k^2l$

d. $17a^3b^3c^2$ e. p^2q^3

❹ **Find the degree of the following algebraic expressions.**

a. $3a^2x + b^2y + c^2z$ b. $9x^3 + 2x^2y + y^3$ c. $8x^5y^3z + 2x^4y^2 + z^9$

❺ **State whether the following sets of terms are like or unlike terms. Give reasons.**

a. $12a^3b^3, -9a^3b^3, 15a^3b^3$ b. $3x^5y^7, -2p^5q^7, 4h^5g^7$

c. $8a^3b^8, -4a^9b^8, 12a^3b^9$ d. $14v^3u^2z, -67zu^2v^3, 3u^2v^3z$

❻ **Classify the following algebraic expressions based on the number of terms present in them.**

a. $2x + 6y + 3z$ b. $14a^3b^3c^3$

c. $12x^2 - 14y^2$ d. $2p^2 + 3q^2 + 4r^2$

e. $a^2 + 2ab + b^2$ f. $x^3 + y^3 + z^3 + 2x^2y + 2y^2z + 2z^2x - 3xyz$

Generating Algebraic Expressions

Look at the following examples and see how algebraic expressions are used to model the real-life situations.

Example 4: Vinod scored 7 marks more than Vishnu. Write an algebraic expression to represent the number of marks scored by Vinod.

Let the marks scored by Vishnu be x. Then, the marks scored by Vinod is $x + 7$.

Example 5: In a marathon, Chitra ran three times more than Preeti. Write an algebraic expression to represent the number of kilometers run by Chitra.

Let the number of kilometers ran by Preeti be k km. Then, the number of kilometers ran by Chitra is $3k$.

Example 6: Arya's age is 3 years more than twice Surya's age. Write an algebraic expression to represent Arya's age.

Let the age of Surya be p years. Then, the age of Arya is $2p + 3$.

Exercise 11.2

Write the algebraic expressions for the given situations.

a. Ravi's age is 32 years less than his father's.

b. The number of tigers in a zoo is 10 less than the number of lions.

c. The deficiency in rainfall this year is 20% compared to last year.

d. What is Tom's age if Tom is 4 years younger than his brother Steve?

e. Ayaan earns ₹300 a day working part time at a supermarket. Write an algebraic expression to represent the amount of money he will earn in d days.

f. A small hotel has ₹10,000 to distribute to all its workers together as bonus. How much money will each employee get?

Addition of Algebraic Expressions

Look at the following example.

Sunil and Sudhir went to a bookshop. Sunil bought 8 books and Sudhir bought 5 books. If the cost of each book is ₹x, what is the amount spent by both of them?

Amount spent by Sunil = ₹ $8x$ (Since the cost of each book is ₹x and Sunil bought 8 books)

Amount spent by Sudhir = ₹ $5x$ (Since the cost of each book is ₹x and Sudhir bought 5 books)

∴ The total amount spent by them is ₹ $(8x + 5x)$.

In order to solve the question, we need to know how to add algebraic expressions. Let us first understand some basic facts.

If there are 3 balloons in one bunch and 5 balloons in another bunch, then the total number of balloons is 3 balloons + 5 balloons = 8 balloons.

We can **add only like terms in algebraic expressions**. The like terms can be added by adding their numerical coefficients.

So, the total amount spent by Sunil and Sudhir = $8x + 5x = (8 + 5)x = 13x$

Example 7: Add the following algebraic expressions.

a. $9a + 15a = 24a$

b. $30xy + (-12xy) = 30xy - 12xy = 18xy$

Addition of Polynomials

Here are the two groups of ice creams and cupcakes. What is the total number of eatables in both the groups? Let us represent the ice creams by x and the cupcakes by y. Then the total number of eatables in A and B would be $(5x + 3y) + (4x + 6y)$

Now, let us see how to add these two algebraic expressions. It can be done in the following two ways.

Row Method or Horizontal Method

Example 8: Add $5x + 3y$ and $4x + 6y$ using the row or horizontal method.

Step 1	Write all the expressions to be added in a row with a '+' symbol in between them.	$(5x + 3y) + (4x + 6y)$
Step 2	Identify the like terms and rearrange them. Take the terms along with their signs while rearranging.	$= (5x + 4x) + (6y + 3y)$
Step 3	Add the coefficients of the like terms and write the resultant expression.	$= (5 + 4)x + (6 + 3)y$ $= 9x + 9y$

Example 9: Add $3p^2 + 12pq - 6q^2$ and $-8q^2 + 5p^2 - 2pq$.

$(3p^2 + 12pq - 6q^2) + (-8q^2 + 5p^2 - 2pq)$

$= (3p^2 + 5p^2) + (12pq - 2pq) + (-6q^2 - 8q^2) = 8p^2 + 10pq - 14q^2$

Column Method or Vertical Method

Example 10: Add $5x^2 - 4y^2 + 2xy$ and $-3xy + 9x^2 - 7y^2$ using the column method.

Step 1	Write the expressions one below the other such that the like terms come in the same column.
Step 2	Add the coefficients of the like terms.
Step 3	Write the results in the respective columns.

$$\begin{array}{rcrcr} 5x^2 & - & 4y^2 & + & 2xy \\ 9x^2 & - & 7y^2 & - & 3xy \\ \hline 14x^2 & - & 11y^2 & - & 1xy \\ \hline \end{array}$$

Example 11: Add $3p^2 + 12pq - 6q^2$ and $-8q^2 + 5p^2 - 2pq$.

$$\begin{array}{rrr} 3p^2 & + \ 12pq & - \ 6q^2 \\ 5p^2 & - \ 2pq & - \ 8q^2 \\ \hline 8p^2 & + \ 10pq & - \ 14q^2 \\ \hline \end{array}$$

Subtraction of Algebraic Expressions

In the subtraction of algebraic expressions we use the concept of additive inverse. In Chapter 2, we have learned that to subtract x from y:

1. we first write y 2. Put '–' sign 3. write x 4. calculate

Subtraction of Monomials

Example 12: Subtract the following.

a. $32x$ from $75x$

$75x - 32x = (75 - 32)x = 43x$

b. $46y$ from $-12y$

$-12y - 46y = (-12 - 46)y = -58y$

c. $-15z$ from $25z$

$25z - (-15z) = 25z + 15z = (25 + 15)z$

$= 40z$

d. $-53p$ from $-23p$

$-23p - (-53p) = -23p + 53p$

$= (-23 + 53)p = 30p$

Subtraction of Polynomials

Let us understand the subtraction of polynomials in both horizontal and vertical methods using an example.

Example 13: Subtract $-3xy + 9x^2 - 7y^2$ from $5x^2 - 4y^2 + 2xy$ using the horizontal and vertical methods.

Horizontal Method

Step 1	Write the expressions in a row by writing a minus symbol in between them.	$5x^2 - 4y^2 + 2xy - (-3xy + 9x^2 - 7y^2)$
Step 2	Find the additive inverse of the expression to be subtracted and add it to the other expression.	$= 5x^2 - 4y^2 + 2xy + 3xy - 9x^2 + 7y^2$
Step 3	Identify and group the like terms.	$= (5x^2 - 9x^2) + (-4y^2 + 7y^2) + (2xy + 3xy)$
Step 4	Add/subtract the numerical coefficeints of the like terms and write the result.	$= -4x^2 + 3y^2 + 5xy$

Vertical Method

Step 1 Write the expressions one below the other such that the expression to be subtracted comes in the second row and the like terms come one below the other.

Step 2 Change the sign of every term in the second expression. Write the changed sign below the old sign of each term in the second line.

Step 3 Add the coefficients of the like terms and write the result in the respective columns.

$$\begin{array}{r} 5x^2 - 4y^2 + 2xy \\ 9x^2 - 7y^2 - 3xy \\ (-) \quad (+) \quad (+) \\ \hline -4x^2 + 3y^2 + 5xy \end{array}$$

Example 14: Subtract $14k^3 + 3k^2 - 7k + 5$ from $19k^3 - 4k + 10$ using horizontal method.

$$(19k^3 - 4k + 10) - (14k^3 + 3k^2 - 7k + 5) = (19k^3 - 14k^3) - 3k^2 + \{-4k - (-7k)\} + (10 - 5)$$

$$= 5k^3 - 3k^2 + 3k + 5$$

Example 15: Subtract $14k^3 + 3k^2 - 7k + 5$ from $19k^3 - 4k + 10$ using vertical method.

$$\begin{array}{rrrr} 19k^3 & + 0k^2 & - 4k & + 10 \\ 14k^3 & + 3k^2 & - 7k & + 5 \\ (-) & (-) & (+) & (-) \\ \hline 5k^3 & - 3k^2 & + 3k & + 5 \end{array}$$

[Since there is no k^2 term in this expression, we have written it as $0 \times k^2$.]

Exercise 11.3

1. **Add the following algebraic expressions.**
   a. $5a - 9b$ and $-16a + 19b$
   b. $41h + 15g$ and $7g - 13h$
   c. $5p^3 - 3p^2 - 6p - 3$ and $3p^3 + 7p - 10$
   d. $-14a^2 + 21b^2 + 9ab$ and $33a^2 - 25b^2 + ab$
2. **Subtract the second expression from the first expression in the following.**
   a. $7b + 16c, 52c - 12b$
   b. $19l^6 + 15l^2 - 12l, 19l^6 + 15l^2 - 12l$
   c. $12k^2 + 2k - 9, 9k^2 - 14k + 6$
   d. $17bc + 19ca - 12ab, -2ab + 5bc + 3ca$
3. **If A = $-4x^2 + 3y^2 + 14xy$, B = $21x^2 - 15xy + 9y^2$ and C = $22x^2 - 25y^2 + 17xy$, then find the following.**
   a. A + A + C
   b. A + C − B
   c. C − A + B
   d. A − B − C
4. What polynomial would you get by adding $7a - 2b + 3c$ and $5a + 6b - 9c$ and then subtracting the sum from $14a - 25b + 30c$?

5. What is to be added to $13x^8 - 12x^3 + x^2 - 19x + 49$ to get $54x^8 - 40x^3 + 72x^2 - 98$?
6. The sides of a rectangle are $-4x + 6y + 3z$ and $12x - 4y + 9z$. Find its perimeter.
7. The perimeter of a scalene triangle is $29a + 9b - 6c$. Two of its sides are $16a + 5b - 2c$ and $-6a + 7b - 12c$. Find the third side.

Summary

1. An ***algebraic expression*** is an expression that consists of variable(s) and constant(s) connected by arithmetic operators.
2. A ***term*** in an algebraic expression is a variable or a constant or combination of variable(s) and constant.
3. A term is the product of its ***factors***.
4. Each factor in a term is called the ***coefficient*** of the product of the other factors in the term.
5. Terms in which the same variables are used and each variable has the same exponent are called ***like terms***.
6. Terms in which variables are different or the same variables have different exponents are called ***unlike terms***.
7. A ***monomial*** is an algebraic expression that has only one term. ***Binomials*** have two terms and ***trinomials*** have three terms. An algebraic expression with one or more terms is called polynomial.
8. **Degree of an algebraic expression** is the highest of all the degrees of the terms of that algebraic expression.
9. Addition and subtraction of algebraic expressions are done by combining the like terms and adding or subtracting their numerical coefficients.

For the Curious Mind

Find the third side of the triangle shown below if its perimeter is given as $15a^2 b + 25c$.

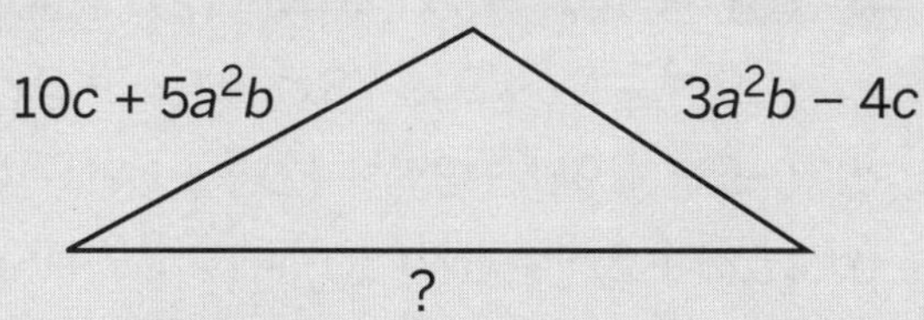

Revision Exercise

1 **State whether the following are true or false.**

a. The number of rivers in Assam is a variable.

b. $2x + 6$ is a single term.

c. $5t \times 4y$ is a single term.

d. The coefficient of x in $4a^2bx$ is $4a^2b$.

e. The coefficient of a in $9a^2b$ is $9b$.

f. The degree of $8x^3y^2z$ is 6.

g. The degree of $10x^3 + 15y^2 - 2z$ is 6.

h. $14x^2y$ and $6xy^2$ are like terms.

i. $15xy^2 + 9xy + 3$ is a binomial.

j. Binomial and trinomial are also polynomials.

2 **Add the following algebraic expressions.**

a. $12xyz + 16xy - 2z$ and $-4xy + 15xyz$

b. $8x^2 + 15xy - 6y^2$ and $19xy + 7y^2 - 12x^2$

c. $18pq - 3p^2q^2 + 5p$ and $22p^2q^2 - 14pq - 8q$

d. $10a^2 - 5b^2 + 12c^2$ and $16b^2 - 8c^2 + 21a^2$

3 **Subtract the following algebraic expressions.**

a. $-26xy$ from $69xy$

b. $9q^2 + 17q$ from $25q + 17q^2$

c. $4h^2g^2 + 12h^2 - 10g^2$ from $3g^2 + 19h^2g^2 - 8h^2$

d. $5k^2x + 19k^2y - 16k^2$ from $15k^2y + 26k^2x - 5k^2$

4 Find how much more is $19ab + 12bc - 4ca$ than $16ab - 12ca + 22cb$?

5 **Write the algebraic expressions for the given situations.**

a. A cassette shop charges ₹15 for renting a video cassette for the first day. It charges ₹2 extra for every additional day. What will be the algebraic expression for the amount that Sarah would pay if she rents a video cassette for n days?

b. Ramya is z years old. Seema is six times Ramya's age increased by 6 years. What is Seema's age?

6 **Match the following.**

Group A	Group B
a. $(2x^2 - 5x - 6) + (x^2 + 8x - 3)$	i. $-7x^3 + 3x^2 + 17x$
b. $(6x^5 + 10x^3 - 7x^2 + 6) + (2x^5 + 4x^2 + 7x - 21)$	ii. $x^3 + 8x^2 - 6x + 11$
c. $(-9x^4 - 5x + 9) - (8x^4 + 5x^2 + 2x)$	iii. $8x^5 + 10x^3 - 3x^2 + 7x - 15$
d. $(-5x^3 + 9x^2 + 2x) - (2x^3 + 6x^2 - 15x)$	iv. $3x^2 + 3x - 9$
e. $(5x^3 + 2x^2 - 6x + 10) + (-4x^3 + 6x^2 + 1)$	v. $-17x^4 - 5x^2 - 7x + 9$

THEME 3

Linear Equations and Inequations

12

Let's Get Started

In English language, a sentence is a collection of words that convey some meaning. Similarly, in mathematics, sentences are used to say something or to convey some meaning. Observe the following examples.

a. $23 + 5 = 28$ b. $46 + 7 > 60$ c. $18 - 6 < 25$

All the three examples contain numbers and other symbols (+, −, ×, ÷, =, >, <, etc.) used in mathematics. Such sentences are known as **mathematical statements/sentences**.

What I shall learn

- To solve linear equations using different methods and to verify the solution of an equation
- To express situations in linear equations and find their solution
- To find solution to simple inequalities (< or >) in one variable

Equation

An **equation** is a mathematical statement containing variable(s) with equality sign.

The condition is that when a specific value is applied to the variable, the expressions on both the sides should have equal value.

For example, $x + 2 = 5$ is an equation with variable x. Here, the equality sign shows that the value of the expression on the LHS is equal to the value of the expression on the RHS.

$$\boxed{x + 2} = \boxed{5}$$

LHS RHS

Example 1: Identify if the following statements are equations and also find the number of variables in the identified equations.

a. $2x + 3 = 5$

It is an equation in one variable x.

b. $y - 3 > 5$

It is not an equation as it does not contain the equality sign.

c. $x + y = 3$

It is an equation in two variables, x and y.

Linear Equation

Linear equation is an algebraic equation consisting of constants and variables, of power 1.

The equations $5x - 3 = 0$, $8y + 4x = -6$ and $9y - 2 = -1x$ are linear equations as the power of each variable is 1. But the equations $3x^2 + 2 = 0$, $\frac{x^2}{3} = 4$ and $4\sqrt{x} + 2x = 6$ are not linear equations.

A linear equation can contain more than one variable. However, in this chapter, we will study linear equations of one variable only.

Solution of a Linear Equation

An equation is a statement of equality wherein a variable satisfies a condition and the value of the equation depends upon the chosen value of the variable. Let us learn different methods of solving the simple linear equations.

Trial and Error Method

Consider the equation $x + 3 = 7$. Here, we have a condition to be satisfied by the variable x. Look at the following table for various values of x.

x	$x + 3 = 7$	Condition satisfied? Yes/No
1	$1 + 3 \neq 7$	No
2	$2 + 3 \neq 7$	No
3	$3 + 3 \neq 7$	No
4	$\mathbf{4 + 3 = 7}$	**Yes**
5	$5 + 3 \neq 7$	No
6	$6 + 3 \neq 7$	No

We find that only if $x = 4$, the condition of the equation $x + 3 = 7$ is satisfied. For any value of x other than 4, the equation is not satisfied, that is, LHS and RHS are not equal. Therefore, the value of the variable in an equation which satisfies the equation is called the **solution or root** of the equation.

Remember

The root of an equation is the value of the variable that satisfies the equation, that is, LHS becomes equal to RHS.

Therefore, $x = 4$ is a solution of the equation $x + 3 = 7$. Here, we substituted different values for x and we picked up the value for x that was the solution to the equation. This method is known as the **trial and error method**.

Method of Balancing

While solving an equation, we must ensure that LHS and RHS are always equal. Therefore, equations are often compared to a weighing balance. Think of an equation as a balance scale where the two scale pans of the balance must be equal. Remember that equal weights will have to be either added or subtracted from both the pans in order to keep the scale balanced.

To find the value of a variable in a linear equation, we perform the operations to both sides of the equation. It is done to ensure that at any given point, LHS is equal to RHS.

Example 2: Solve the following.

a. $x + 8 = 18$

Subtracting 8 from both sides of the equation, we get

$x + 8 - 8 = 18 - 8$

$\therefore x = 10$

b. $n - 10 = 15$

Adding 10 to both sides, we get

$n - 10 + 10 = 15 + 10$

$\therefore n = 25$

Remember

To maintain the balance in an equation, if any number is added to or subtracted from one side of an equation, then it must also be added to or subtracted from the other side of the equation respectively.

Method of Transposing

'Transposing' means 'moving something from one side to the other'. This method is used to transpose a number or a variable or a term instead of adding it to or subtracting it from both sides of the equation. Remember that while transposing a number, we inverse the operation associated with it. That is, + changes to − and vice versa, and × changes to ÷ and vice versa.

Consider the equation $12x - 5 = 19$.

Here, $12x - 5$ is the LHS and 19 is the RHS of the given equation.

Let us transpose −5 from LHS to RHS. On transposing, − 5 becomes +5.

That is, $12x = 19 + 5 \Rightarrow 12x = 24$

Remember

Change side ⇄ Change sign

Now, make the coefficient of x as 1 by transposing 12 to RHS. Observe that in LHS, 12 is a multiplier. So, if we transpose it to RHS, it becomes the divisor of 24.

$12x = \frac{24}{\square}$ That is, $x = \frac{24}{12} = 2$

Therefore, $x = 2$ is the required solution.

Verification: Verify the answer by substituting the value of x in the LHS of the equation.

That is, LHS $= 12x - 5 = 12(2) - 5 = 24 - 5 = 19 =$ RHS

Now, let us solve some more equations using the method of transposing.

Example 3: Solve $4n - 5 = 11$.

Transposing −5 to RHS, we get

$4n = 11 + 5$

$\Rightarrow 4n = 16$

Transposing 4 to RHS, we get

$n = \frac{16}{4} = 4$

$\therefore n = 4$

Example 4: Find the value of a in $2a - 3 = 4$.

$2a - 3 = 4$

$\Rightarrow 2a = 4 + 3$

$\Rightarrow 2a = 7$

$\Rightarrow a = \frac{7}{2}$

Example 5: Solve $2(5 - y) + 3 = -5$.

$$2(5 - y) + 3 = -5$$
$$\Rightarrow 2(5 - y) = -5 - 3$$
$$\Rightarrow 2(5 - y) = -8$$
$$\Rightarrow 5 - y = \frac{-8}{2}$$
$$\Rightarrow 5 - y = -4 \Rightarrow 5 + 4 = y$$
$$\therefore y = 9$$

Exercise 12.1

Solve the following.

1. $2x + 6 = 12$
2. $3n - 7 = 11$
3. $2y - 5 = 9$
4. $13 - x = 1$
5. $\frac{a}{5} = -15$
6. $\frac{3x}{5} = 18$
7. $7c + 15 = 40$
8. $4v + 2 = -4$

Applications of Linear Equations

Let us solve some word problems involving linear equations. There are different techniques to solve these word problems.

The steps to be followed are given below.

1. Read and understand the given word problem.
2. Determine what is to be found and assume that the quantity is a variable (x, y, z, etc.).
3. Frame the LHS and RHS of the linear equation using the variable and the given data.
4. Find the value of the variable in the equation using any of the methods discussed above.
5. Verify the solution by substituting the answer for the variable in the linear equation.

Example 6: If 5 is subtracted from 3 times a number, the result is 40. Find the number.

Let the required number be x. Then 3 times x is $3x$.

It is given that if 5 is subtracted from it, the result is 40.

So, we get the following equation.

$$3x - 5 = 40$$

Solving this equation, we get $3x = 40 + 5 = 45$

$$\Rightarrow 3x = 45 \Rightarrow x = \frac{45}{3} = 15$$

Hence, the required number is 15.

Verification: Substituting $x = 15$ in LHS of the equation, we get $3(15) - 5 = 45 - 5 = 40 = \text{RHS}$.

Example 7: The sum of three consecutive odd numbers is 63. Find the numbers.

Let the first odd number be x. Then, the second number is $x + 2$ and the third number is $x + 4$.

Their sum is given as 63.

$\therefore x + (x + 2) + (x + 4) = 63 \Rightarrow 3x + 6 = 63 \Rightarrow x = \frac{57}{3} = 19$

Substituting the value of x in $(x + 2)$ and $(x + 4)$, we get

$x + 2 = 19 + 2 = 21$ and $x + 4 = 19 + 4 = 23$

Therefore, the three consecutive odd numbers are 19, 21 and 23. It can be seen that the sum of these three numbers is 63.

Example 8: Ravi's father is 4 times as old as Ravi. After 20 years, he will be twice the age of his son. Find their present ages.

Let Ravi's present age be a. Then, his father's age is $4a$.

After 20 years, Ravi's age will be $a + 20$ and his father's age will be $4a + 20$.

$\therefore 4a + 20 = 2(a + 20)$

$\Rightarrow 4a + 20 = 2a + 40 \Rightarrow 4a - 2a = 40 - 20 \Rightarrow 2a = 20 \Rightarrow a = 10$

Ravi's age = 10 years. His father's age = $4a = 4 \times 10 = 40$ years

Exercise 12.2

1. If the sum of four times a number and 5 is 10, what is the number?
2. If twice the sum of three consecutive natural even numbers is 36, find the numbers.
3. I am three times as old as my sister. Nine years later, I shall be one and a half times as old as my sister. What is my present age?
4. A man is 37 years old and his two sons are 8 years and 3 years old. After how many years will he be twice as old as the sum of the ages of his sons?
5. The sum of two numbers is 46. One of the numbers exceeds the other by 8. Find the numbers.
6. The sum of two consecutive multiples of 6 is 78. Find these multiples.
7. The cost of five books and three pens is ₹730. If a book costs ₹50 more than a pen, find the cost of a book and a pen.
8. Four times a number is 5 less than three times the same number. Find the number.
9. Ankit's father has presented a gift card of worth ₹700 for his birthday. He bought few T-shirts of worth ₹100 each and few pants of worth ₹150 each. If the number of T-shirts is twice the number of pants, then find how many t-shirts and pants did Ankit buy.
10. A cab driver charges ₹30 above the meter charge which is ₹6 per km. If the bill is ₹150, then find how many kilometers did a person travel?

Linear Inequations

In our day-to-day life, we come across inequalities quite often. Look at the following examples.

- The maximum number of free messages per month is 100.
- The speed limit of the vehicles in the school zone is 40 kmph.
- The minimum marks required to pass in an examination is 35%.
- To avail a discount, the minimum bill of purchase is ₹1000.
- Maximum baggage allowed per person in an international flight is 45 kg.

An inequality shows the relationship between the two quantities that are not equal.
To represent an inequality, let us learn the following symbols and their meanings.

Symbol	Meaning (Read as)	Example	Words used in a problem statement
$>$	Is greater than	$2 > -1$	More than
$\geq$	Is greater than or equal to	$b \geq 8$	At least, minimum, no less than
$<$	Is less than	$5 < 6$	Less than
$\leq$	Is less than or equal to	$x \leq 3$	At most, maximum, no more than
$\neq$	Is not equal to	$8 \neq 10$	Not equal to

An inequation with a variable having 1 as the highest power is known as a **linear inequation**.

Linear inequation looks exactly like a linear equation, with inequality sign replacing the equality sign.

Examples:

i. $3y + 1 > 0$ ii. $10x \leq 0$ iii. $15 - 8x < 0$ iv. $-5x \geq 0$

The Replacement Set

The set of elements that are used to replace the variable in an inequation is called the replacement set or domain of the variable.

For example: Consider an inequation $y < 6$. Let the replacement set be N (the set of Natural Numbers).

Then, we can replace y by certain numbers of N, that is, for some values of the variable from N, the given inequation is satisfied and for some values, it is not.

Here, for $y = 1, 2, 3, 4$ and 5 the given inequation is satisfied and for the remaining values of y, the given inequation is not satisfied.

The set of values of the variable which satisfy the given inequation is called the solution set.

Solution Set

The subset of the replacement set containing those values of the variable for which the given inequation is satisfied is called the solution set.

Example 9: Find the solution set of $x < 8$, where x is a subset of W.

Here, $x = \{0, 1,2,3,4, 5, 6, 7\}$, which satisfies the given inequation $x < 8$. Therefore, it is the solution set of the inequation $x < 8$.

Solving Linear Inequations

Given below are some points to remember while solving linear inequations.

- We can add or subtract the same number on both sides of the inequation.
- We can multiply or divide both sides of the inequation by any positive number.
- When multiplying or dividing an inequation by a negative number, we reverse the inequality sign.

Examples:

a. $-2x > 6 \Rightarrow -2x \times -3 < 6 \times -3 \Rightarrow 6x < -18$

b. $4x < 8 \Rightarrow \frac{4x}{-2} > \frac{8}{-2} \Rightarrow -2x > -4$

Example 10: Solve the inequation $2x + 5 < 5x - 7$.

$2x + 5 < 5x - 7$

$2x < 5x - 12$ (Transposing +5 to RHS)

$-3x < -12$

Dividing by -3, we get $x > 4$

Thus, $x > 4$ is the solution.

Remember

We reverse the inequality sign while dividing or multiplying a linear inequality with a negative number.

Example 11: Solve $-11 \leq 5x - 6 \leq 9, x \in Z$.

The above inequation is the combination of two inequations and we need to solve this separately.

First, we have $-11 \leq 5x - 6$

$5x - 6 \geq -11$

$5x \geq -11 + 6$ (Transposing the -6 to RHS)

$5x \geq -5 \Rightarrow x \geq -1$ (Dividing both sides by 5)

Then, we have $5x - 6 \leq 9$

$\Rightarrow 5x \leq 9 + 6 \Rightarrow 5x \leq 15 \Rightarrow x \leq 3$

$\therefore x = \{-1, 0, 1, 2, 3\}$

Verification: Substituting $x = 2$, we get $-11 \leq 10 - 6 \leq 9$

$-11 \leq 4 \leq 9$

Exercise 12.3

Solve the following linear inequations.

1. $x - 3 \geq 2; x \in N$
2. $15 < 2x + 3 < 9; x \in Z$
3. $17 \leq 5x + 3 \leq 18; x \in Z$
4. $3x + 9 < 12; x \in Z$
5. $4y - 6 \leq 10; y \in N$
6. $14 \leq 2p + 8 \leq 18; p \in N$

1 Fill in the blanks.

a. In a linear equation, the highest power of the variable is ________.

Summary

- An **equation** is an open statement containing variable(s) with equality sign.
- **Linear equation** is an algebraic equation consisting of constants and variables, of power 1.
- The value of the variable in an equation which satisfies the equation is called the **solution or root** of the equation.
- Solution of the linear equation can be found by (i) trial and error method (ii) Method of balancing (iii) Method of transposing
- An inequation with a variable having 1 as the highest power is known as a **linear inequation**.
- The set of elements that are used to replace the variable in an inequation is called the **replacement set or domain** of the variable.
- The subset of the replacement set containing those values of the variable for which the given inequation is satisfied is called the **solution set**.

Revision Exercise

b. The variable in the equation $5x - 9 = -3$ is ________.

c. A mathematical sentence that contains the equality sign is called ________.

d. The mathematical sentence $5 < 2x - 1$ is an example of ________.

e. The value of the variable in an equation which satisfies the equation is called ________.

2. **Solve the following equations.**

a. $x - 8 = 12$ b. $5x - 4 = 16$ c. $8x + 3 = 51$ d. $9x + 12 = 57$ e. $17x - 3 = -37$

3. **Find the solution set of *x* in the following inequations.**

a. $2x < 5 + 7x$ b. $2x - 4 \geq 3$ c. $11 \leq 6x - 1 \leq 17$ d. $-5 < x < 3$

4. **Solve the following word problems.**

a. Find the three consecutive odd numbers whose sum is equal to 273.

b. Dhanya has saved some 10-rupee and 5-rupee coins in her piggy bank. If the there are 25 coins in the piggy bank which amounts to ₹200, find the number of coins of each denomination.

c. The length of a rectangle is 2 more than its breadth. If the perimeter of the rectangle is 36 cm, find the dimensions of the rectangle.

d. Five years from now, Sunil will be twice his present age. How old is he now?

For the Curious Mind

Sum of the digits of a two digit number is 9. The number formed by reversing the digits is 45 less than the original number. Find the original number.

Theme Worksheet 3

Which question never gets a reply if the answer is "yes"? To find out, answer the questions given below. Then write the code letter in the box corresponding to the correct answer at the bottom of the page. Some are done for you.

Degree of the polynomial $4x^3 - 2x^5 + 2x + 3$ is

S

Coefficient of y^2 in the polynomial $y^2 - 1$ is

A

Coefficient of x in $12x^2$

G

Factors of $12yz$

O

$15x^2z$ is a ____________.

L

$(7x + 12) + (-2x + 3)$

R

$(-8x + 3y) - (5x - 6y)$

Y

$6z + 18 = 12$ is a ______________.

E

$x - 6 = 3$, then $x =$ ______

P

$5x - 2 = -7$, then $x =$ ________

U

The subset of the replacement set containing those values of the variable for which the given inequation is satisfied is called ________.

E

If $1 < 2x + 7 < 5$, $x \in I$ then find the solution.

I

The set of elements that are used to replace the variable in an inequation is called _________of the variable.

N

The number t is atleast 7.

E

A			Y		
1	$5x + 15$	Linear Equation	$-13x + 9y$	$2, 2, 3, y, z$	-1

S								
5	Monomial	$t \geq 7$	Solution Set	9	-2	Domain	$12x$	?

Skill-based Worksheet - Solving Daily Life Problems

Solve the following.

1. Akhil is elder to Nikhil by 5 years. After 3 years, Akhil will be thrice as old as Nikhil was two years ago. What are their present ages?

2. Mr. Jaydev opened a mobile showroom. He gets ₹125 on selling a mobile. His monthly expense to run the showroom is ₹10,000. What is the minimum number of mobiles that he should sell in a month to make a profit?

3. In a competitive exam, there are 100 multiple choice questions. For every correct answer, 3 marks are given and for every incorrect answer or un-attempted question, 1 mark is deducted. If Vinod has scored 160 marks, find the number of questions that he has answered correctly.

4. Joe called some of his friends to home for celebrating Christmas. His mom prepared 35 cakes to distribute to his friends. He gave 2 cakes to each of them and there were 5 cakes left. How many of his friends came home for the celebration?

5. Rohan bought 60 units of fencing to fence his garden. The length of the garden is 3 units more than twice its breadth. Find the length and breadth of the garden.

6. Vikki has planted a rose plant which has 30 cm height, on occasion of his birthday. Every day it grows by 5 cm. How many days will it take to grow to a height of 150 cm?

7. A mobile service provider is giving the following plan:

Monthly Rental	₹ 100
Free talk time	60 minutes
Call rate	₹ 1 per minute

   If the monthly bill of a person for a particular month is ₹350, find the number of minutes of talk time apart from the free talk time.

8. Mr. Abhijeet went to US on a business trip. He wants to exchange his Indian currency with US dollars. If he has ₹1,00,000, how many US dollars will he get on exchange? (1USD = ₹68)

Mental Maths

Chapter 11 - Operations on Algebraic Expressions

Answer the following:

1. The factors of the term $15k^3x^2$
2. The coefficient of b^3 in the term $14b^4c^2$
3. The numerical coefficient in the term $16a^2b^3c^4$
4. The degree of the polynomial $14a^2 + 2b^2 - 5ab$
5. The degree of the constant polynomial.
6. Write any three like terms to $3m^4x^2$.
7. $5a^2n^6h^2$ is a ____________ (trinomial/monomial).
8. The sum of $2x^2$ and $-12x^2$ is________.
9. The sum of $(3k^3 - 2b^2)$ and $(-12b^2 + 5k^3)$ is________.
10. $(-15c^6 + 3c^3) - (5c^6 - 6c^3) =$ ________.

Chapter 12 - Linear Equations and Inequations

Solve the following.

1. $4x + 3 = 7$
2. $x + 6 = -10$
3. $3x - 2 = 7$
4. $\frac{x}{6} = 2$
5. $18 - x = 2$
6. $y - 10 = 10$
7. $-z + 5 = 4$
8. $x + 2 < 5, x \in N$
9. $\frac{x}{2} \geq 3, x \in Z$
10. $-3 \leq x + 2 \leq 3, x \in Z$

Geometry

Chapters Covered

13. Lines and Angles

14. Properties of Triangles

15. Symmetry

16. Visualising solid shapes

17. Mapping space around us

18. Congruence of Triangles

19. Constructions

Why this Theme Matters

Geometry is a branch of mathematics concerned with the shapes, sizes, positions and properties of different figures. Since ancient times, geometry has been used by people to measure lands and construct buildings and canals. In the present times, geometry is used in fields like robotics, space science, etc.

Bridges and other similar structures are often designed to include triangular shapes, as these shapes are able to withstand a great amount of pressure. Hence triangular shapes are used in civil engineering and architecture. It is also used in astronomy, navigation and computer graphics. Therefore, it is necessary to understand and study triangles and its properties.

Pythagoras is a Greek philosopher and a Mathematician. A major contribution by Pythagoras in the field of Geometry is '***Pythagoras Theorem***' for right angled triangles. It helps to solve many real life problems such as finding the length of a side when the lengths of other two sides of a right angled triangle are known.

We will learn about Geometry and its applications under this theme.

THEME 4

Lines and Angles

13

What I shall learn

- To identify the different types of angles made by the transversal intersecting two lines
- To verify the properties of different types of angles made by the transversal in case of parallel lines
- To check whether two given lines are parallel or not

Let's Get Started

We know that an **angle** is a geometrical shape formed when two rays emerge from a common point. The common point is called the **vertex** and the rays are called the **arms** of the angle.

Look at the following pictures. Identify and classify the angles as acute, obtuse and right angles.

Naming an Angle

In the given figure, $\overrightarrow{BA}$ and $\overrightarrow{BC}$ are the arms of an angle and B is the vertex. The angle is denoted by the symbol ∠ and named as ∠ABC or ∠CBA or simply as ∠B.

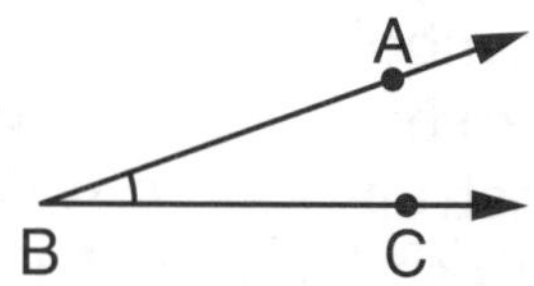

Interior and Exterior of an Angle

The plane in which an angle lies is divided into three regions.

The region bounded by the arms of an angle is called the **interior** of the angle. The region outside the arms of an angle is called the **exterior** of the angle. All the points on the arms of an angle are said to lie on the angle. In the figure, points P, Q and R lie in the interior of ∠AOB, points M and N lie on the exterior of ∠AOB and points E and F lie on ∠AOB.

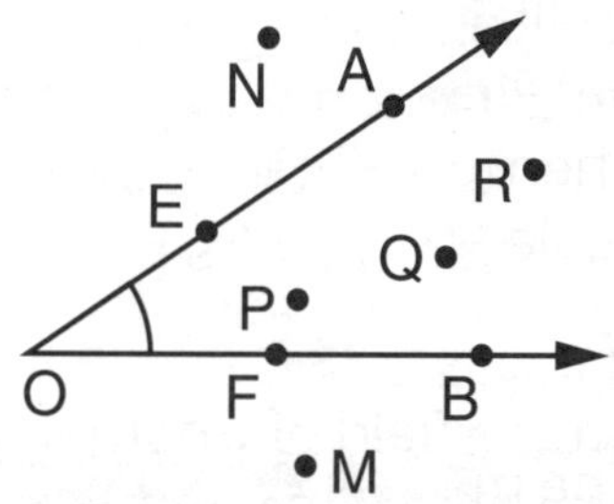

Measurement of an Angle

An angle is measured by a unit called **degree**, which is represented by the symbol °.

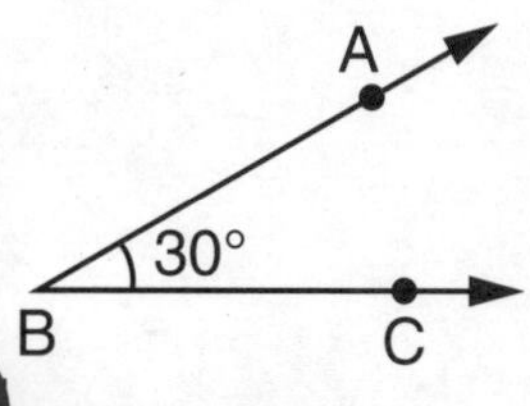

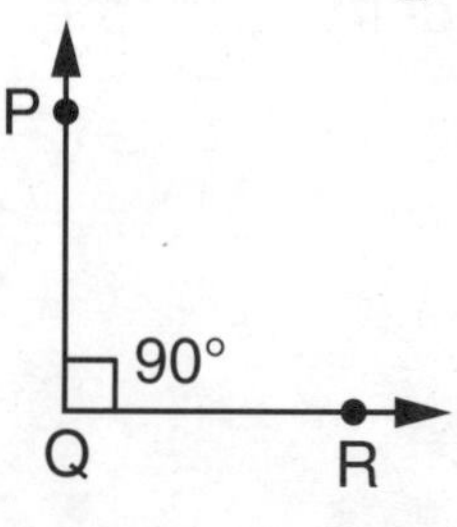

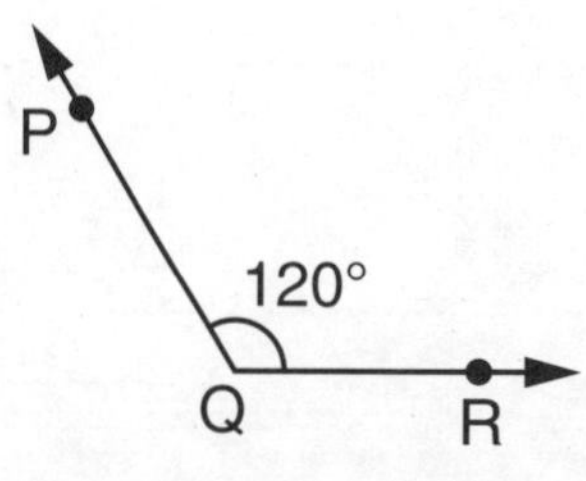

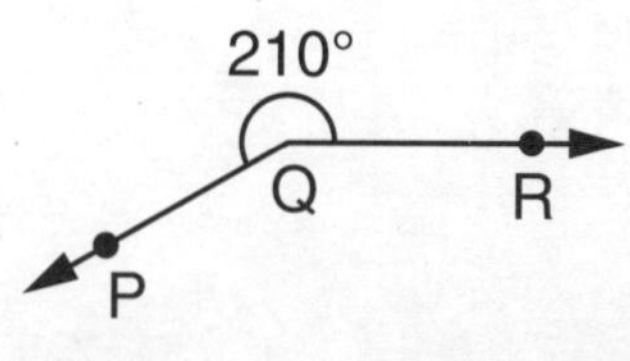

Classification of Angles

Zero angle
∠AOB = 0°

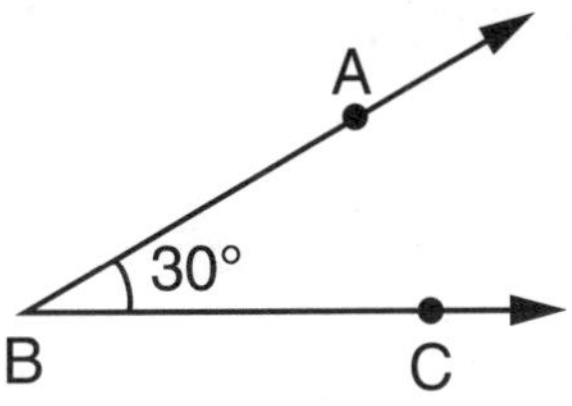

Acute angle
∠ABC = 30°
(0° < 30° < 90°)

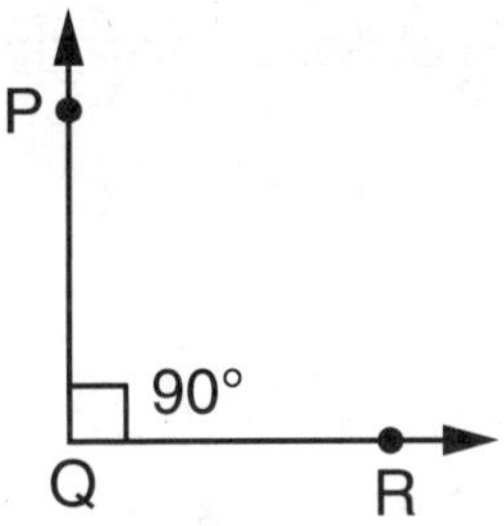

Right angle
∠PQR = 90°

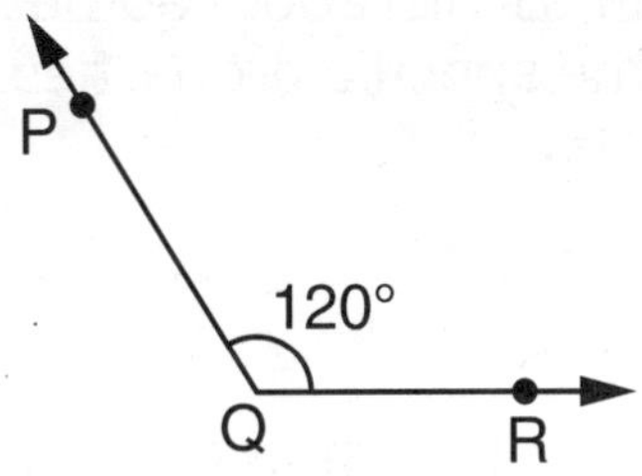

Obtuse angle
∠PQR = 120°
(90° < 120° < 180°)

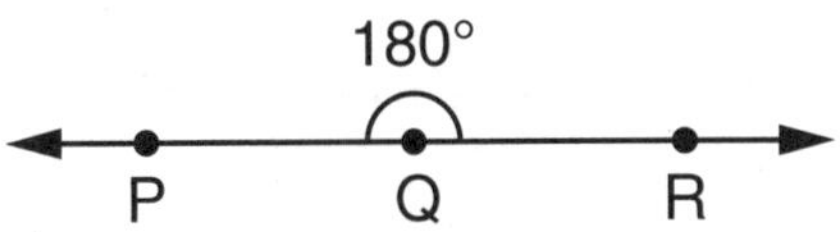

Straight angle
∠PQR = 180°

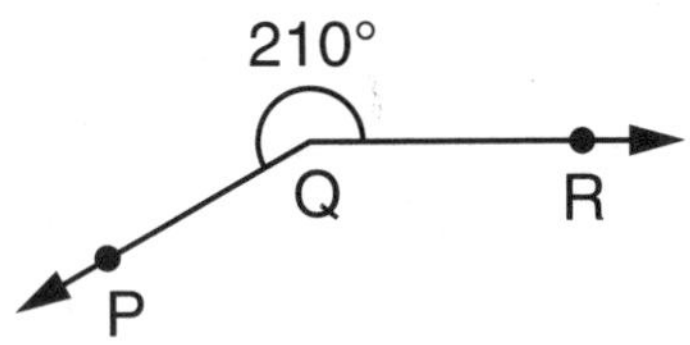

Reflex angle
∠PQR = 210° (180° < 210° < 360°)

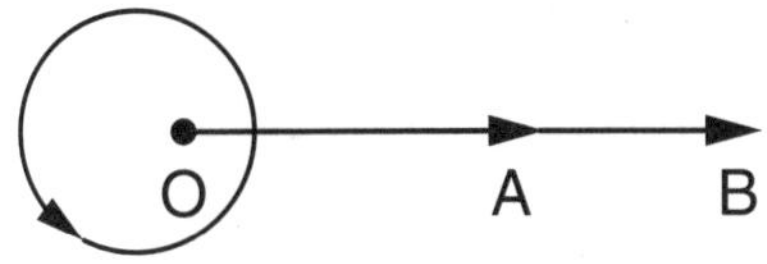

Complete angle
∠AOB = 360°

Measuring Angles Using Protractor

A degree is a unit of measurement of an angle. The symbol used for representing degrees is °. Angles can be measured with the help of the D-shaped instrument called **protractor**. A protractor consists of centre, base line, outer scale and inner scale as shown in the adjacent figure.

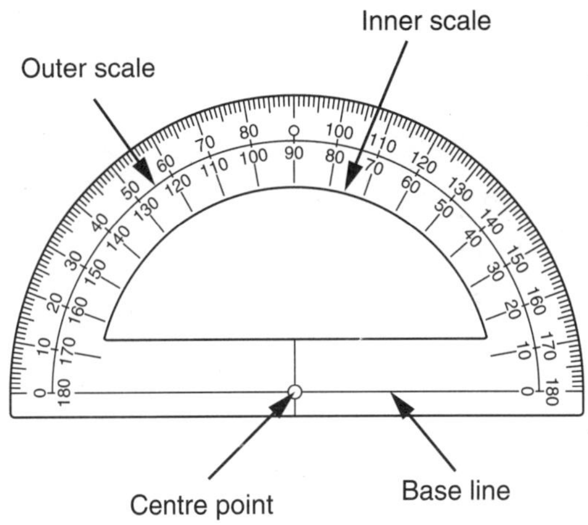

To measure an angle using a protractor, place it over the angle to be measured such that the centre point of the protractor coincides with the vertex of the angle and base line coincides with one of the arms of the angle.

Then, choose the appropriate scale (choose the scale where the base line arm is pointing to 0°) and read the angle by identifying to which degree the other arm of the angle is coinciding.

The measure of the ∠POR shown in the figure given below is 120°.

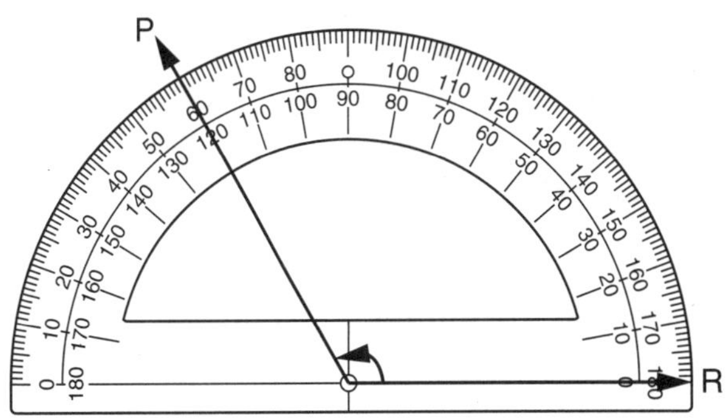

Pairs of Angles

Let us learn about some special pairs of angles which satisfy some specific properties.

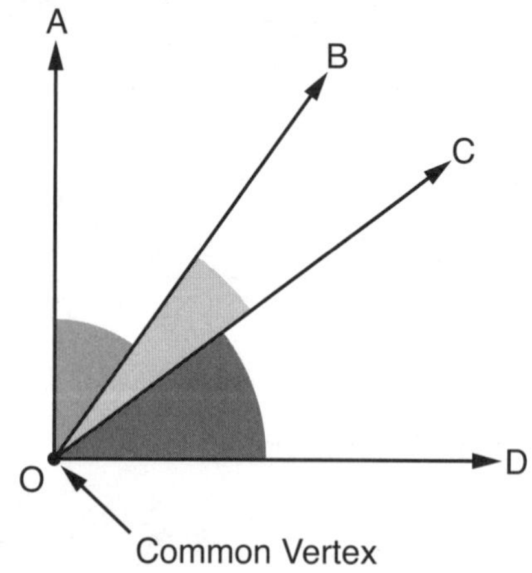

Adjacent Angles

In mathematics, **two angles are said to be adjacent if they have a common arm, common vertex and the other arms lie on the opposite sides of the common arm**. In the figure, ∠AOB and ∠BOC are adjacent. Identify the other pair of adjacent angles.

Are ∠AOB and ∠COD adjacent? Why or why not? Are ∠BOD and ∠COD adjacent?

No, they are not adjacent. Even though they share a common vertex and a common arm, the other arms don't lie on the opposite sides of the common arm.

Complementary and Supplementary Angles

Consider a pair of angles 25° and 65°. Stick them together and notice that the sum of these two angles is 90°.

That is, ∠25° + ∠65° = ∠90°.

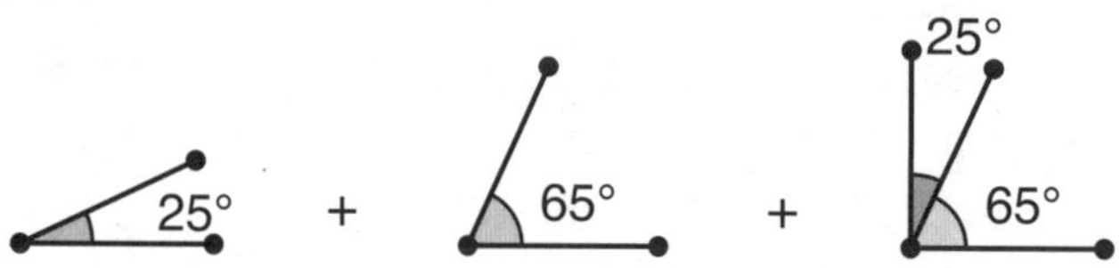

Consider a pair of angles 64° and 116°. Stick them together and notice that the sum of these two angles is 180°.

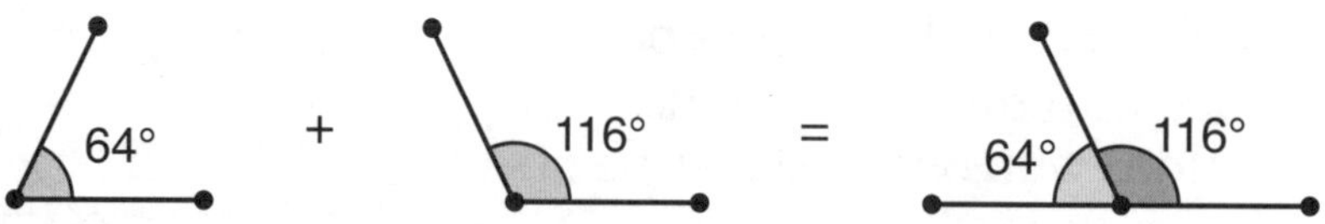

The pair of angles whose sum is 90° are known as complementary angles. Each angle is the complement of the other. For example, 30° is complement to 60° and vice versa. **The pair of angles whose sum is 180° are known as supplementary angles.** Each angle is the supplement of the other. For example, 135° is supplement to 45° and vice versa.

Linear Pair

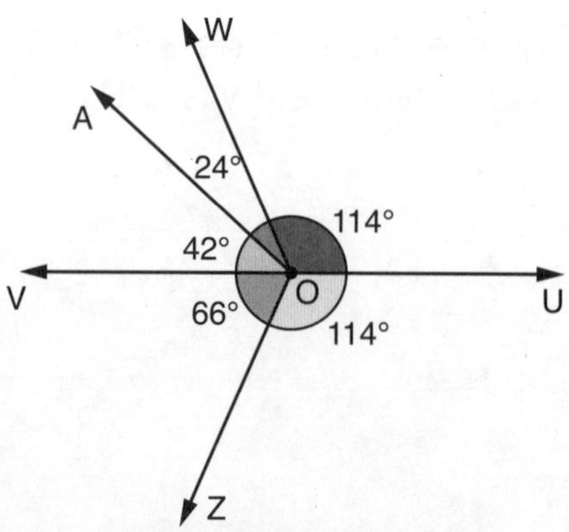

Observe the figure shown here.

Which are the angles adjacent to ∠VOZ?

The answer is ∠VOA and ∠ZOU

Which are the supplementary angles of ∠VOZ?

The answer is ∠WOU and ∠ZOU

Which is the angle which is adjacent as well as supplementary to ∠VOZ? The answer is ∠ZOU

The pair of angles that are adjacent as well as supplementary is known as a linear pair.

∠VOZ + ∠ZOU = 180° (66° + 114° = 180°)

So, ∠VOZ and ∠ZOU form a linear pair. Identify the other linear pairs in the figure.

Real-life Examples:

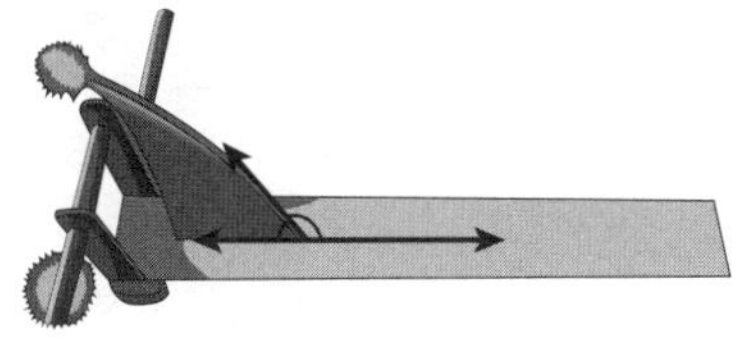

Vertically Opposite Angles

Take two sticks and paste them on a chart as shown here so as to form intersecting lines and name them. Observe the angles so formed.

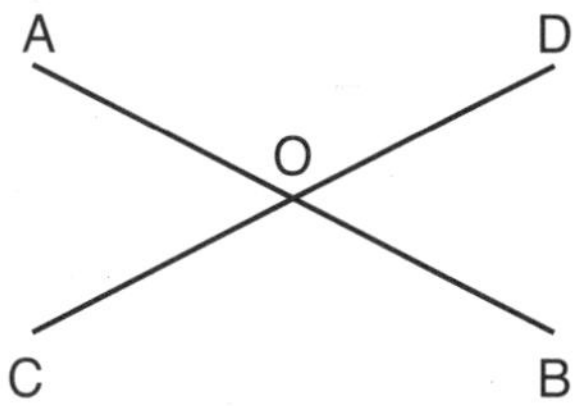

∠AOD and ∠COB share a common vertex (O) but no common arm.

Similarly, ∠AOC and ∠DOB also share a common vertex (O) but no common arm.

Two angles that share a common vertex, such that the arms of the angles form a pair of opposite rays, are called vertically opposite angles. Vertically opposite angles are equal.

Remember

Measure of two vertically opposite angles are always equal.

Real-life Examples:

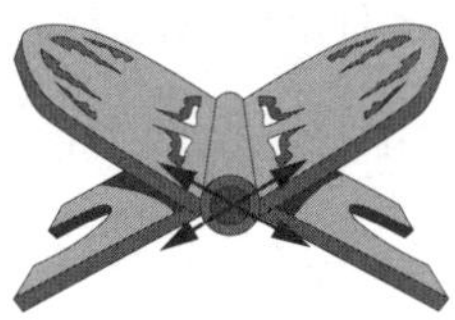

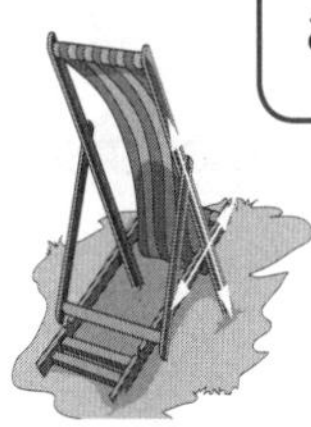

Note: 1. The sum of all the angles formed on the same side of a straight line at a point is 180°, that is, ∠1 + ∠2 + ∠3 + ∠4 = 180°.

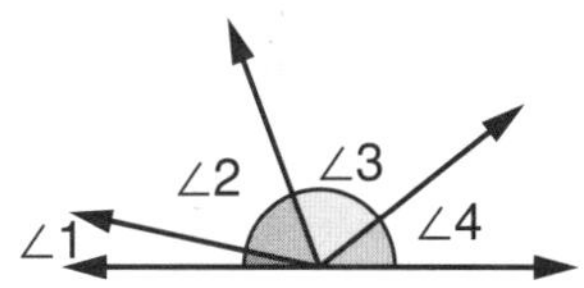

2. The sum of all the angles formed around a point is 360°, that is, ∠1 + ∠2 + ∠3 + ∠4 = 360°.

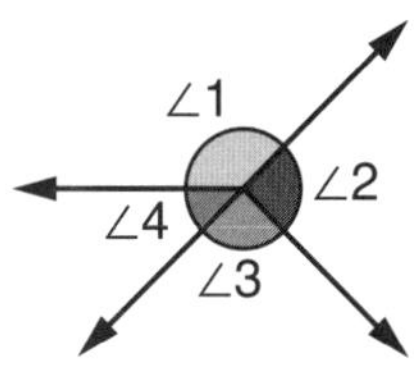

Example 1: Two complementary angles are in the ratio 3 : 7. Find the angles.

Let the required angles be $(3x)°$ and $(7x)°$.

$\therefore 3x + 7x = 90° \Rightarrow 10x = 90° \Rightarrow x = 9°$

Hence, the required angles are $(3 \times 9)°$ and $(7 \times 9)°$, that is, 27° and 63°.

Example 2: Find the angle which is triple of its supplement.

Let the measure of required angle be $x°$.

Then, the measure of its supplement will be $(180 - x)°$.

$\therefore x = 3(180 - x) \Rightarrow x = 540 - 3x$

$\Rightarrow 4x = 540 \Rightarrow x = 135°$

Example 3: How many degrees are there in $\frac{1}{2}$ right angle?

Let the measure of the required angle be $x°$.

$\therefore x = \frac{1}{2} \times 90° = 45°$

Exercise 13.1

1. An angle is 40° more than a straight angle. Find the angle.
2. At 7 o' clock, the hands of a clock make an obtuse angle and a reflex angle. Find the measure of each of these angles.
3. At 11 o'clock, the hands of a clock make an acute angle and a reflex angle. Find the measure of each of these angles.
4. **How many degrees are there in each of the following angles?**
   - i. Two straight angles
   - ii. $1\frac{1}{3}$ of a right angle
   - iii. $\frac{1}{2}$ of a straight angle
   - iv. $\frac{1}{6}$ of a straight angle
5. If $x°$ and $(x + 40)°$ are complements of each other, find the value of x.
6. If $x°$ and $(x + 60)°$ are supplements of each other, find the value of x.
7. Two complementary angles are in the ratio 3 : 6. Find the angles.
8. Two supplementary angles are in the ratio 10 : 8. Find the angles.
9. An angle is double its supplement. Find the angle.
10. Find the measure of an angle that is 40° more than its complement.
11. Find the measure of an angle that is 60° less than its supplement.
12. Find an angle that is 10° more than five times its supplement.

13 Find all the angles in the following figures.

a.

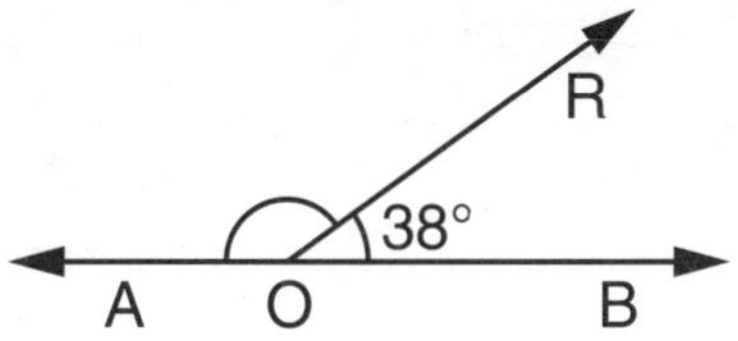

b.

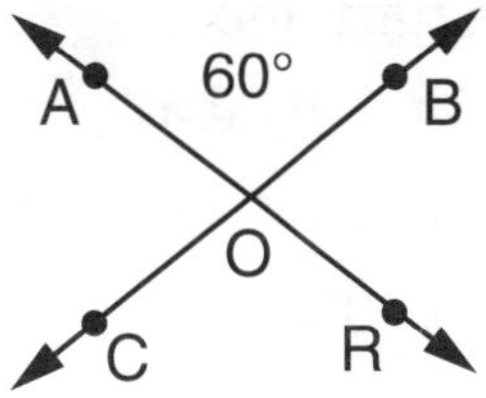

c.

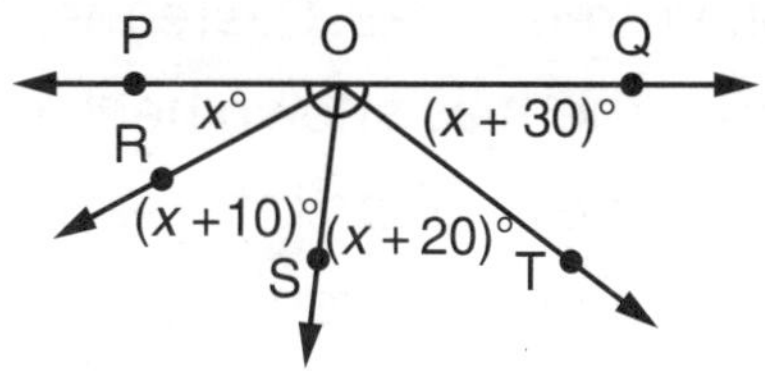

d.

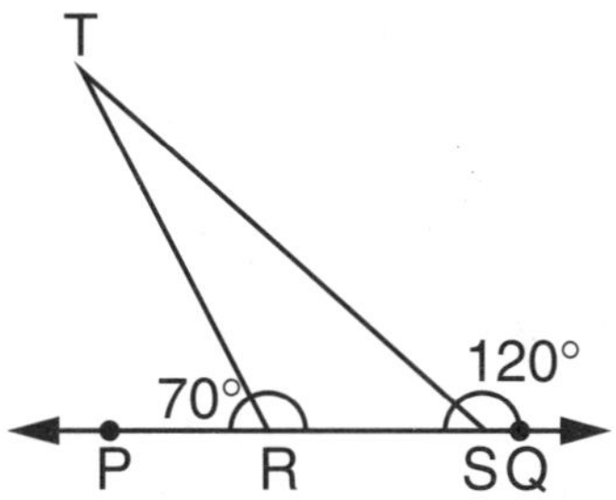

e.

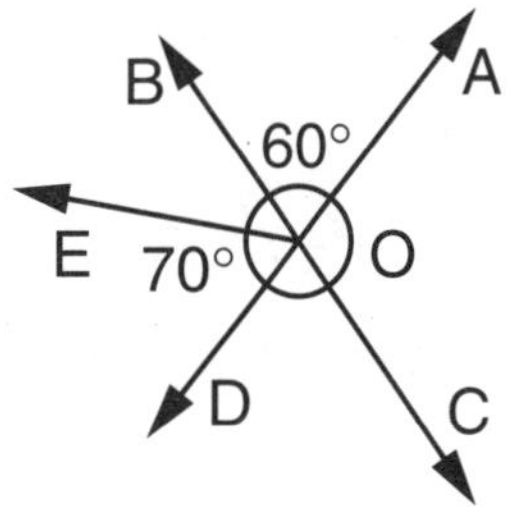

f.

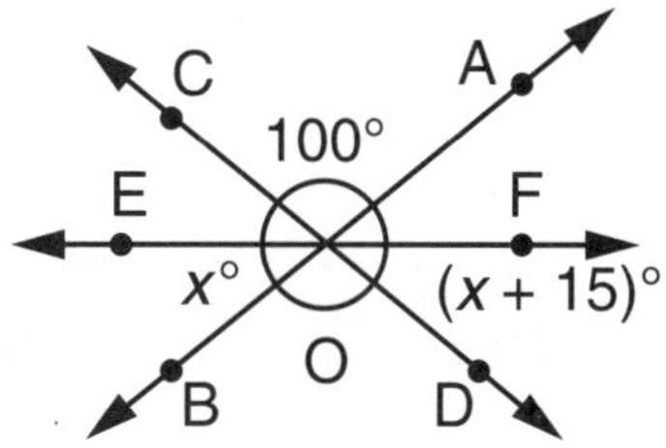

Example 4: In the given figure, AOB is a straight line. Find ∠AOR and ∠BOR.

∠AOR + ∠BOR = 180° (Linear Pair/Sum of adjacent angles on a straight line)

$\therefore x + 25 + 3x + 35 = 180$

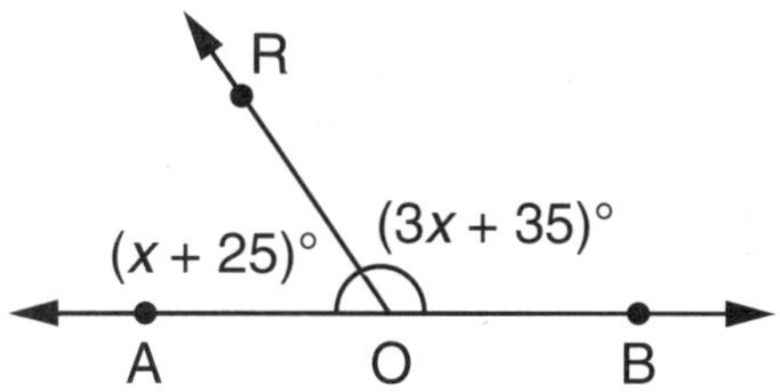

$\Rightarrow 4x + 60 = 180 \Rightarrow 4x = 180 - 60 = 120 \Rightarrow x = \frac{120}{4} = 30$

So, we have:

$\therefore$ ∠AOR = $(x + 25)° = (30 + 25)° = 55°$ and ∠BOR = $(3x + 35)° = (3 \times 30 + 35)° = 125°$

Example 5: In the given figure, AB, CD and EF are three straight lines intersecting each other at point O. If ∠AOC = 60°, find the other angles.

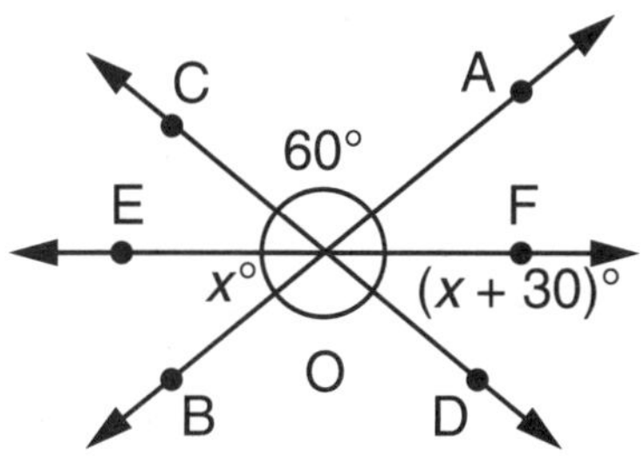

∠BOD = ∠AOC = 60° (Vertically opposite angles)

∠EOB + ∠BOD + ∠FOD = 180° (Sum of adjacent angles on a straight line)

$\therefore x + 60 + x + 30 = 180$

$\Rightarrow 2x + 90 = 180 \Rightarrow 2x = 90 \Rightarrow x = 45$

So, we have:

∠EOB = x = 45° = ∠FOA (Vertically opposite angles), ∠FOD = $x + 30 = 75°$

∠EOC = ∠FOD = 75° (Vertically opposite angles)

Parallel Lines

Two lines that will never meet even if they are extended endlessly on both sides are called **parallel lines**. The perpendicular distance between parallel lines always remains constant. Parallel lines are represented by the symbol ||.

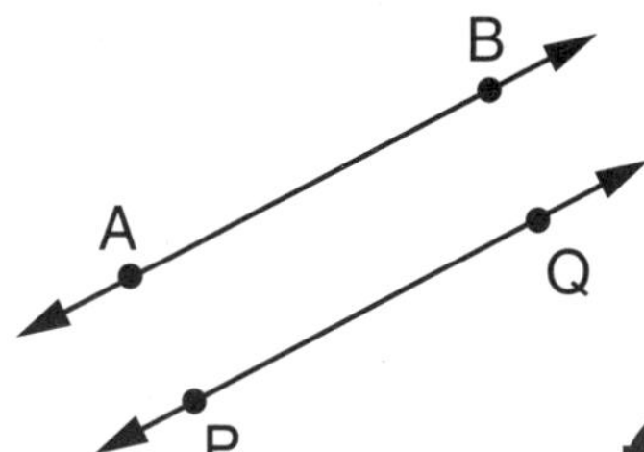

In the given figure, AB || PQ.

Angles Made by the Transversal

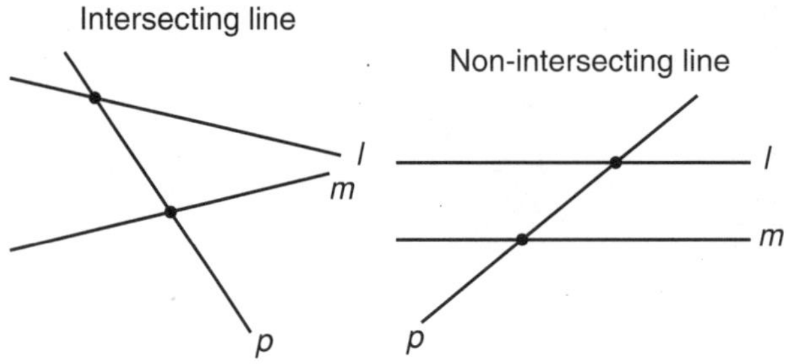

Take three sticks. Paste them on a chart and name them as shown here. *l* and *m* are any two lines. They can be intersecting or non-intersecting lines. Line *p* is intersecting the lines *l* and *m* at two distinct points.

The line that intersects two or more lines at two distinct points is known as a **transversal.**

Let AB and CD be any two intersecting lines and EF be the transversal intersecting the lines at points X and Y. Observe the different angles formed by the transversal.

$\angle 1$, $\angle 2$, $\angle 7$ and $\angle 8$ are the **exterior angles** and $\angle 3$, $\angle 4$, $\angle 5$ and $\angle 6$ are the **interior angles** formed between the lines.

Real-life Examples:

Alternate interior angles: The pair of interior angles formed on the opposite sides of a transversal and do not form a linear pair are called alternate interior angles. $\angle 3$ and $\angle 6$, and $\angle 4$ and $\angle 5$ are two pairs of alternate interior angles.

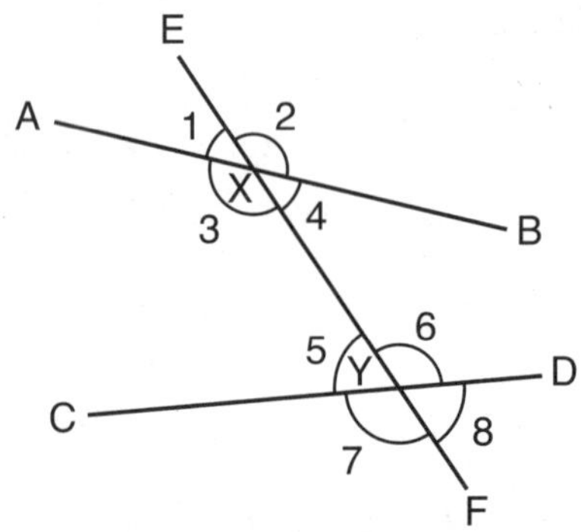

Alternate exterior angles: The pair of exterior angles formed on the opposite sides of a transversal and do not form a linear pair are called alternate exterior angles. $\angle 1$ and $\angle 8$, and $\angle 2$ and $\angle 7$ are two pairs of alternate exterior angles.

Corresponding angles: The pair of angles formed on the same side of a transversal, one being an exterior angle and the other an interior angle, which do not form a linear pair are called corresponding angles. $\angle 2$ and $\angle 6$, and $\angle 3$ and $\angle 7$ are two pairs of corresponding angles. Find the other two pairs.

Parallel Lines and a Transversal

Two lines in a plane are said to be parallel if they do not intersect at any point even if they are extended indefinitely in both the directions.

How to check whether the two lines are parallel or not?

Observe the distance between any two parallel lines like two bars of a window, opposite edges of a book, etc. You will find that the distance between them is constant throughout.

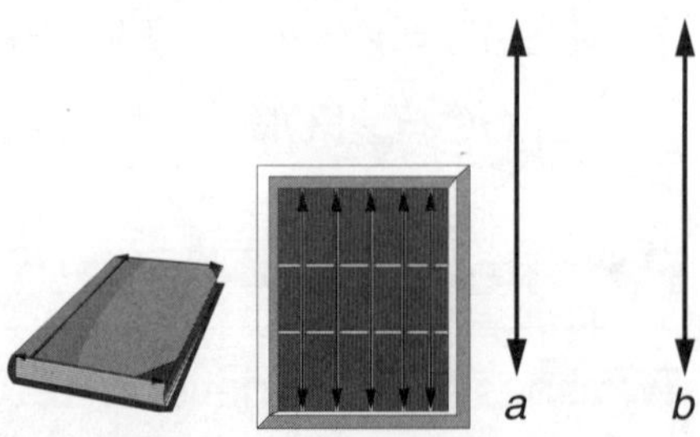

Properties of angles made by the transversal with parallel lines

Take a sheet of paper. Fold it twice horizontally and crease the lines to form two parallel lines. Then fold it slantingly as shown here and crease the line to form the transversal. Take a patty paper and trace the parallel lines and the transversal on it. Label the parallel lines and the transversal on both the papers.

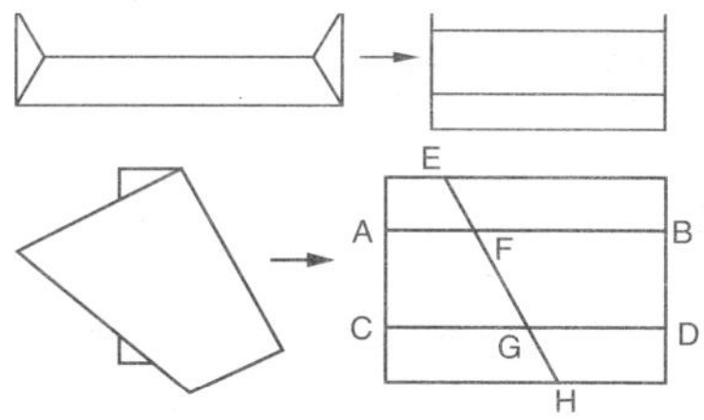

Mark the different pairs of corresponding angles using different colours. Place the papers one above the other and slide the top patty paper along the transversal EH, until the line CD of the top paper coincides with the line AB. Observe different pairs of corresponding angles.

You observe that **all the pairs of corresponding angles are equal.**

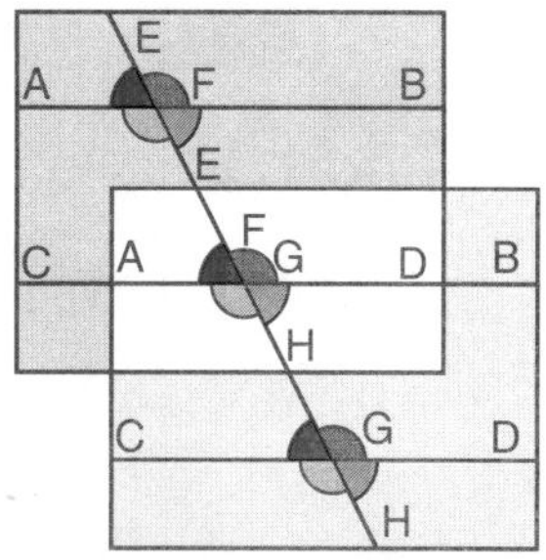

Similarly, mark the different pairs of alternate interior angles. Rotate the figure on second patty paper by 180° and place it over the first such that the line CD of Fig. 2 coincides with AB of Fig. 1 and the transversals coincide. Observe the angles. You observe that **the two pairs of alternate interior angles are equal**.

Fig. 1 Fig. 2 (Rotated by 180°)

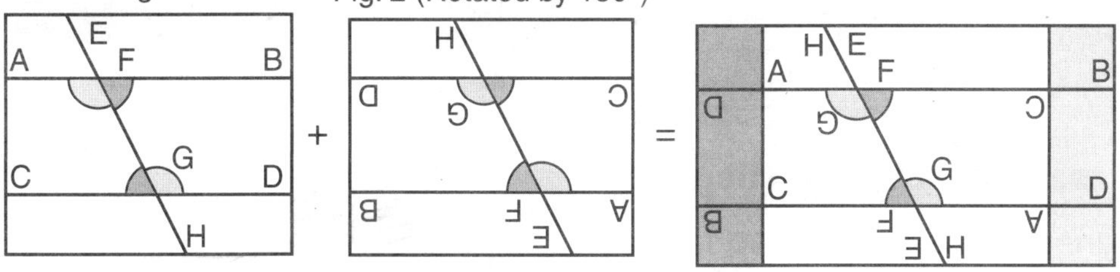

Mark one pair of the interior angles on the same side of the transversal on both the patty papers with the same colour.

Rotate Fig. 2 by 180° and place it over Fig. 1 in such a way that the line CD of Fig. 2 coincides with AB of Fig. 1 and transversals coincide. You can observe that the sum of interior angles on the same side of the transversal form a straight angle, that is, 180°. Therefore, **the interior angles on the same side of the transversal are supplementary**.

Properties of the Angles Formed When a Transversal Intersects Two Parallel Lines

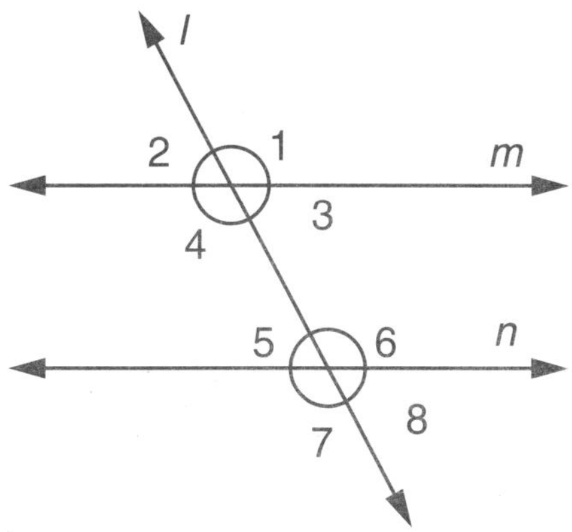

a. The pairs of alternate interior as well as the pairs of alternate exterior angles are equal.

   In the given figure, $\angle 4 = \angle 6$, $\angle 3 = \angle 5$, $\angle 2 = \angle 8$ and $\angle 1 = \angle 7$.

b. The pairs of corresponding angles are equal.

   In the given figure, $\angle 2 = \angle 5$, $\angle 4 = \angle 7$, $\angle 1 = \angle 6$ and $\angle 3 = \angle 8$.

c. The pairs of consecutive interior angles on the same side of the transversal are supplementary.

   In the given figure, $\angle 4 + \angle 5 = 180°$

   $\angle 3 + \angle 6 = 180°$

Two lines are parallel if each pair of

a. the corresponding angles are equal.
b. the alternate interior or the alternate exterior angles are equal.
c. the co-interior angles on the same side of the transversal are supplementary.

Example 6: In the given figure, AB || PQ and RC is the transversal. If $\angle AUV = 130°$, find all the other angles.

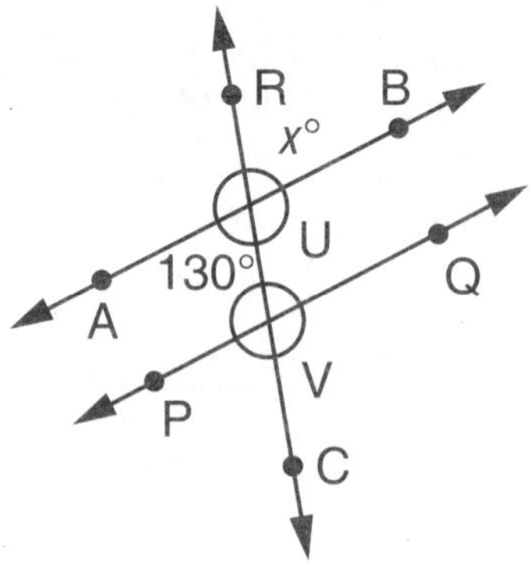

$\angle AUV = \angle RUB = 130°$ (Vertically opposite angles)

$\angle RUB + \angle BUV = 180°$ (Adjacent angles on a straight line add up to 180°)

$\therefore \angle BUV = 180° - 130° = 50°$

$\angle RUB = \angle UVQ = 130°$ and $\angle CVQ = \angle VUB = 50°$ (Corresponding angles)

$\angle QVU = \angle AUV = 130°$ (Alternate interior angles)

$\angle RUA = \angle BUV = 50°$ and $\angle PVC = \angle QVU = 130°$ (Vertically opposite angles)

Example 7: In the given figure, AB || CD, $\angle ABM = 60°$ and $\angle CDM = 30°$. Find the measure of $\angle BMD$.

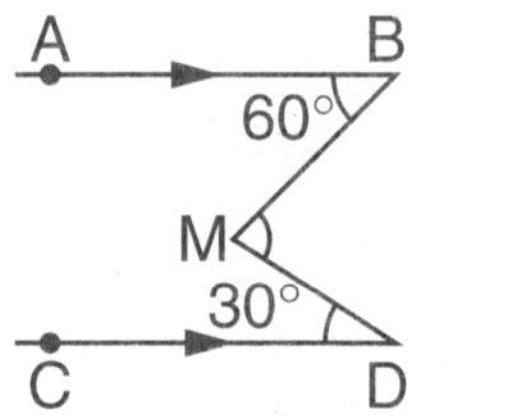

Through M, we draw PMQ || AB || CD.

Let $\angle BMQ = x°$ and $\angle DMQ = y°$. AB || PQ and BM is a transversal.

So, $\angle ABM = \angle BMQ = 60°$ (Alternate angles) $\therefore x = 60°$

Again, CD || PQ and MD is a transversal.

So, $\angle CDM = \angle DMQ = 30°$ (Alternate angles)

$\therefore y = 30°$ therefore, $\angle BMD = x + y = 60° + 30° = 90°$

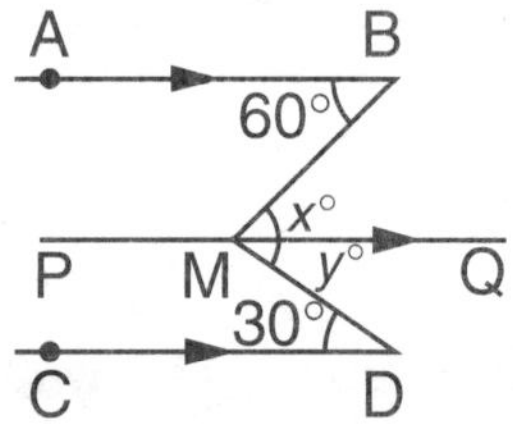

Example 8: In the given figure, PQ || RS, $\angle RST = 140°$, $\angle STQ = 60$ and $\angle PQT = x°$. Find the value of x.

Through T, we draw MTN || PQ || RS. Let $\angle MTQ = y°$. Then $\angle MTS = (60 - y)°$.

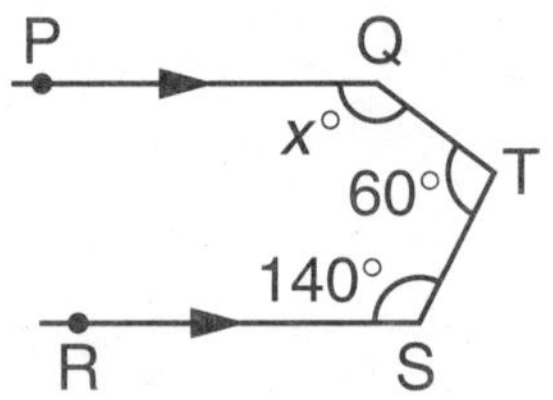

Now MN || RS and ST is a transversal.

$\therefore 140 + 60 - y = 180$ (The sum of co-interior angles on the same side of
the transversal is 180°.)

$\Rightarrow y = 200 - 180 = 20$

Again, PQ || MN and QT is a transversal.

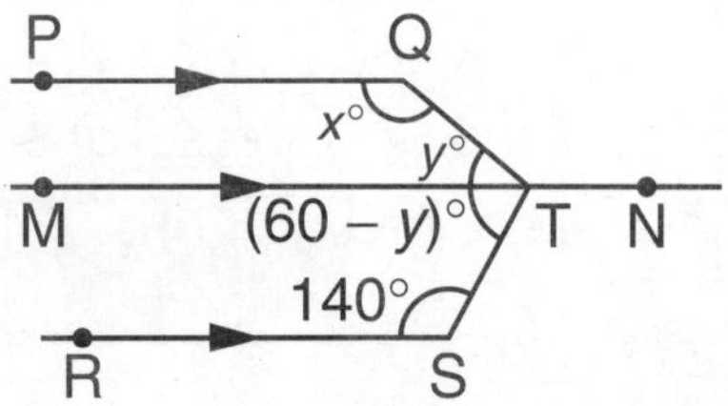

$\therefore x + y = 180°$ (The sum of co-interior angles on the same side of the transversal is 180°.)

$\Rightarrow x + 20 = 180 \Rightarrow x = 180 - 20 \Rightarrow x = 160$ $\therefore \angle PQT = 160°$

Exercise 13.2

1 **In each of the following figures, find all the unknown angles.**

a.

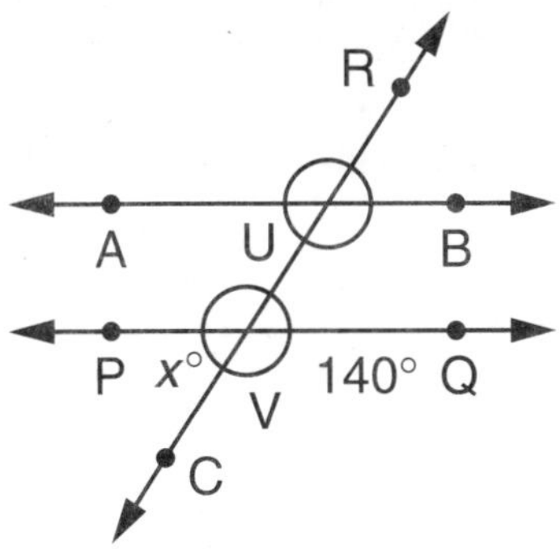

b.

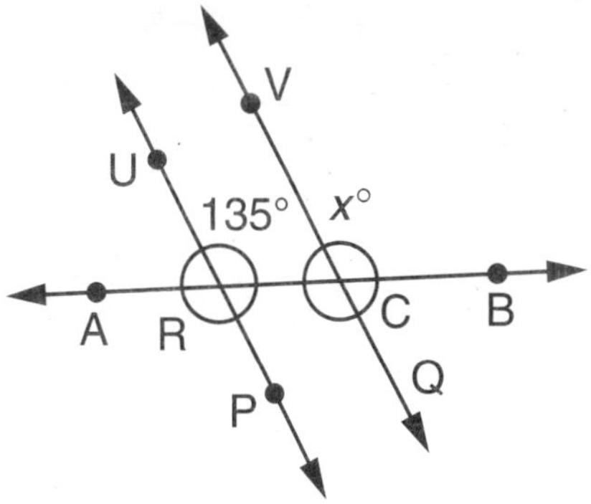

c.

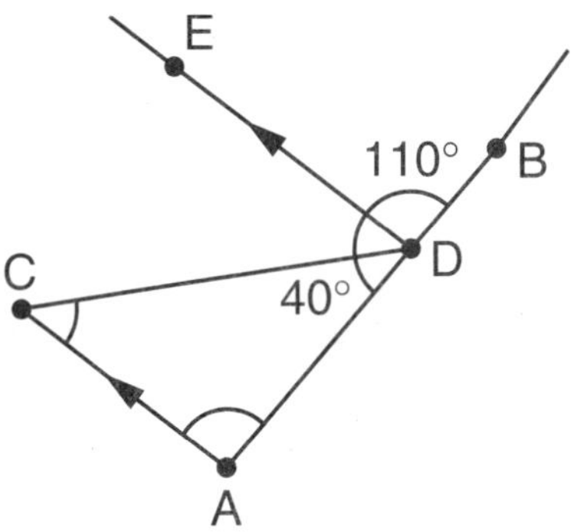

d.

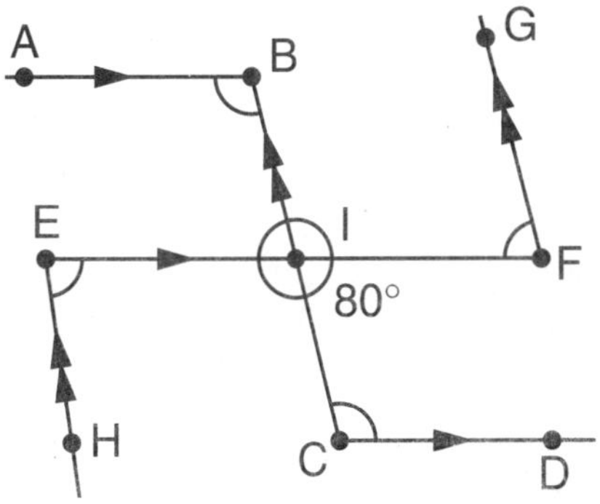

e.

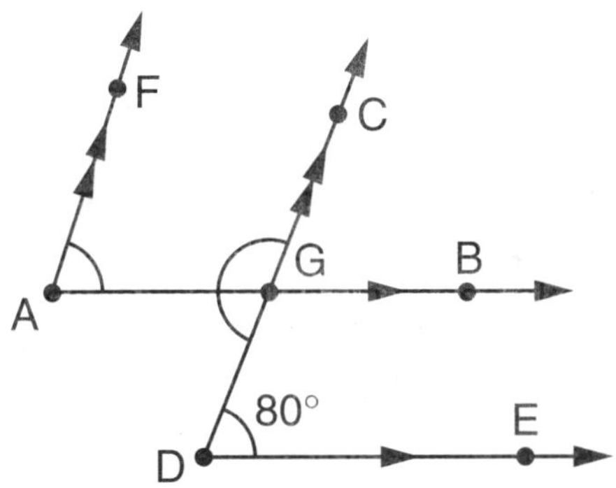

f.

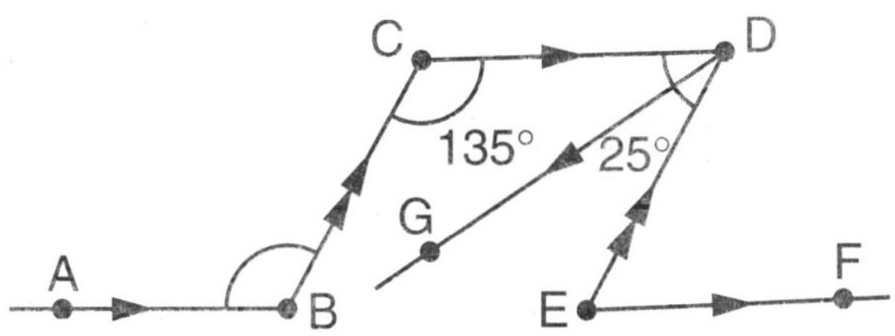

g.

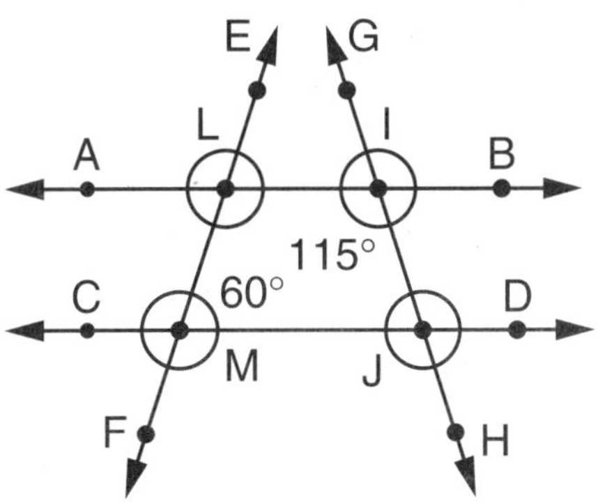

h.

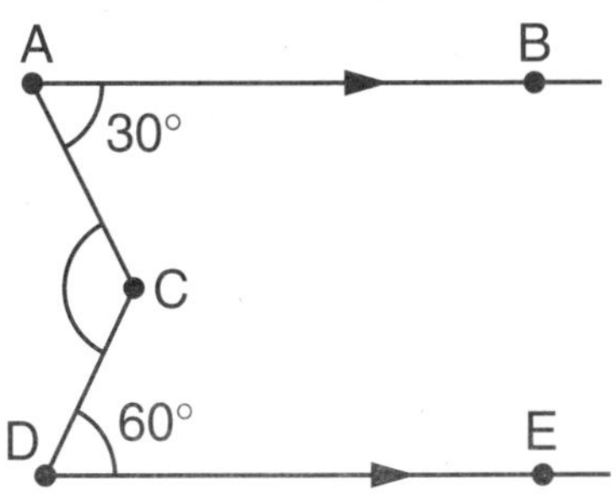

Summary

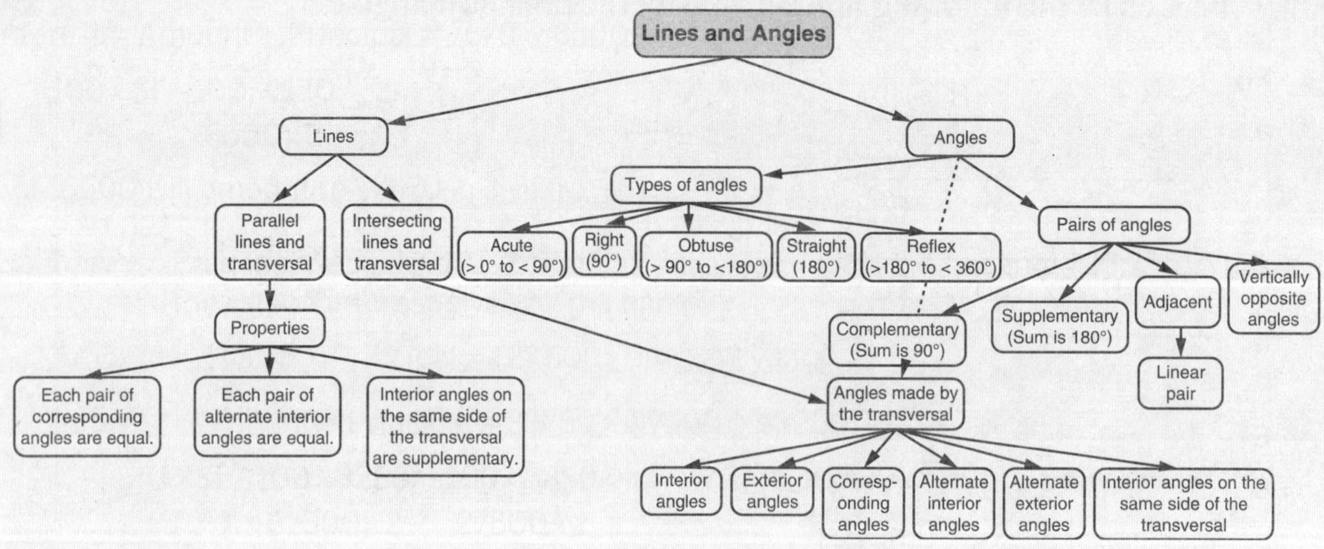

For the Curious Mind

Do all the pairs of supplementary angles form a linear pair? Are all linear pairs supplementary? Why?

Revision Exercise

1 **Fill in the blanks.**

a. Two lines are __________ if each pair of corresponding angles are equal.

b. The two pairs of angles that are formed on the opposite sides of a vertex when two straight lines intersect each other are known as __________ angles.

c. If an angle measures exactly 90°, then it is known as a __________ angle.

d. The sum of the measures of __________ angles is 90°.

e. Adjacent angles have a common __________ and a common __________.

2 **State whether the following statements are true or false.**

a. If an angle measures 360°, then it is known as a complete angle.

b. Two angles are supplementary when their sum is 180°.

c. If two angles are adjacent to each other and their sum is 90°, then they are a linear pair of angles.

d. If two lines that are extended infinitely on both sides never meet and the distance between them remains constant, then the lines are called concurrent lines.

e. If a line intersects two or more lines, then it is a transversal.

3 **Match the following.**

a. Adjacent angles whose sum is 180°	i. Vertically opposite angles
b. Two angles whose sum is 90°	ii. Complete angle
c. Angles formed when two lines intersect	iii. Supplementary angles
d. Angle measuring 90°	iv. Complementary angles
e. Angle measuring 0°	v. Linear pair of angles
f. Angle measuring 360°	vi. Right angle
g. Angles whose sum is 180°	vii. Zero angle

4 An angle is 60° more than a straight angle. Find the angle.

5 At 8 O' clock, the hands of a clock make an obtuse angle and a reflex angle. Find the measure of each of these angles.

6 How many degrees are there in three right angles?

7 If x° and $(x + 50)$° are complements of each other, find the value of x.

8 Two complementary angles are in the ratio 4 : 5. Find the angles.

9 For a transversal intersecting two parallel lines, the alternate exterior angles are equal to the corresponding alternate interior angles. Do you agree? Justify your answer.

10 Find an angle which is two-third of its complement.

THEME 4

Properties of Triangles

14

What I shall learn

- To list the properties of triangles
- To understand Pythagoras theorem and Pythagorean triplets

Let's Get Started

Triangular shapes are frequently used in civil engineering and architecture. This makes it necessary for us to understand and study triangles and their properties. Triangles are also used in astronomy, navigation and computer graphics.

Identify the shape of the triangles in the following figures and classify them as acute-angled, right-angled and obtuse-angled triangles.

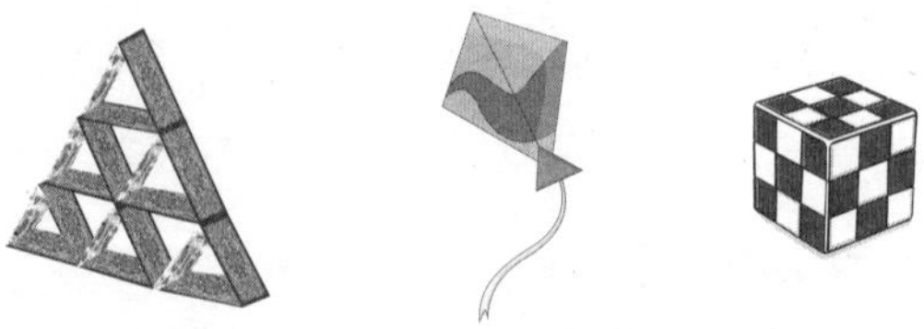

Triangle

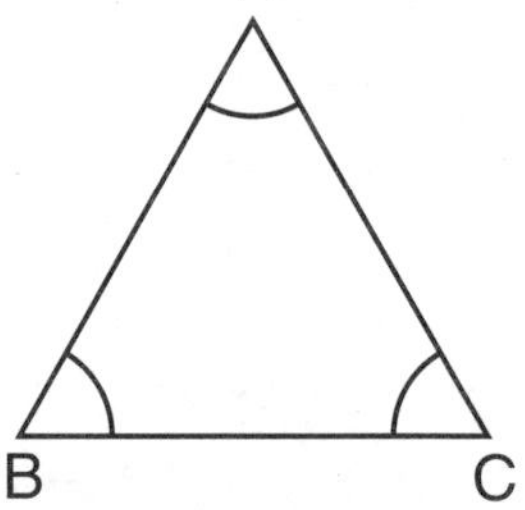

A triangle is a simple closed figure made up of three line segments. Let A, B and C be any three points in a plane which are not in a straight line. The figure formed by connecting these three points is a triangle.
It is denoted by the symbol Δ (Greek letter 'delta') and is written as ΔABC (read as 'triangle ABC'). It can also be named as ΔBCA or ΔCAB.

Elements of a Triangle

A triangle has 3 sides and 3 angles. Thus, a triangle has 6 elements. The line segments ($\overline{AB}$, $\overline{BC}$ and $\overline{CA}$ in the above triangle) that form the triangle are known as the **three sides** of the triangle. Two sides of a triangle meeting at a common point (called **vertex**) form an **angle** at that point. For example, the sides $\overline{AB}$ and $\overline{BC}$ form the angle $\angle ABC$. It is also be written as $\angle CBA$ or $\angle B$.

Hence, $\angle A$, $\angle B$ and $\angle C$ are the **three angles** and A, B and C are the **three vertices** of the triangle. The three sides and three angles of a triangle are known as the **six elements** of a triangle.

Interior and Exterior of a Triangle

The region within the boundary of a triangle is known as the **interior region**. The region outside the boundary of a triangle is known as the **exterior region**. In the figure, A, B and C are in the interior region, K, L and M are in the exterior region and P, Q and R are on the boundary of ΔXYZ. The interior region along with the boundary is known as the **triangular region**.

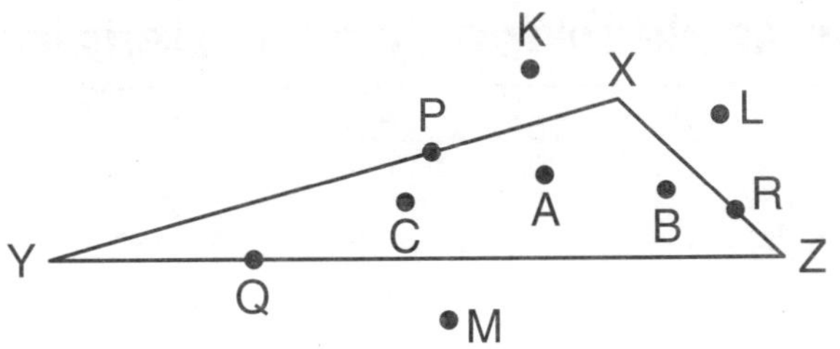

Note

When we say ΔXYZ, it refers only to the boundary of the triangle and not its interior.

Classification Based on Sides

Equilateral Triangle: A triangle in which the lengths of all sides are equal is known as an equilateral triangle.

All the angles of an equilateral triangle are equal to 60°.

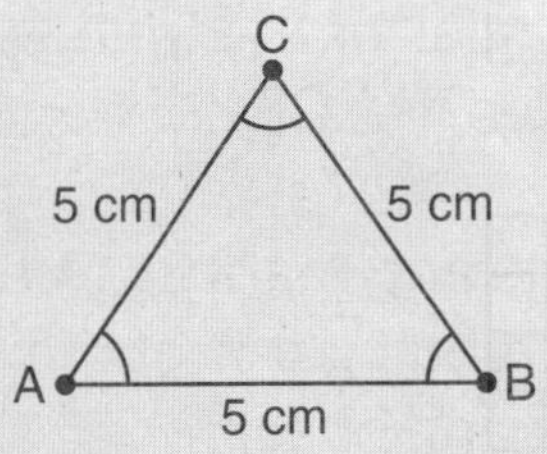

Isosceles triangle: A triangle in which the lengths of only two sides are equal is known as an isosceles triangle.

The angles opposite to the equal sides are also equal. Therefore, an isosceles triangle has 2 equal sides and 2 equal angles.

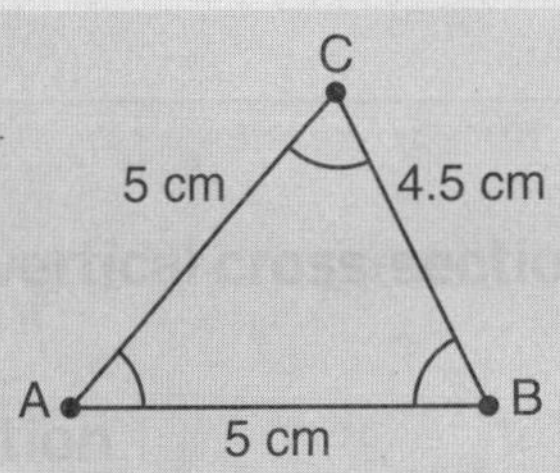

Scalene triangle: A triangle in which the lengths of all sides are different is known as a scalene triangle.

All the angles of a scalene triangle are of different measures.

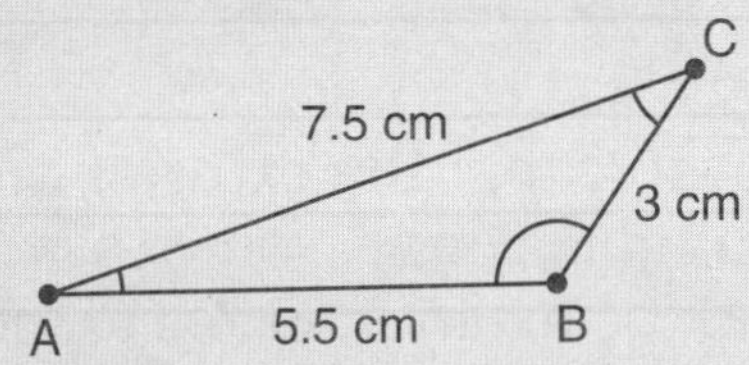

Classification Based on Angles

Acute-angled triangle: A triangle in which all the angles are less than 90° is known as an acute-angled triangle.

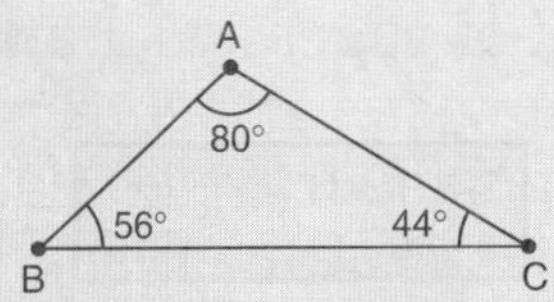

Right-angled triangle: A triangle in which one angle is 90° and the other angles are acute is known as a right-angled triangle.

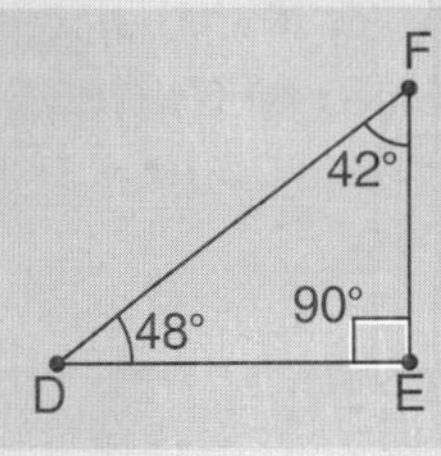

Obtuse-angled triangle: A triangle in which one angle is greater than 90° and the other angles are acute is known as an obtuse-angled triangle.

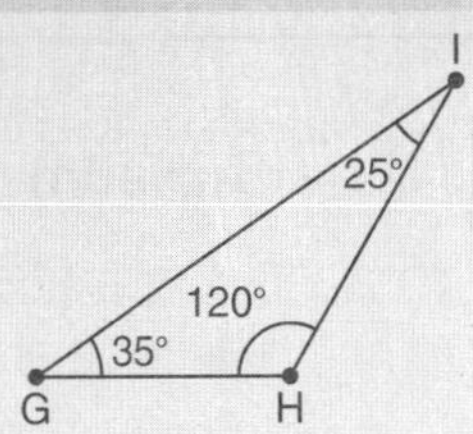

Angle Sum Property and Exterior Angle Property of a Triangle

Exterior Angle of a Triangle

Consider a triangle ABC. You know that ∠A, ∠B and ∠C are the interior angles of the triangle. Let us extend the side AB. ∠CBE formed between the lines BC and AB produced is known as the exterior angle. Observe that ∠CBE forms a linear pair with the interior angle ∠CBA of the triangle. An **exterior** angle of a triangle is an angle that forms a linear pair with one of the interior angles of the triangle. ∠A and ∠C are the interior opposite angles to ∠CBE. Extend the other sides and find five more exterior angles.

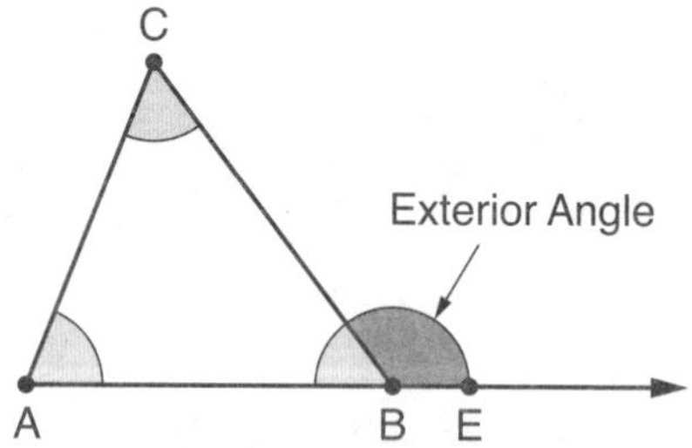

Draw a triangle and mark its interior angles on a patty paper. Draw an exterior angle for the triangle by extending one of the sides. Cut the interior opposite angles and place them on the exterior angle and observe.

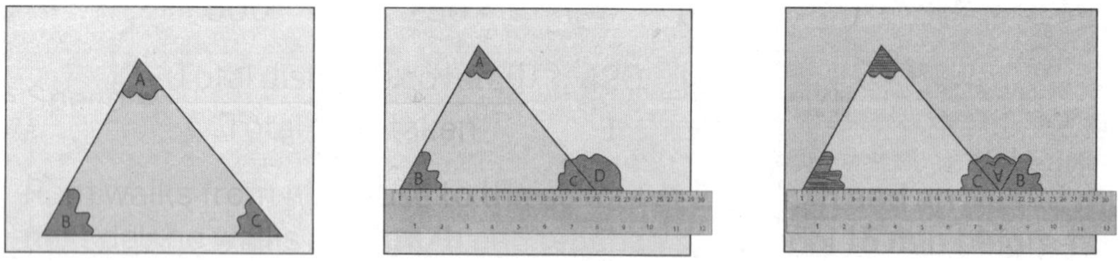

You will observe that **the exterior angle of the triangle is equal to the sum of its interior opposite angles**. This is known as **the exterior angle property of a triangle**. Measure the interior and the exterior angles of the triangle that you have drawn and verify the above property for all the exterior angles. Hence, ∠CBE = ∠CAB + ∠ACB.

Angle Sum Property of a Triangle

Take a sheet of paper and draw three different triangles—an acute, an obtuse and a right-angled triangle. Mark the interior angles of all the triangles. Cut all the interior angles of one triangle and arrange them to form a straight line. Repeat the same for other triangles also.

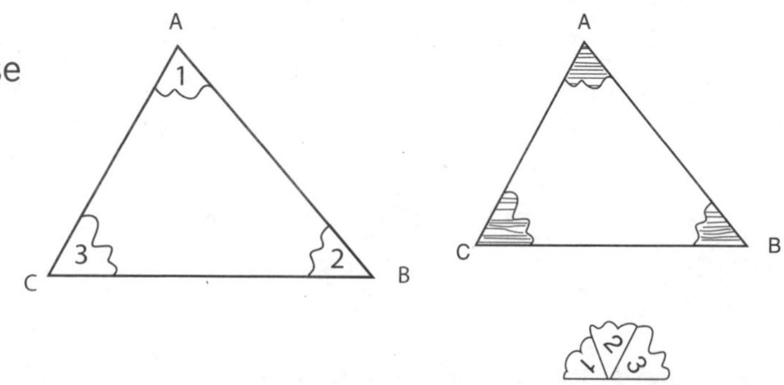

From the above activity, we can conclude that **the sum of interior angles of a triangle is 180°**.

This is known as the **angle sum property of triangles**. In triangle ABC, ∠A + ∠B + ∠C = 180°

Theorem 1: The sum of the angles of a triangle is 180°.

Given: $\triangle ABC$

To prove: $\angle ACB + \angle CAB + \angle CBA = 180°$

Construction: Produce AB to D.

From B, draw BE II AC.

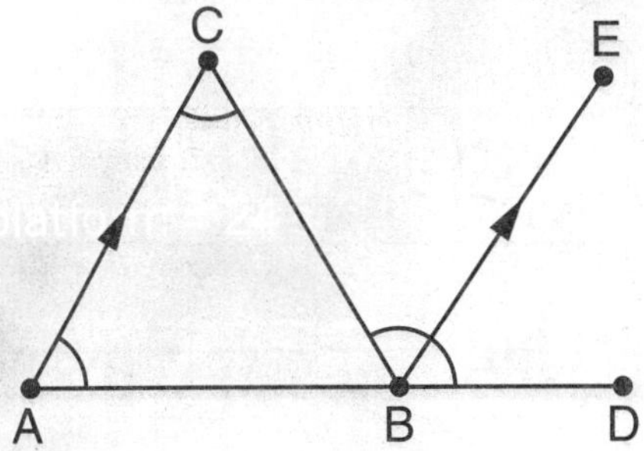

Proof: Since BE II AC and CB is a transversal,

$\angle ACB = \angle CBE$ ...(i)
[Alternate interior angles]

Again, since BE II AC and ABD is a transversal,

$\angle CAB = \angle EBD$ ...(ii) [Corresponding angles]

Adding the corresponding sides of (i) and (ii), we get

$\angle ACB + \angle CAB = \angle CBE + \angle EBD = \angle CBD$ ...(iii)

Adding $\angle CBA$ to both sides of (iii), we get

$\angle ACB + \angle CAB + \angle CBA = \angle CBD + \angle CBA = 180°$ [$\because$ $\angle CBD$ and $\angle CBA$ form a linear pair]

Theorem 2: When a side of a triangle is produced, the exterior angle so formed is equal to the sum of its interior opposite angles.

Proof: Since $\angle CBD$ is the exterior angle at B and from (iii) above, we have

$\angle ACB + \angle CAB = \angle CBE + \angle EBD = \angle CBD$

Thus, an exterior angle = sum of two interior opposite angles.

Angles in Equilateral and Isosceles Triangles

Draw an equilateral triangle and an isosceles triangle of any size on patty paper. Mark all the three angles and cut them. Overlap the angles and observe. Are all the angles equal? If not, which angles are equal?

You will observe that, **in an equilateral triangle, all the angles are equal and in an isosceles triangle, the angles opposite to the equal sides are equal**.

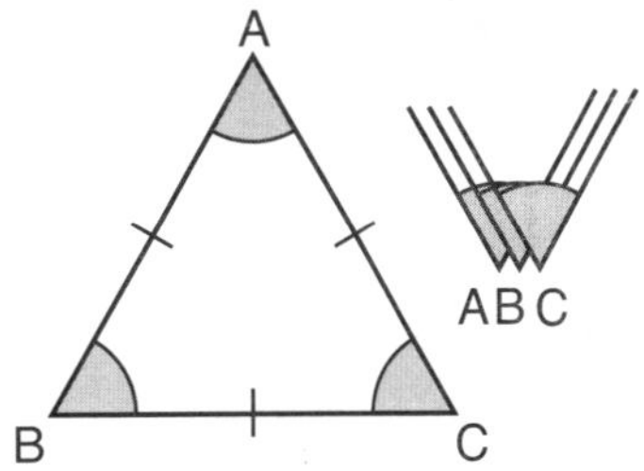

Equilateral Triangle

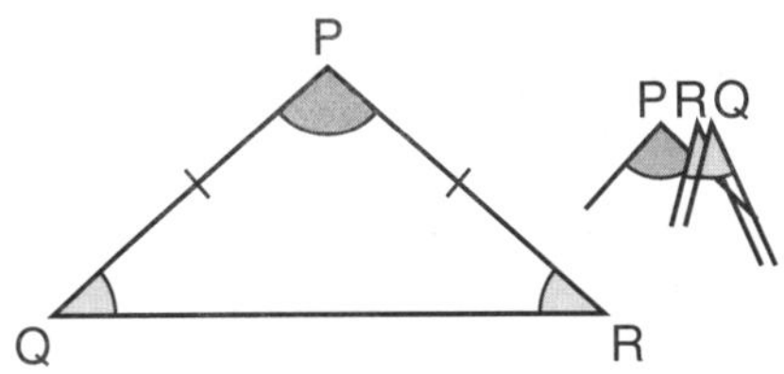

Isosceles Triangle

What will be the measure of each angle in an equilateral triangle? (Use angle sum property and find the angle). Similarly, if the isosceles triangle is a right-angled triangle, then the other two angles are 45° each. Why?

Sum of the Sides of a Triangle

Take two sticks each of different lengths, say 2 cm, 3 cm, 4 cm, 6 cm and 8 cm (total 10 sticks). Try to form triangles with different combinations of side lengths. Copy the following table in your notebook and note down the measurements of side lengths which can form a triangle and which cannot form a triangle.

Measurements of the Sides which Form a Triangle	Measurements of the Sides which Do not Form a Triangle

A few examples of both cases are given. In each case, find the sum and difference of any two sides of a triangle and compare it with the third side.

Combinations That Form a Triangle	Sum of Any Two Sides	Difference of Any Two Sides	Combinations That Do Not Form a Triangle	Sum of Any Two Sides	Difference of Any Two Sides
3, 3, 4	$3 + 3 = 6$	$3 - 3 = 0$	3, 3, 6	$3 + 3 = 6$	$3 - 3 = 0$
	$3 + 4 = 7$	$4 - 3 = 1$		$3 + 6 = 9$	$6 - 3 = 3$
3, 4, 4	$4 + 3 = 7$	$4 - 3 = 1$	2, 8, 6	$2 + 8 = 10$	$8 - 2 = 6$
	$4 + 4 = 8$	$4 - 4 = 0$		$8 + 6 = 14$	$8 - 6 = 2$
				$2 + 6 = 8$	$6 - 2 = 4$

We observe that in any triangle, **the sum of any two sides is always greater than the third side** and **the difference between any two sides is always less than the third side**. These are known as **the inequalities of a triangle**.

Solved Examples

Example 1: In an isosceles triangle, if the non-equal angle is 80°, then find the equal angles.

Let each equal angle be x.

Then, we have, by angle sum property

$x + x + 80° = 180° \Rightarrow 2x + 80° = 180° \Rightarrow 2x = 180° - 80° \Rightarrow 2x = 100° \Rightarrow x = \frac{\overset{50}{\cancel{100}}}{\underset{1}{\cancel{2}}} \Rightarrow x = 50°$

Therefore, the measure of each of the equal angles is 50°.

Example 2: Is it possible to draw a triangle whose sides are 8 cm, 6 cm and 14 cm?

In order to form a triangle, the sum of any two sides must be greater than the third side. Here, $8 + 6 = 14 \not> 14$. Hence, we cannot form a triangle with the given sides.

Example 3: If two sides of a triangle are 3 cm and 5 cm, then what are the possibilities for the third side?

Let the third side be x cm.

Then we have, $3 + 5 > x$ (Sum of any two sides is greater than the third side.)

$\Rightarrow x < 8$

$5 - 3 < x$ (Difference of any two sides is less than the third side.)

$\Rightarrow 2 < x$

Therefore, the length of the third side must be greater than 2 cm and less than 8 cm.

Example 4: The angles of a triangle are in the ratio 3 : 4 : 5. Find the measure of each angle of the triangle.

Let the measures of the given angles be $(3x)^\circ$, $(4x)^\circ$ and $(5x)^\circ$.

$3x + 4x + 5x = 180$ (Sum of all the angles of a triangle is 180°.)

$\Rightarrow 12x = 180 \Rightarrow x = 15$

Thus, the required angles are $(3 \times 15)^\circ$, $(4 \times 15)^\circ$ and $(5 \times 15)^\circ$, i.e., 45°, 60° and 75°.

Example 5: In the given triangle ABC, BC has been produced to D. $\angle BAC = y^\circ$, $\angle ABC = (3b)^\circ$, $\angle BCA = (2b)^\circ$ and $\angle ACD = (4b)^\circ$. Find the values of b and y.

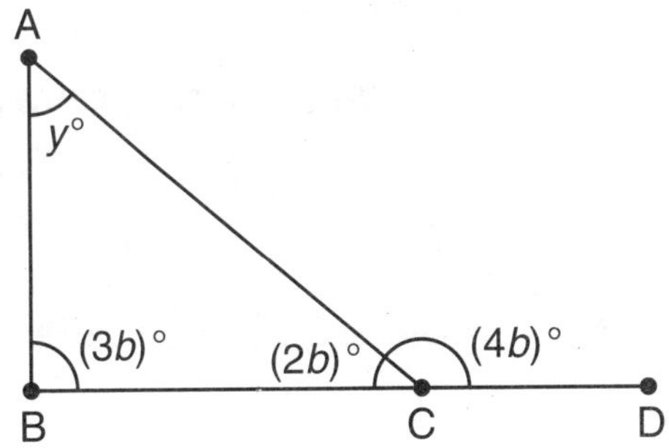

$\angle BCA + \angle ACD = 180^\circ$ (Linear pair)

$\therefore 2b + 4b = 180^\circ \Rightarrow 6b = 180^\circ \Rightarrow b = 30^\circ$

$\angle ACD = \angle ABC + \angle BAC$ [Exterior angle = sum of interior opposite angles]

$4b = 3b + y \Rightarrow 4b - 3b = y \Rightarrow b = y = 30^\circ$

Hence, $b = 30^\circ$ and $y = 30^\circ$.

Example 6: Calculate the value of x in each of the following figures.

i. In ΔACF,

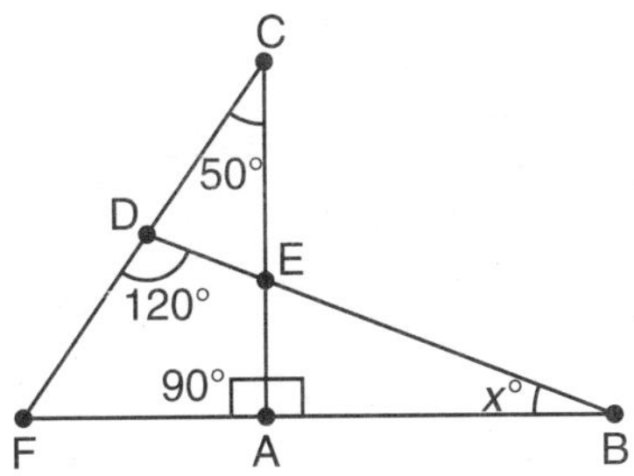

$\angle AFC + \angle FCA + \angle CAF = 180^\circ$

$\Rightarrow \angle AFC + 50^\circ + 90^\circ = 180^\circ$

$\Rightarrow \angle AFC + 140^\circ = 180^\circ$

$\Rightarrow \angle AFC = 180^\circ - 140^\circ$

$\Rightarrow \angle AFC = 40^\circ$

In ΔFDB,

$\angle FDB + \angle DBF + \angle BFD = 180^\circ$

$\Rightarrow 120^\circ + x + 40^\circ = 180^\circ$

$\Rightarrow x = 180^\circ - 160^\circ = 20^\circ$

ii. In ΔAQC,

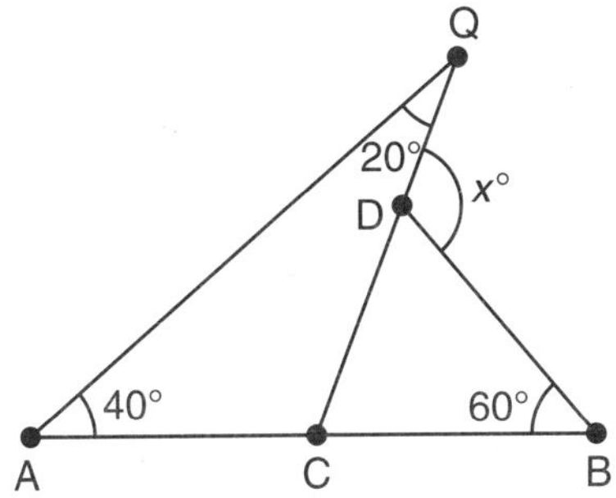

$\angle QCB = \angle QAC + \angle AQC$ [Exterior angle property of a triangle]

$\Rightarrow \angle QCB = 40^\circ + 20^\circ \Rightarrow \angle QCB = 60^\circ$

In ΔBCD,

$\angle QDB = \angle DBC + \angle DCB$ [Exterior angle property of a triangle]

$\Rightarrow \angle QDB = 60^\circ + 60^\circ \Rightarrow \angle QDB = 120^\circ$

$\therefore x = 120^\circ$

Example 7: In ΔABC, the angle bisectors of $\angle A$ and $\angle B$ meet at D. If $\angle C = 60°$, find $\angle ADB$.

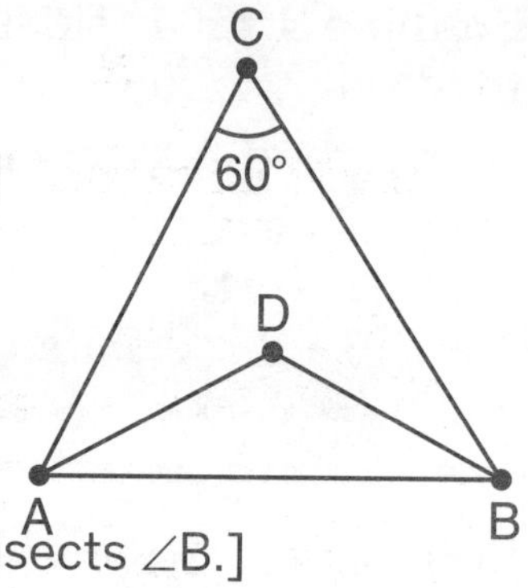

$\angle CAB + \angle ABC + \angle BCA = 180°$ [Sum of all the angles of a triangle]

$\Rightarrow \angle CAB + \angle ABC = 180 - \angle BCA$

$= 180 - 60 = 120°$

$\angle DAB + \angle ABD + \angle BDA = 180°$ [Angle sum property of a triangle]

$\Rightarrow \frac{1}{2}\angle CAB + \frac{1}{2}\angle ABC + \angle BDA = 180°$ [AD bisects $\angle A$ and DB bisects $\angle B$.]

$\Rightarrow \angle BDA = 180° - \frac{1}{2}\angle CAB - \frac{1}{2}\angle ABC$

$\Rightarrow \angle BDA = 180° - \frac{(\angle CAB + \angle ABC)}{2} = 180 - \frac{120}{2} = 180 - 60 = 120°$

Exercise 14.1

1. **Does each of the following sets of line segments form a triangle?**

   a. 7 cm, 7 cm, 7 cm b. 5 cm, 7 cm, 10 cm c. 6 cm, 6 cm, 14 cm
   d. 7 cm, 5 cm, 10 cm e. 3 cm, 8 cm, 15 cm f. 4.4 cm, 7 cm, 5.6 cm

2. **Does each of the following sets of angles form a triangle?**

   a. 25°, 75°, 80° b. 80°, 80°, 30° c. 20°, 60°, 100° d. 40°, 110°, 30°
   e. 140°, 50°, 10° f. 80°, 70°, 30° g. 55°, 35°, 90° h. 62°, 38°, 80°

3. In ΔABC, if $\angle A = 75°$ and $\angle B = 55°$, find the measure of $\angle C$.
4. In ΔRST, if $\angle R = 80°$ and $\angle S = \angle T$, find the measure of each of the equal angles of the triangle.
5. The angles of a triangle are in the ratio 4 : 5 : 6. Find the measure of each of the angles.
6. One angle of a triangle measures 80° and the other two angles are in the ratio 3 : 2. Find these angles.
7. One of the two equal angles of an isosceles triangle measures 50°. Find the measure of each angle of the triangle.
8. In a right-angled triangle, the two acute angles are in the ratio 3 : 6. Find these angles.
9. Find the measure of the angles of an isosceles right-angled triangle.
10. Find the measure of the angles of an equilateral triangle.

11 **Find the unknown angles marked in each of the following.**

a.

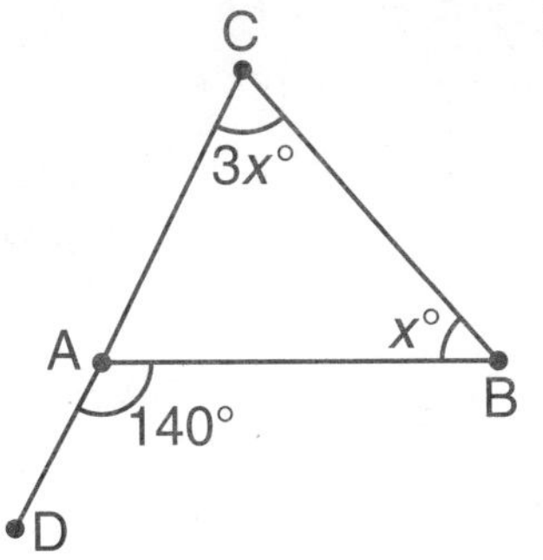

b.

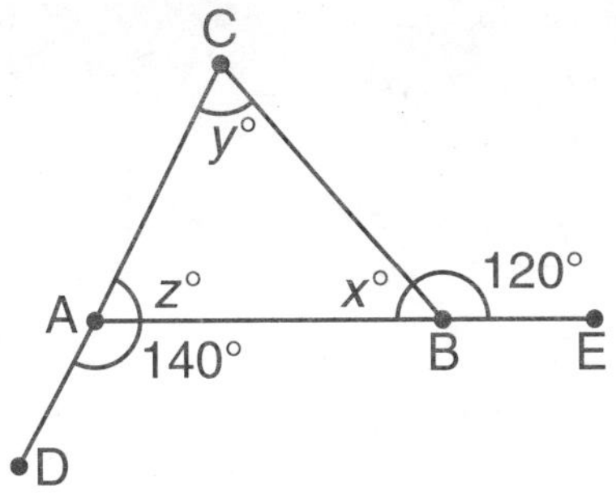

c.

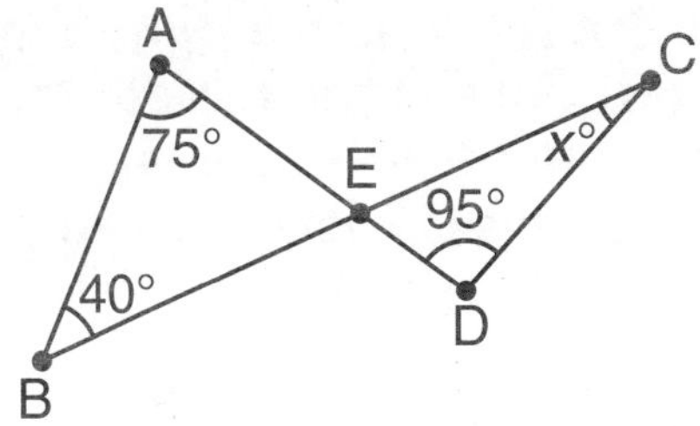

d.

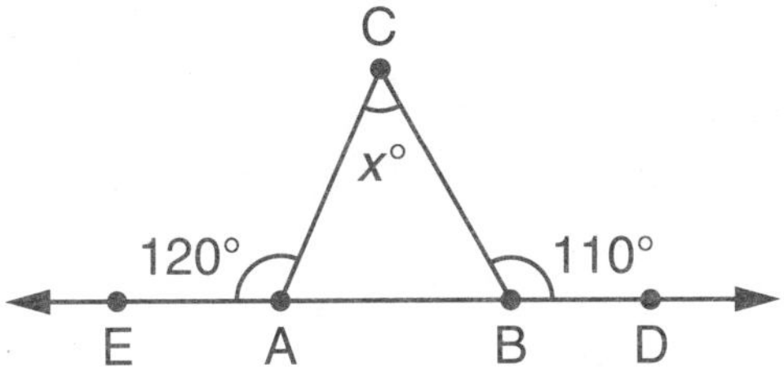

e.

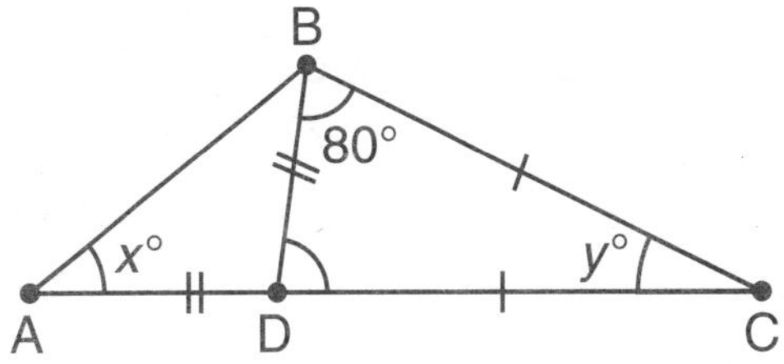

f.

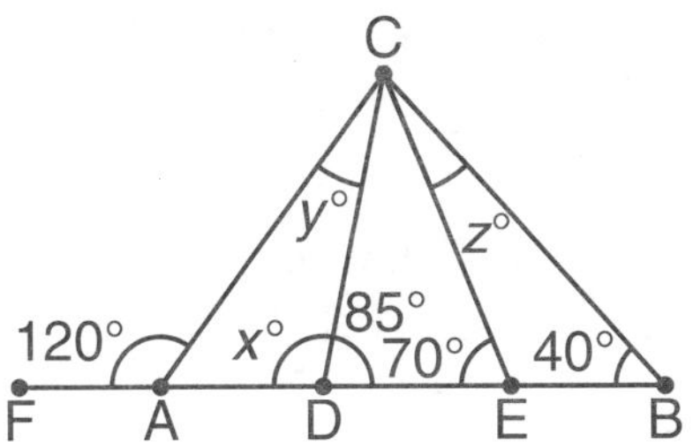

g.

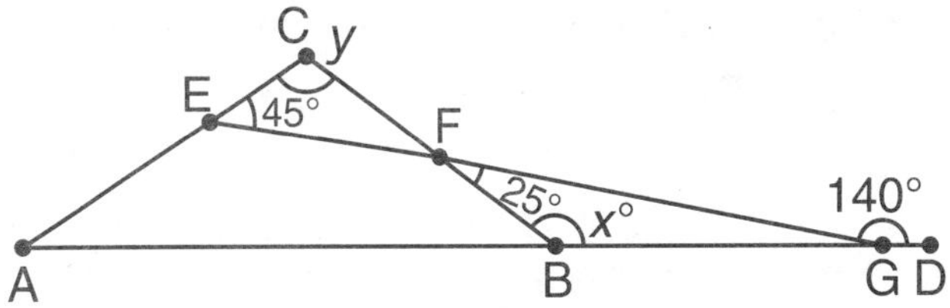

12 Each base angle of an isosceles triangle is 30° more than its vertical angle. Find the measures of all the angles of the triangle.

13 The vertical angle of an isosceles triangle is four times the sum of its base angles. Find each angle of the triangle.

14 In an isosceles triangle, one of the equal angles is 35°. Find the other angles.

Pythagoras Theorem

Consider a right-angled triangle. The side opposite to the right angle (90°) is known as the **hypotenuse** and the other two sides are called **legs**.

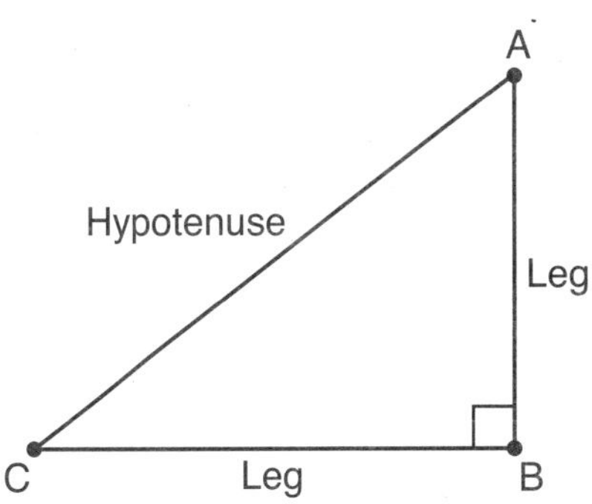

Take a grid paper and construct a right-angled triangle ABC, right-angled at B. Draw squares on sides $\overline{AB}$, $\overline{BC}$ and $\overline{AC}$ as shown in the first figure. Colour the squares drawn on the legs of the triangle. Cut all the unit squares which are coloured and try to fill the square on the hypotenuse with them as shown in the second figure. What do you observe? Can you fill the square completely?

You will observe that the unit squares of the two squares on the legs completely cover the square on the hypotenuse. Therefore, we can say that **in a right-angled triangle, the square of the hypotenuse is equal to the sum of the squares of the other two sides**. This is known as **Pythagoras Theorem**, named after a famous Greek mathematician.

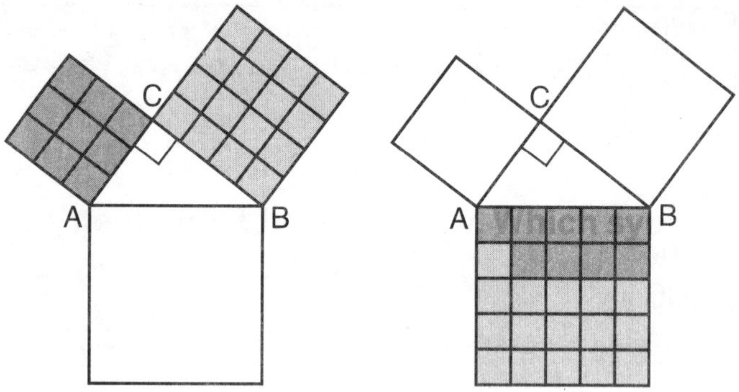

Is the converse also true? That is, if the square of one side is equal to the sum of the squares of the other two sides, then is the triangle a right-angled triangle? You can verify this by doing the following activity.

Cut out squares of side lengths 5 cm, 12 cm and 13 cm. Join the three squares such that they form a triangle. Trace the triangle and measure the angles of the triangle.

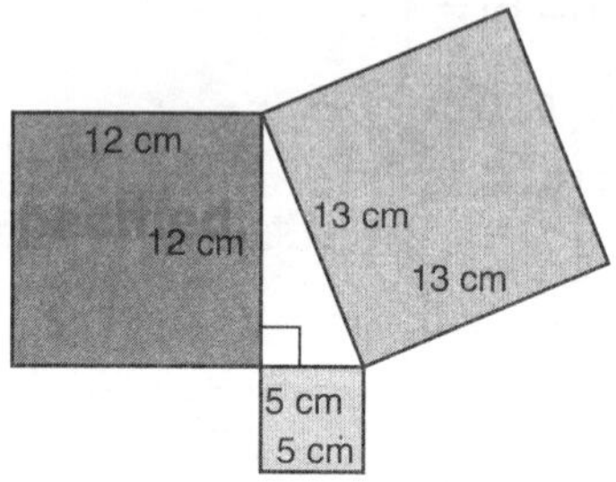

Repeat the same activity with side lengths 8 cm, 15 cm and 17cm.

You will observe that in both the cases, one of the angles is 90°, that is, the triangles formed are right-angled triangles. Also, observe that the side lengths satisfy the property that the square of one side is equal to sum of the squares of other two sides ($13^2 = 12^2 + 5^2$; $17^2 = 15^2 + 8^2$). Therefore, the **converse of Pythagoras theorem** is also true.

The integers which satisfy the Pythagoras theorem are known as **Pythagorean triplets. Three positive integers *a*, *b* and *c* are said to be a Pythagorean triplet if they satisfy the condition $c^2 = a^2 + b^2$**. (3, 4, 5), (5, 12, 13) and (8, 15, 17) are a few examples of Pythagorean triplets. Find out a few more examples.

Some Results

1. Observe the following right-angled triangles. In each triangle, the hypotenuse measures the longest. Therefore, we can say that **in a right-angled triangle, the hypotenuse is the longest side**. Draw a few more right-angled triangles and verify this result.

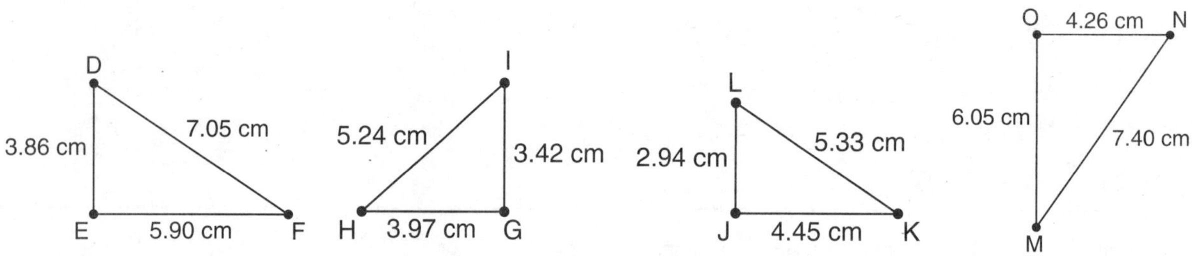

2. Draw a line *m* and mark a point P not lying on *m*. Draw different line segments from P to *m*. Measure the lengths of all the line segments that are drawn. What do you observe? You will notice that among all the line segments, the perpendicular has the shortest length. Therefore, **the shortest distance from any point to a line is the perpendicular distance from the point to the line**.

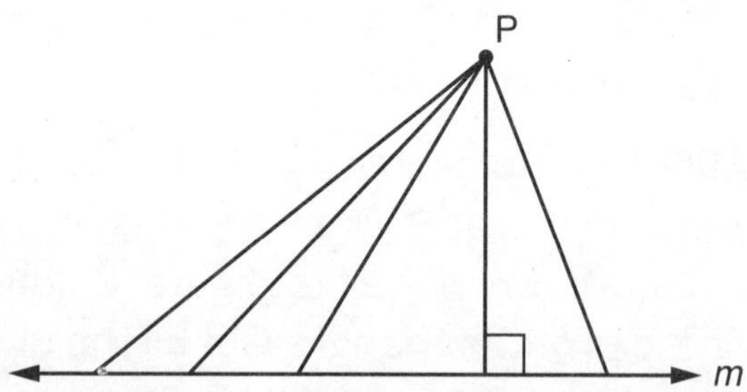

The above results can be proved by using the Pythagoras theorem.

Solved Problems

Example 8: In a right-angled triangle, if the lengths of hypotenuse and one of the legs are 29 cm and 21 cm respectively, find the length of the other side.

Let the length of the other side be x cm.

Then, by Pythagoras theorem, we have, $29^2 = x^2 + 21^2 \Rightarrow x^2 = 29^2 - 21^2 = 841 - 441$ $= 400 = 20^2 \Rightarrow x = 20$

Therefore, the length of the other side is 20 cm.

Example 9: A bus travels 8 km south and then 6 km east. How far is the bus from the starting point?

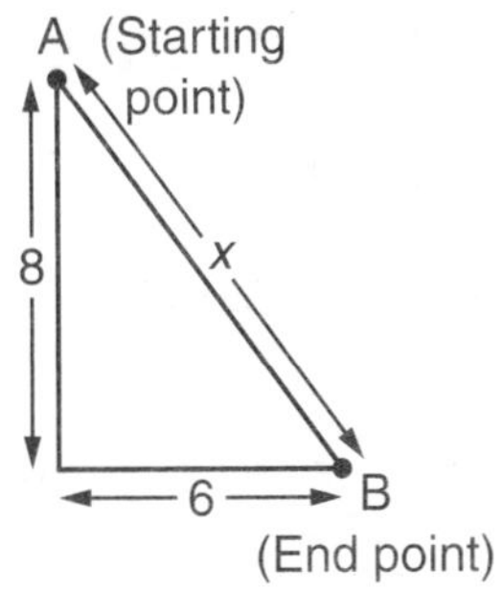

Let the distance of the bus from starting point be x km.

Then, by Pythagoras theorem, we have,

$x^2 = 8^2 + 6^2 \Rightarrow x^2 = 64 + 36 = 100 = 10^2 \Rightarrow x = 10$

Therefore, the bus is at a distance of 10 km from the starting point.

Example 10: A ladder is leaning against a wall and reaches a window at a height of 15 ft. The foot of the ladder is placed 8 ft away from the wall. How long should the ladder be to reach the window?

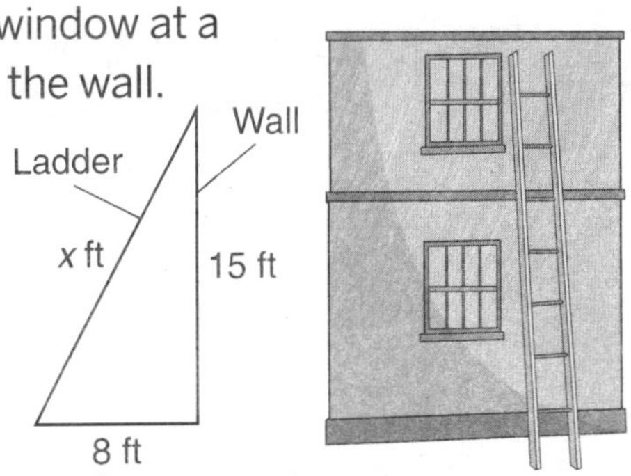

Let the length of the ladder be x ft.

Then, by Pythagoras theorem, we have,

$x^2 = 8^2 + 15^2 \Rightarrow x^2 = 64 + 225 = 289 = 17^2 \Rightarrow x = 17$

Therefore, the required length of the ladder is 17 ft.

Example 11: A boat carrying passengers moves across a river that is 800 m wide from one shore to the opposite shore. It starts its journey by moving perpendicular to the shore but ends up 600 m down the river due to rapidly flowing water. What is the actual distance covered by the boat?

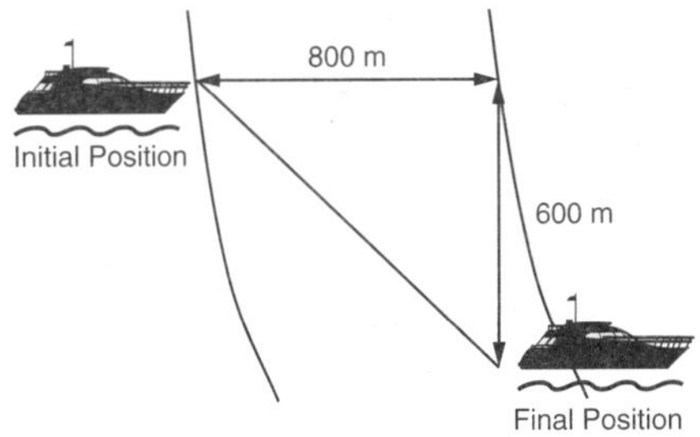

Let the actual distance covered by the boat be x m.

Then, by Pythagoras theorem, we have,

$x^2 = 800^2 + 600^2 \Rightarrow x^2 = 640000 + 360000 = 1000000$
$= 1000^2$

$\Rightarrow x = 1000$

Therefore, the actual distance travelled by the boat is 1000 m.

Exercise 14.2

1. **Verify whether the following sets of lengths can form a right-angled triangle or not.**

   a. 9 cm, 40 cm and 41 cm b. 6 ft, 8 ft and 10 ft c. 14 m, 40 m and 50 m

2. **Find the third side of the following right-angled triangles.**

   a. Hypotenuse–13 cm, One side–5 cm b. Sides–10 cm, 24 cm

   c. Hypotenuse–50 cm, One side–48 cm d. Sides–18 cm, 80 cm

3. Sudheer rides his bicycle 9 km east and then rides 12 km north. How far is he from his starting point?

4. A ladder of length 29 ft is leaning against the wall of a building and is placed such that the foot of the ladder is 21 ft from the base of the building. How far above the ground does the ladder touch the building?

5. Find the width of the rectangular carpet if its length is 12 ft and it has a diagonal of length 20 ft.

6. Find the height of an equilateral triangle whose side is 4 cm.
   Hint: The altitude of an equilateral triangle bisects the opposite side..

7. The length and breadth of Lalita's house are 15 m and 8 m respectively.
   What is the length of the diagonal of the house?

Summary

1. A triangle is a simple closed figure made up of three line segments.
2. The three sides and three angles of a triangle are known as the six elements of a triangle.
3. The interior region of a triangle along with the boundary is known as the triangular region.
4.

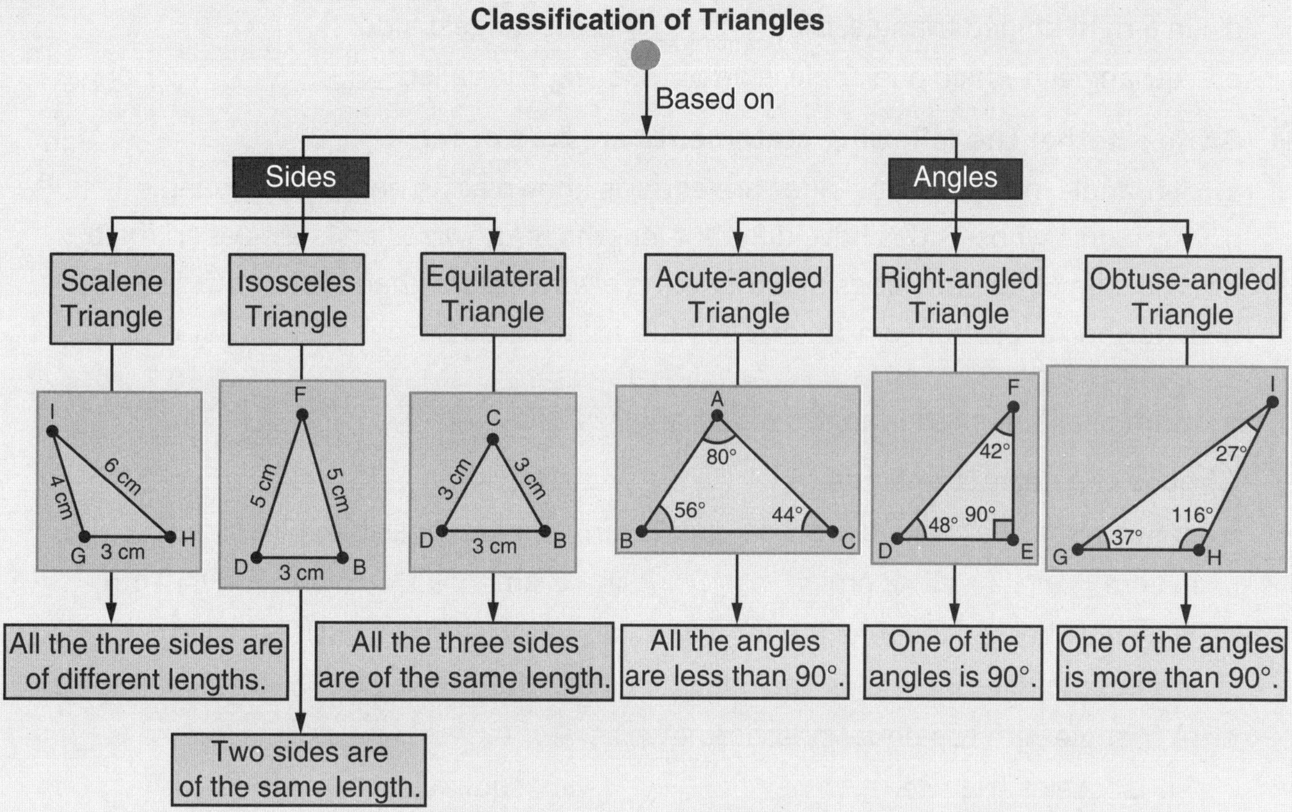

5. In an equilateral triangle, all the angles are equal to 60°. In an isosceles triangle, the angles opposite to the equal sides are equal. In a scalene triangle, none of the angles are equal.
6. In a triangle, the sum of any two sides is less than the third side and the difference of two sides is less than the third side.
7. An exterior angle of a triangle is an angle that forms a linear pair with one of the interior angles of the triangle.
8. The exterior angle of a triangle is equal to the sum of its opposite interior angles. This is known as exterior angle property of a triangle.
9. The sum of the interior angles of a triangle is 180°. This is called the angle sum property of a triangle.
10. In a right-angled triangle, square of the hypotenuse is equal to the sum of the squares of the other two sides. This is know as Pythagoras theorem.

Revision Exercise

1 Fill in the blanks.

a. The sum of all the angles of a triangle is ________.

b. There are __________ elements in a triangle.

c. A triangle is a simple closed figure made up of _______________ line segments.

d. In a right angled triangle, the _________ is the longest side.

e. A triangle in which one angle is an obtuse angle is called _____________ triangle.

2 State whether the following statements are true or false.

a. A triangle in which three sides are equal is known as an equilateral triangle

b. A triangle whose sides have different lengths is known as an isosceles triangle.

c. The sum of any two sides of a triangle is always lesser than the third side.

d. The shortest distance from any point to a line is the perpendicular distance from the point to the line.

e. Sum of all the interior angles of a triangle is 180°.

3 Choose the correct options.

a. If two sides of a triangle are 8 cm and 11 cm, then the possible third side is

i. 1 cm ii. 2 cm iii. 3 cm iv. 4 cm

b. If a circle passes touches the three vertices of a triangle, then it is called

i. circumcircle ii. incircle iii. full circle iv incentre circle

c. A triangle with two equal sides is known as

i. isosceles triangle ii. equilateral triangle

iii. scalene triangle iv. acute-angled triangle

d. If XYZ is a right-angled triangle and $\angle Z = 90°$, then

i. $XY^2 + YZ^2 = XZ^2$ ii. $YZ^2 + ZX^2 = XY^2$ iii. $ZY^2 + XY^2 = YZ^2$ iv. All of these

e. A triangle in which one angle is a right angle and the other angles are acute angles is

i. acute-angled triangle ii. obtuse-angled triangle

iii. right-angled triangle iv. scalene triangle

4 Answer the following questions

a. The angles of a triangle are in the ratio 1 : 2 : 3. Find the measure of each of the angles.

b. One angle of a triangle measures 90°and the other two angles are in the ratio 2 : 4. Find these angles.

c. One of the two equal angles of an isosceles triangle measures 70°. Find the measure of each angle of the triangle.

d. In a right-angled triangle, the two acute angles are in the ratio 1 : 5. Find these angles.

e. One of the unequal angles of an isosceles triangle measures 100°. Find the measure of each angle of the triangle.

f. If one of the exterior angles of a triangle is 105° and the interior opposite angles are in the ratio 3:4, then find all the interior angles of the triangle.

g. In a triangle, the measurements of two sides are 7 cm and 5 cm. List all the possible measurements for the third side.

h. **Identify the Pythagorean triplets among the following.**

   i. 12, 35, 37 ii. 11, 60, 61 iii. 13, 80, 85 iv. 20, 100, 101

i. The width and height of a TV screen are 16 inches and 30 inches respectively. What is the screen size? (Hint: screen size is the length of the diagonal of the screen.)

j. Ramesh rides his car 150 km west and then 200 km south to reach his office. How far is he from the house?

For the Curious Mind

1. Prove that the sum of the angles of a quadrilateral is 360°. (Hint: Join A and C and use the angle sum property of triangles for ΔABC and ΔADC.).

2. In the given figure, ΔABC is an equilateral triangle whose side $\overline{AC}$ has been produced in both directions to points D and E respectively. Prove that $\angle BAD = \angle BCE$.

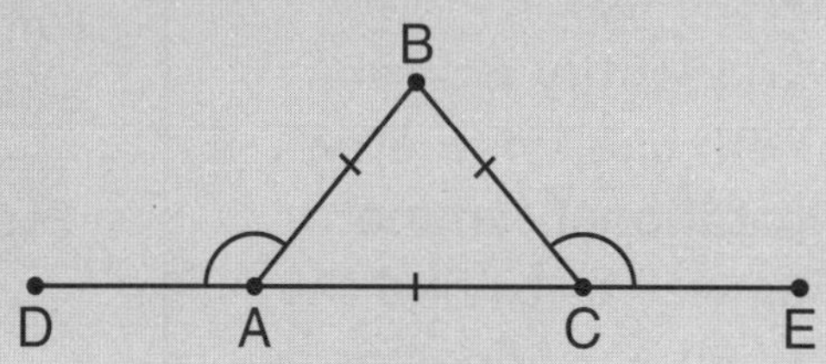

THEME 4

Symmetry

15

What I shall learn

- To define the terms reflection and rotational symmetry
- To identify figures with line symmetry/ rotational symmetry as well as to find the number of lines of symmetry/order of rotation
- To identify figures with a combination of symmetries

Let's Get Started

Symmetry occurs everywhere in nature. Look around and you can see many symmetrical objects. Symmetry is used in various fields like art, architecture, design, etc. Observe the symmetrical objects given below.

Line Symmetry

In the previous classes, we have learned what symmetry is and identified figures with different lines of symmetry. Let us recall them.

A figure has **line symmetry** if there exists a line which divides the figure into two equal coinciding or congruent halves. Such a line is known as the **line of symmetry** or the **mirror line**.

Examples:

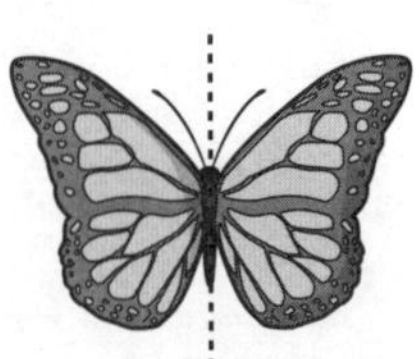

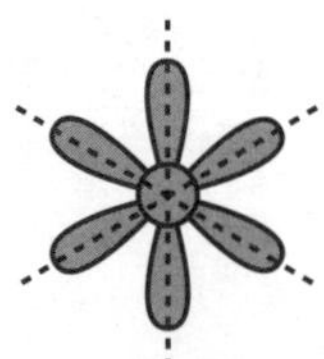

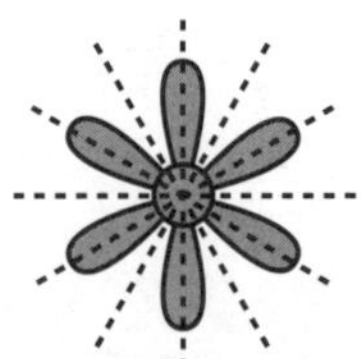

Remember

A figure is said to be symmetrical if it has mirror halves. One half will be a reflection of the other.

In the above figures, the dotted lines are the lines of symmetry.

A circle has infinite number of lines of symmetry.

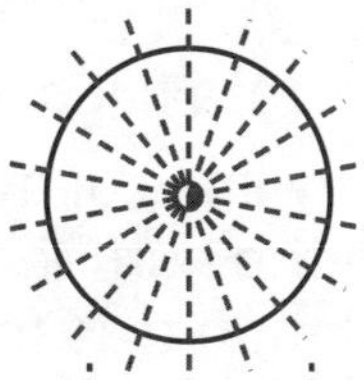

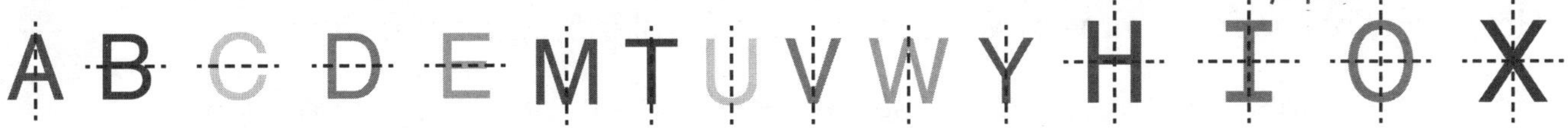

Note

1. The lines of symmetry in an equilateral triangle are also the angle bisectors of the triangle. And the line of symmetry in an isosceles triangle is the bisector of the angle contained by the two equal sides.
2. If a polygon has *n* sides, its largest number of lines of symmetry is *n*.

The figure above shows a few letters of the English alphabet that have one or more than one lines of symmetry.

Observe the following table showing the lines of symmetry in different triangles

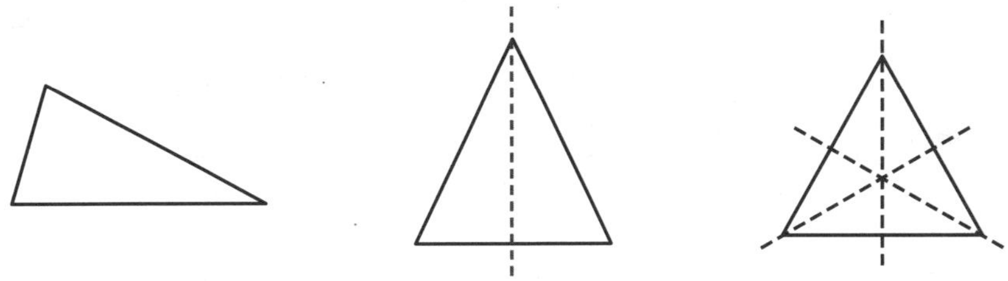

From the above figures, we can conclude that, a scalene triangle has no lines of symmetry, an isosceles triangle has 1 line of symmetry and an equilateral triangle has 3 lines of symmetry.

Lines of Symmetry for Regular Polygons

A **polygon** is a simple closed figure made up of only line segments. Identify the polygons among the following figures.

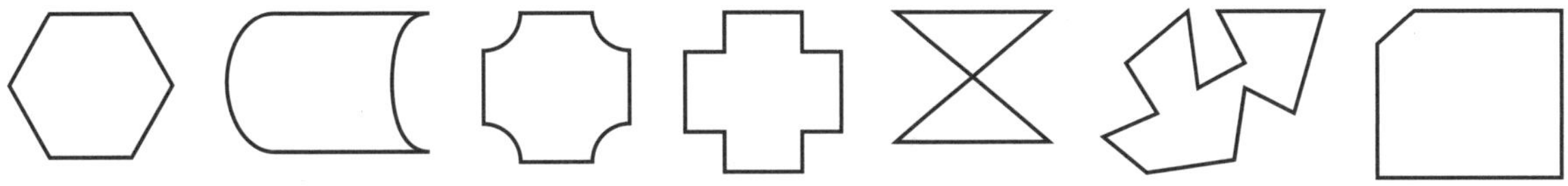

Polygons in which all the sides and angles are equal are known as **regular polygons**. Equilateral triangle, square and regular pentagon are a few examples of regular polygons. Let us find out whether the regular polygons are symmetrical and how many lines of symmetry they have.

Activity 1

Draw regular polygons of different sides—equilateral triangle, square, regular pentagon, hexagon, heptagon, octagon, nonagon and decagon on a patty paper. Cut out each regular polygon separately. Find the lines of symmetry of all these polygons by folding them along the lines which make the halves exactly match each other. As an example, lines of symmetry of an equilateral triangle are shown alongside. Copy the table given below in your notebook and record your observations.

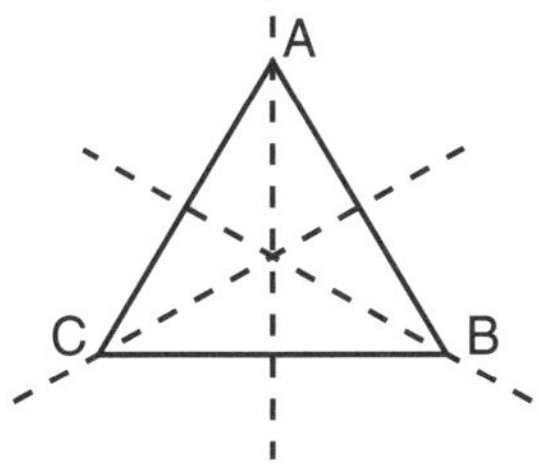

Regular Polygon	Number of Sides	Number of Lines of Symmetry

Observe the data filled in the above table and answer the following questions.

1. How many lines of symmetry does an equilateral triangle have? Is there any relation between the number of sides of an equilateral triangle and its lines of symmetry?
2. Is the relation true for other regular polygons?
3. How many of lines of symmetry will be there in a regular polygon of *n* sides?

The following table summarizes the number of lines of symmetry in regular polygons.

Regular Polygon	Equilateral Triangle	Square	Regular Pentagon	Regular Hexagon	Regular Heptagon	Regular Octagon	Regular Nonagon	Regular Decagon	Regular *n*-gon
Figure		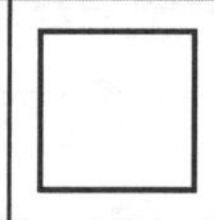	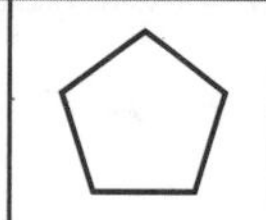		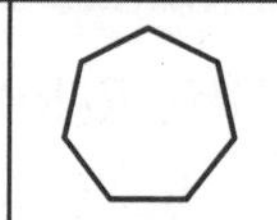	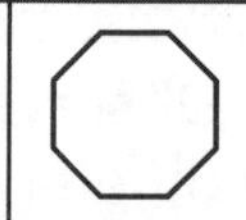	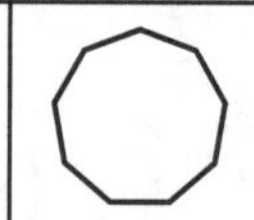	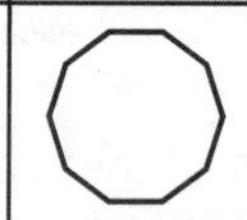	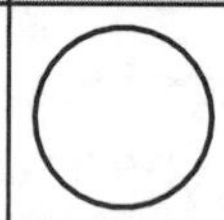
Lines of Symmetry		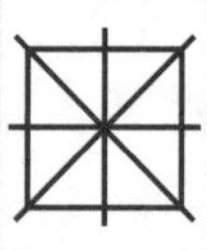				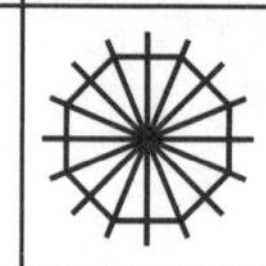	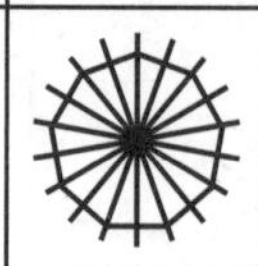	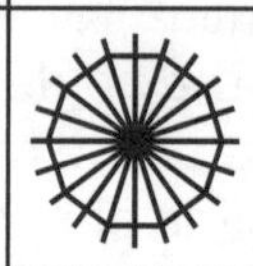	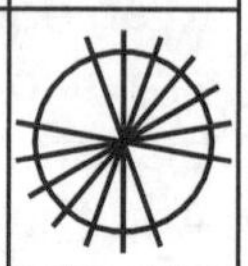
	3	4	5	6	7	8	9	10	*n*
	A regular polygon of *n* sides has *n* number of lines of symmetry.								

Exercise 15.1

1 Fill in the blanks.

a. A square has ________ sides and ________ lines of symmetry.

b. A regular nonagon has __________ lines of symmetry.

c. A regular polygon with 12 sides will have ________ lines of symmetry.

2 Draw the lines of symmetry for the given figure and fill in the blanks.

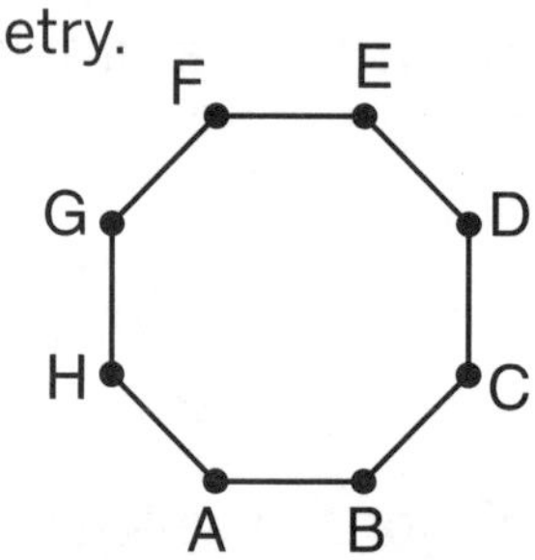

a. The number of sides is __________.

b. The number of lines of symmetry is __________.

c. The name of the regular polygon is __________.

3 Draw all the lines of symmetry and write the number of lines of symmetry for each of the following figures.

a. 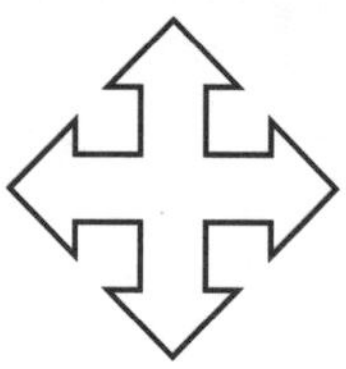

b. 

c. 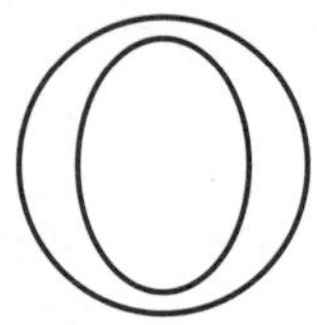

d. 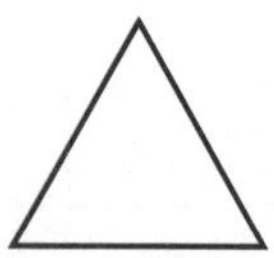

e. 

f. 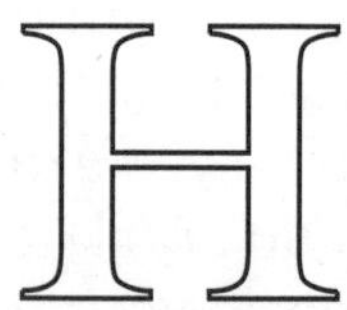

Do all of them have the same number of lines of symmetry? Which figure is having maximum number of lines of symmetry? Give reasons.

Rotational Symmetry

Rotations

Have you ever observed how the hands of a clock rotate? Do they rotate in both directions? No, the hands of a clock rotate only in one direction, which is known as the clockwise rotation. Rotation in the opposite direction is known as the anticlockwise or counterclockwise direction/rotation.

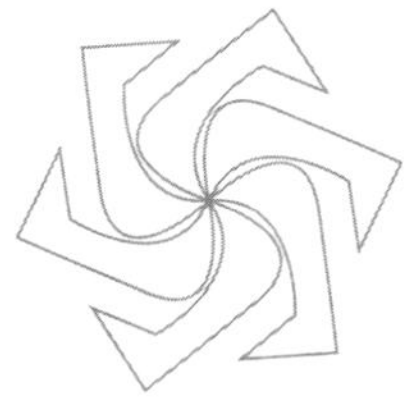

Look at the figure shown here. Can you find the line of symmetry for this figure? Copy this figure on a patty paper and fold it and try to find the lines of symmetry. You will find that this figure has no lines of symmetry. This figure has another type of symmetry called rotational symmetry.

A figure is said to have rotational symmetry if it looks exactly the same when rotated by a certain angle.

Order and Angle of Rotation

Now, make another copy of this figure on a patty paper. Place one over the other on a 360° angle board by coinciding their centres as shown here. Rotate the top figure, keeping the bottom figure constant. Observe how many times the figure coincides with itself in one complete, i.e., in 360° rotation. This gives the **order of rotation**. You can observe that the order of rotation of the above figure is 6. The smallest angle with which the figure is rotated in order to coincide with itself is known as the **angle of rotation** of that figure. The centre along or around which the figure is rotated is known as the **centre of rotation**.

> **Note**
> If the figure has rotational symmetry then the order of symmetry is more than 1.

Example 1: Find the order of rotation and angle of rotation of an equilateral triangle ABC.

If an equilateral triangle ABC is rotated through 360° about a point (Centre of rotation of an equilateral triangle is the point of intersection of all the perpendicular bisectors of its sides), It attains the original position three times (when rotated through 120°, 240° and 360°) as shown below.

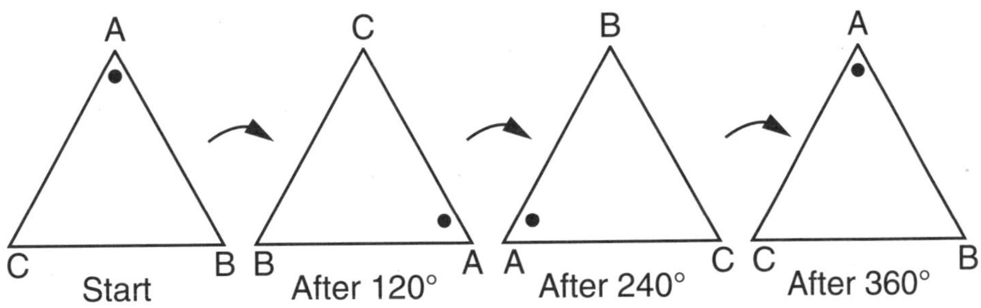

Therefore, the equilateral triangle possesses a rotational symmetry of order 3 and the angle of rotation is $\frac{360^\circ}{3} = 120^\circ$.

> **Remember**
> 1. When an object is rotated through 360°, the number of times the object looks exactly similar to what it looked originally is known as order of rotation or order of rotational symmetry.
> 2. The angle of rotation is $\frac{360^\circ}{r}$, where r is the order of rotation.

Operations of the Rotation of simple figures

The following table shows the position of some simple figures after the rotation of figures by 90°, 180°and 270°.

Figure	Position after rotation by			Observations
0° or 360°	90°	180°	270°	
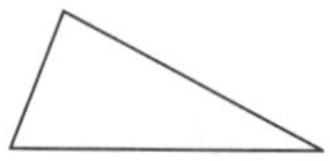 Scalene Triangle		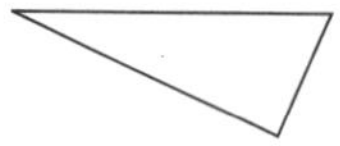		Scalene triangle does not have rotational symmetry.
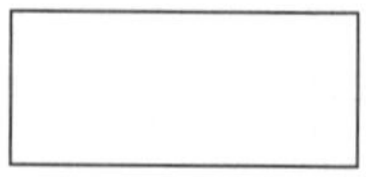 Rectangle		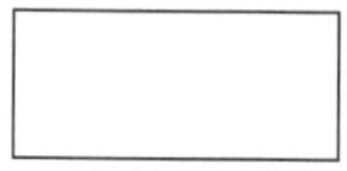		Rectangle looks the same after rotation by 180°. Hence, it has rotational symmetry of order 2 and the angle of rotation is 180°.
 Square				Square looks the same after the rotation by 90°, 180° and 270°. Hence, it has rotational symmetry of order 4 and the angle of rotation is 90°.
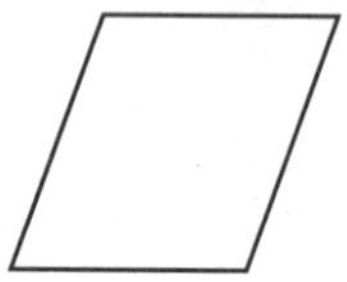 Parallelogram	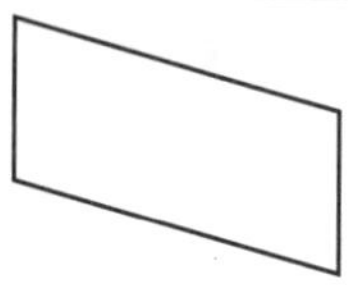	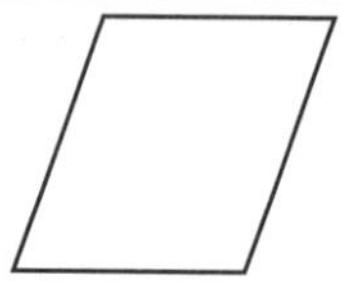	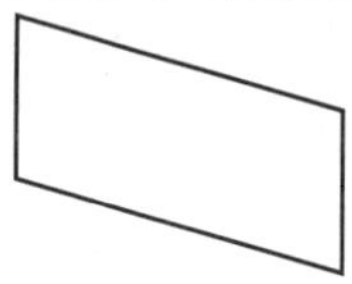	Parallelogram looks the same after rotation by 180°. Hence, it has rotational symmetry of order 2 and the angle of rotation is 180°.
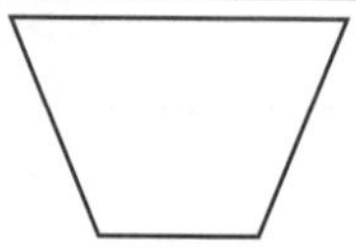 Trapezium	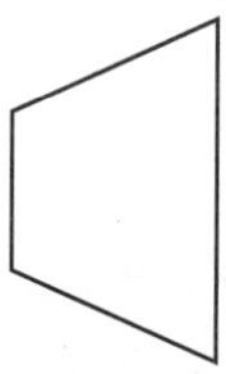	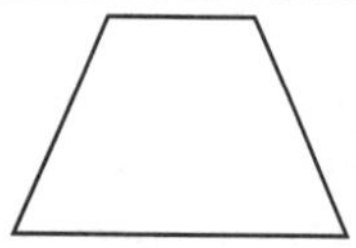	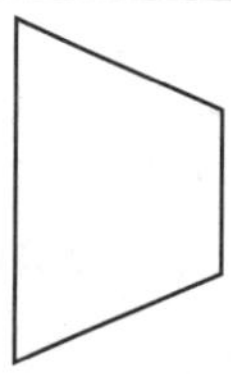	Trapezium does not have rotational symmetry.
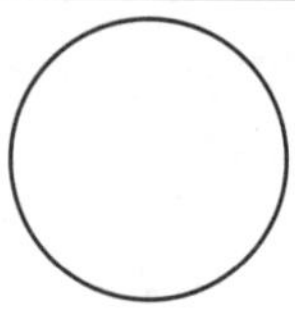 Circle	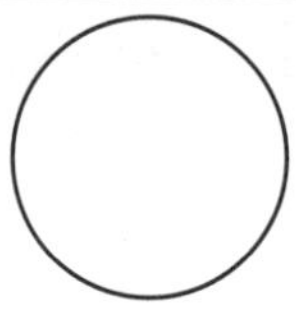	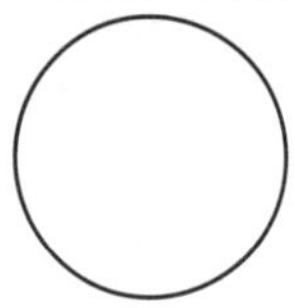	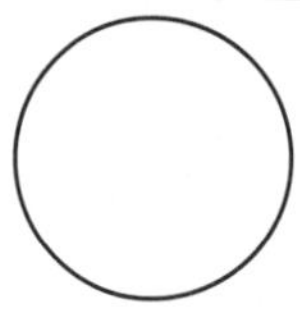	Circle looks the same after the rotation by 90°, 180° and 270°. You can also verify that it looks the same after any angle of rotation. Hence, circle has rotational symmetry of infinite order.

Figures with Combination of Symmetries

We have seen a few examples of figures which have line symmetry or rotational symmetry. Let us observe the following figure. It has line symmetry and rotational symmetry.

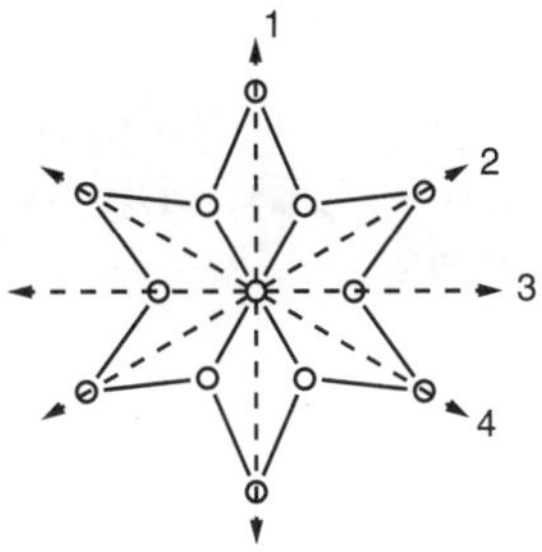

Four lines of symmetry

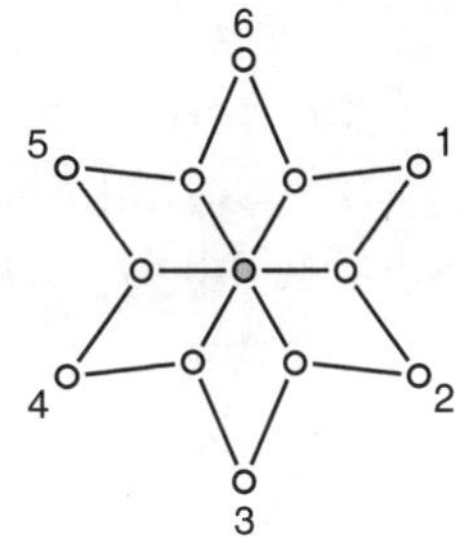

Rotational symmetry of order 6

The following figures have line symmetry as well as rotational symmetry.

Rectangle	Square
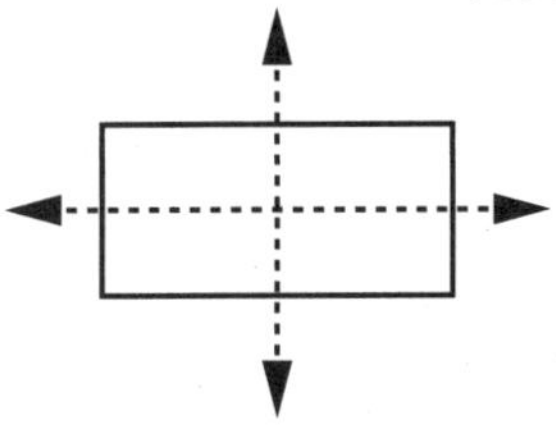 Two lines of Symmetry 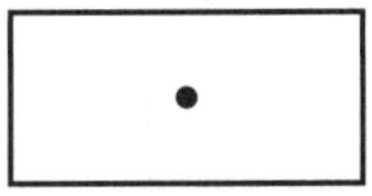 Rotational Symmetry of order 2	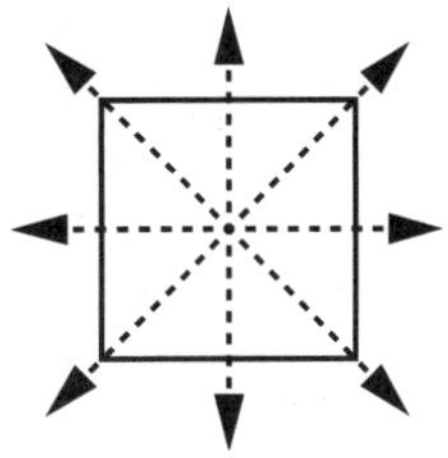 Four lines of Symmetry 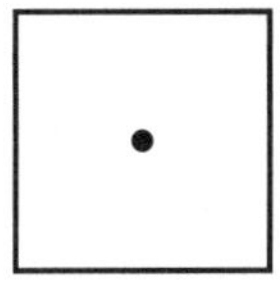 Rotational Symmetry of order 4
Rhombus	**Circle**
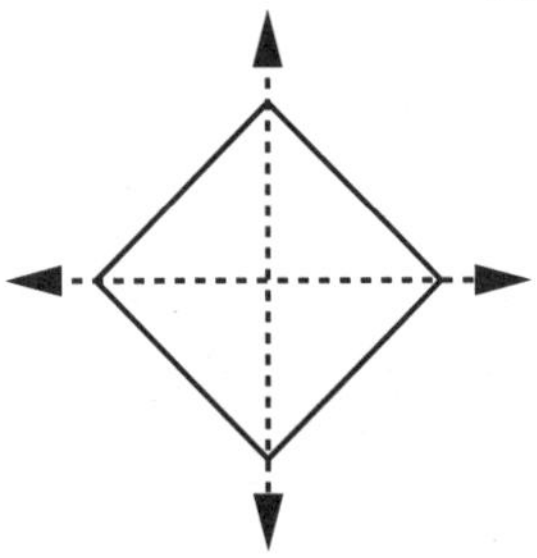 Two lines of Symmetry 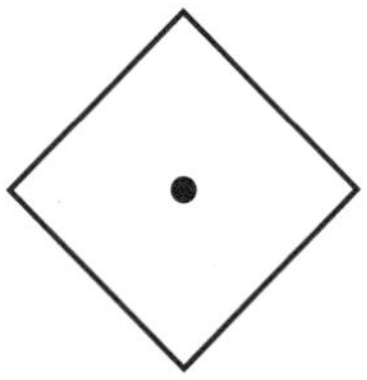 Rotational Symmetry of order 4	 Infinite lines of Symmetry 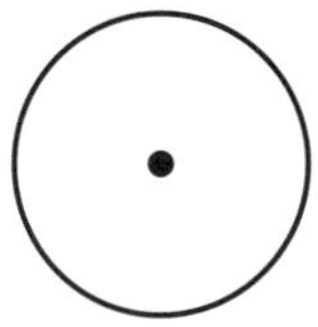 Rotational Symmetry of infinite order
Letter O	**Letter H**
 Two lines of Symmetry  Rotational Symmetry of order 2	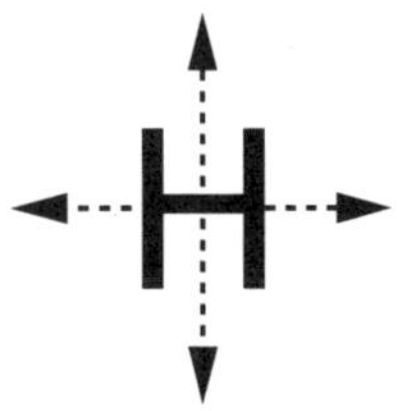 Two lines of Symmetry  Rotational Symmetry of order 2

Activity 2

Prepare patty paper cut-outs of the figures given below. For each figure, first guess and then test for each kind of symmetry (use circular board for testing rotational symmetry). Copy the following table in your notebook and fill in your observations.

Figures

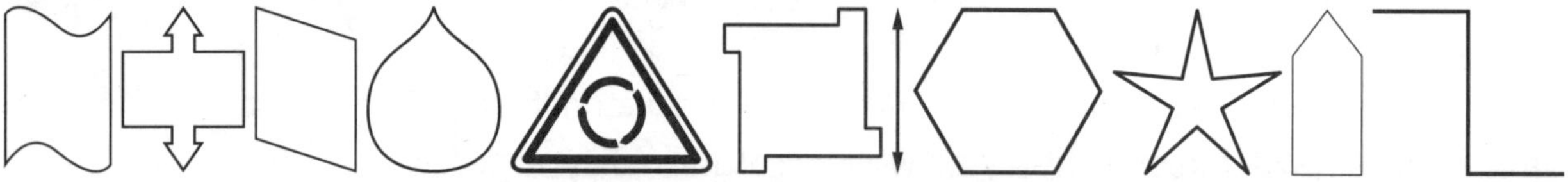

Figure (Rough Sketch)	Line Symmetry (Yes/No)	Rotational Symmetry (Yes/No)

Now, study the table and classify the figures as shown below:

Has Only Line Symmetry	Has Only Rotational Symmetry	Has Line and Rotational Symmetries

Applications of Symmetry in Everyday Life

You can find many day-to-day applications of symmetry. A few examples are shown below.

Note: Different names are used for 'Rangoli' in different parts of India.

TheTaj Mahal has line symmetry.

Rangolis have line/rotational symmetry.

Rotational Symmetry for Regular Polygons

In earlier classes, we have learned about the line of symmetry for regular polygons. Let us see whether regular polygons have rotational symmetry or not. If yes, what is their order of rotation, angle of rotation, etc.?

Activity 3

Prepare two copies of patty paper cut-outs of each of the following regular polygons. Find the order of rotation and angle of rotation for each of them using the above procedure. Copy the following table in your notebook and record your observations.

Regular Polygons

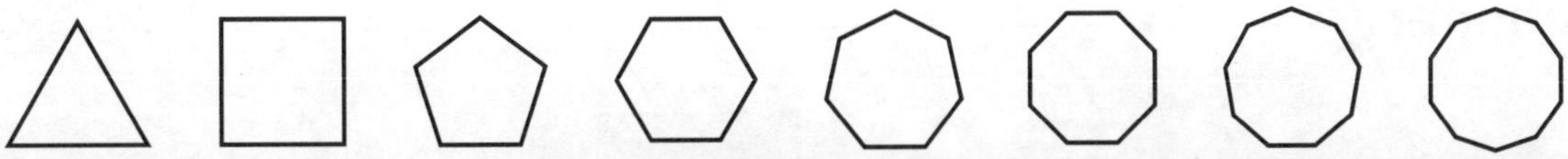

Regular polygon	Number of sides	Angle of rotation	Order of rotation
Equilateral Triangle	3	120°	3

Observe the table. Do you find any relationship between the number of sides and the order of rotation?

Inference: A regular polygon of n sides has the rotational symmetry of order n and the angle of rotation is given by $\frac{360°}{n}$.

Exercise 15.2

1. **Find whether the following figures have rotational symmetry. If yes, find their order of rotation and the angle of rotation.**

a. 
b. 
c. 
d. 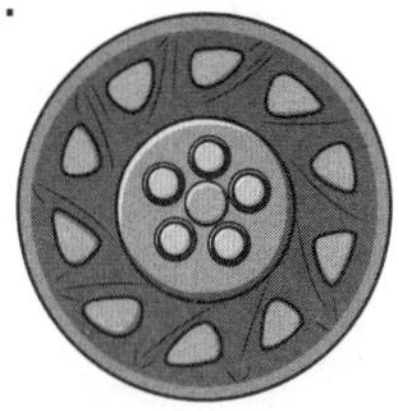

a. b. c. d.

2. **Find the order of the rotational symmetry of the following figures.**

a. 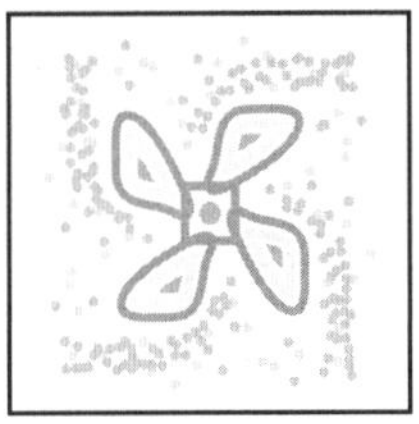
b. 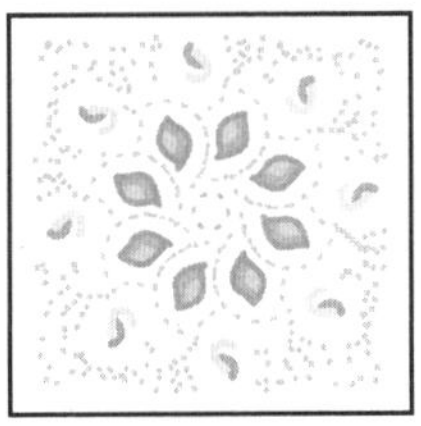
c. 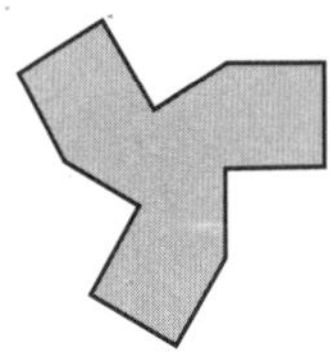
d. 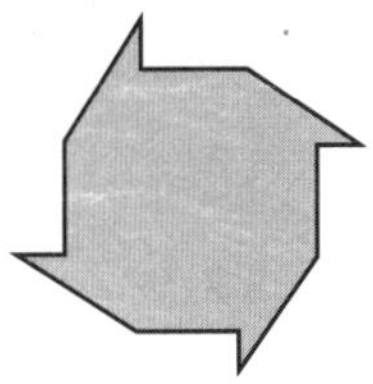

3. State the types of symmetries possessed by a circle. Also, mention the number of lines of symmetry and order of rotational symmetry.

4. **Identify the types of symmetries possessed by each of the following figures.**

a. 
b. 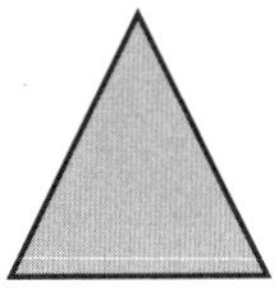
c. 
d. 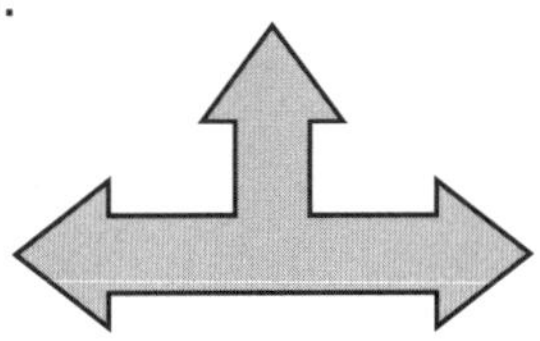

Summary

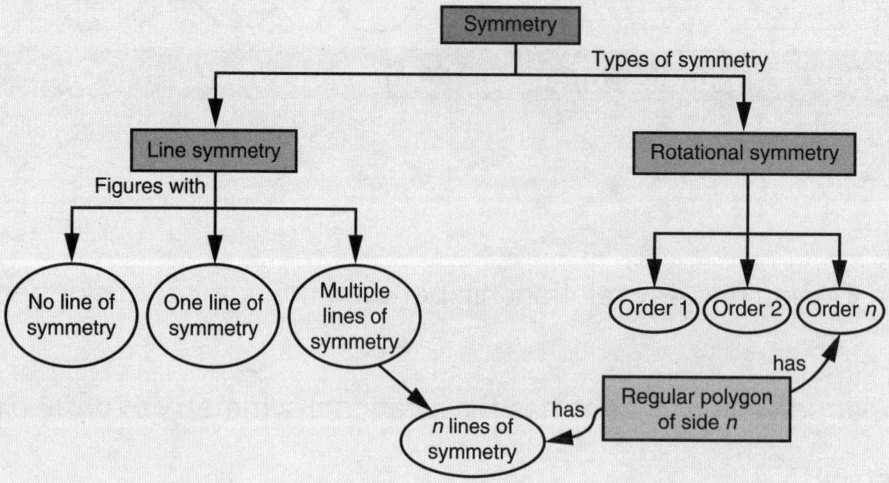

Symmetry
Types of symmetry
Line symmetry
Rotational symmetry
Figures with
No line of symmetry
One line of symmetry
Multiple lines of symmetry
Order 1
Order 2
Order n
has
Regular polygon of side n
has
n lines of symmetry

Revision Exercise

1 **State whether the following statements are true or false.**

a. A regular polygon with eight sides has nine lines of symmetry

b. For any figure, it is not possible to have all types of symmetry.

c. If a figure has rotational symmetry, then its order of rotational symmetry is one.

d. The angle of rotation for a square is 90°.

e. The order of rotation for both rectangle and parallelogram is 2.

2 **Fill in the blanks.**

a. A regular polygon of *n* sides has ________ lines of symmetry.

b.  has rotational symmetry of order ________.

c. The angle of rotation of a figure whose order of rotation is *r* is ________.

d. The order of rotation of a regular polygon of *n* sides is ________ and hence its angle of rotation is ________.

3 Can we say that the figure which has n lines of symmetry is a regular polygon with n sides? For example, can we say that the figure which has four lines of symmetry is a square?

4 Draw all the possible lines of symmetries for the figures shown here.

a. 

b. 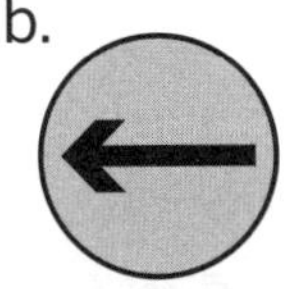

5 **What is the order of the rotational symmetry of the following?**

a. A regular hexagon

b. The capital letter 'S'

6 Does the given figure have rotational symmetry? Justify your answer. Write its order of rotational symmetry.

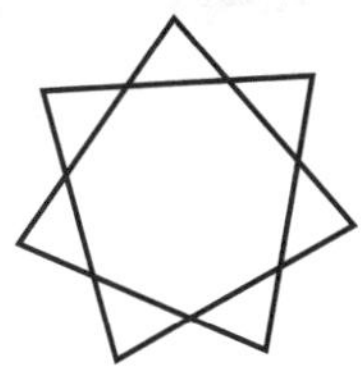

7 **Draw reflection of the following figures along the dotted axes of reflection.**

a. 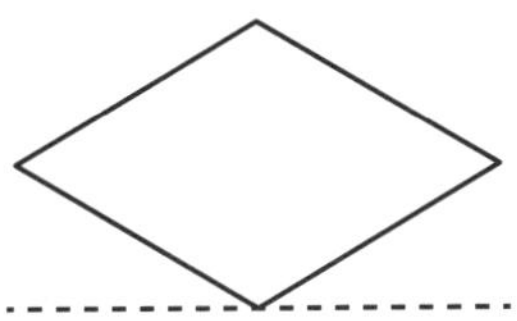

b. 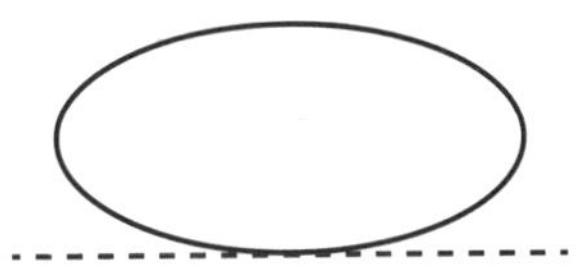

c. 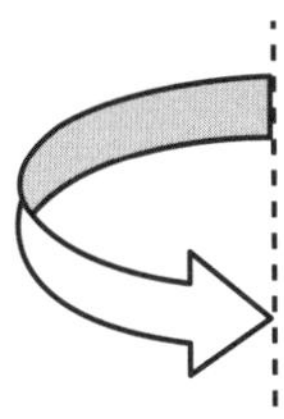

For the Curious Mind

Create shapes for the following, if possible. Otherwise, give reasons.

a. Only line of symmetry

b. Only rotational symmetry

c. Line and rotational symmetry

d. Line symmetry but no rotational symmetry.

e. Rotational symmetry but no line symmetry.

THEME 4

16 Visualising Solid Shapes

What I shall learn

- To identify faces, edges, vertices and nets of 3D shapes
- To draw oblique sketches and isometric sketches of different solid shapes
- To view different sections of a solid by slicing, by shadow play and by viewing from different angles (front view, side view and top view)

Let's Get Started

Classify the following figures into two groups by drawing the arrow marks and name of groups. What is the difference between them?

All figures in Group A are **solid shapes** or **3D shapes**, whereas all figures in Group B are **plane figures** or **2D shapes**. A plane figure has only two dimensions—length and breadth—and has only area, whereas a solid shape has three dimensions—length, breadth and height/depth—and has surface area and volume.

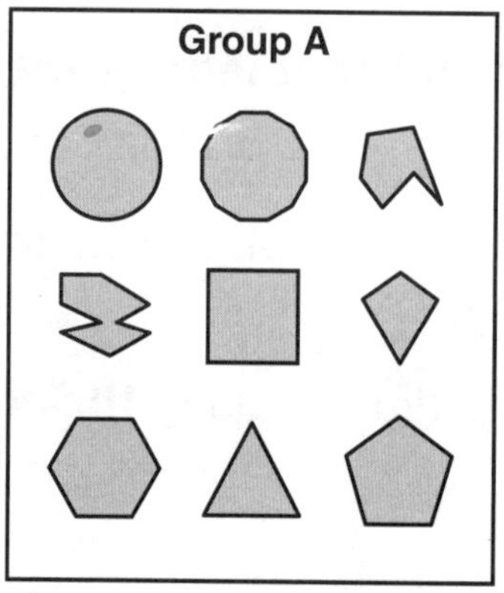

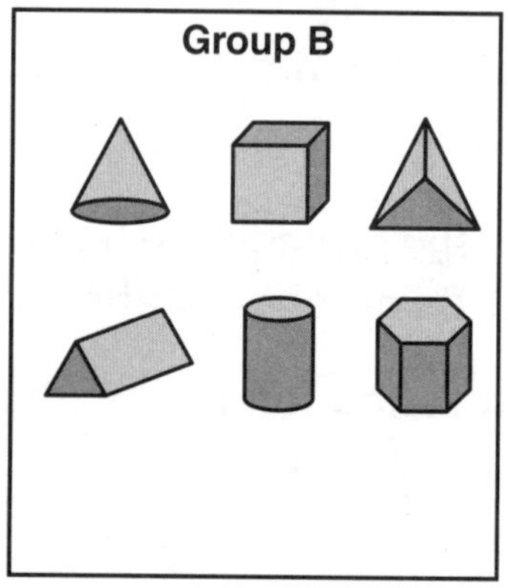

Faces, Edges, Vertices and Nets of 3D Shapes

Face: The surface of a solid is called a **face**.

Edge: The line where two faces meet is called an **edge**.

Vertex: The point where two or more edges meet is called a **vertex**.

Net of a solid is a two-dimensional pattern that can be folded to get the solid.

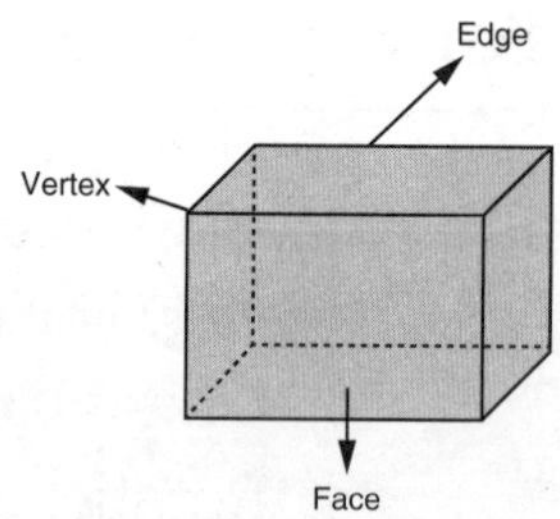

In previous classes, we have learned about different solid shapes—their vertices, faces and edges and their nets. Let us recall them using the following table.

Solid Shape	Faces, Vertices and Edges	Net
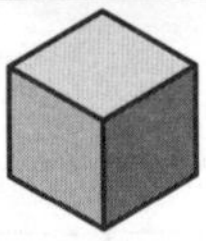 Cube	6 Faces 12 Edges 8 Vertices	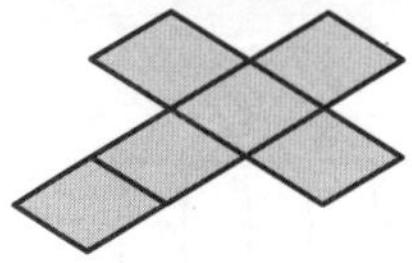
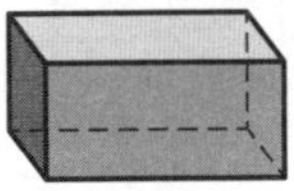 Cuboid	6 Faces 12 Edges 8 Vertices	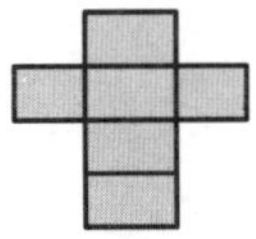
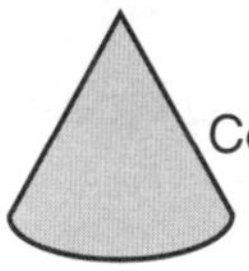 Cone	1 Flat Face, 1 Curved face 1 Curved Edge One Vertex	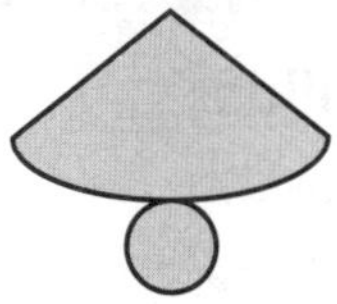
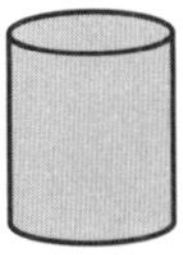 Cylinder	2 Flat Faces, 1 Curved Face 2 Curved Edges No Vertices	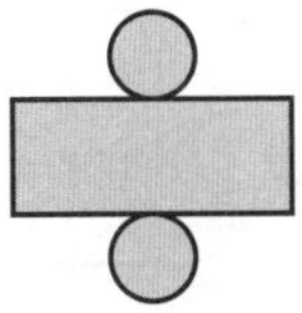
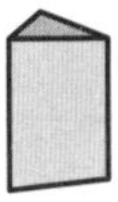 Triangular Prism	5 Faces 9 Edges 6 Vertices	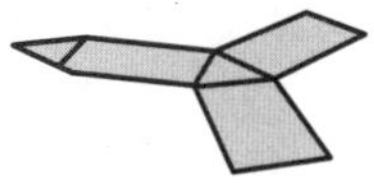
 Triangular Pyramid	4 Faces 6 Edges 4 Vertices	

Exercise 16.1

1 **Which of the following is not the net of the solid shown here?**

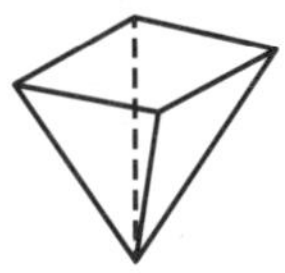

(a) 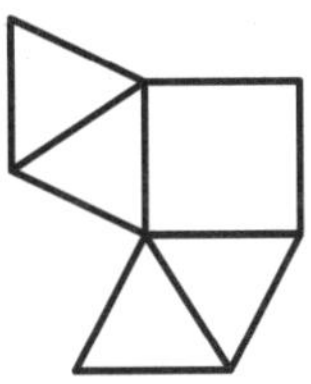
(b) 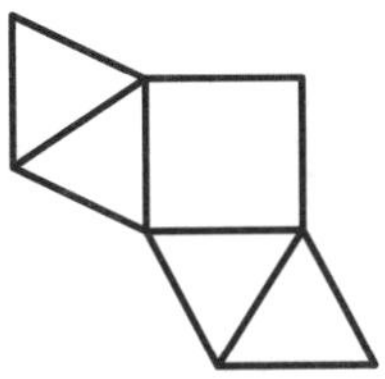
(c) 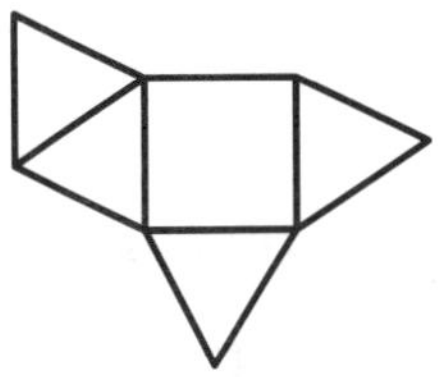
(d) 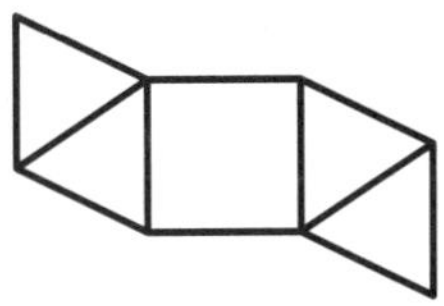

2 **Which solid can be formed by folding the adjacent net?**

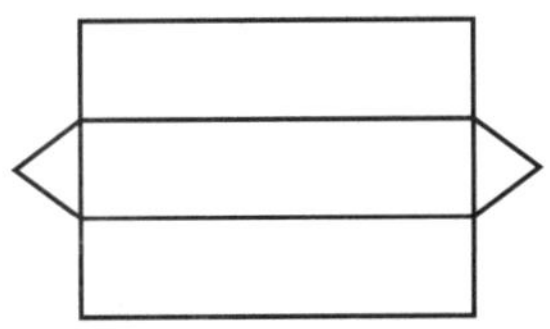

(a) Triangular pyramid
(b) Rectangular pyramid
(c) Triangular prism
(d) Rectangular prism

❸ **Which of the following is the net of the solid shown here?**

(Hint: Prepare the following nets and fold them to form the solid.)

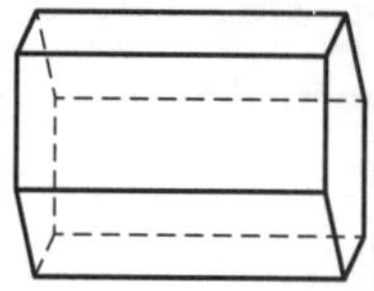

(a)

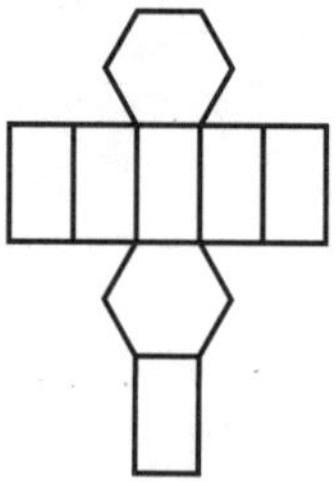

(b)

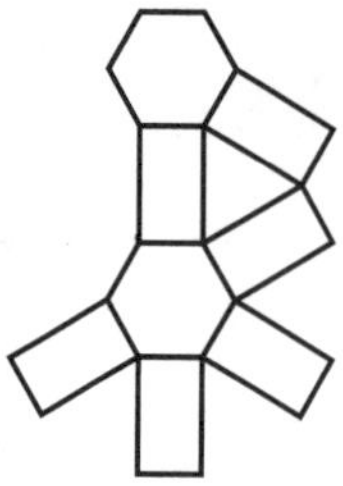

(c)

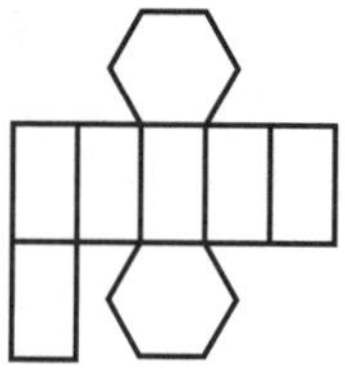

(d)

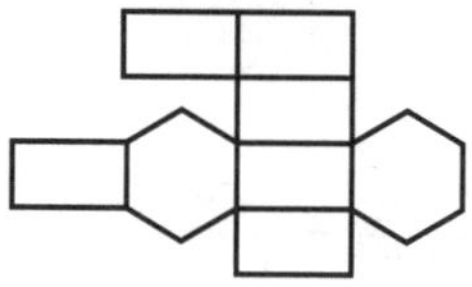

❹ **Match the following:**

Solids	**Number of faces, edges and vertices**
a. Cube	i. Faces - 4, Edges - 6, Vertices - 4
b. Cylinder	ii. Faces - 6, Edges - 12, Vertices - 8
c. Cone	iii. Faces - 2, Edges - 1, Vertices - 1
d. Triangular prism	iv. Faces - 3, Edges - 2, Vertices - 0
e. Triangular pyramid	v. Faces - 5, Edges - 9, Vertices - 6

Drawing Solid Shapes on Flat Surfaces

You know how to represent 2D figures such as circles, squares, rectangles, quadrilaterals, etc. on a plane surface. How do you represent 3D figures like cubes, cuboids, etc. on a plane surface?

There are different ways of drawing solid shapes on flat surfaces; two of them are shown below.

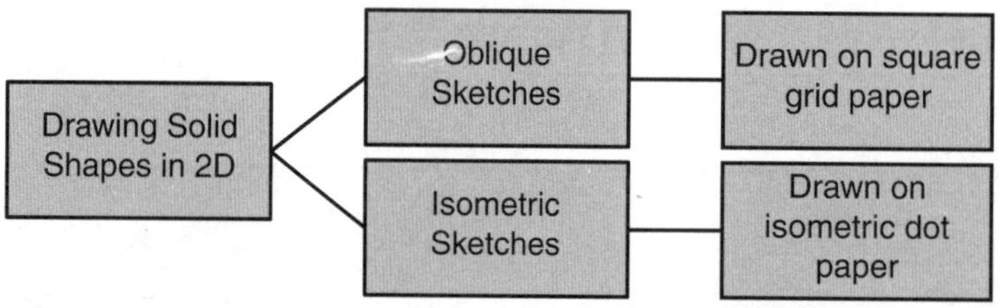

Oblique Sketches

Let us draw an oblique sketch of a cuboid using a square grid paper (we use grid paper initially for practice; later they can be drawn on plain paper). We know that the faces of a cuboid are rectangles and the opposite faces are equal.

Step 1: First draw the front face of a cuboid.

Step 2: Draw the back face slightly above and to the side of the front face. Sizes of both the faces should be the same.

Step 3: Join the corresponding vertices. Use dotted lines for hidden edges.

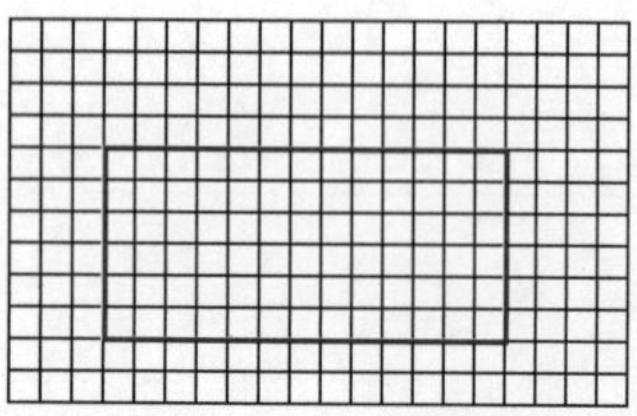

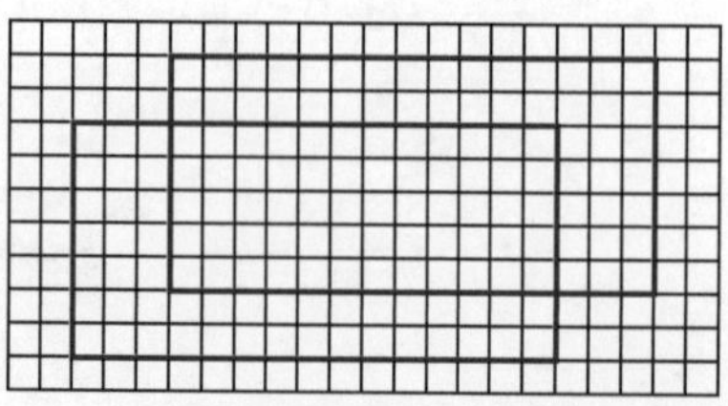

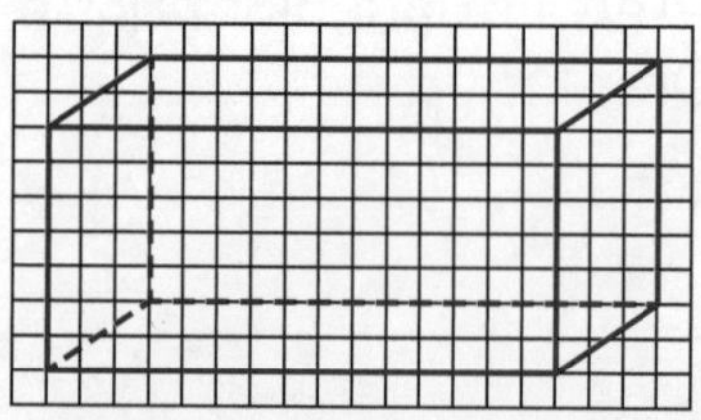

Isometric Sketches

Isometric sketches are drawn on an isometric dot paper which divides the paper into small equilateral triangles with dots. In isometric sketches, the measurements will also be the same as that of the original solid.

Let us draw the isometric sketch of a cube of side 3 units.

Step 1: Draw a square of side 3 units.

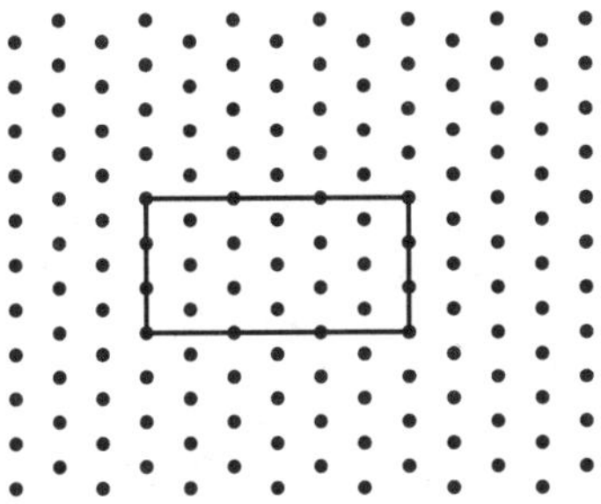

Step 2: From all the four corners of the square draw slanting lines of 3 units.

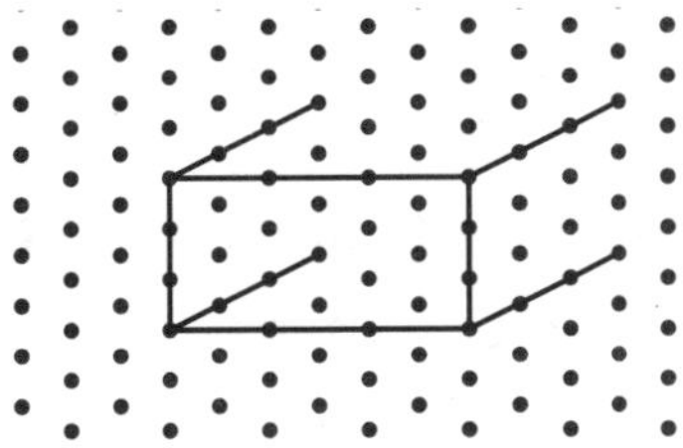

Step 3: Draw another square of side 3 units touching the corners of all the slanting lines drawn. We get the isometric sketch of a cube of side 3 units.

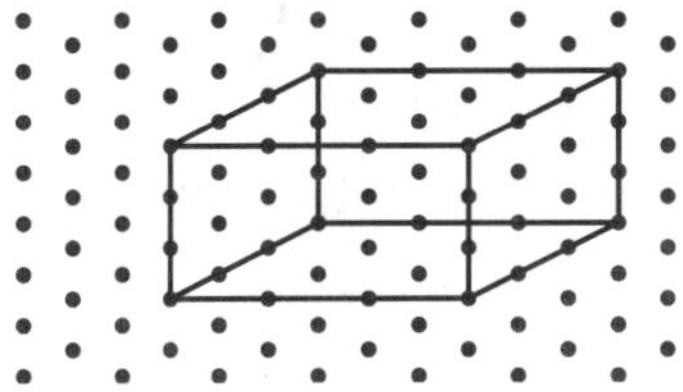

Similarly, the steps of drawing an isometric sketch of a cuboid of dimensions 5 units, 3 units and 2 units are given below.

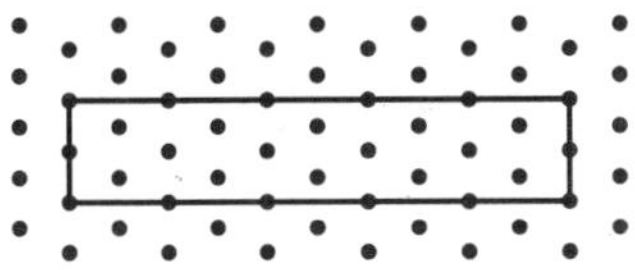

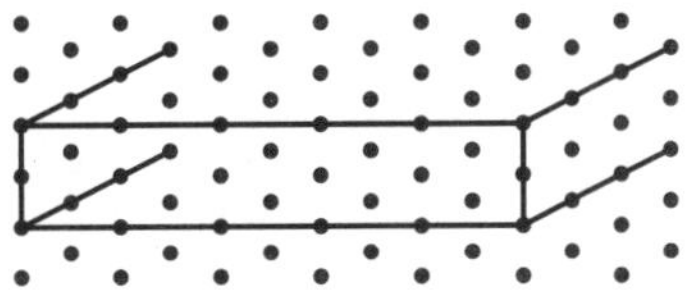

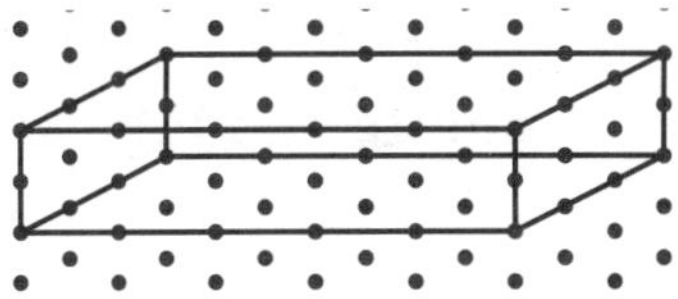

Do You Know?

Isometric dot paper is also known as triangular dot paper. 'Iso' means same and 'metric' means measure. In these sketches, the measurements will be the same as that of the original; hence, they are called isometric sketches.

Example 1: Draw an isometric sketch of a triangular prism whose oblique sketch is given below.

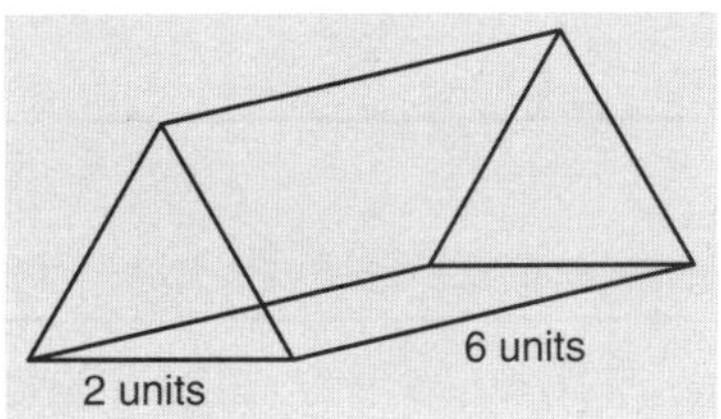

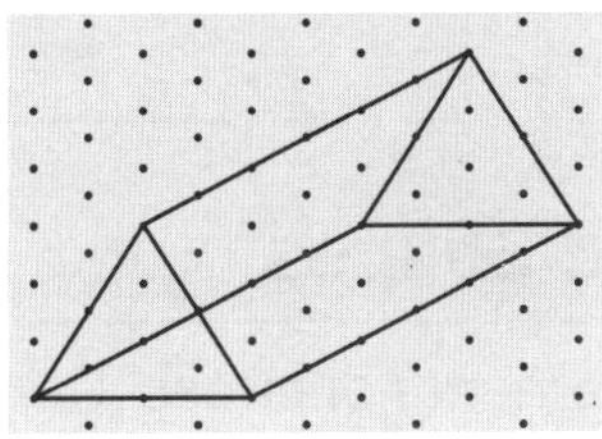

Steps:

1. Draw an equilateral triangle of side 2 units.
2. Draw parallel line segments of length 6 units from all the corners of the triangle.
3. Draw another equilateral triangle by joining the corresponding edges.

Think and Discuss: Mohan has drawn the isometric sketches of a cylinder and a cone whose dimensions are shown here. Is he correct? Can we draw isometric sketches of solids with curved edges? Discuss your observations in the class.

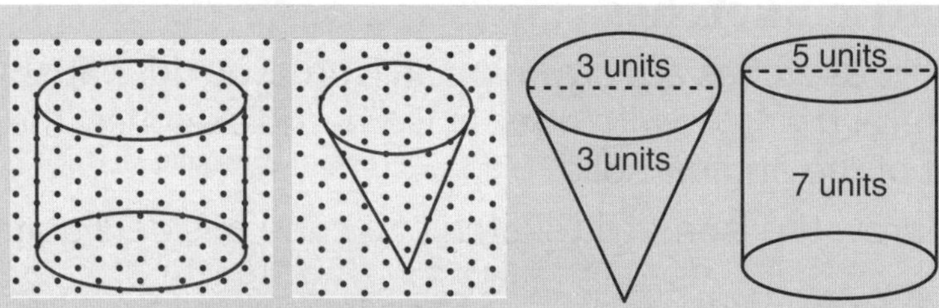

Exercise 16.2

1. **Draw the oblique and the isometric sketches of the following solids.**

   a. Cube of length 6 units b. Cuboid of dimensions 8 × 6 × 4 units

2. **Draw the following solids on an isometric dot paper and write their dimensions.**

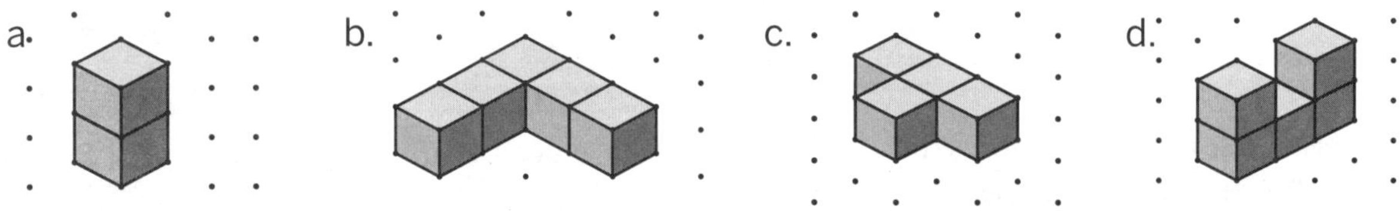

(Note: Form the above solids using connecting cubes and identify the dimensions.)

3. **Complete the following isometric sketches of cubes or cuboids.**

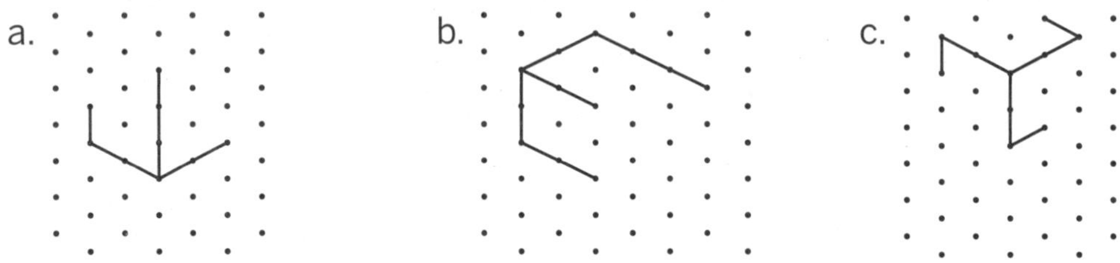

4. Imagine a structure with 5 unit cubes and draw it on an isometric dot paper.
5. Draw three different solids using 6 unit cubes on an isometric dot paper.

Visualising Solid Shapes

Look at these arrangements of cubes. Can you guess how many cubes are there in each arrangement? We can easily guess that there are 6 cubes and 4 cubes in the first and the second arrangements respectively.

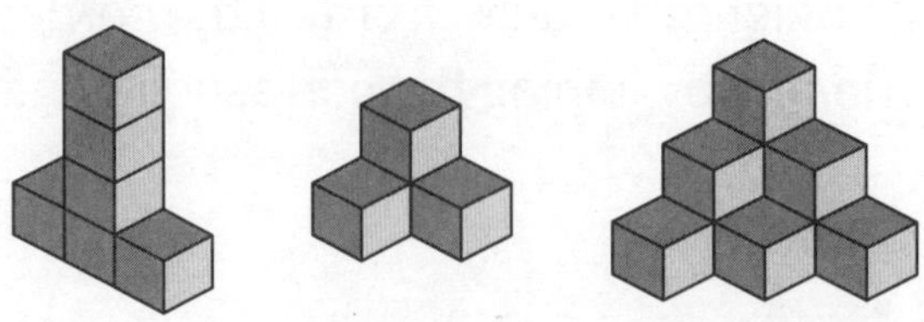

In the third arrangement, it is little difficult to guess because all the cubes are not visible. Only 6 cubes are visible. Look at the figure shown here. The same arrangement has been shown with each layer separately. Now, you can count that there are 10 cubes.

Solids look different from different perspectives. Let us learn various ways of viewing solid objects.

(a) Viewing the cross-sections by cutting

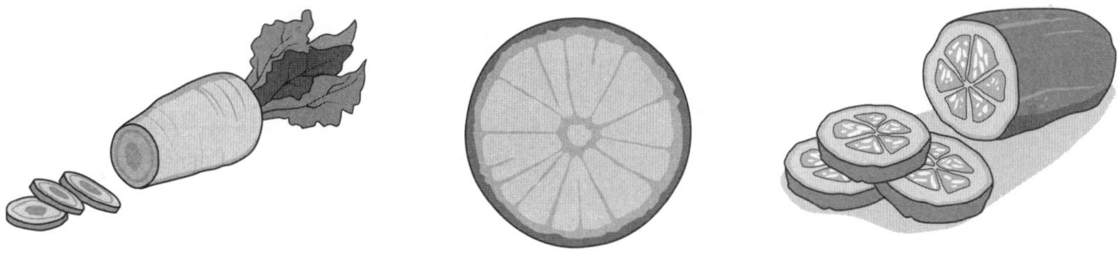

Activity 1

Take an orange, a cucumber and a carrot, and cut them horizontally at right angles with a knife. What shape do you observe?

The surface obtained when an object is cut straight across is known as its **cross-section**. You observe that the cross-sections of orange, cucumber and carrot are circles. Similarly, cut different vegetables and identify the shapes of their cross-sections.

Note: Cut them at different angles and observe their cross-sections.

The horizontal cross-sections of different solid shapes are given below.

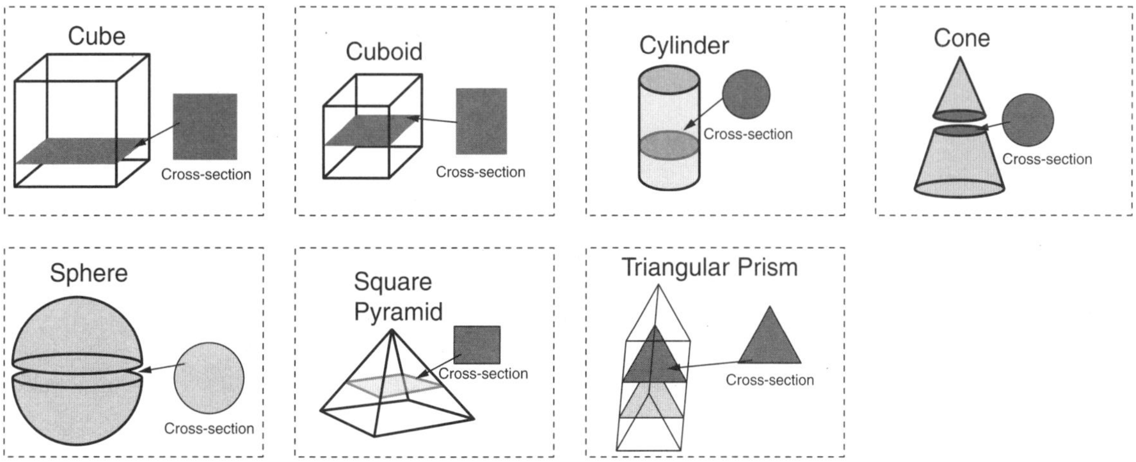

Take a few more solids like triangular pyramid, square prism, pentagonal prism, pentagonal pyramid, etc. and observe their horizontal cross-sections. In prisms, the horizontal cross-sections will have the same shape and size as that of their bases, whereas in pyramids, the shape is the same as that of their bases, but their sizes go on reducing when the cross-section is taken towards the apex.

Think: If you cut the above solids vertically, do you get the same cross-sections? Write the shape of the vertical cross-sections of the above solids.

(b) By Shadow Play

Activity 2

Project a torch light on an empty white wall. Place the following objects one by one in front of the torch light and observe the shadows cast by them on the wall.
Objects: dice, book, ice-cream cone, ball, soft drinks can, etc.
Copy the following table in your notebooks and fill it.

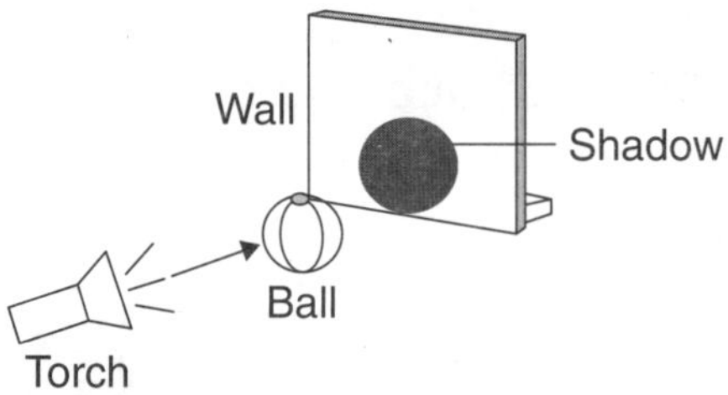

Object	Name of the Solid	Shape of the Shadow
Ball	Sphere	Circle

Move the torch light nearer and farther from the object and observe how the shadow changes. You can also observe the size and the position of your shadow in the sunlight during the different times of the day.

Cross-curricular Link: State the reason for forming shadows.

Note: Carry out the Maths Lab Activity given at the end of this chapter before this concept.

(c) By Different Views

Activity 3

Take a glass and look at it from different positions—from the top, from the front, from the side—and observe how it looks. Does it look the same? Take a few more objects, like book, water bottle, lunch box, etc. and try to look at them from different views.

Here are a few objects and their views from different positions.

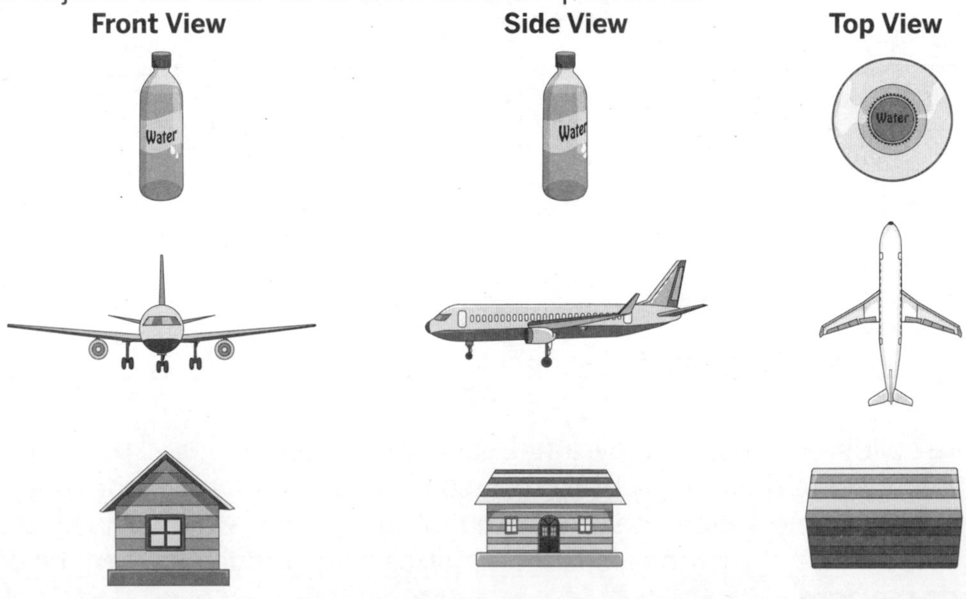

* The roof of the house may not be flat but it looks so when it is viewed from the top (bird's view).

Look at the following solids, which are formed using the connecting cubes, and their different views.

Solid	**Front View**	**Top View**	**Side View**

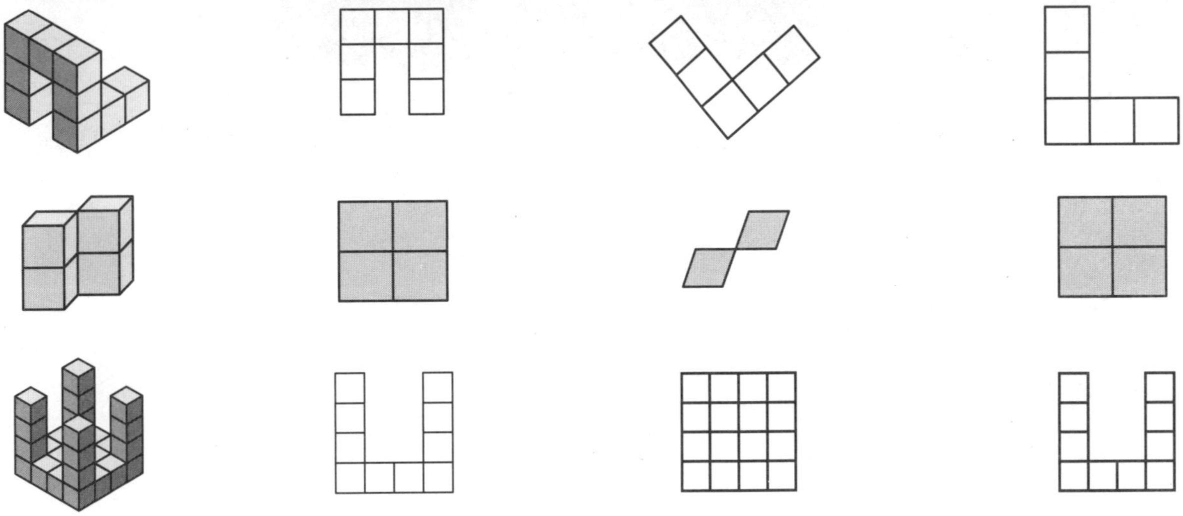

Exercise 16.3

1. **Write the shapes obtained by the horizontal and the vertical cross-sections of the following solids.**

	Horizontal Cross-section	**Vertical Cross-section**
a. Cylinder	______	______
b. Cone	______	______
c. Cube	______	______
d. Sphere	______	______
e. Rectangular prism	______	______
f. Square pyramid	______	______

2. **Write the names of the solids whose shadows are given below. Is there a unique answer for this? Why?**

a. b. c. d. e.

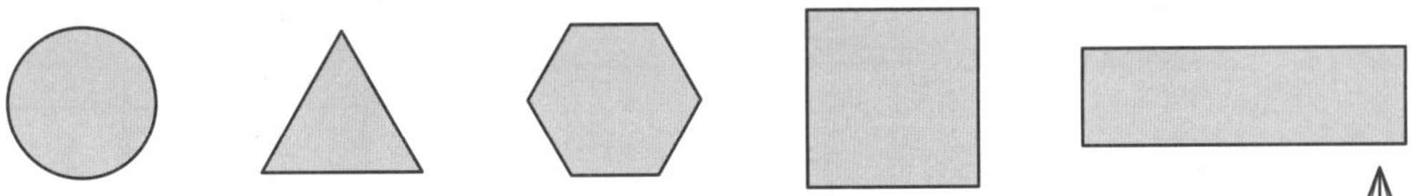

3. Draw the top, side and front view of the solid shown here.

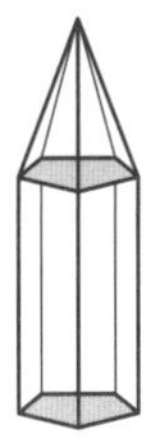

4 **Identify and write the different views of the following solids in the boxes below the figures.**

How are these two views different?

a.

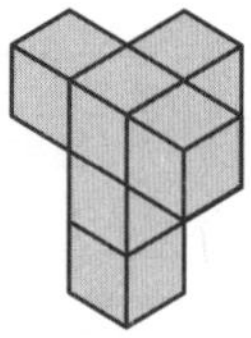

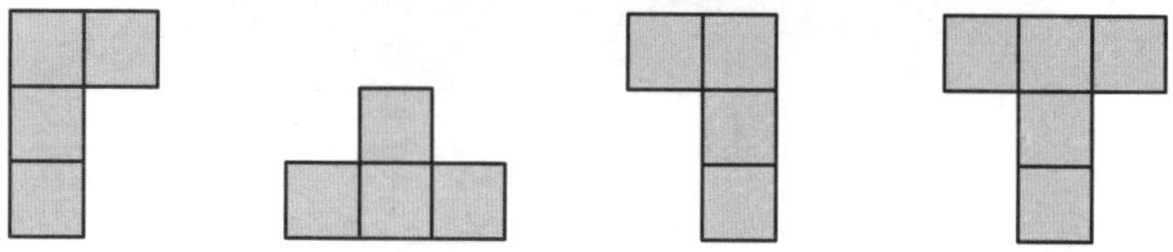

b.

Summary

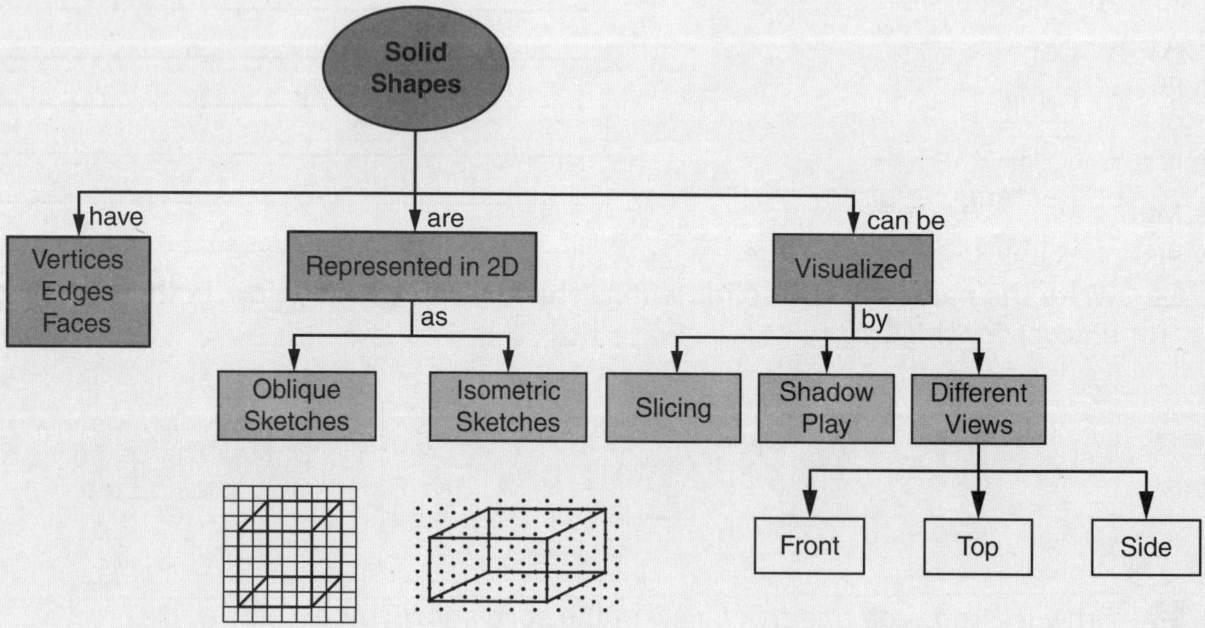

Revision Exercise

1 Write the names of the solid shapes corresponding to the following objects.

a. Sweet box b. Globe c. Chalk piece box

d. Chalk piece e. Candle f. Toy top

(Note: The above examples are the nearest approximations of the solids.)

2 Which solid shapes will be formed when each of the following nets are closed?

a.  b.  c. 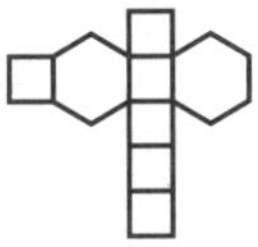 d. 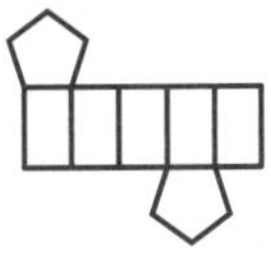 e. 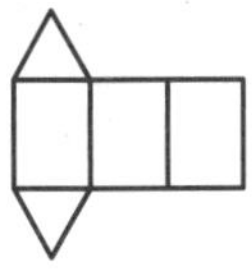 f. 

3 Priya calculated the number of vertices of a triangular pyramid (tetrahedron) as follows: there are in total 4 triangular faces with 3 vertices each. Therefore, there are $4 \times 3 = 12$ vertices. But when she counted actually, there were only 4 vertices. What went wrong?

4 A cuboid has sides of dimensions 4 cm, 2 cm and 1 cm. Draw two possible views of the cuboid on isometric sheet and name them.

5 A projector is placed at some height above this solid to get a shadow on the chart kept below. Draw the shape of the shadow. What happens to the shadow if the solid is rotated?

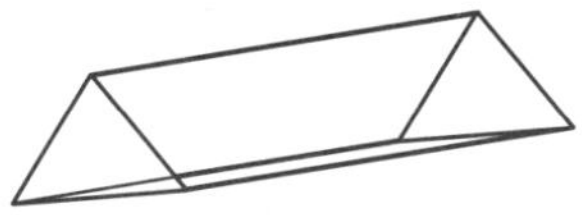

6 Match the objects with their views by drawing arrows. Write their views on the top of the arrows.

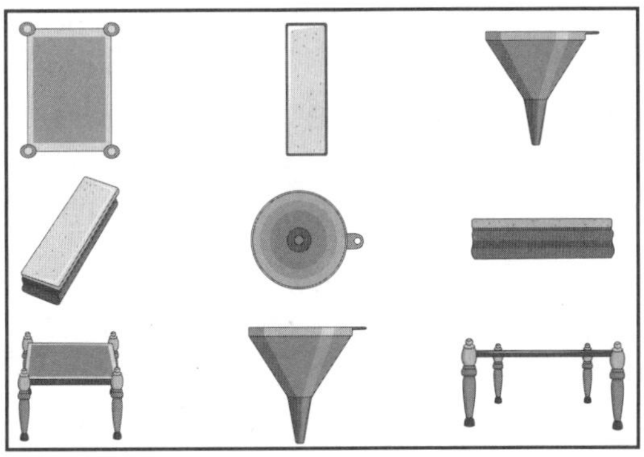

7 Draw the top, side and front view of the solid shown here. What do you observe?

8 Identify and draw the solid whose different views are given below.

Top view

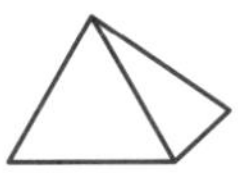

Side view

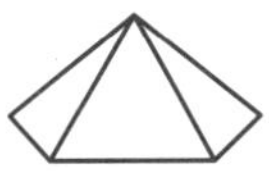

Front view

Solid:

9 Draw the front view, side view and top view of the following solids formed by joining the connecting cubes.

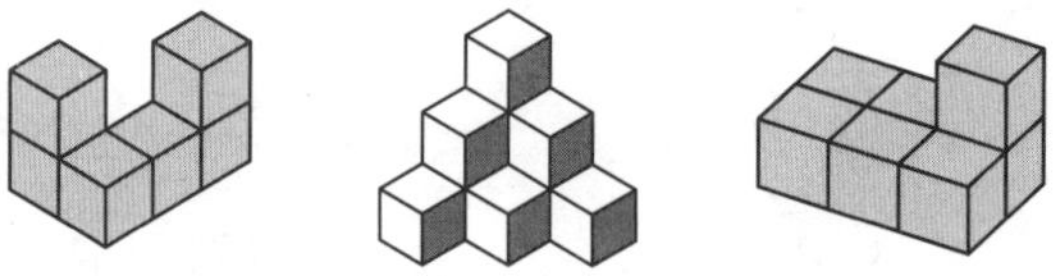

10 **Fill in the following table.**

Solid	Top View	Front View	Side View
a. Cube			
b. Cuboid			
c. Cone			
d. Cylinder			
e. Sphere			

Which solids have the same top, front and side views?

11 **Draw different views of the following solids.**

a. 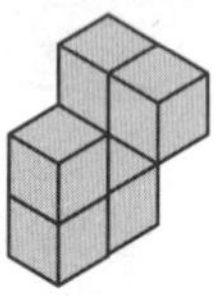

b. 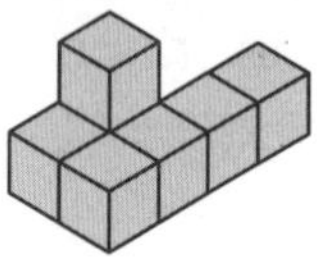

c. 

For the Curious Mind

1. Find the number of cubes in the arrangements of cubes shown here.

a. 

b. 

2. Identify and draw the solids whose different views are shown here. Is there a unique solid possible with these views? Use the connecting cubes to build the solid.

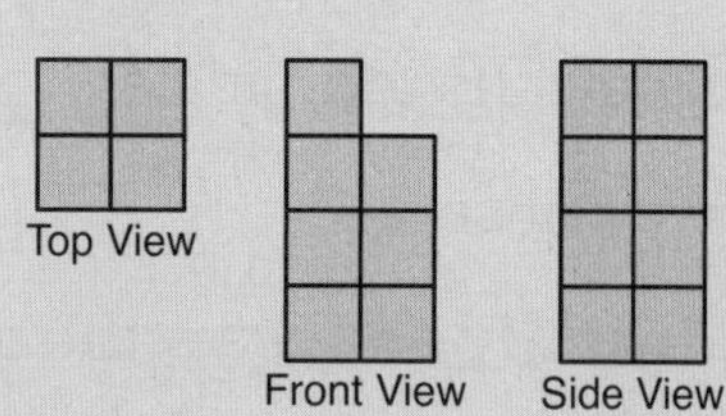

THEME 4

Mapping Space Around Us

17

What I shall learn

- To identify the location of different places in a map
- To draw a map

Let's Get Started

Let us take an instance to see how we can utilize maps in our day-to-day life. Jahnavi is a news reporter working for a news channel in Delhi. She has come to Mumbai for some official work and is staying near Chhatrapati Shivaji Terminus. She has to go to Andheri East for covering some news. As she is new to the place, she wants to know the distance from Chhatrapati Shivaji Terminus to Andheri East. Also, she wants to find out the best route to reach Andheri East, etc. As she is travelling there for the first time, she is taking the help of the Mumbai road map to get all the information she wants.

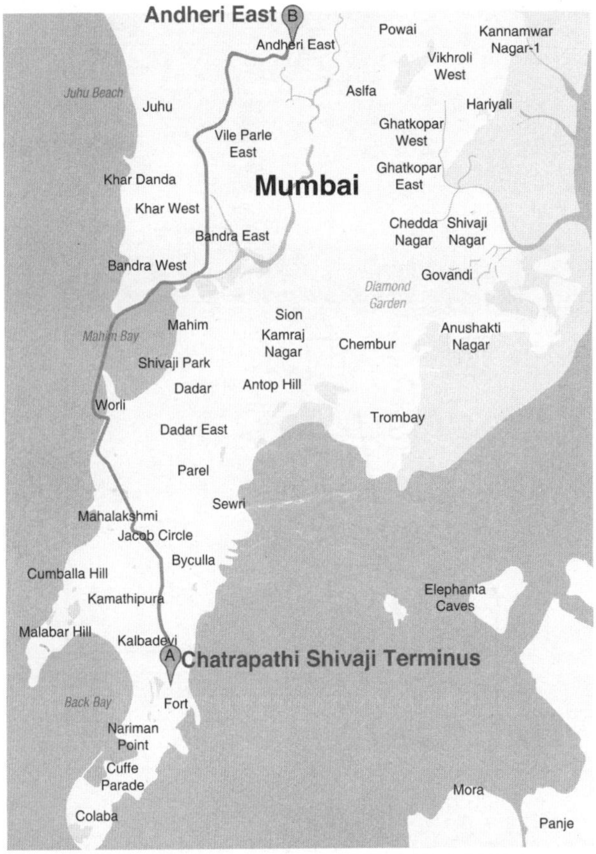

A **map** is a drawing that shows the position of things such as countries, cities, towns, streets, rivers, mountains, etc. There are different kinds of maps which are meant for different purposes.

Did You Know?

One of the first maps of the world was drawn around 510 B.C. by a Greek traveller, Anaximander. But that map is lost and there is no evidence of the existence of the map he created.

Directions in Maps

Look at the road map shown below. Let us mark the direction from Bus Stand to Jai Niwas Guest House. Move straight towards East and take second left towards North till you reach Gopinath Marg. From there, take a right turn towards East and the first left turn towards North to reach Jai Niwas Guest House.

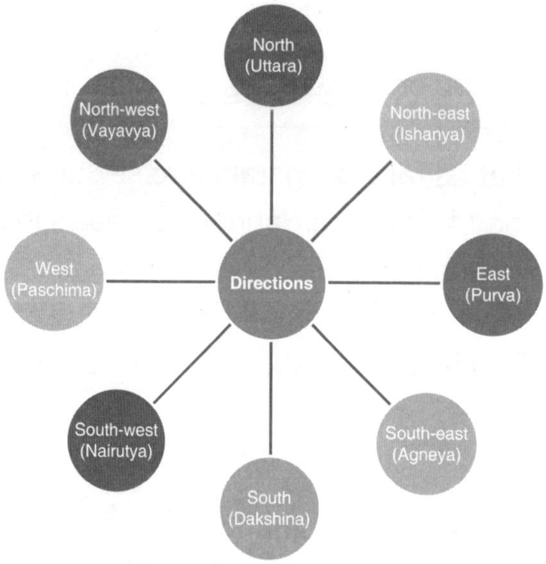

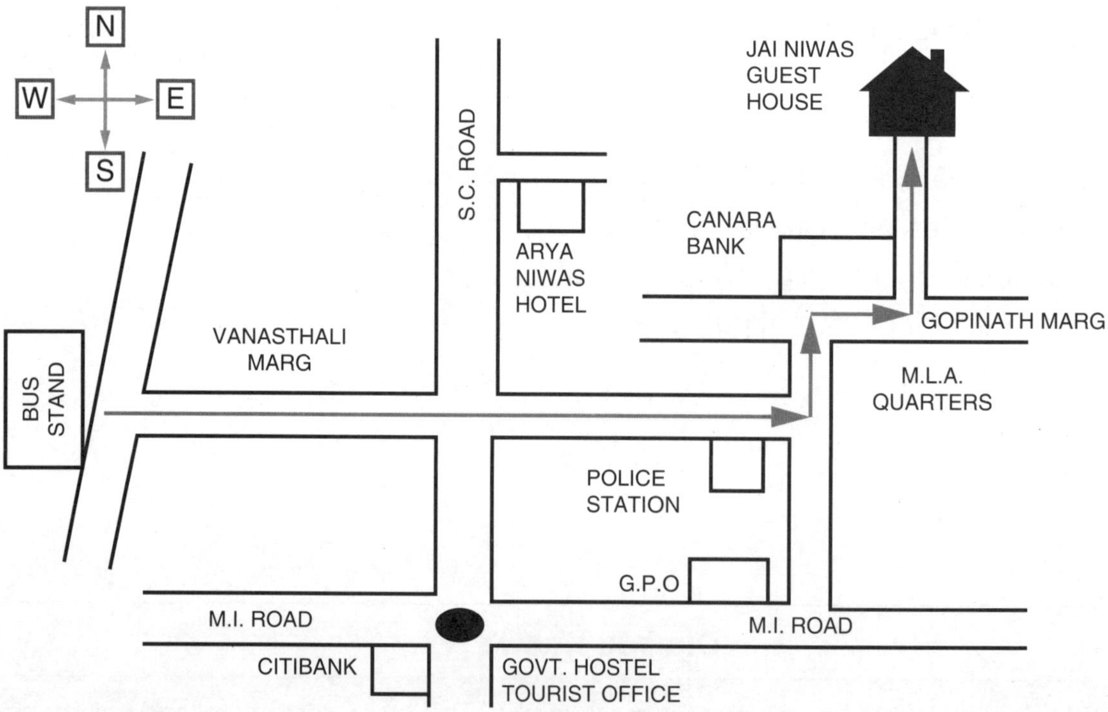

Symbols or Legends in the Map

Look at the tourist map of Ooty shown here. There are some symbols used in the map, which represent a specific location. They are also called **map legends**. If we use symbols in a map, we need to specify which symbol stands for what at the end of the map. This is called the **key**. Observe the symbols used for highway, railway, hotel, hospital, educational building, etc. in the map.

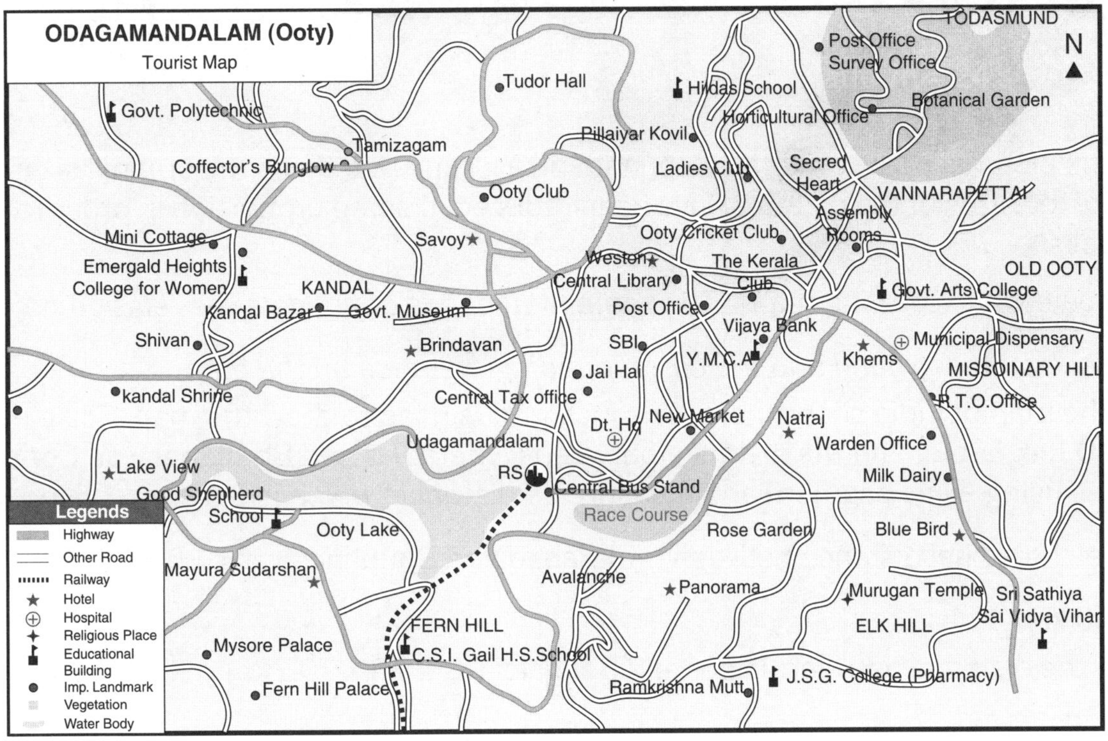

Some of the standard symbols used in maps are given below.

Bridge	Educational Building	Railway	Gate / Toll Gate
Highway Route Number	Electric Power Station	Religious Building	Fire Station
Tunnel	Footbridge	Sports Track/ Race Track	Electric Facility: large
Telephone Line	Airport	Stadium	Museum
Restaurant	Boating	Golf Course	Forest/Trees
Hospital	Hotel/Guest House	Library	Parking
Post Office	Rest Rooms	Fuel/Gas/Petrol	Telephone

Scale in the Map

Look at the pictures of a bicycle, an elephant and a giraffe. Are these the original sizes of them? No, the sizes of the pictures have been reduced in some proportion in order to draw it in our books.

We use scale while drawing maps. *The **scale** of a map is defined as the relation between the distance on the ground and the corresponding distance on the map.*

Look at the map of India shown here. One inch grid is used to draw the map. Scale used is **1 in = 700 km**. Let us find the distance between Hyderabad and Bhubaneswar. Connect the two places using a line segment and measure its distance, which is 3.8 cm = 1.5 in.

Therefore, the actual distance between Hyderabad and Bhubaneswar = 1.5 × 700 km = 1050 km.

Similarly, the distance between Jaipur and Bangalore is 2.83 × 700 km = 1981 km.

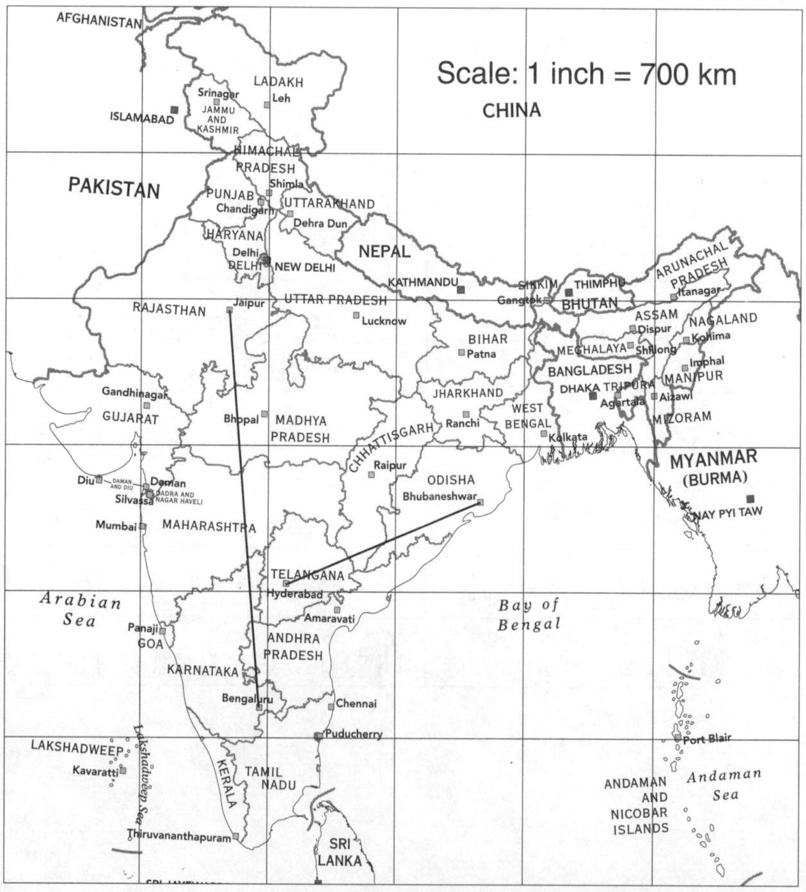

Draw Maps

To draw a map showing the route from your house to school, it is important to show your neighbourhood, special places and the space all around that you were allowed to travel. For this, you should have a good spatial literacy of your region or city.

Remember: Spatial literacy is the confident use of maps, mapping and spatial thinking to solve our day-to-day problems in the society and the world around us. Before that, you should be able to draw and measure a map of a house or a school campus.

Observe the house plan given below.

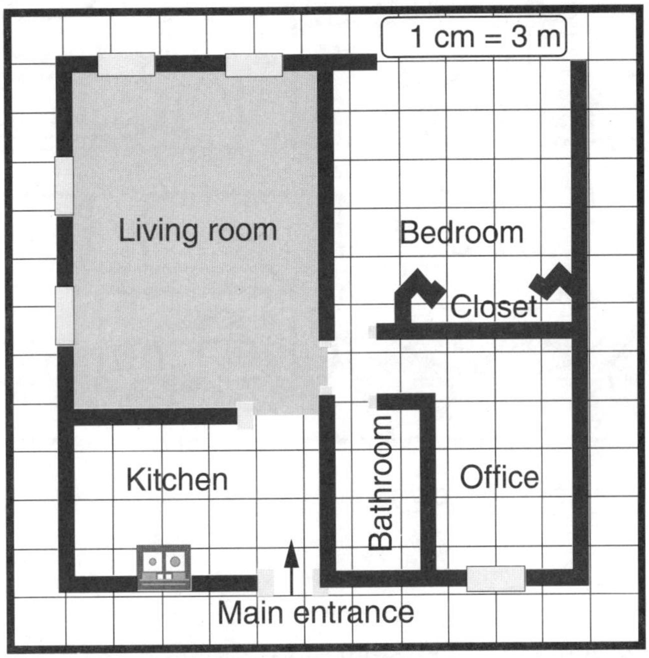

Measure the actual dimension of the following rooms in the house plan using the scale given. (One has been done for you):

	Length in the house plan	Breadth in the house plan	Actual Length	Actual Breadth
Living Room	7 cm	5 cm	21 m	15 m
Kitchen				
Bedroom				
Office				
Bathroom				

Observe the map showing the route from your house to school.

List all the roads and all the special places that are located en route to your school one after the other.

Now, how do you place these things on your map?

To help you with it, just have a recall about the basics of maps like directions, scales, legends and symbols. So, you can draw roads and buildings that are finalized from your list using geometrical shapes.

For example, the following map shows the neighbourhood of David's and his friends houses from the school.

Similarly, you can draw a map of your town.

Project

Draw a map of your town and mark the special places in your town.

Summary

Maps help us to:

1. Know the roads when we go to the new places.
2. Know different routes between the two places and the shortest route among them.
3. Calculate the actual distance between any two places using the scale and so on.

For the Curious Mind

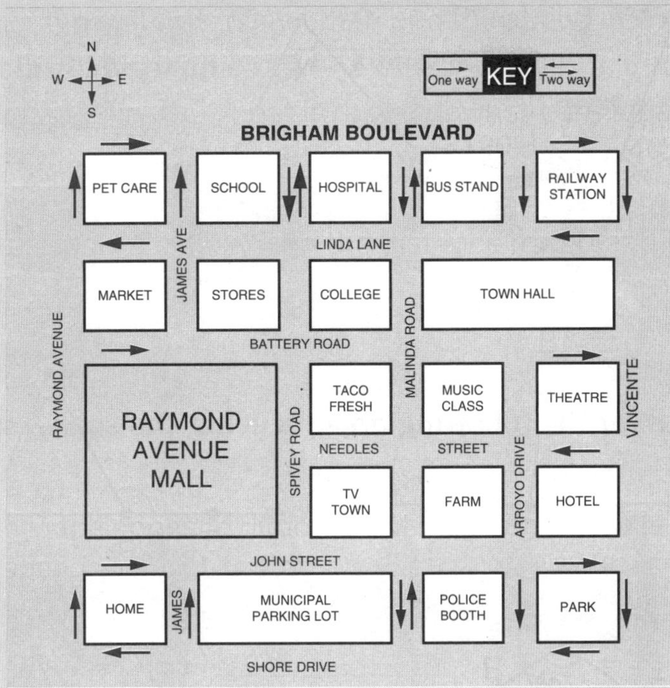

John has to drop his parents to the railway station. He has to pick up his daughter from the school and son from the college. He has to buy some fruits from the market and then return home. Draw the best route for John in the above plan.

Revision Exercise

1 **You are going on a trip and you want to know the nearest hotel to stay. Which symbol will you look for in the map?**

(a) 

(b) P

(c) 

(d) 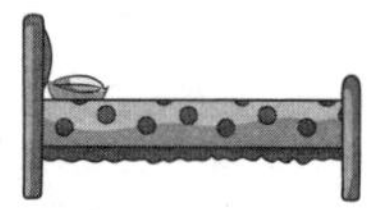

2 **Find the actual length of the following objects using the scales specified.**

(a)

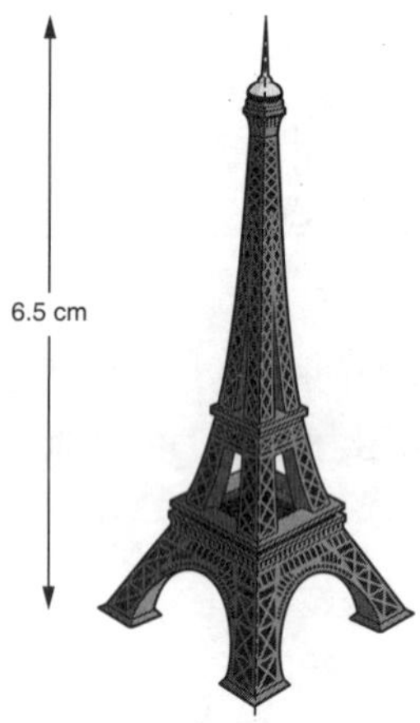

Scale:
1 cm = 58.9 m

Actual Height =

(b)

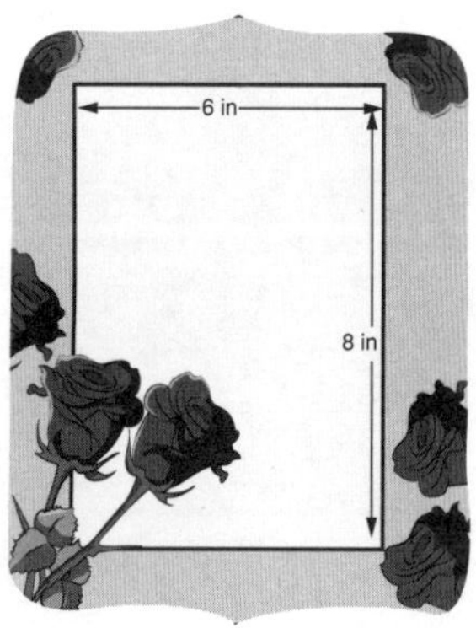

Scale:
1 in = 2.5 cm

Actual Length =
Actual Width =

3. Draw your school campus in a chart. Create and use your own symbols to represent different places such as library, classrooms, office room, playground, etc. in the chart.

4. **Refer the map of India as shown and answer the following questions.**

(a) Which are the neighbouring states to Madhya Pradesh?

(b) Find the distance between the capital of Madhya Pradesh and the capitals of each of its neighbouring states.

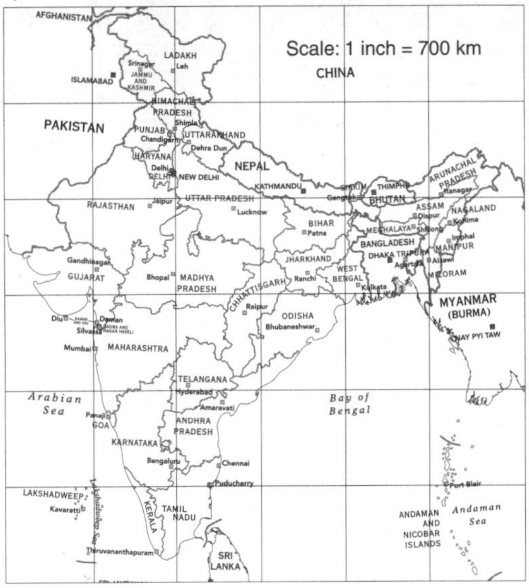

Given below are the distances on the map.

Bhopal to Mumbai: 0.94 in

Bhopal to Gandhinagar: 0.86 in

Bhopal to Jaipur: 0.62 in

Bhopal to Lucknow: 0.95 in

Bhopal to Raipur: 0.89 in

(c) Which is the nearest capital place to Bhopal among them and what is the distance in km?

5. **Find out the scale used to draw the map using the distance information given.**

Places	Actual distance	Distance on map
From Bengaluru to Lucknow	1855 km	5.3 cm

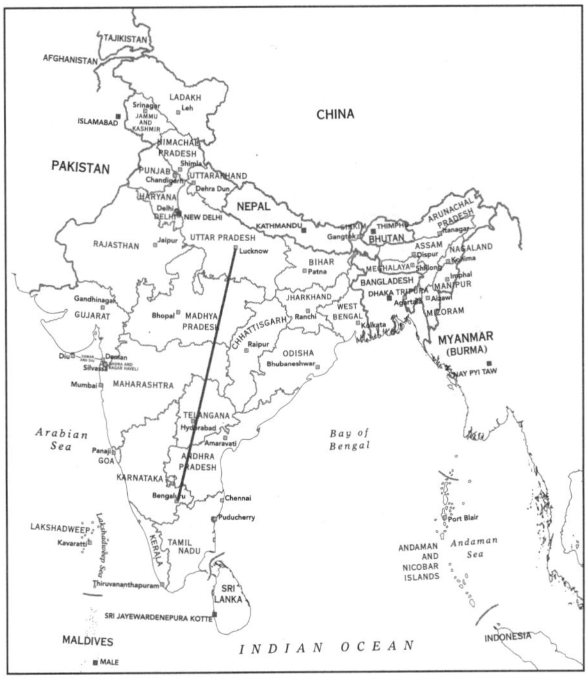

THEME 4

Congruence of Triangles

18

What I shall learn

- To understand the concept of congruency for plane figures
- To define various criteria for congruence of triangles

Let's Get Started

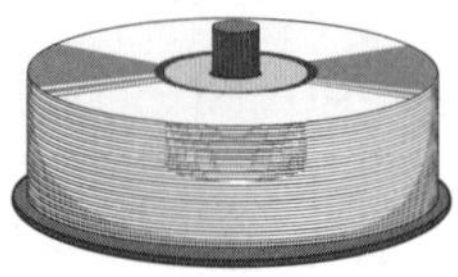

Look at the picture shown here. This is a pile of CDs placed one above the other. Do they cover each other exactly? Yes, they do so because they are of the same shape and size. You can observe the same when you pile 5 rupee coins or ten rupee notes one over the other. The objects which are of the **same shape and same size** are said to be **congruent** to each other.

Look at a few examples and non-examples in the following pictures.

Congruent objects

Non-congruent objects

Congruence

Congruence through Superimposition

To find out the congruent shapes, trace them on a patty paper and cut them. Place the shapes one over the other, that is, superimpose and observe whether they cover each other exactly. This method of identifying the congruent figures is known as the **method of superimposition**. Look at the following shapes. Identify the congruent shapes among them and fill them with the same colour. One has been done for you.

Congruency Symbol

The symbol used to denote congruence is '≅'. This symbol was given by Carl Brandan Mollweide in 1824.

Example: 'Figure F_1 is congruent to Figure F_2' is written as $F_1 \cong F_2$.

$$F_1 \cong F_2$$

Congruence of Line Segments

Take two matchsticks from a matchbox and place one over the other and check whether they are congruent or not. Repeat the same with needles of the same size. What do the matchsticks and the needles represent? They represent line segments. How do we check whether the following line segments are congruent or not?

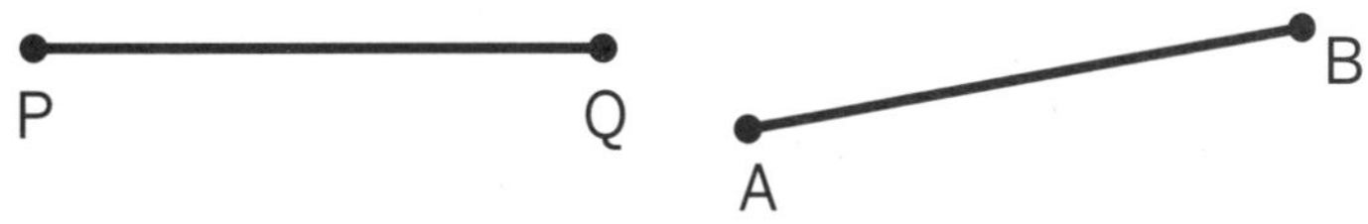

Yes, we use the method of superimposition. Trace one of the line segments, say $\overline{AB}$, on a patty paper. Place it on the line segment $\overline{PQ}$ such that A coincides with P. If B also coincides with Q, then the line segments $\overline{AB}$ and $\overline{PQ}$ are congruent and it is written as $\overline{AB} \cong \overline{PQ}$.

Measure the lengths of $\overline{AB}$ and $\overline{PQ}$. You will find that both of them have the same length.

Therefore, **two line segments are said to be congruent if they have the same length**.

Congruence of Angles

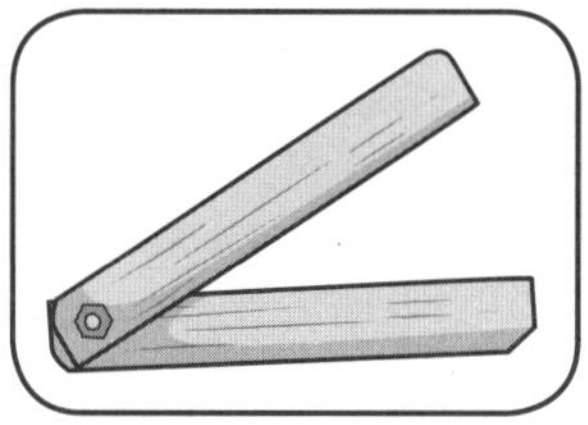

Look at a few angles shown below. How do we check which of them are congruent? We can use the same method of superimposition by tracing the angles on a patty paper and overlapping one over the other. Can you think of any other way of checking for congruence of angles? Take two sticks and make an angle by fixing a screw at one end such that the arms are movable. Open it equal to one of the angles, say $\angle LMN$. Without moving the arms, place it one by one on the other angles and check whether it coincides or not.

We check to see whether the angles have the same measure. So, **two angles are said to be congruent if they have the same measure**.
Measure the given angles using a protractor and verify your findings.

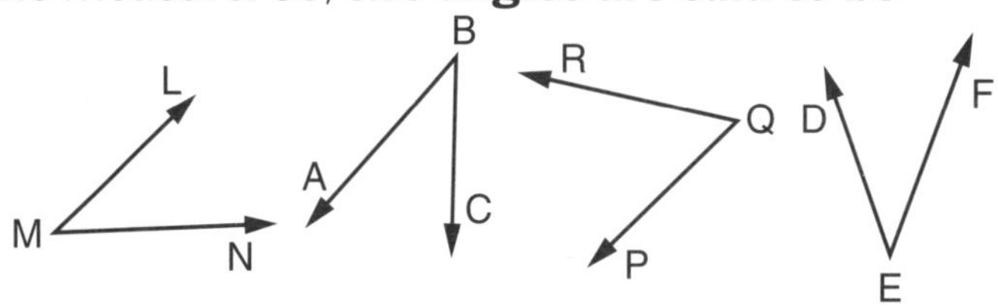

Congruence of Circles

Look at the following circles. Identify the congruent circles among them using the tracing method.

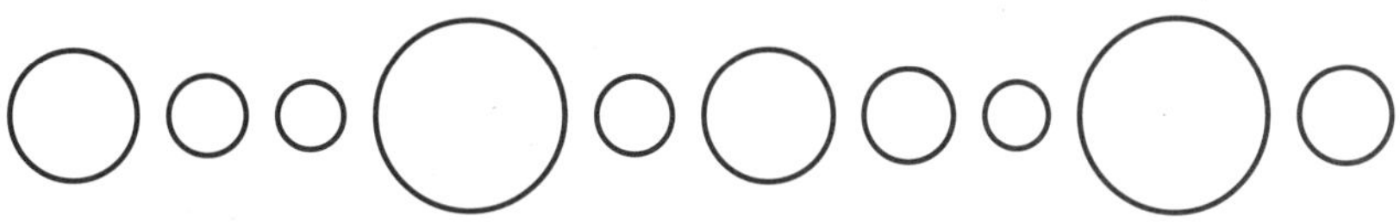

Find the radius (by folding) of all the congruent circles. What do you observe? You will observe that the radii of the congruent circles are equal. Therefore, **two circles are said to be congruent if they have the same radii**. The following are a few examples of congruent circles. Identify a few more examples from your daily life.

Congruence of Regular Polygons

Regular Polygon	Figures		Congruence Relation	Explanation
Equilateral Triangle	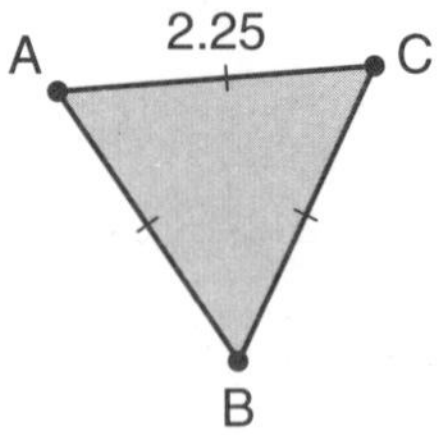	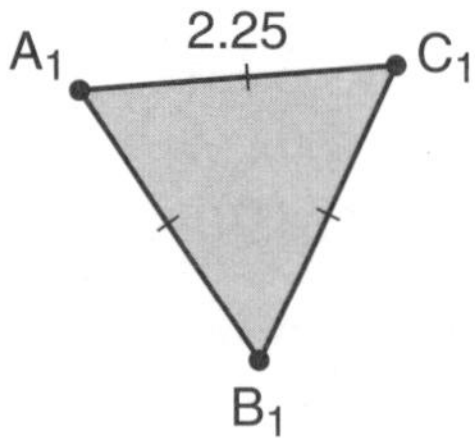	$\Delta ABC \cong \Delta A_1B_1C_1$	The equilateral triangles ABC and $A_1B_1C_1$ have the same side length i.e., 2.25 units. Trace one of the equilateral triangles on a transparent sheet and overlap on the other. You can observe that they are congruent. ***Hence, two equilateral triangles are said to be congruent if they have the same side lengths.***
Square	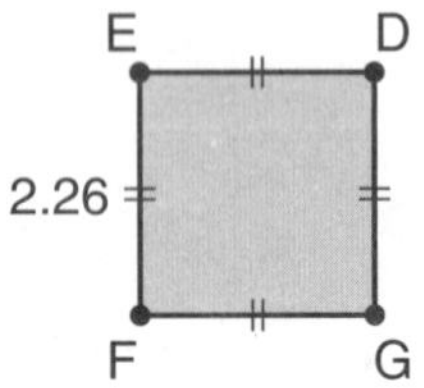	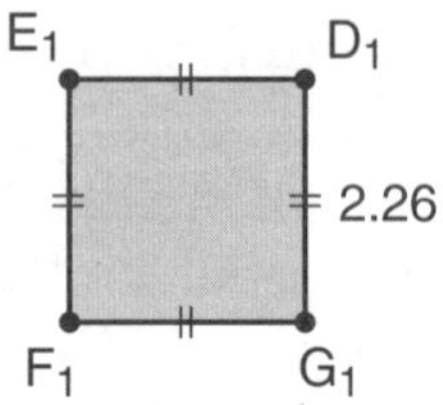	Sq. DEFG ≅ Sq. $D_1E_1F_1G_1$ =	The squares DEFG and $D_1E_1F_1G_1$ have the same side length i.e., 2.26 units. Trace one of the squares on a transparent sheet and overlap on the other. You can observe that they are congruent. ***Hence, two squares are said to be congruent if they have the same side lengths***.
Regular Pentagon	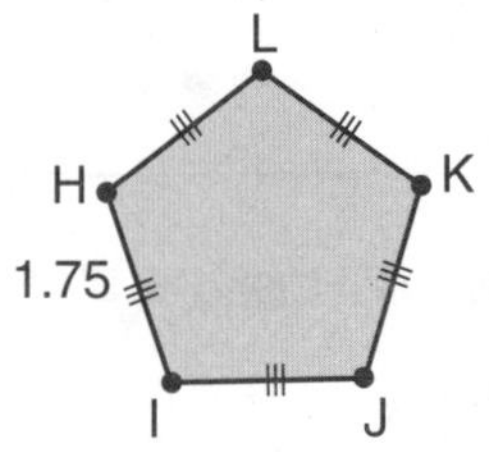	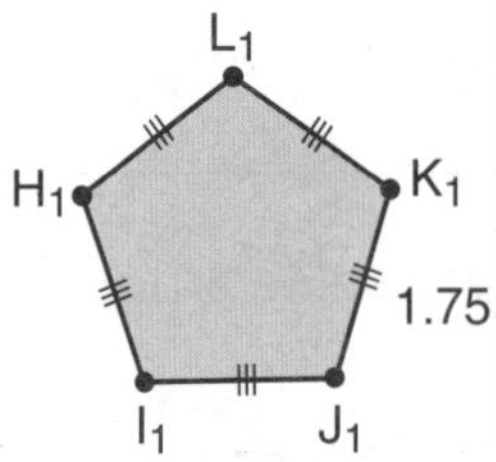	Pent. HIJKL ≅ Pent. $H_1I_1J_1K_1L_1$	The regular pentagons HIJKL and $H_1I_1J_1K_1L_1$ have the same side length i.e., 1.75 units. Trace one of the regular pentagons on a transparent sheet and overlap on the other. You can observe that they are congruent. ***Hence, two regular pentagons are said to be congruent if they have the same side lengths.***

Continue the above table for regular hexagons, heptagons, etc. and you can generalize that **two regular polygons are said to be congruent if they have the same side lengths**. Check whether this is true for non-regular polygons also.

Corresponding Parts of the Congruent Figures

(a)

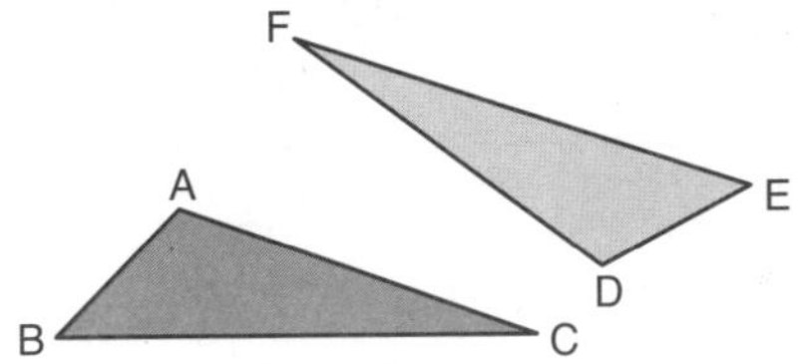

(b)

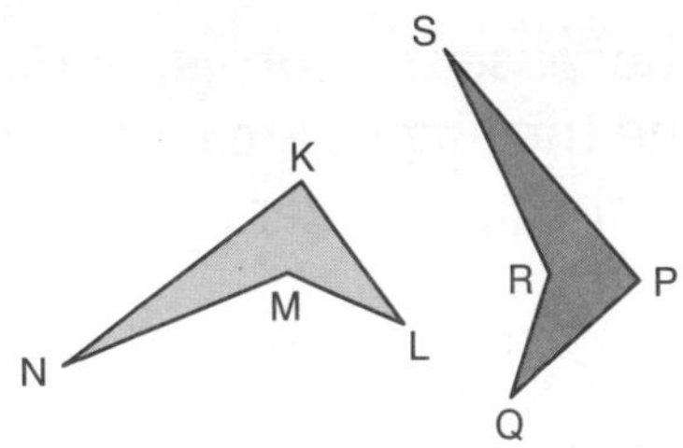

Consider the above two sets of congruent figures. ΔABC ≅ ΔDEF and Quad. KLMN ≅ Quad. PQRS. Trace one of the congruent figures, say ΔDEF, on a patty paper. Superimpose ΔDEF on ΔABC and observe which line segments and angles are equal. You will observe that $\overline{AB} = \overline{ED}$, $\overline{BC} = \overline{EF}$ and $\overline{AC} = \overline{DF}$, and ∠A = ∠D, ∠B = ∠E and ∠C = ∠F. Rotate ΔDEF and see whether any other line segments and angles of the two figures are equal. Repeat the same with figures of set (b). We observe that $\overline{KL} = \overline{PQ}$, $\overline{LM} = \overline{QR}$, $\overline{MN} = \overline{RS}$, $\overline{KN} = \overline{PS}$ and ∠K = ∠P, and ∠L = ∠Q, ∠M = ∠R and ∠N = ∠S. These are known as the **corresponding parts of congruent figures**. No other parts are equal other than the corresponding parts in congruent figures.

Congruence of Triangles

Two triangles are congruent if their corresponding sides and corresponding angles are equal.

Let ΔABC be congruent to ΔDEF.

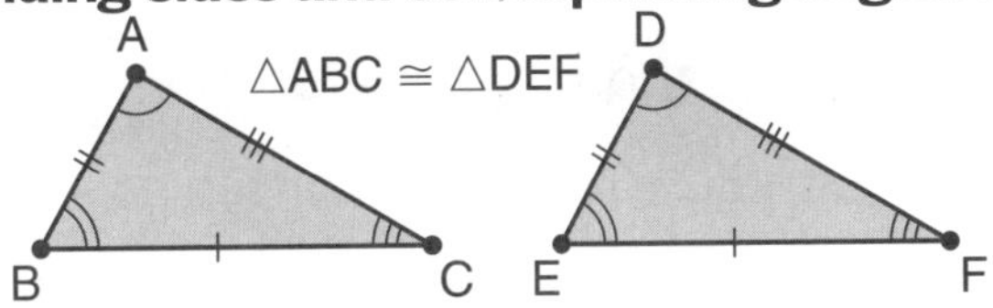

Correspondence: **A ↔ D**
B ↔ E
C ↔ F

All the corresponding parts—vertices, sides and angles of ΔABC and ΔDEF are shown below:

Corresponding Parts

Corresponding Vertices

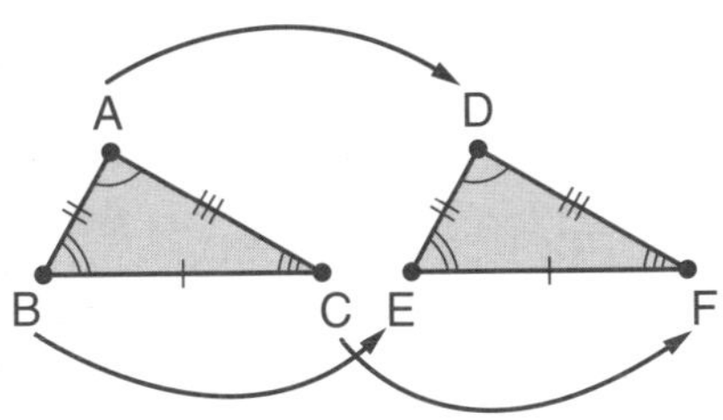

A and D
B and E
C and F

Corresponding Sides

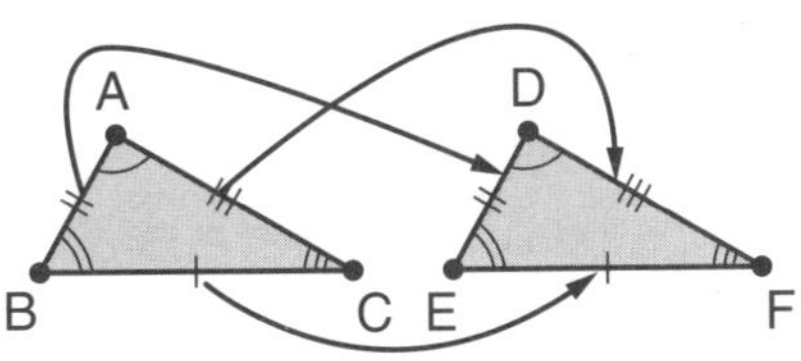

$\overline{AB}$ and $\overline{DE}$
$\overline{BC}$ and $\overline{EF}$
$\overline{AC}$ and $\overline{DF}$

Corresponding Angles

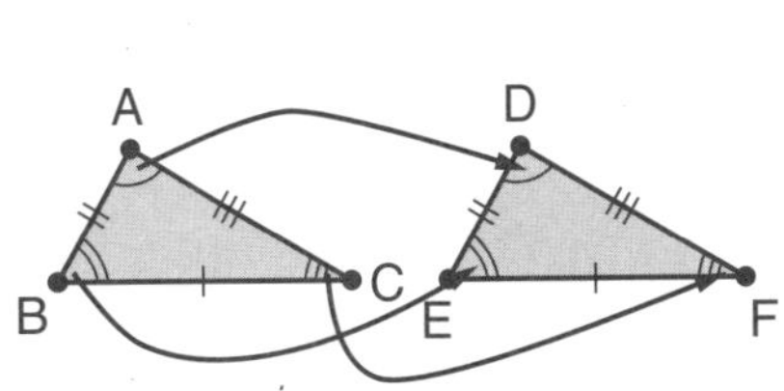

∠A and ∠D
∠B and ∠E
∠C and ∠F

Example 1: Write all the corresponding elements of the pair of triangles shown below.

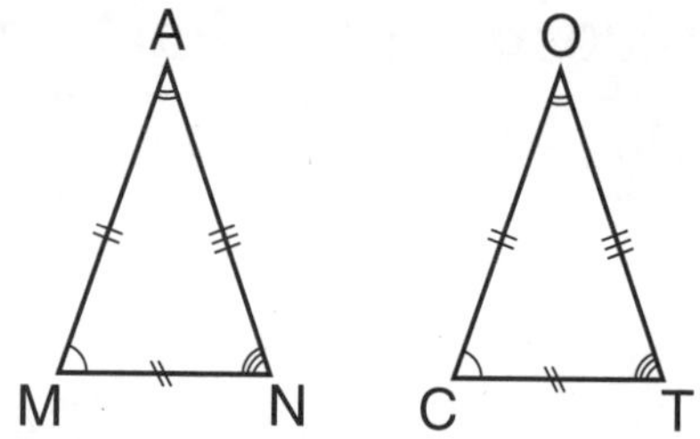

$\Delta MAN \cong \Delta COT$ because the corresponding elements, i.e., the sides and the angles are equal. You can use a tracing paper to check whether the two triangles are congruent or not.

In figures, congruence is denoted by the same number of small ticks on the corresponding sides and same number of arcs on the corresponding angles and is written using the symbol '$\leftrightarrow$', which is read as 'corresponds to'.

In the above figures,

1. Side MA corresponds to side CO.
2. Side MN corresponds to side CT.
3. Side AN corresponds to side OT.
4. $\angle M$ corresponds to $\angle C$.
5. $\angle A$ corresponds to $\angle O$.
6. $\angle N$ corresponds to $\angle T$.

Corresponding sides: 1. $MA \leftrightarrow CO$ 2. $MN \leftrightarrow CT$ 3. $AN \leftrightarrow OT$

Corresponding angles: 1. $\angle M \leftrightarrow \angle C$ 2. $\angle A \leftrightarrow \angle O$ 3. $\angle N \leftrightarrow \angle T$

In ΔMAN and ΔCOT, correspondence between the vertices of the triangles would be $M \leftrightarrow C$, $N \leftrightarrow T$ and $A \leftrightarrow O$.

Number of Correspondences in a Pair of Triangles

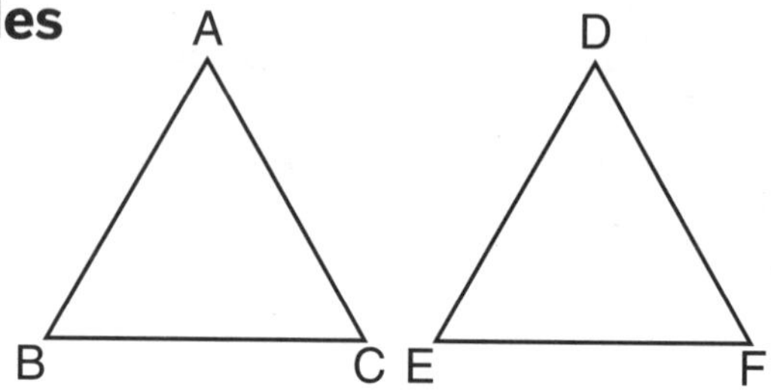

Six correspondences are possible in a pair of triangles.
Let us consider the triangles ΔABC and ΔDEF.

The six possible correspondences are:

- $A \leftrightarrow D$, $B \leftrightarrow E$ and $C \leftrightarrow F$; this is written as $ABC \leftrightarrow DEF$.
- $A \leftrightarrow E$, $B \leftrightarrow F$ and $C \leftrightarrow D$; this is written as $ABC \leftrightarrow EFD$.
- $A \leftrightarrow F$, $B \leftrightarrow D$ and $C \leftrightarrow E$; this is written as $ABC \leftrightarrow FDE$.
- $A \leftrightarrow D$, $B \leftrightarrow F$ and $C \leftrightarrow E$; this is written as $ABC \leftrightarrow DFE$.
- $A \leftrightarrow E$, $B \leftrightarrow D$ and $C \leftrightarrow F$; this is written as $ABC \leftrightarrow EDF$.
- $A \leftrightarrow F$, $B \leftrightarrow E$ and $C \leftrightarrow D$; this is written as $ABC \leftrightarrow FED$.

If $\Delta ABC \cong \Delta DEF$, then ΔABC will superimpose on ΔDEF in accordance with any one of these correspondences, and the corresponding sides and the corresponding angles will be congruent. Hence, we will have three pairs of corresponding sides and three pairs of corresponding angles.

Therefore, two triangles are congruent if and only if there is a correspondence between their vertices such that the corresponding sides and the corresponding angles are equal or congruent.

If $\Delta ABC \cong \Delta DEF$ and $ABC \leftrightarrow DEF$, then we write:

$\Delta ABC \cong \Delta DEF$ if and only if $AB = DE$, $BC = EF$, $CA = FD$, $\angle A = \angle D$, $\angle B = \angle E$ and $\angle C = \angle F$.

Example 2: Write all the corresponding elements if $\Delta WEB \cong \Delta TOP$ and $WEB \leftrightarrow TOP$.

1. $WE = TO$ 2. $EB = OP$ 3. $WB = TP$
4. $\angle W = \angle T$ 5. $\angle E = \angle O$ 6. $\angle B = \angle P$

Exercise 18.1

1 Name all the congruent shapes given in the following figures.

a. 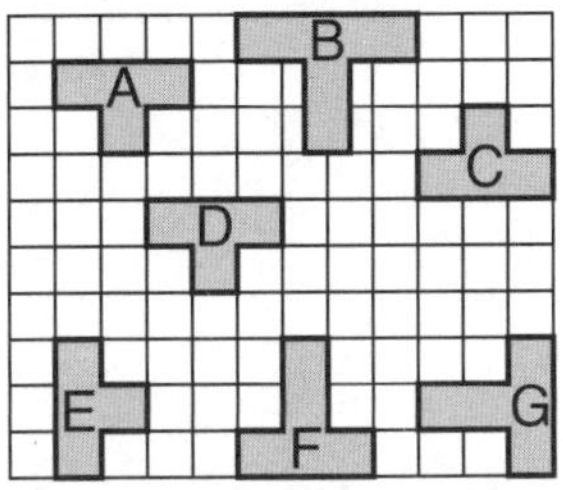

b. 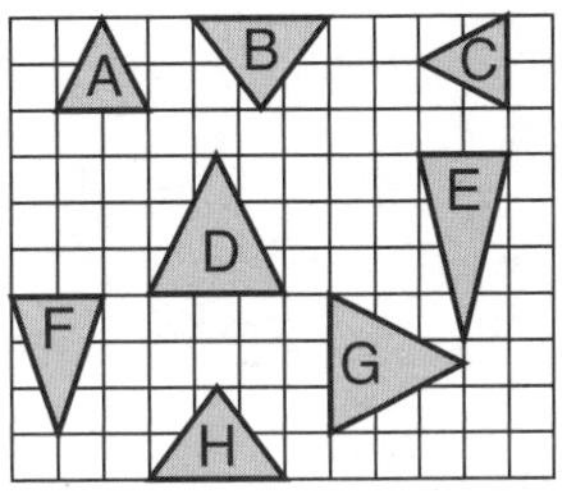

2 Check whether the following shapes are congruent by using the method of superimposition.

a. 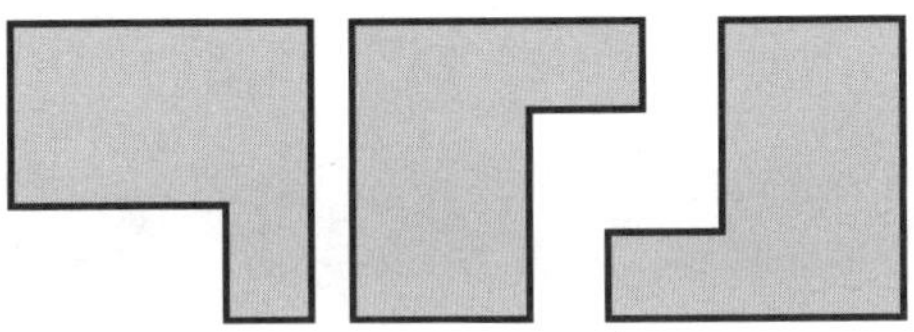

b. 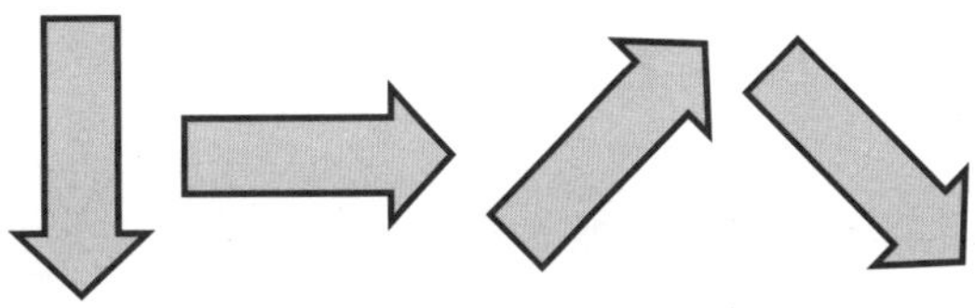

3 Draw line segments congruent to each of the line segments given below.

a. 

b. 

c. 

4 Draw angles congruent to each of the angles given below.

a. 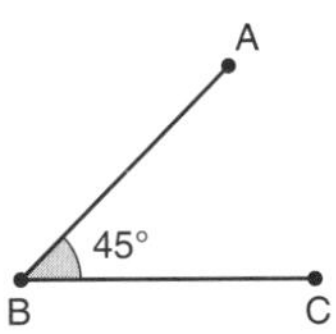

b. 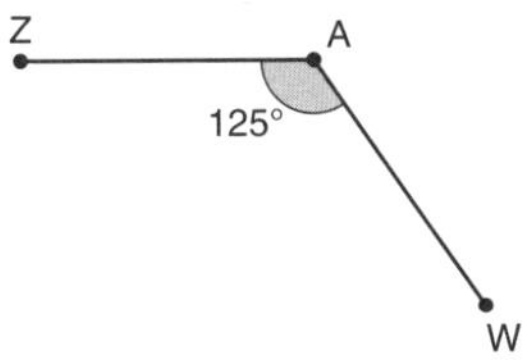

c. 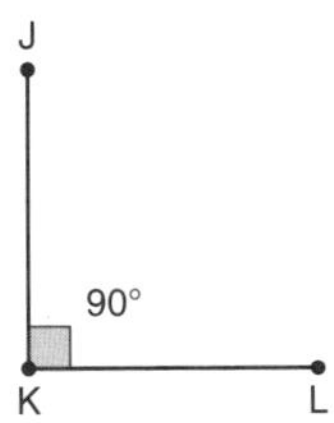

d. 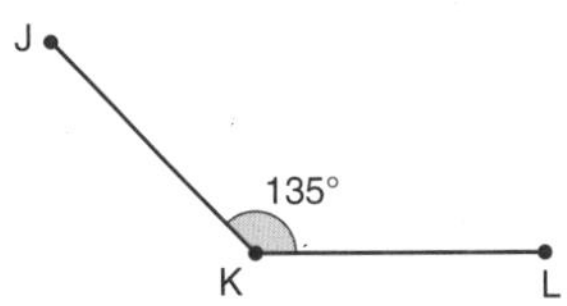

5. The figures given alongside are congruent to each other. Name all the congruent line segments and the congruent angles.

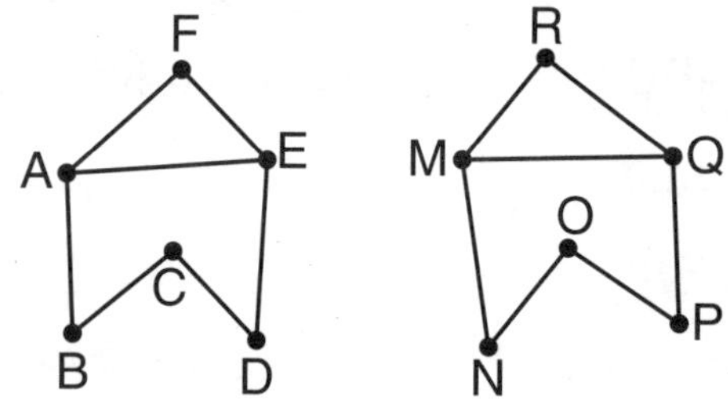

6. ΔDRP ≅ ΔUVW. Write all the corresponding elements if DRP ↔ UVW.

7. **Write the congruence relation between two triangles based on the congruency of its corresponding parts. Also, draw rough sketches of the triangles.**

Correspondence	Congruent relation	Rough sketches
A ↔ E, B ↔ D, C ↔ F AC ↔ EF, BC ↔ DF		
∠M ↔ ∠Q, MN ↔ QR ∠N ↔ ∠R, NP ↔ RS ∠P ↔ ∠S, PM ↔ SQ		
∠A ↔ ∠X ∠B ↔ ∠Y ∠C ↔ ∠Z AB ↔ XY, BC ↔ YZ		
B ↔ C T ↔ E A ↔ I BT ↔ CE, BA ↔ CI		

8. **Identify the shape of the following figures and check whether they are congruent.**

a. 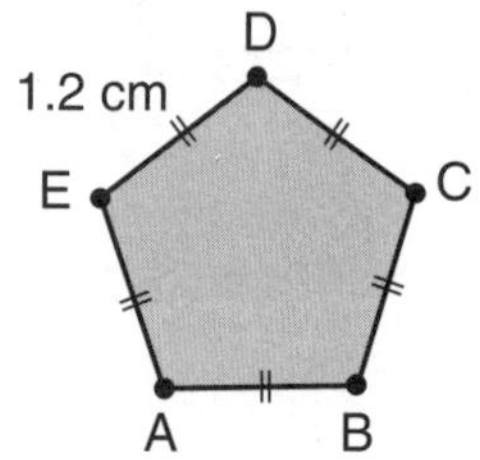

b. 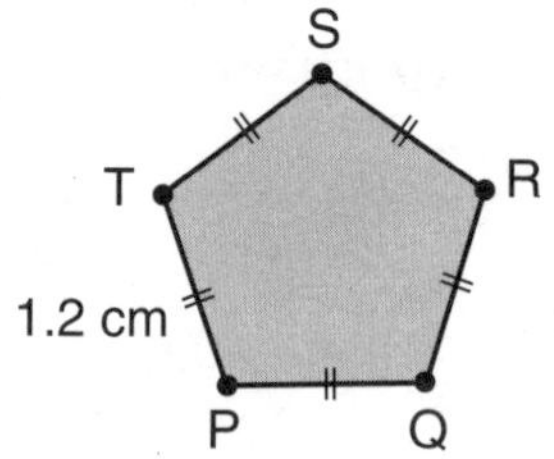

9. **Are the triangles congruent? Justify.**

a. 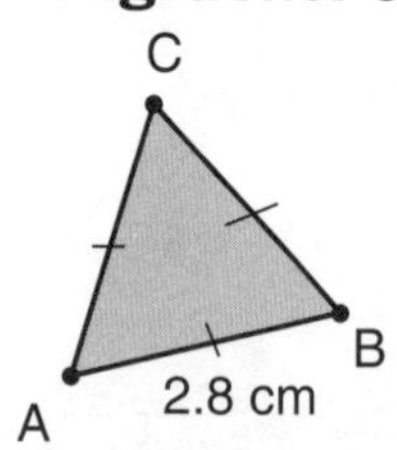

b. 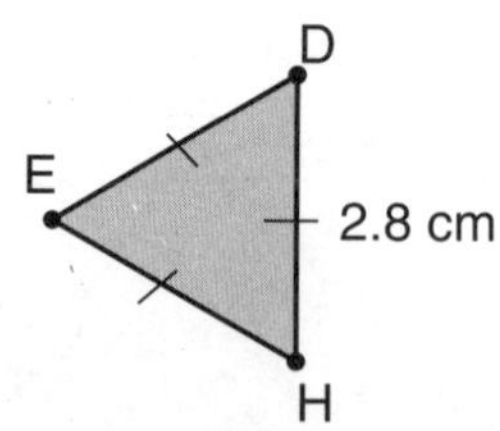

Criteria for Congruency of Triangles

Recall the construction of triangles. We have learned that if any 3 measurements are known, then a triangle can be constructed.

The different combinations of measurements required to construct a triangle are:

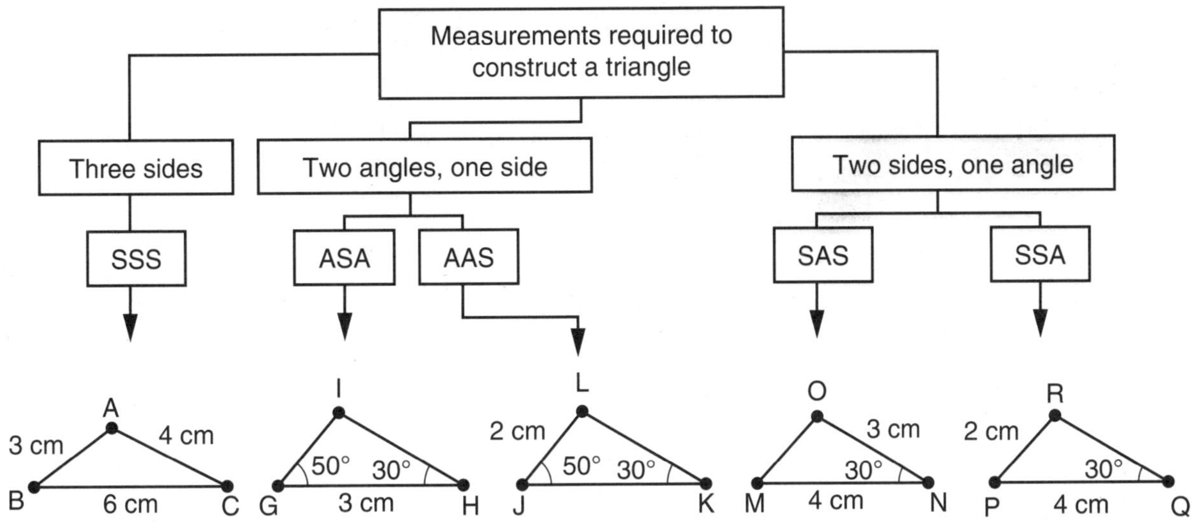

The congruence of two triangles also depends on these minimum criteria that are required for the construction of triangles.

Side–Side–Side (SSS)

Two triangles are congruent if the three sides of one triangle are respectively equal to the three sides of the other triangle.

This criteria is called side–side–side (or SSS) criteria for checking whether two triangles are congruent or not.

Construct two triangles ABC and XYZ such that AB = XY, BC = YZ and AC = XZ.

Use a tracing paper to check whether the two triangles superimpose on each other.

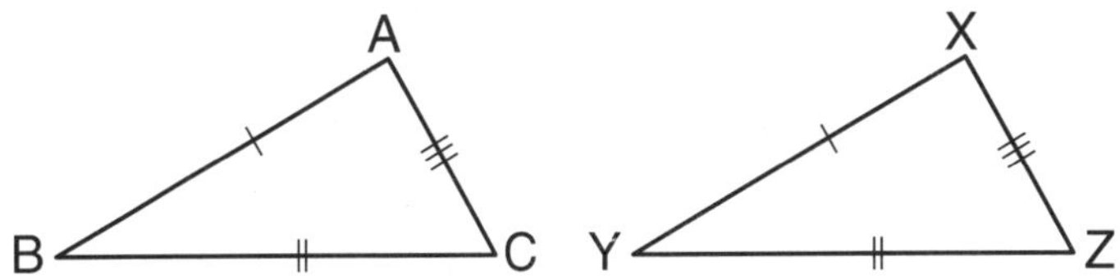

If they superimpose, then $\Delta ABC \cong \Delta XYZ$ (by SSS congruence) and the other three pairs of corresponding elements are equal too, i.e., $\angle A = \angle X$, $\angle B = \angle Y$ and $\angle C = \angle Z$.

Example 3: In the figure, VS = FM and VM = FS. Show that $\Delta VSM \cong \Delta FMS$.

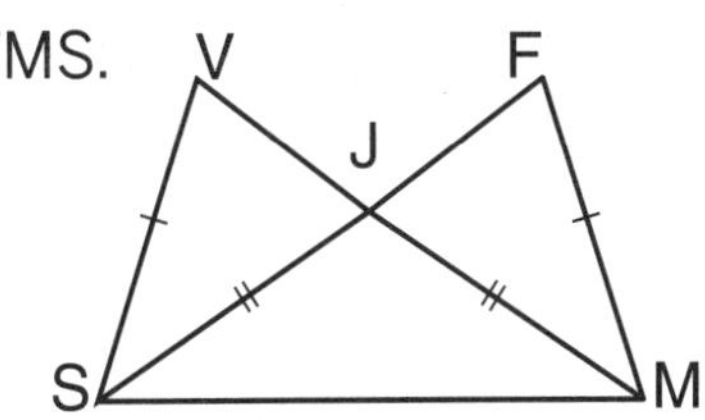

In ΔVSM and ΔFMS,

VS = FM (given)

VM = FS (given)

SM = SM (common side)

$\Delta VSM \cong \Delta FMS$ (By SSS congruence)

Side–Angle–Side (SAS)

Two triangles are congruent if two sides and the included angle of one triangle are equal to two sides and the included angle of the other triangle.

> **Note**
>
> 'Included Angle' means the angle formed by the sides of a triangle which are congruent to sides of the other triangle.

This criteria is called side–angle–side (or SAS) criteria for checking whether two triangles are congruent or not.

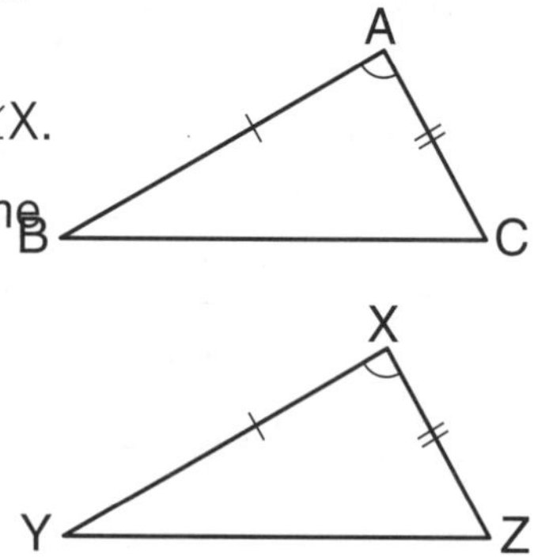

Construct two triangles ABC and XYZ such that AB = XY, AC = XZ, and ∠A = ∠X.

Use a tracing paper to check whether the two triangles coincide on superimposing

If they coincide, then ΔABC ≅ ΔXYZ (by SAS congruence) and the other three pairs of corresponding elements are equal too, i.e.,
BC = YZ, ∠B = ∠Y and ∠C = ∠Z.

Example 4: In the figure, M is the midpoint of PR and LN. Show that LP = RN and LP || RN.

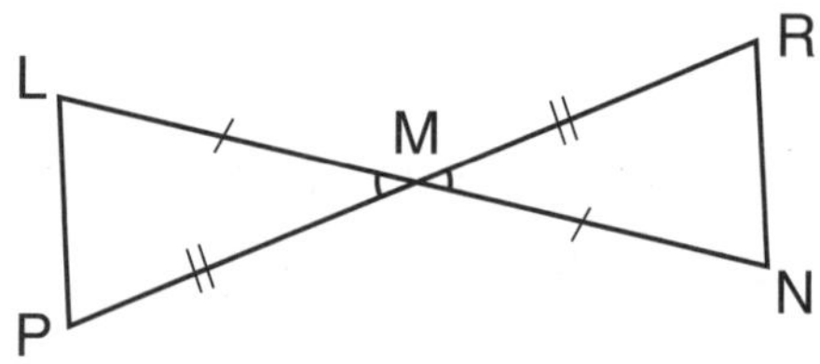

In ΔLMP and ΔNMR,

LM = MN (M is the midpoint of LN)

PM = MR (M is the midpoint of PR)

∠LMP = ∠NMR (Vertically opposite angles)

ΔLMP ≅ ΔNMR (By SAS congruence criterion)

∴ LP = RN (Corresponding parts of congruent triangles are equal)

And ∠PLM = ∠RNM (CPCT)

The lines LP and RN are intersected by the transversal PR and ∠PLM = ∠RNM, which are alternate angles. Therefore, LP || RN.

Angle–Side–Angle (ASA)

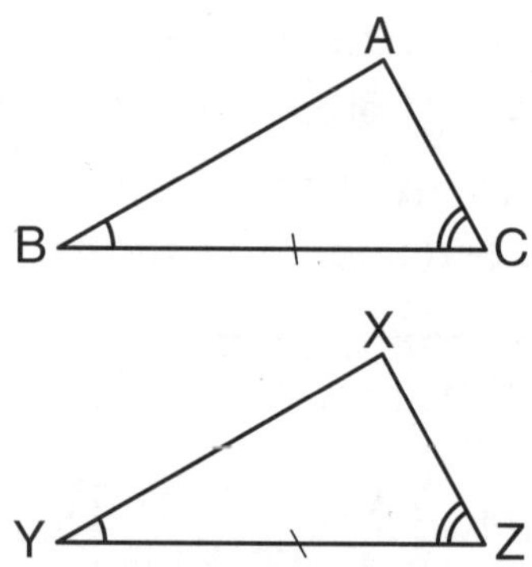

Two triangles are congruent if two angles and the included side of one triangle are equal to two angles and the included side of the other triangle.

This criteria is called angle–side–angle (or ASA) criteria for checking whether two triangles are congruent or not.

Construct two triangles ABC and XYZ such that ∠B = ∠Y, ∠C = ∠Z and BC = YZ.

Use a tracing paper to check whether the two triangles coincide on superimposing.

If they coincide, then ΔABC ≅ ΔXYZ (by ASA congruence) and the other three pairs of corresponding elements are equal too, i.e., AB = XY, AC = XZ and ∠A = ∠X.

Example 5: In the figure, the diagonal SA of the quadrilateral STAR bisects the angles S and A. Show that SR = ST and RA = TA.

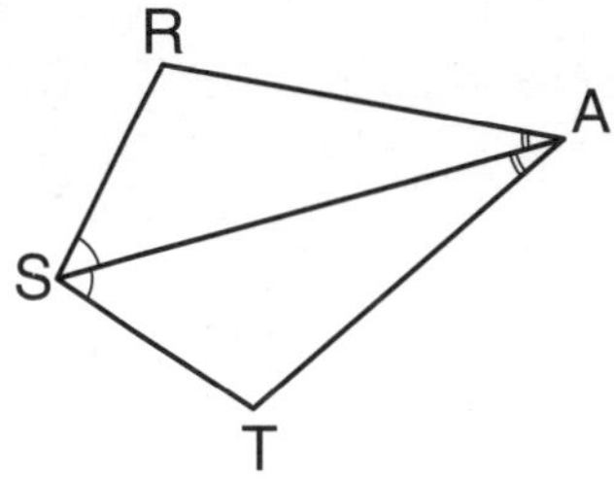

As the diagonal SA bisects $\angle S$ and $\angle A$,

$\angle TSA = \angle RSA$ and $\angle RAS = \angle TAS$

In ΔSRA and ΔSTA,

$\angle TSA = \angle RSA$ (given)

$\angle RAS = \angle TAS$ (given)

SA = SA (common side)

$\Delta SRA \cong \Delta STA$. (By ASA congruence criterion)

$\therefore$ SR = ST and RA = TA (CPCT)

Note

CPCT is the abbreviation for 'corresponding parts of congruent triangle'.

Angle–Angle–Side (AAS)

Two triangles are congruent if two angles and a non-included side of one triangle are equal to two angles and a non-included side of the other triangle.

This criteria is called angle–angle–side (or AAS) criteria for checking whether two triangles are congruent or not.

Construct two triangles ABC and XYZ such that $\angle A = \angle X$, $\angle B = \angle Y$ and BC = YZ.

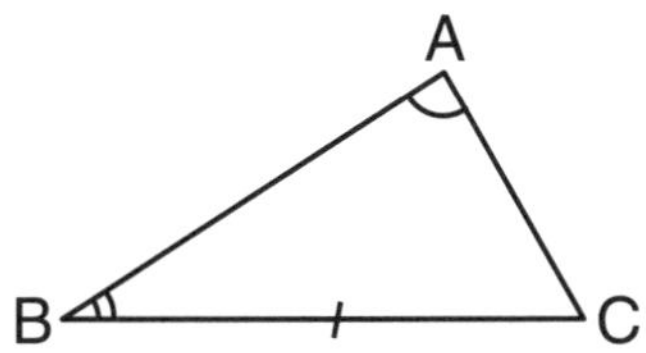

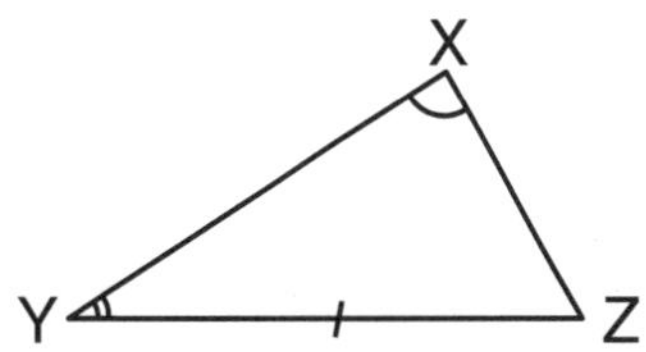

Use a tracing paper to check whether the two triangles coincide on superimposing.

If they coincide, then $\Delta ABC \cong \Delta XYZ$ (by AAS congruence) and the three pairs of corresponding elements are equal too, i.e., AB = XY, AC = XZ and $\angle C = \angle Z$.

The congruence criterion ASA is equivalent to AAS.

If the given side is not the included side, then will the triangles be congruent? For example, consider the triangle PQR in which $\angle PRQ = 75°$, $\angle PQR = 35°$ and PQ = 5 cm, which is not the included side. Since we know two angles, we can calculate the third angle using angle sum property, i.e., $\angle RPQ = 180° - (75° + 35°) = 70°$. Then, PQ becomes the included side for angles P and Q.

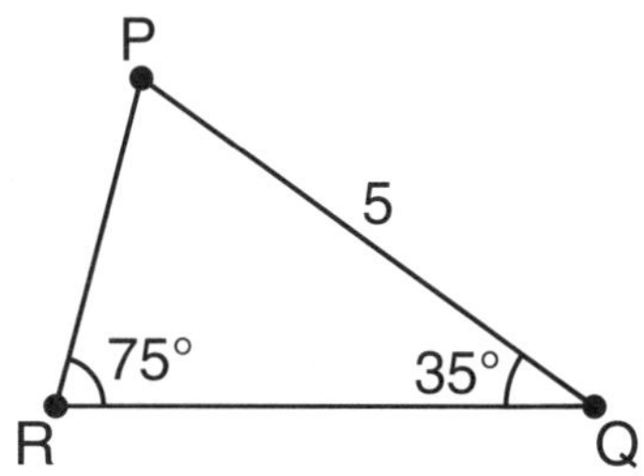

If two angles of one triangle are equal to two angles of another triangle, then the third angle will be equal as well.

Therefore, ASA and AAS criteria for congruence are equivalent.

Example 6: In the figure, $p \parallel q$. Z is the midpoint of GO. Show that Z is also the midpoint of IN.

In ΔGZN and ΔOZI,

∠ZNG = ∠ZIO (alternate angles)

∠GZN = ∠OZI (vertically opposite angles)

GZ = OZ (given)

So, by AAS congruence criterion, ΔGZN ≅ ΔOZI.

Therefore, ZN = ZI (CPCT)

Therefore, Z is also the midpoint of IN.

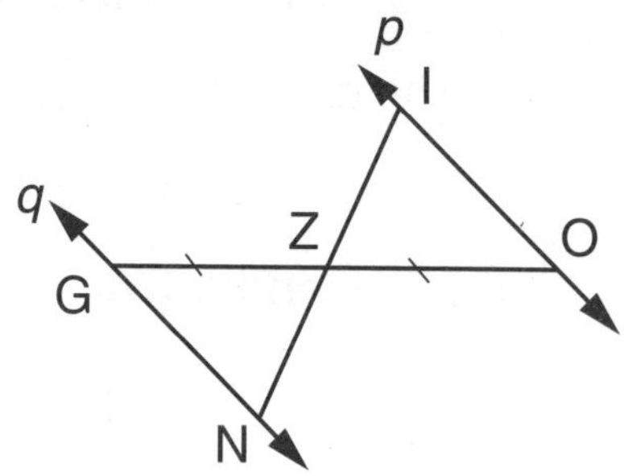

Right Angle–Hypotenuse–Side (RHS)

Two right triangles are congruent if the hypotenuse and one side of one triangle are equal to the hypotenuse and one side of the other triangle.

This criteria is called the right angle–hypotenuse–side (or RHS) criteria for checking whether two triangles are congruent or not.

Construct two right triangles ABC and XYZ such that
∠B = ∠Y = 90°, hypotenuse AC = hypotenuse XZ and BC = YZ.

Use a tracing paper to check whether the two triangles superimpose on each other.

If they superimpose, then ΔABC ≅ ΔXYZ (by RHS congruence) and the three pairs of corresponding elements are equal, i.e., AB = XY, ∠C = ∠Z and ∠A = ∠X.

Example 7: Triangle UVW is an isosceles triangle in which UV = UW. Show that the altitude UP bisects VW.

In the right triangles UPV and UPW,

Angle UPV=Angle UPW (UP is the altitude). UV = UW (given)

UP = UP (common side)

ΔUPV ≅ ΔUPW So, (by RHS congruence criterion)

Therefore, VP = PW (CPCT)

Thus, the altitude UP bisects VW.

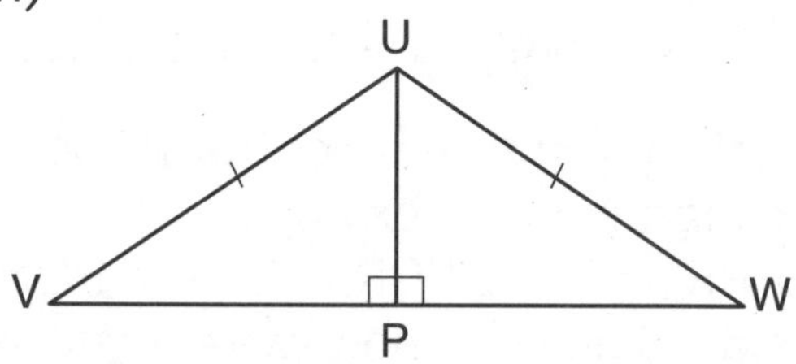

Why the AAA (Angle–Angle–Angle) Criteria is Not Used to Check Congruency

Look at the following figures of triangles.

Observe that the triangles in figures a. and b. have equal angles.

Are these groups of triangles congruent?

a.

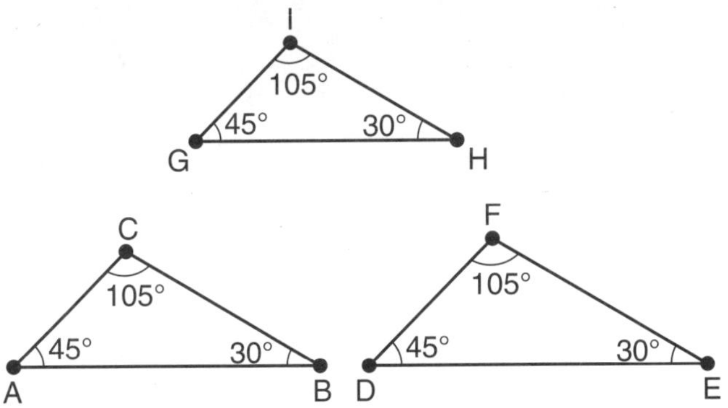

b.

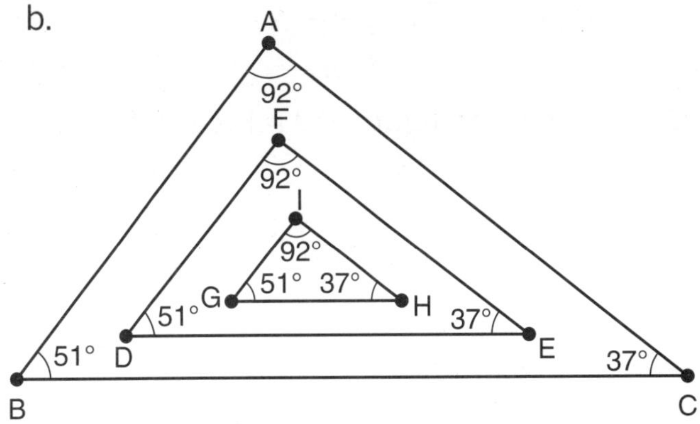

By observation, you can say that they are not congruent. If you place them one over the other they will not coincide .

Therefore, even if all the three angles of one triangle are equal to the three angles of another triangle, they need not be congruent.

Therefore, AAA (angle–angle–angle) criteria cannot be used to check the congruency of triangles.

Exercise 18.2

1 Write the congruence relation between triangles given below and also write the congruence criteria.

a.

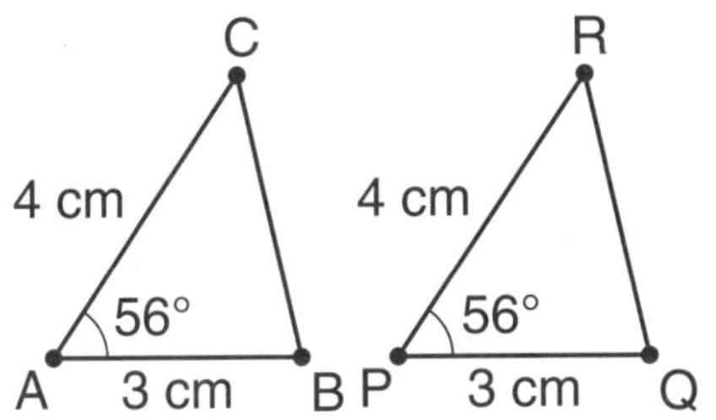

b.

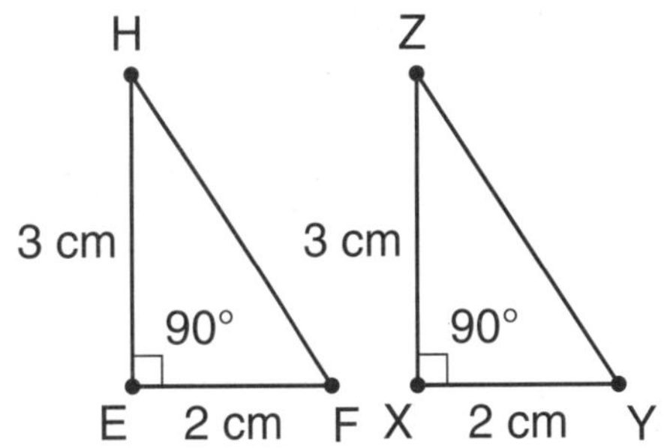

c.

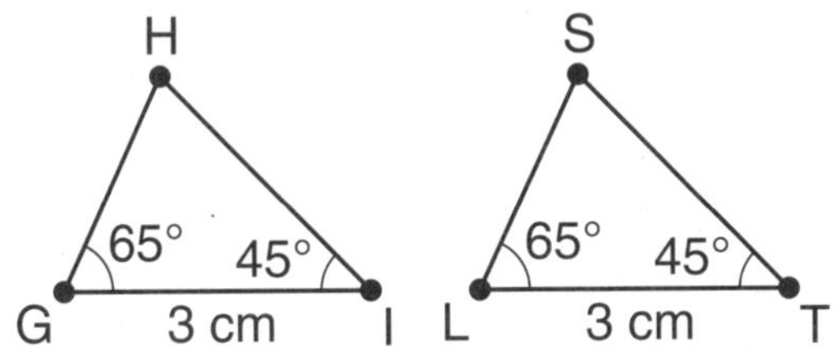

d.

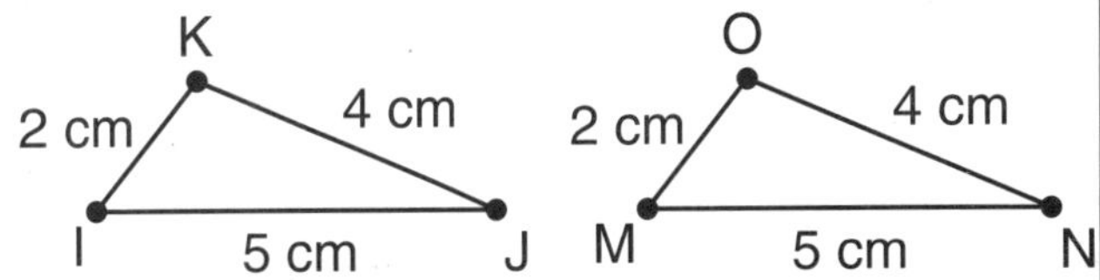

2 In the given figure, PQ || TS and PR = RS. Is $\Delta PQR \cong \Delta RST$? If not, find the correct congruence relation and write it using symbols.

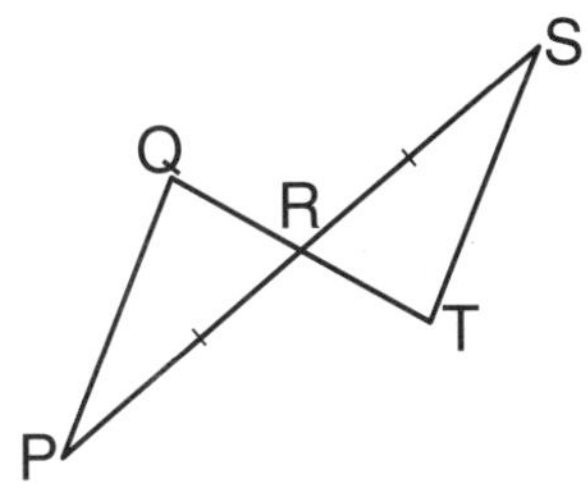

3 In the given figure, MP = MQ. MR is the bisector of $\angle PMQ$. Prove that $\Delta MPR \cong \Delta MQR$. Is $\angle P = \angle Q$?

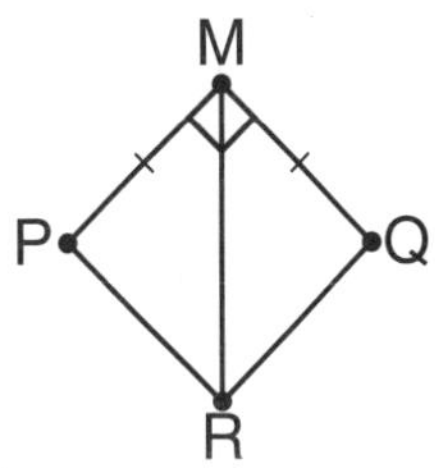

4. Find the triangles that are congruent in the given figure.

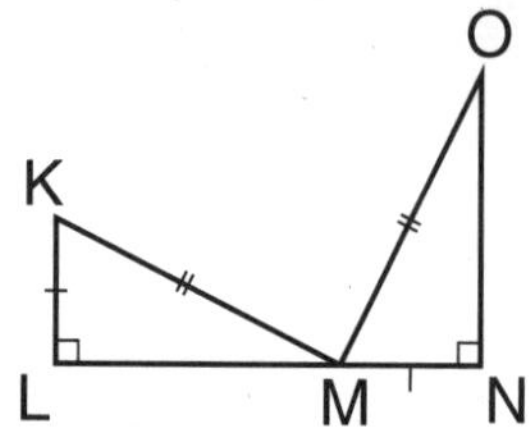

5. In the given figure, PQ = PR and S is the midpoint of QR. Is $\Delta PQS \cong \Delta PRS$? If so, prove it using any congruence criteria. Also, write the corresponding parts.

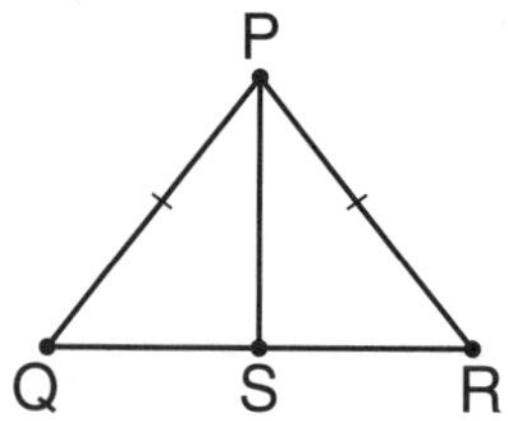

6. In the given figure, AB || CD, AB = CD and $\Delta AOB \cong \Delta DOC$. Prove that $AO = \frac{1}{2}AD$ and BC = 2OC.

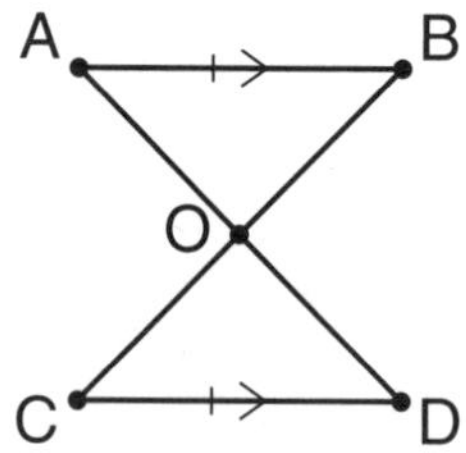

Summary

Congruence

- Two figures of the same size and the same shape are said to be congruent.
- Congruence of 3D objects

- Congruence of Plane figures
  - Line segments (Same length)
  - Angles (Same angle measure)
  - Triangles (Same sides and same angles)
    - Criteria
      - **SSS**: If three sides of one triangle are equal to the corresponding three sides of another triangle, then the two triangles are congruent.
      - **SAS**: If two sides and the included angle of one triangle are equal to the corresponding two sides and the included angle of another triangle, then the two triangles are congruent.
      - **ASA**: If two angles and the included side of one triangle are equal to the corresponding two angles and the included side of another triangle, then the two triangles are congruent.
      - **RHS**: If the hypotenuse and one side of a right-angled triangle are equal to the corresponding hypotenuse and one side of another right-angled triangle, then the triangles are congruent.

Revision Exercise

1 Choose the correct options.

a. The two given figures are

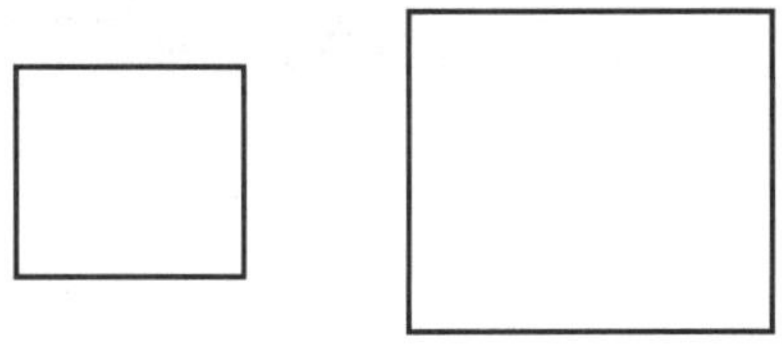

i. congruent because they are squares.
ii. not congruent because they are not rectangles.
iii. not congruent because they are not identical.
iv. congruent because they are geometrical shapes.

b. If ΔHNG is congruent to ΔSTV, then

i. $HN = TV$, $NG = ST$, $GH = VS$
ii. $HN = ST$, $NG = VS$, $GH = TV$
iii. $HN = ST$, $NG = TV$, $GH = VS$
iv. None of the above

c. $\angle X \cong \angle Y$. This symbol means

i. $\angle X$ is equal to $\angle Y$.
ii. $\angle X$ is congruent to $\angle Y$.
iii. $\angle X$ is equal to $\angle Y$ but not congruent.
iv. $\angle X$ is congruent to $\angle Y$ but not equal.

d. If we keep two congruent figures one over the other,

i. one will not cover the other completely.
ii. they will overlap each other exactly.
iii. one will be bigger than the other.
iv. they will be similar in shape.

2 Show that ΔLMN is isosceles if the median LD is perpendicular to the base MN.

3 In ΔABC and ΔPQR shown below, $AB = PQ$, $BC = QR$, CB and RQ are extended to X and Y respectively, and $\angle ABX = \angle PQY$. Show that $\Delta ABC \cong \Delta PQR$.

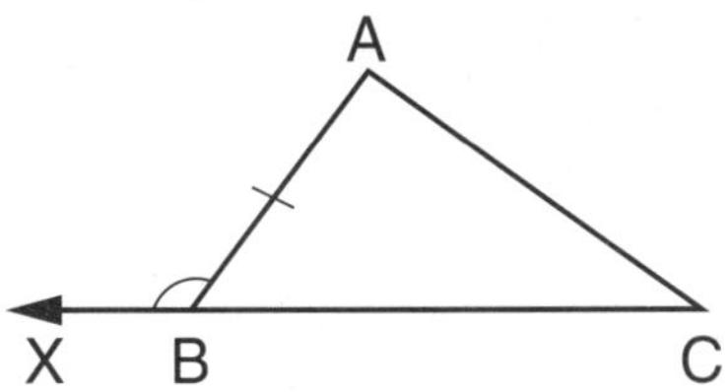

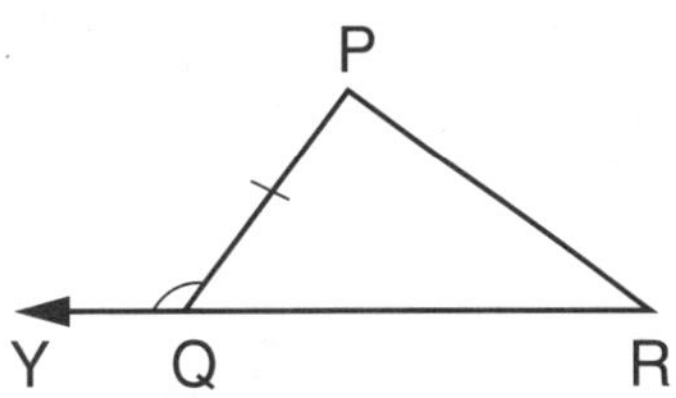

4 In the given figure, $\angle CPD = \angle BPD$. AD is the bisector of $\angle BAC$. Show that $\Delta CAP \cong \Delta BAP$ and hence, $CP = BP$.

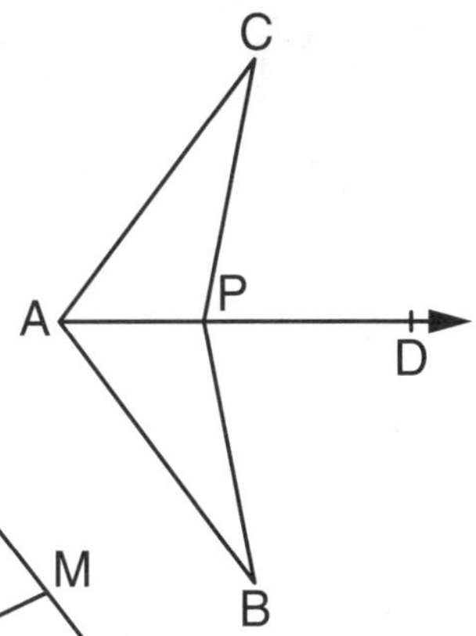

5 The altitudes UM, NH and SP of ΔSUN are equal. Prove that ΔSUN is an equilateral triangle.

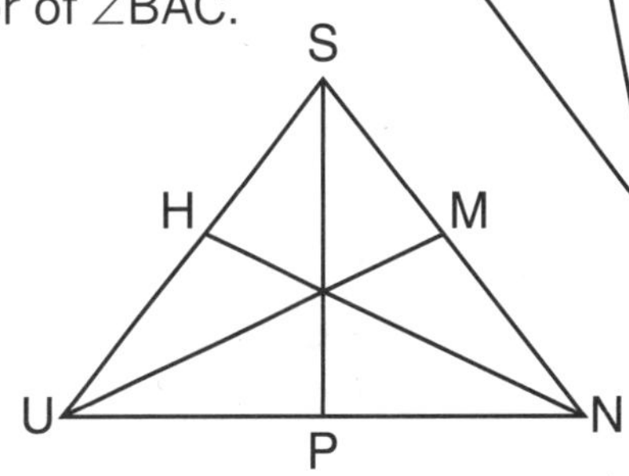

For the Curious Mind

1. Is it possible to construct a unique right-angled triangle when only the hypotenuse is given? Justify your answer.
2. The length of the side of each square in the following figure is 1 unit. How many congruent squares can you find in the following figure?

THEME 4

Constructions 19

What I shall learn

- To construct a line parallel to a given line through a point outside it
- To construct triangles using SSS, SAS, ASA and RHS criteria

Let's Get Started

In this chapter, let us learn how to construct a line parallel to a given line and to construct triangles when different dimensions are known.

We know that **two or more lines are said to be parallel if they do not intersect at any point on the plane. It follows that the perpendicular distance between any two points on the lines remains the same.**

Here are a few real-life examples of parallel lines. Collect more examples of similar kind.

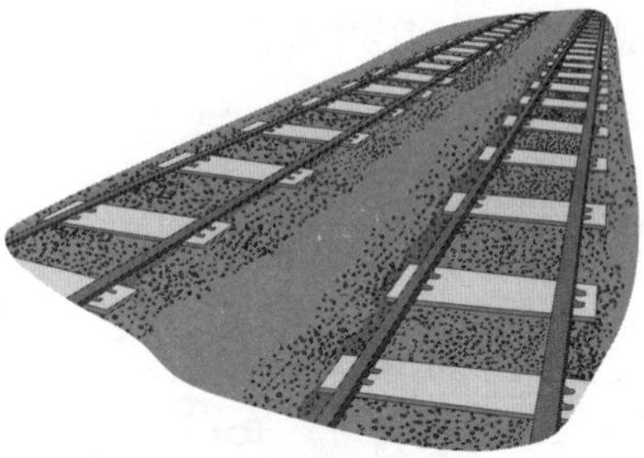

Railway tracks

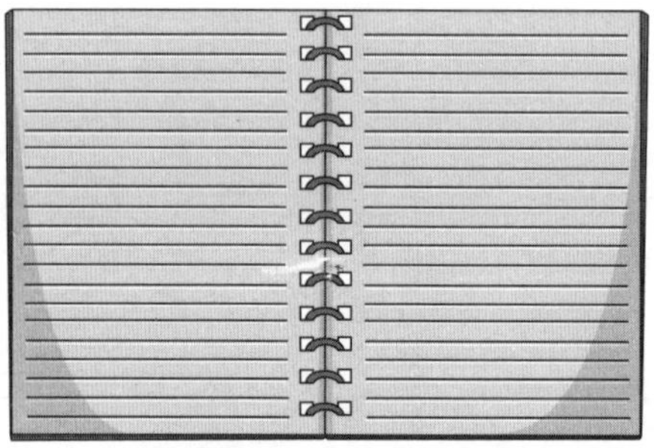

Lines on a notebook

Dividers between bowling tracks

Let us recall the properties of parallel lines and a transversal. Let *l* and *m* be two parallel lines intersected by a transversal. Then,

(a) Pairs of corresponding angles are equal.
($\angle 1 = \angle 5$; $\angle 4 = \angle 8$; $\angle 2 = \angle 6$ and $\angle 3 = \angle 7$)

(b) Pairs of alternate interior angles are equal.
($\angle 4 = \angle 6$ and $\angle 3 = \angle 5$)

(c) Interior angles on the same side of the transversal are supplementary.
($\angle 4 + \angle 5 = 180°$ and $\angle 3 + \angle 6 = 180°$)

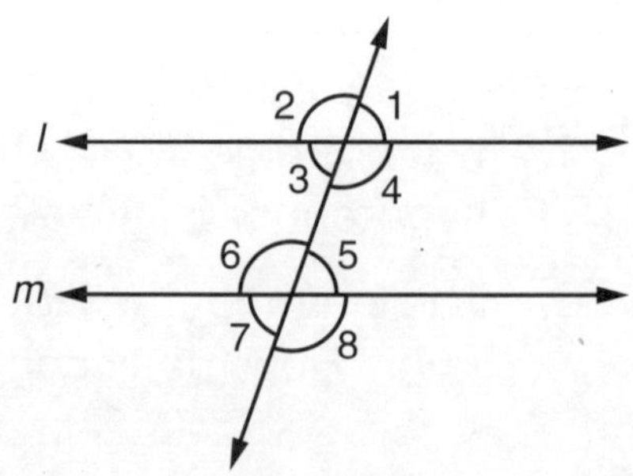

Construction of a Line Parallel to a given Line through a Point Outside it

We will use one of the above properties to construct parallel lines.

Step 1: A line *l* and a point X, not on it are given.

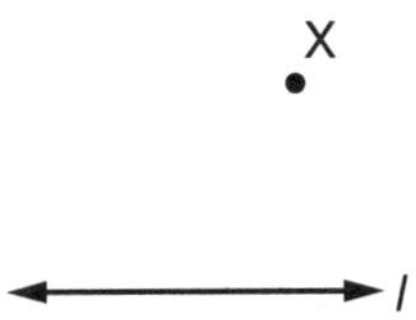

Step 2: Mark a point Y on line *l*.

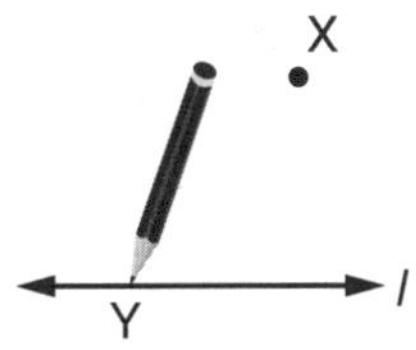

Step 3: Join X and Y using a ruler.

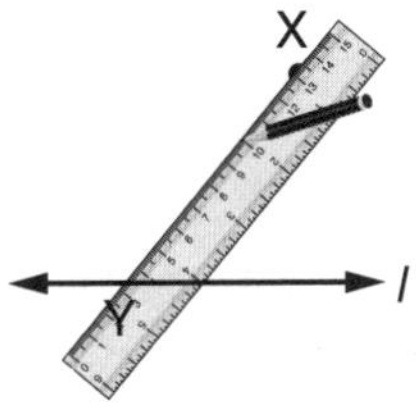

Step 4: Draw an arc with Y as the centre and any radius cutting line *l* at M and line segment $\overline{XY}$ at N.

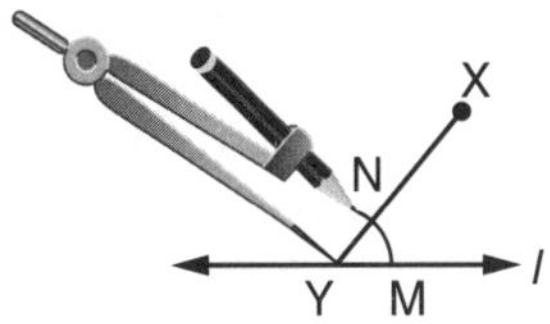

Step 5: With X as centre and with the same radius, draw an arc AB cutting $\overline{XY}$ at O.

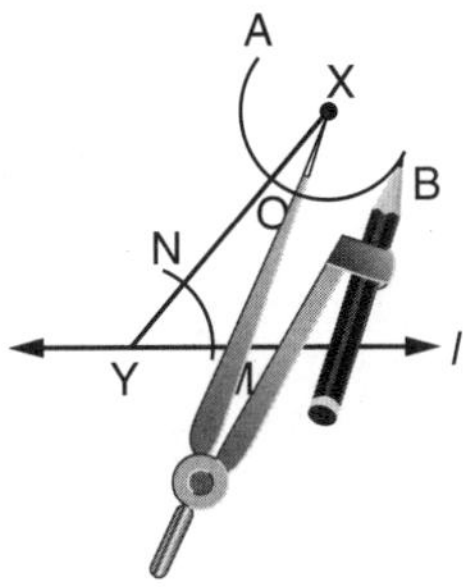

Step 6: Keeping the pointed tip of the compass at N, adjust the width such that the opening is at M.

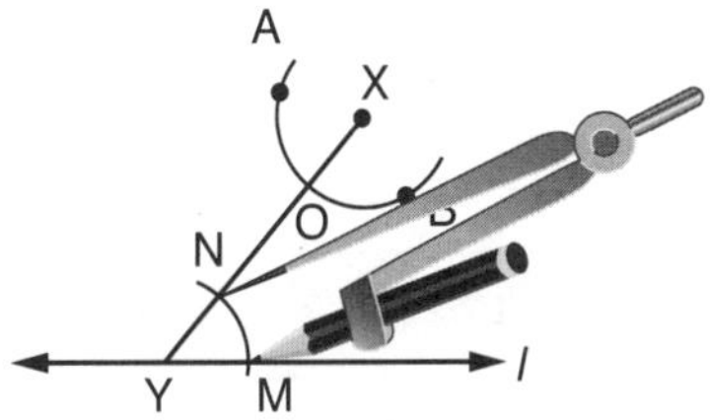

Step 7: With this radius and O as centre, draw an arc cutting arc AB at P.

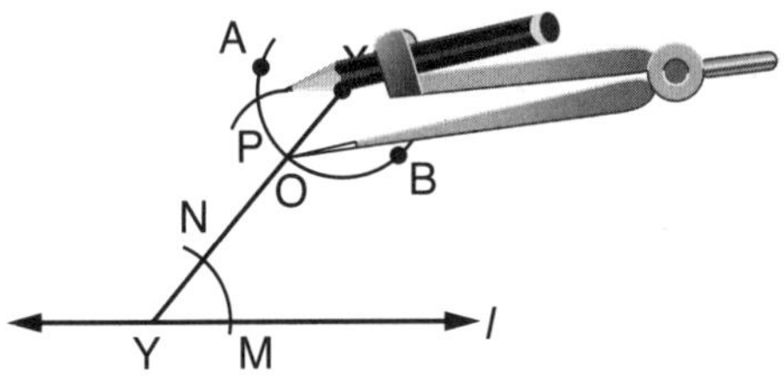

Step 8: Join P and X to get the required parallel line *m*.

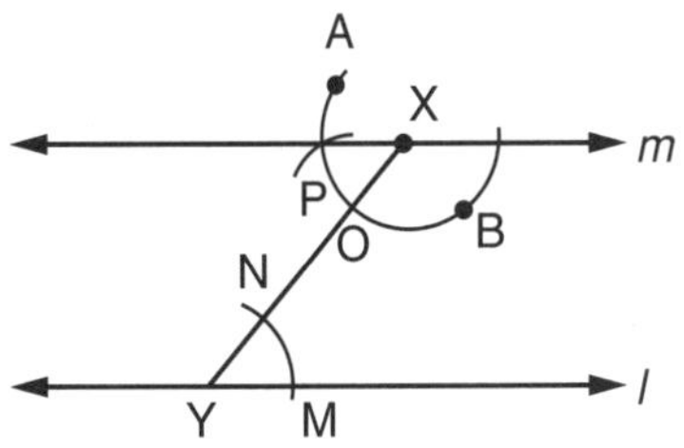

Verify whether the lines *l* and *m* are parallel or not using the set squares. Which property of parallel lines has been used in this construction and in which steps?

Solved Example:

Construct a line parallel to line *l* through a point which is at a distance of 5 cm from the given line.

Step 1: A line *l* is given.

Step 2: Consider any point outside the line *l* and construct a perpendicular line to it.

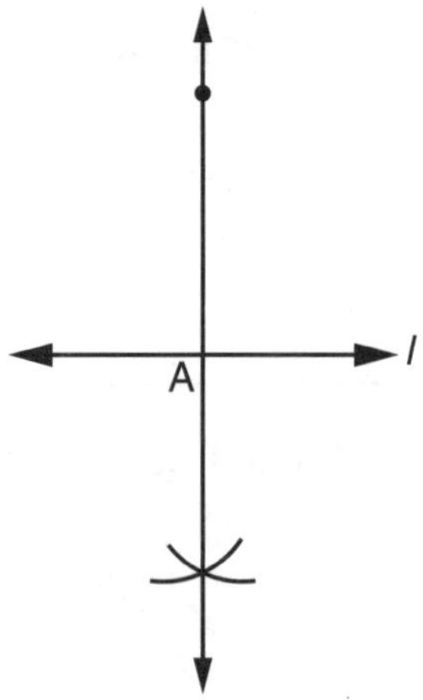

Step 3: Take a ruler and compass and open the compass to measure 5 cm.

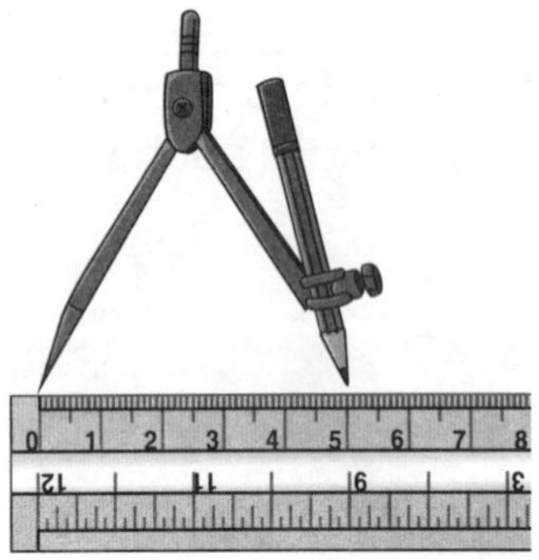

Step 4: Keeping A as a centre without changing the radius draw an arc on the perpendicular line.

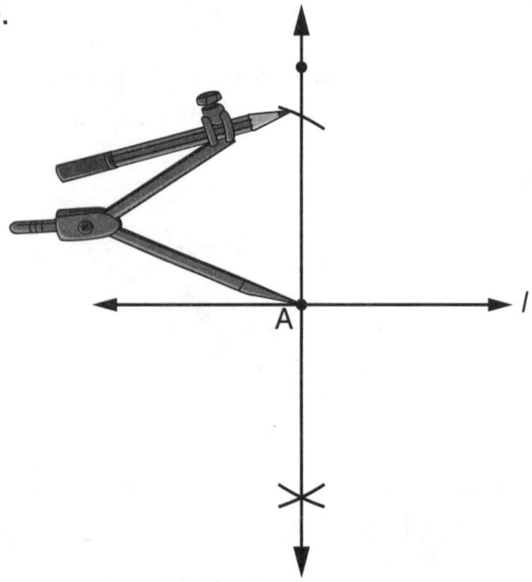

Step 5: Mark the intersection of the arc and perpendicular line as P which is the required point which is at a distance of 5 cm from the given line.

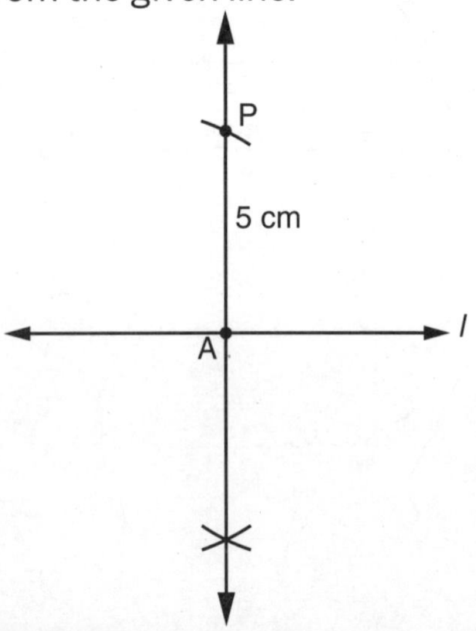

Step 6: Follow the above method and construct a parallel line to *l* passing through the point P. Line *m* is the required parallel line.

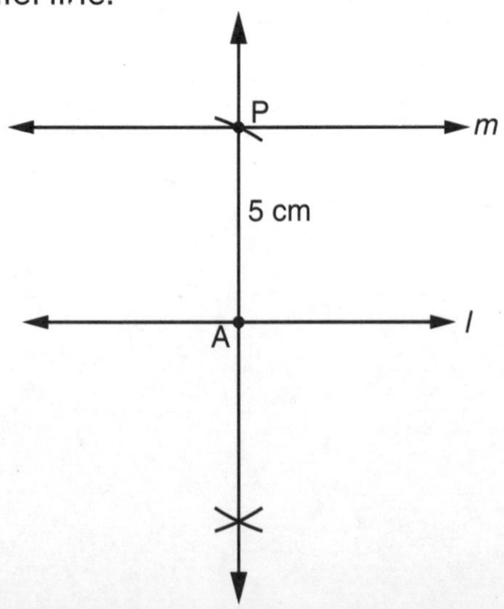

Construction of Triangles

We know that there are 6 elements in a triangle. Then how many measurements do we require to construct a triangle? Take two sticks and try to form a triangle. Is it possible? Take three sticks and try to form a triangle. Can you form a triangle now? You can observe that a minimum of three measurements are required to construct a triangle. Let us learn about the different criteria for construction of triangles.

Constructing a Triangle When Three Sides Are Given (SSS Construction)

With the help of an example, let us see how to construct a triangle using a ruler and a compass when the lengths of the three sides are known.

Example 1: Construct a triangle whose side lengths are 6 cm, 4 cm and 3 cm.

Hints and Tips

In SSS construction, it is convenient to start the construction by drawing the longest side first.

Step 1: Draw a rough sketch of the triangle.

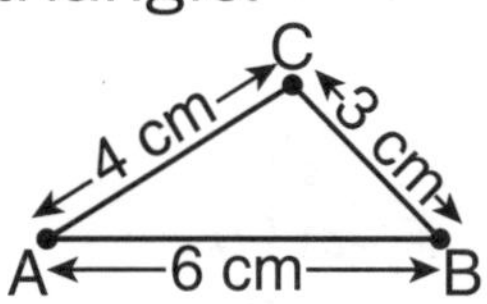

Step 2: Draw a line segment AB of length 6 cm.

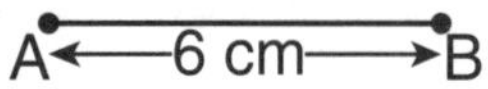

Step 3: With A as centre and 4 cm as radius, draw an arc on one side of AB.

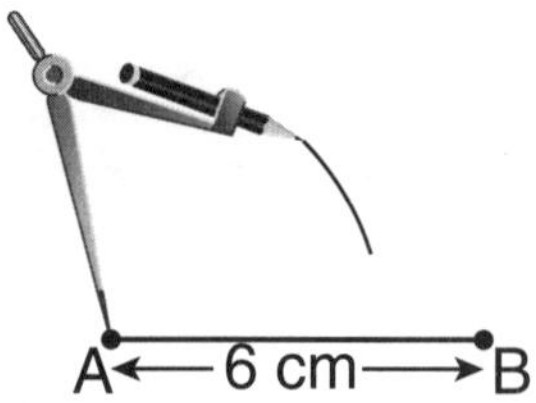

Step 4: With B as centre and 3 cm as radius, draw another arc cutting the previous arc at C.

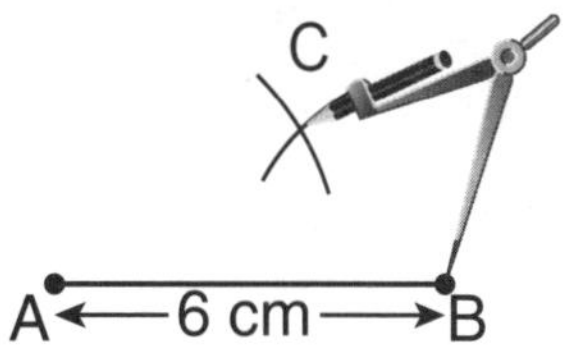

Step 5: Join A and C, and B and C to get the required triangle ABC.

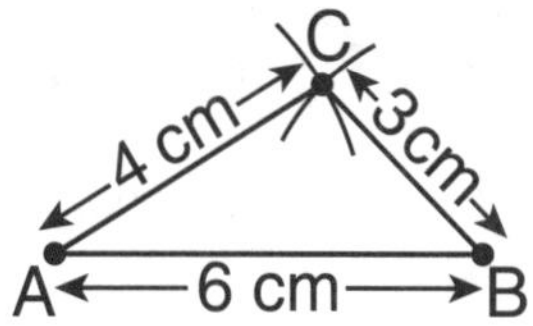

Constructing a Triangle When Two Sides and the Included Angle Are Given SAS Construction

Let us learn how to construct a triangle when the lengths of two of its sides and the angle between them are known.

Example 2: Construct a triangle ABC with AB = 5 cm, AC = 3 cm and ∠BAC = 60°.

Step 1: Draw a rough sketch of the triangle.

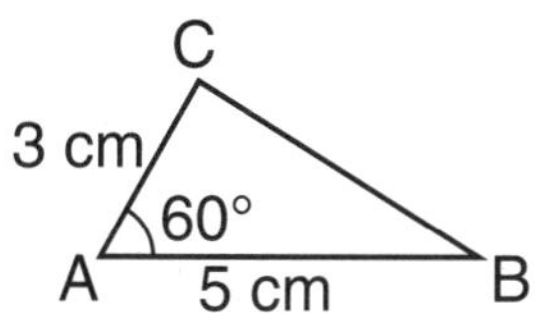

Step 2: Draw a line segment AB of length 5 cm.

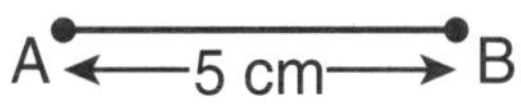

Step 3: Using a compass, draw a ray AX such that ∠XAB = 60°.

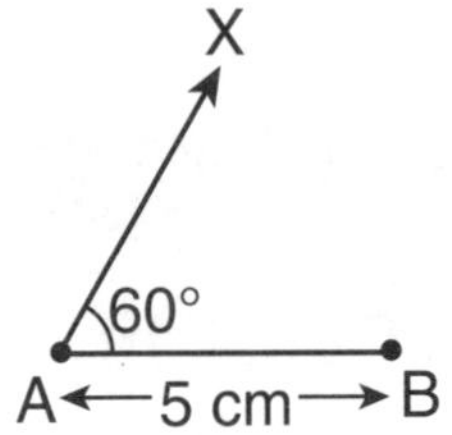

Step 4: With A as centre and 3 cm radius, draw an arc cutting ray AX at C.

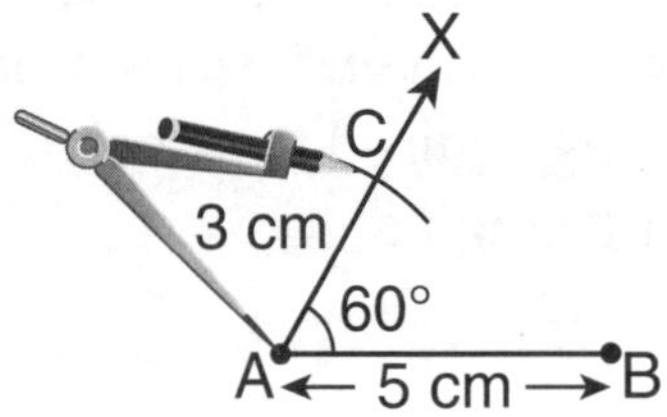

Step 5: Join B and C to get the required triangle ABC.

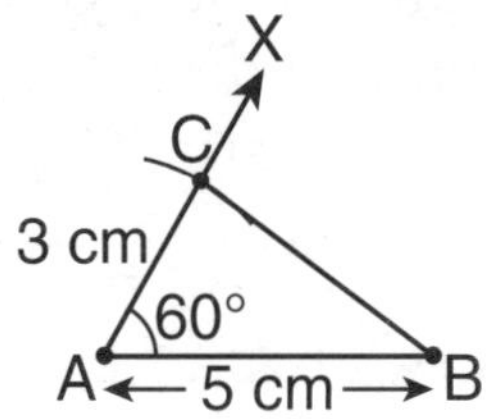

Exercise 19.1

1. Construct a triangle PQR with PQ = 5 cm, QR = 5.5 and PR = 4 cm.
2. Construct a triangle XYZ with XY = 6 cm, XZ = 8 cm and YZ = 10 cm. Name the type of triangle obtained.
3. Construct an equilateral triangle of side 6.5 cm.
4. Construct a triangle PQR with PQ = QR = 6 cm and ∠PQR = 75°.
5. Construct a triangle ABC with BC = 3.5 cm, ∠ACB = 80° and AC = 5.4 cm.

Constructing a Triangle When Two Angles and the Included Side Are Given (ASA Construction)

Let us learn how to construct a triangle when the measure of two of its angles and the length of the side between them are known.

Example 3: Construct a triangle PQR with QR = 4 cm, ∠Q = 60° and ∠R = 70°.

Step 1: Draw a rough sketch of the triangle.

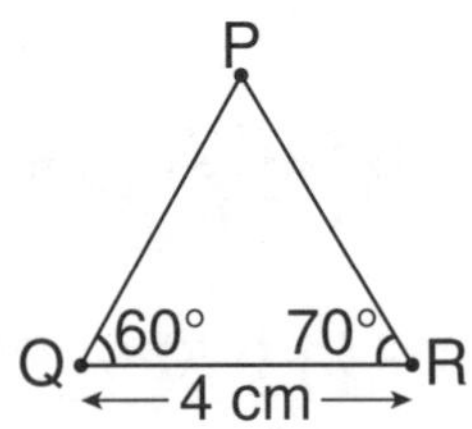

Step 2: Draw the line segment QR of length 4 cm.

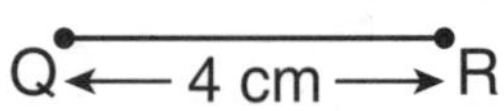

Step 3: Using a protractor, construct ∠Q of measure 60° at point Q.

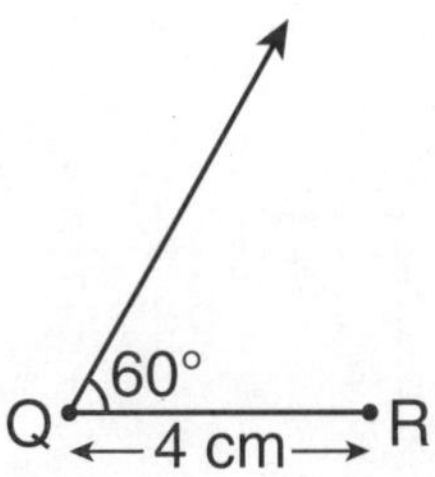

Step 4: Using a protractor, construct ∠R of measure 70° at point R.

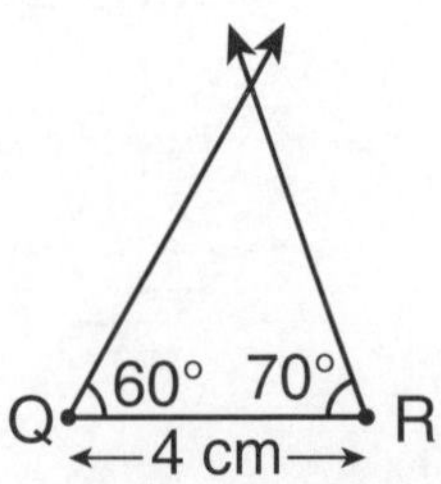

Step 5: The point of intersection is P. ΔPQR is the required triangle.

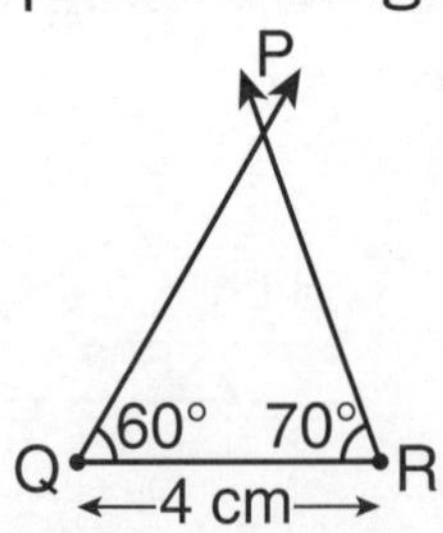

Note:

1. We have seen that while constructing a triangle with two sides and one angle, the angle known must be an included angle, otherwise, the triangle constructed will not be unique. Is it true in case of ASA also? Should the known side be the included side? Can you draw a unique triangle with the following measurements? Try drawing it in your notebook.

   Construct a ΔABC with AB = 5 cm, $\angle A = 55°$ and $\angle C = 45°$. (Hint: Use angle sum property and find the third angle.)

2. To construct an isosceles triangle, we require only two independent measurements since two sides and two opposite angles of an isosceles triangle are already equal.

3. To construct an equilateral triangle, it is enough if we know the length of only one side of the triangle because all the sides are of equal length and all the angles are 60°.

Construction of a Right-angled Triangle (RHS Criterion)

We know that in a right-angled triangle, one of the angles is 90°. If we know the length of the sides that make the right angle, then we can use the SAS criterion and construct the triangle. If we know the length of one of the sides that make the right angle and the measure of the angle adjacent to this side, then we can use ASA method to construct the triangle. In case of a right-angled triangle, even if the angle given is not the included angle, we can construct a unique triangle, which is not true in case of other triangles.

Example 4: Construct a right-angled triangle ABC, right angled at B with AB = 4 cm and BC = 4.5 cm.

Step 1: Draw a rough sketch of the triangle.

Step 2: Draw the line segment BC of length 4.5 cm.

Step 3: Construct $\angle B$ of measure 90° at point B.

Step 4: With B as the centre and radius 4 cm, draw an arc cutting BY at A.

Step 5: Join A and C. Δ ABC is the required right-angled triangle.

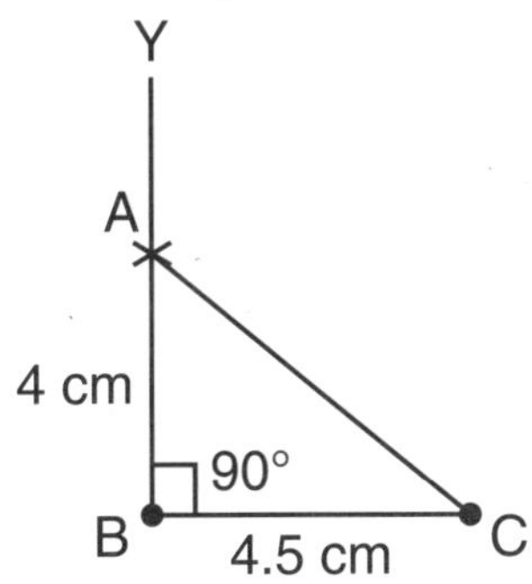

Example 5: Construct a triangle LMN with MN = 5 cm, $\angle L = 60°$ and a right angle at M.

Since one angle is 90° and the other angle is given to be 60°, we can find the third angle using the angle sum property.

$\angle L + \angle M + \angle N = 180° \Rightarrow 60° + 90° + \angle N = 180° \Rightarrow \angle N = 30°$

Therefore, we know three independent measurements—$\angle M$, MN (which is the included side) and $\angle N$. So, we can use the ASA criterion and construct the triangle.

Step 1: Draw the line segment MN of length 5 cm.

Step 2: Construct a ray at point M making an angle of 90°.

Step 3: Construct a ray at point N making an angle of 30°.

Step 4: Mark the intersection point of the two rays as L.

Step 5: ΔLMN is the required triangle. Measure ∠L and verify whether it is 60°.

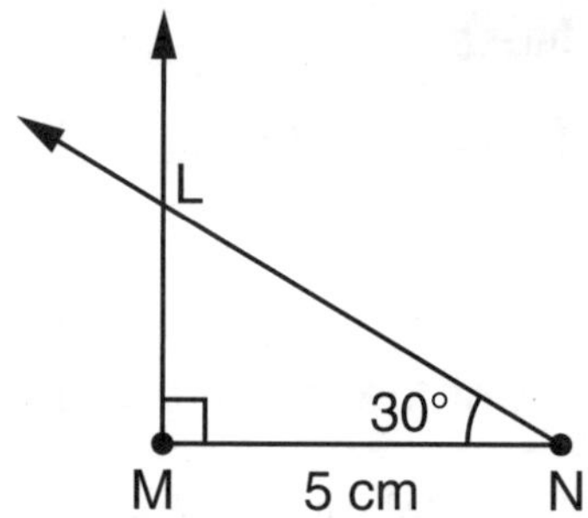

Cases Where Constructing Unique Triangles Is Not Possible

Case I: When Only the Measures of the Three Angles Are Given

Construct a triangle ABC with ∠A = 75°, ∠B = 65° and ∠C = 40° on a patty paper with any convenient side lengths. Take the triangles constructed by your friends and coincide with your triangle. You will observe that the triangles constructed by all of you are not the same.

Hence, we cannot construct a unique triangle even if all the angles of the triangle are known.

The following diagram illustrates this. There are many triangles, ΔABC, ΔA_2BC_2, ΔA_3BC_3, ΔA_4BC_4 and so on which have the same angle measurements.

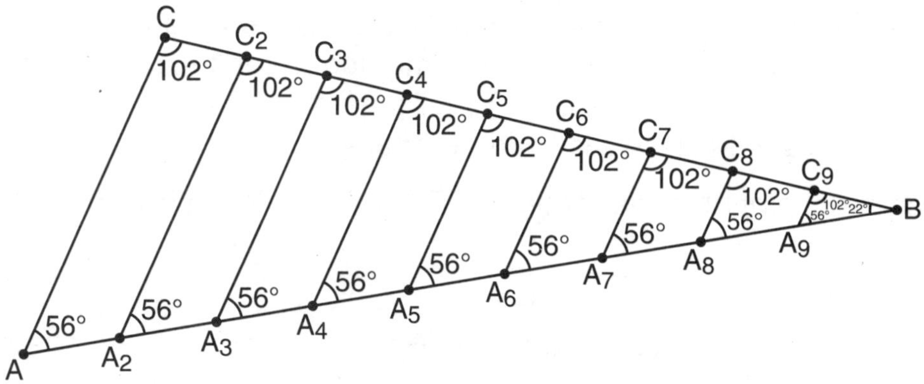

Why are we not able to construct a unique triangle in this case?

This is because even if only two angles are given, the third angle can be calculated using the angle sum property. So, it is same as knowing only two independent measurements and we know that to construct a triangle, we need a minimum of three independent measurements.

Case II: When Only Two Sides and an Angle Other Than the Included Angle Are Given

Example 6: Construct a triangle ABC with AB = 4.3 cm, BC = 4.5 cm and ∠BCA = 60°.

Steps of construction:

1. Draw BC = 4.5 cm.
2. Construct ∠BCM = 60°.
3. Since AB = 4.3 cm, so draw an arc with B as the centre and radius of 4.3 cm. We find that the arc intersects ray CY at two points, both of which can be point A.

Therefore, we get two different triangles A_1BC and A_2BC with the given information. So, we cannot get a unique triangle in this case.

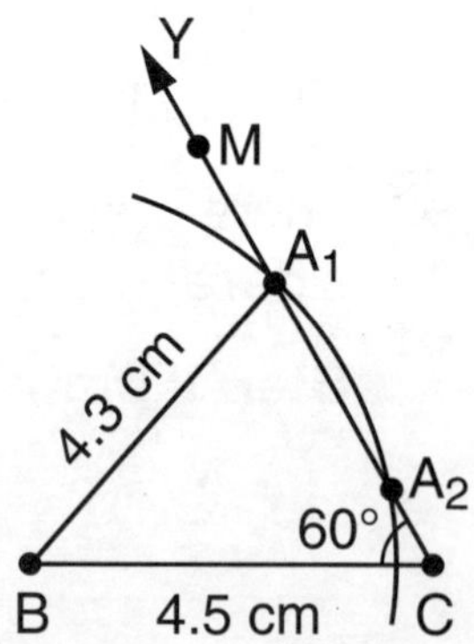

Now, observe the following.

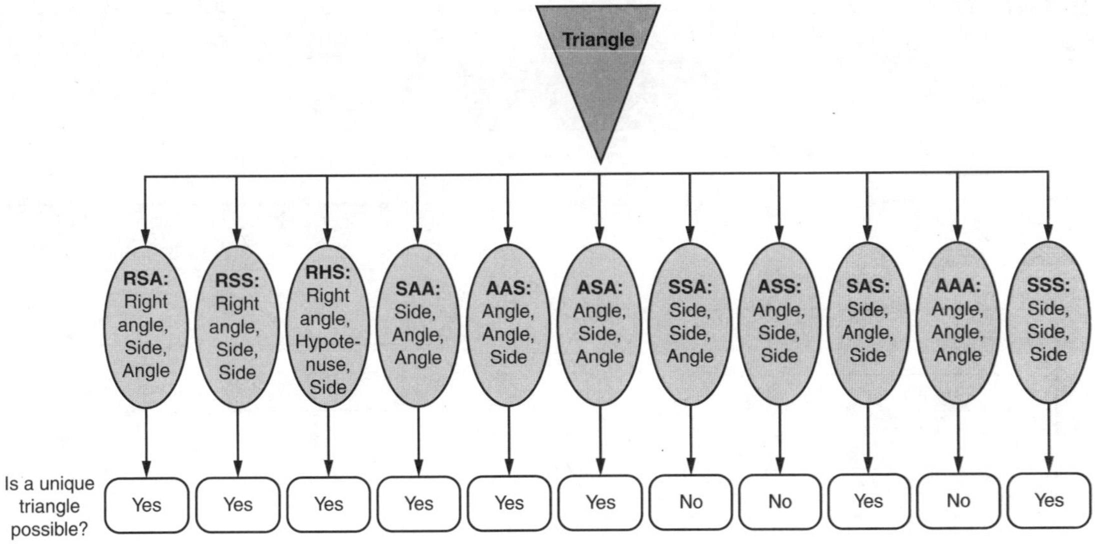

Exercise 19.2

1. Construct a triangle ABC with AB = 3 cm, ∠B = 80° and ∠C = 50°.
2. Construct a triangle PQR with PQ = 5.5 cm, ∠P = 110° and ∠Q = 40°.
3. Construct a right-angled triangle PQR with PQ = 5 cm, QR = 13 cm and a right angle at P.
4. Construct a right-angled triangle ABC with AB = 6 cm, AC = 5 cm and a right angle at A.

Summary

Construction

- of **Triangles**, when
  - Three sides are given (SSS)

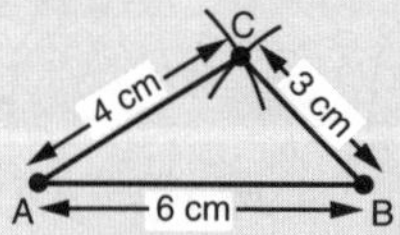

  - Two sides and the included angle are given (SAS)

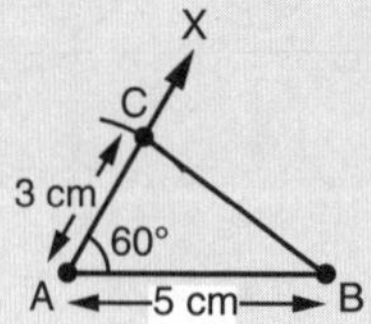

  - Two angles and a side are given (ASA/AAS/SAA)

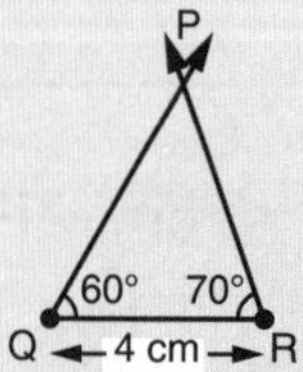

  - Hypotenuse and one side of a right-angled triangle are given (RHS)

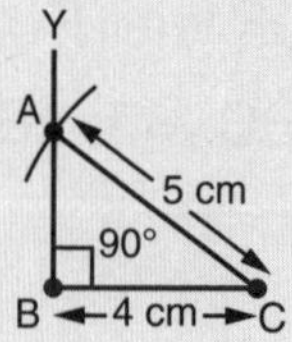

  - Two sides of a right-angled triangle are given (RSS)

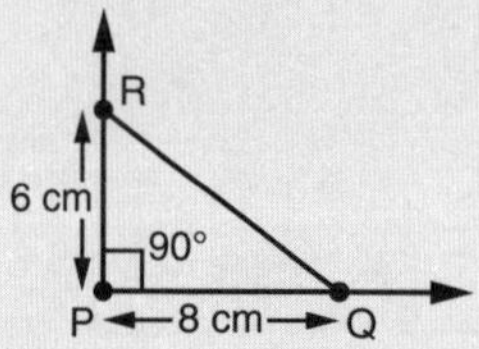

  - One side and one angle of a right-angled triangle are given (RSA)

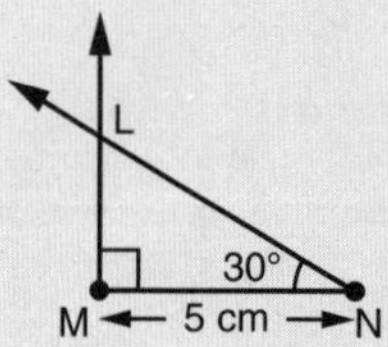

- of **Line parallel to a given line through a point outside the given line**
  - Using **Paper folding**

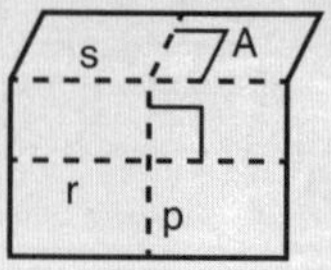

  - Using **Ruler and Compass**

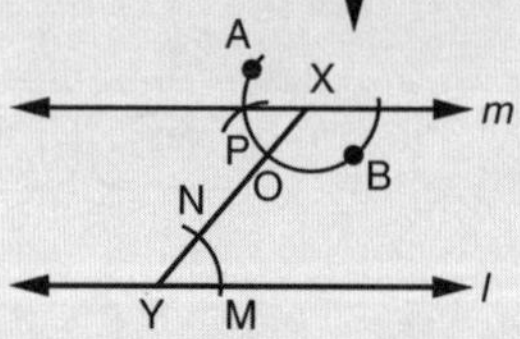

Revision Exercise

1 Construct a line *m* parallel to a given line *l* through a point P not on the given line using a ruler and compass. Construct another line *n* parallel to the line *m* passing through a point Q not on the line. Will the first line *l* be parallel to the third line *n*? Justify your answer.

2 Construct a line parallel to the given line through a point outside it using the property that states 'corresponding angles are equal'. Write the steps of construction.

3 **Take a bundle of sticks of the lengths shown below. Identify the maximum number of triangles that can be constructed with these sticks and write their measurements.**

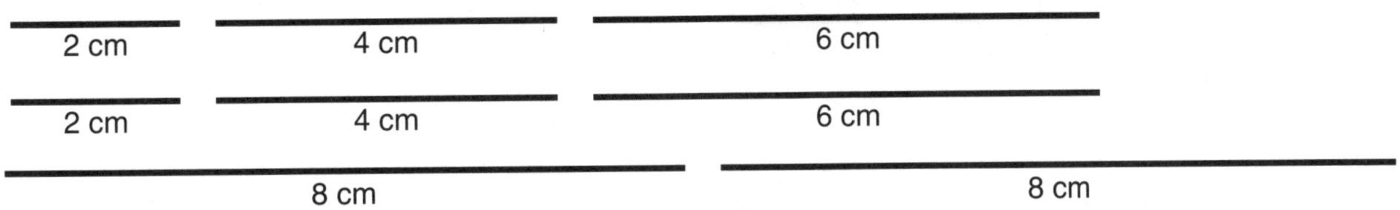

4 Is it possible to construct a triangle ABC with $\overline{BC} = 9$ cm, $\overline{AC} = 5$ cm and $\angle B = 40°$? Justify your answer with a diagram.

5 **Identify the minimum number of measurements required to construct the following triangles. Draw their rough sketches and label the measurements.**

a. Equilateral triangle
b. Isosceles triangle
c. Right-angled triangle
d. Obtuse-angled triangle

6 **Choose the correct answers for the following questions.**

(a) Which of the following measures form a unique right-angled triangle?

(i) Triangle ABC with $\angle B = 90°$, $\overline{BC} = 5$ cm and $\overline{CA} = 8$ cm

(ii) Triangle ABC with $\angle B = 90°$ and $\overline{CA} = 7$ cm

(iii) Both (i) and (ii)

(iv) Triangle ABC with $\angle B = 90°$, $\overline{BC} = 5$ cm and $\angle C = 60°$

(v) Both (i) and (iv)

(b) A unique right-angled triangle can't be constructed when

(i) two side lengths are given
(ii) one side length and hypotenuse are given

(iii) the length of the base having right angle and the other base angle are given

(iv) two angles apart from the right angle are given

7. Construct a right-angled isosceles triangle, whose equal sides measure 6.3 cm each.

8. **Construct the following triangles.**

   a. ΔABC with AB = 5 cm, BC = 5.5 cm and AC = 7 cm

   b. ΔPQR with PQ = 6.5 cm, $\angle P = 65°$ and Q = 75°

   c. ΔXYZ with XY = 5 cm, YZ = 6.5 cm and a right angle at Y

   d. ΔPQR with PQ = 4.5 cm, $\angle P = 60°$ and PR = 5.5 cm

For the Curious Mind

Construct the triangles ABC and DCE using the ASA criteria by finding the measurements required from the given figure. CD is the angle bisector of $\angle ACE$.

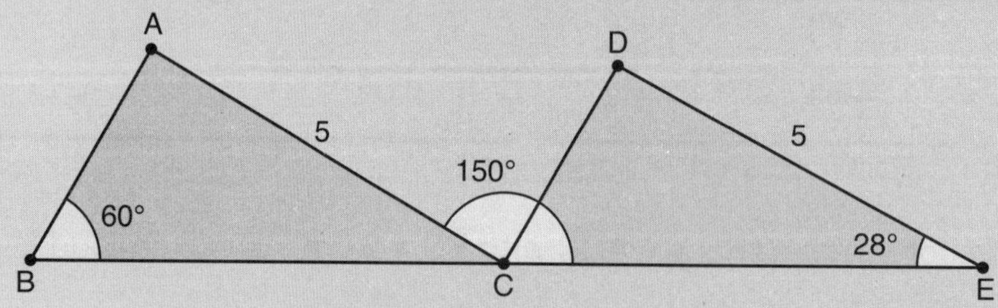

Theme Worksheet 4

1 Complete the following table containing the classification of triangles by drawing a rough figure, if possible. (One has been done for you)

Type of triangle	Scalene	Isosceles	Equilateral
Acute- angled	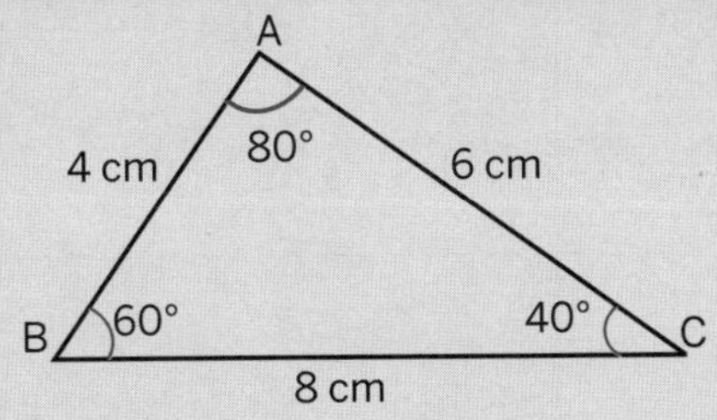		
Right- angled			
Obtuse-angled			

2 Write the congruence relation between the triangles given below and also write the congruence criteria. (One has been done for you)

Congruent triangles		Congruence relation	Congruence criteria
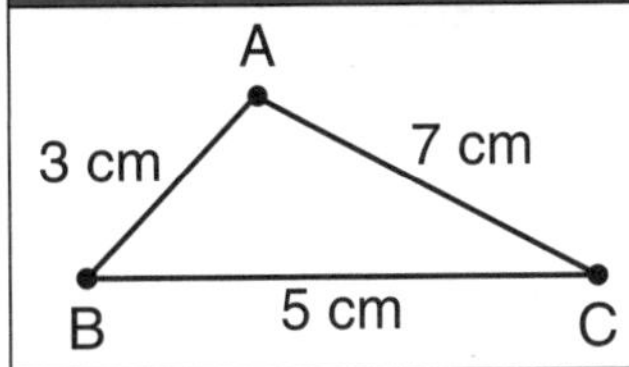	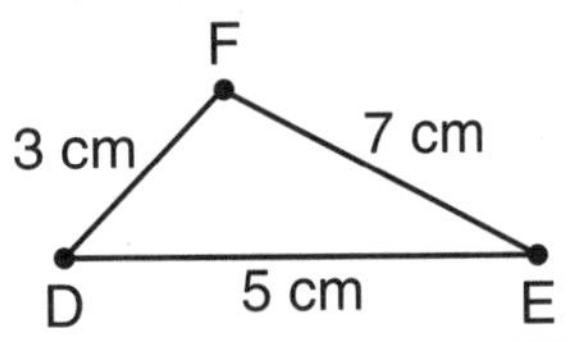	$\Delta ABC \cong \Delta FDE$	SSS
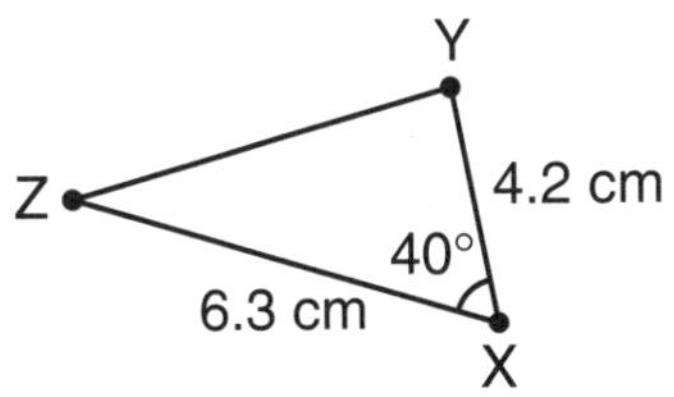	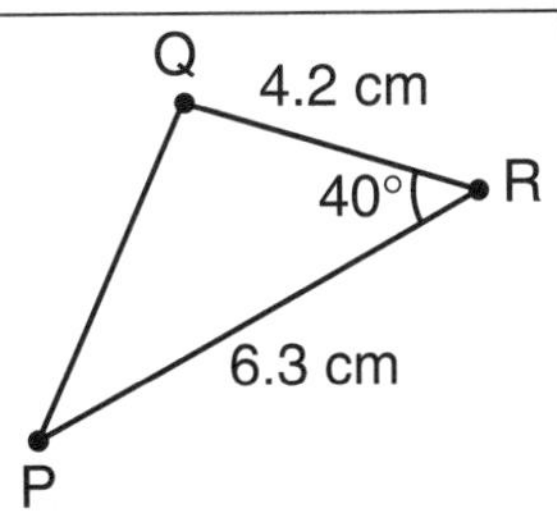		

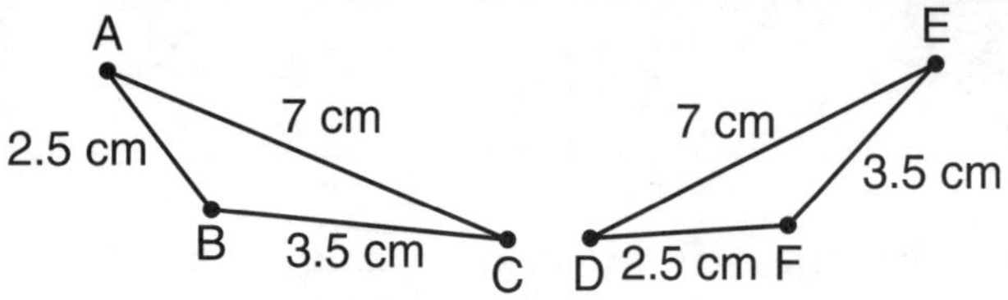A E 7 cm 2.5 cm 7 cm 3.5 cm B 3.5 cm C D 2.5 cm F		
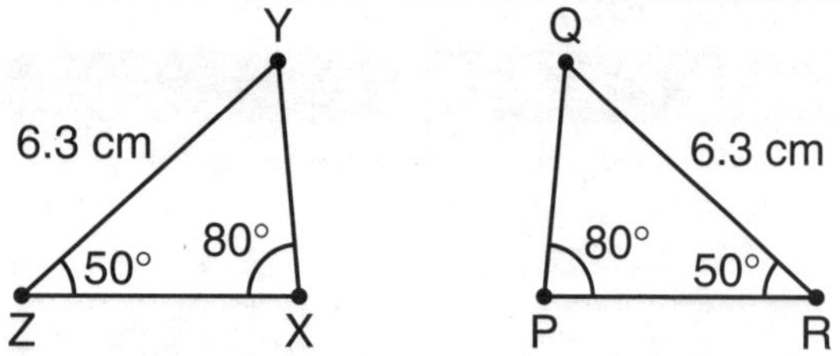Y Q 6.3 cm 6.3 cm 80° 50° 80° 50° Z X P R		
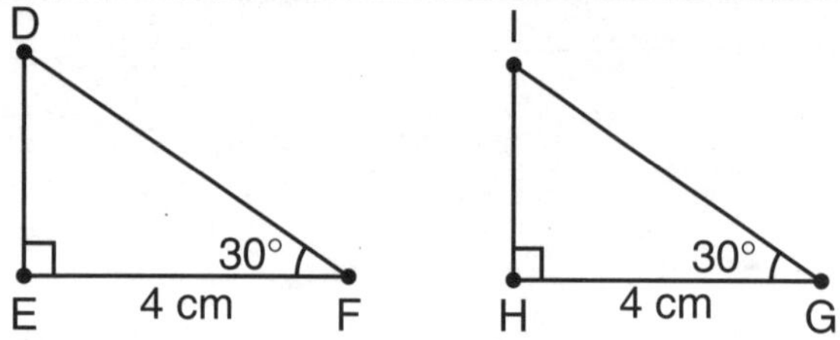D I 30° 30° E 4 cm F H 4 cm G		
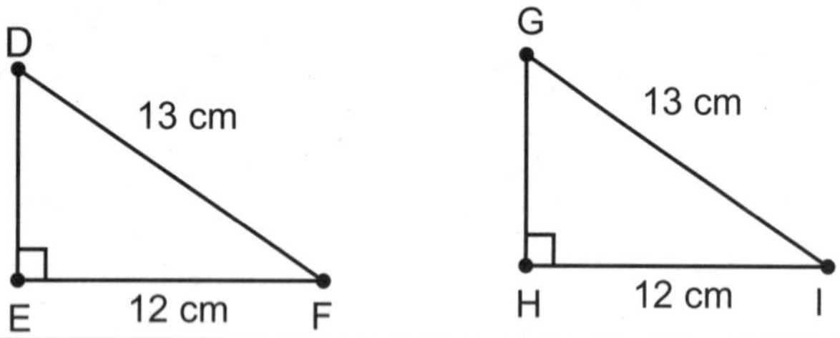G D 13 cm 13 cm E 12 cm F H 12 cm I		

Skill-based Worksheet - Identify, visualize and quantify measures of shapes and objects

1 Identify the different polygons in the following pictures.

a. 

b. 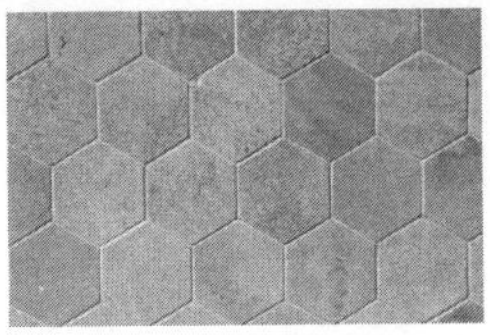

c. 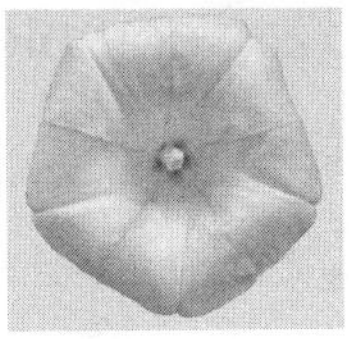

d. 

e. 

2 Identify the different 3D shapes in the following pictures.

a. 

b. 

c. 

d. 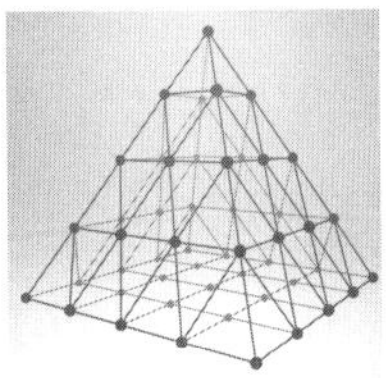

e. 

f. 

g. 

h. 

i. 

j. 

k. 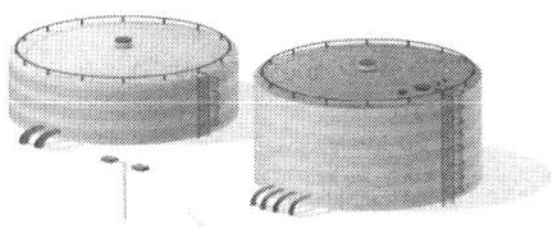

Mental Maths

Chapter 13 - Lines and Angles

1. Find the complements of the following angles.

   a. 17° __________ b. 23° __________ c. 42° __________

   d. 55° __________ e. 89° __________

2. Find the supplements of the following angles.

   a. 45° __________ b. 84° __________ c. 98° __________

   d. 115° __________ e. 179° __________

3. If two complementary angles are equal then the measure of each angle is __________
4. If two supplementary angles are equal then the measure of each angle is __________
5. What is the name of the line which can intersect two or more lines at distinct points? __________
6. How many pairs of adjacent angles are formed for two intersecting lines? __________
7. How many pairs of vertically opposite angles are formed for two intersecting lines? __________
8. How many angles are formed when a transversal intersects two lines? __________
9. If a pair of two corresponding angles formed is equal, then the two lines are __________
10. If a transversal is intersecting two parallel lines then the interior angles on the same side of the transversal are __________

Chapter 14 - Properties of Triangles

1. What are the measures of the angles in an isosceles right-angled triangle? __________
2. What are the measures of the angles in an acute angled triangle with equal side lengths? __________
3. What is the name of the longest side in a right-angled triangle? __________
4. The sum of two sides of a triangle is __________
5. The difference between the two sides of a triangle is __________
6. The shortest distance from a point to a line is __________
7. If the angles of a triangle are in the ratio 1 : 1 : 2, what type of triangle is it? __________
8. If the measurements of two sides of a triangle are 17 cm and 8 cm, what type of triangle is it? __________
9. If the measurements of two sides in a right-angled triangle are 16 m and 30 m then find the measure of the longest side. __________

10. If the exterior angle is 120° and one of the interior angles is 50°, what type of triangle is it? ________

Chapter 15 - Symmetry

1. Write the name of a regular polygon having three axes of symmetry. ____________
2. Write the name of a quadrilateral having maximum number of axes of symmetry. ____________
3. Find the number of axes of symmetry for a regular heptagon. ____________
4. An object has a rotational symmetry, only when the order of symmetry is ____________
5. Name the regular polygon whose angle of rotation is 45 . ____________
6. What is the angle of rotational symmetry of a regular hexagon? ____________
7. Which quadrilaterals have the same angle of rotation? ____________
8. What is the order of rotation in a regular pentagon? ____________
9. Write the name of the triangle which has line symmetry and no rotational symmetry.
10. Find the centre of rotation in a parallelogram. ____________

Chapter 16 - Visualising Solid Shapes

1. Which solid shapes have the same horizontal and vertical cross-sections? ____________
2. Which solid shapes have the same number of edges, faces and vertices? ____________
3. Which solid shapes have their horizontal cross-sections of same shape and size as that of their bases? ____________
4. Which 3D shape looks like a circle from all the sides? ____________
5. Which 3D shape looks like a triangle from the side and circle from the top? ____________
6. Which 3D shape looks like an octagon from the top and rectangle from the side? ____________
7. Which 3D shape looks like a hexagon from the top and triangle from the side? ____________
8. Which solids have the same number of vertices and faces? ____________
9. Which solid net has one rectangle and two circles? ____________
10. Which solid net has four triangular faces? ____________

Chapter 18 - Congruence of Triangles

1. Two geometrical figures are said to be congruent if they have same ____________ and same ____________
2. If the measures of two angles are equal, then the angles are ____________

3. Two regular polygons are said to be congruent if they have same ___________

4. The radius of the circle which is congruent to a circle of diameter 3.8 cm is ___________

5. Two triangles are congruent if and only if two sides and ___________ of two triangles are equal.

6. An equilateral triangle has a side length of 6 cm. The side length of the equilateral triangle which is congruent to this is ___________.

7. How many pairs of corresponding parts must be equal for two congruent triangles? ___________

8. Write the congruent relation for the given corresponding elements. Corresponding sides: $\overline{AB}$ and $\overline{PS}$, $\overline{BC}$ and $\overline{SR}$, $\overline{CA}$ and $\overline{RP}$.

9. The corresponding parts of two triangles are ___________.

10. Write the correct congruency criteria for the given figure. ___________

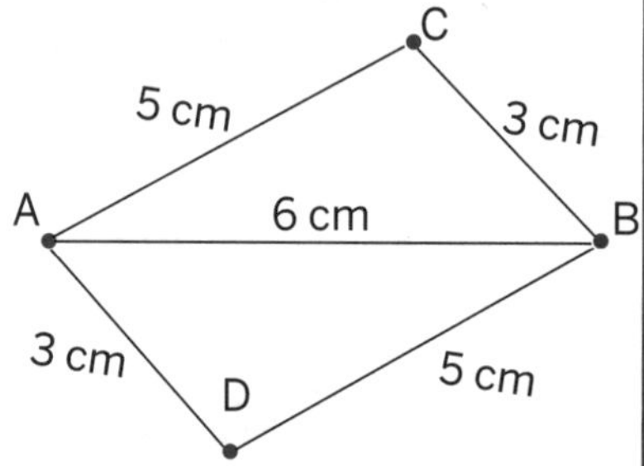

Chapter 19 - Constructions

1. How many measurements are required to construct a unique triangle? ___________

2. How many measurements are required to construct an isosceles triangle? ___________

3. How many measurements are required to construct an equilateral triangle? ___________

4. In a right angled triangle, which is always regarded as the longest side and why? ___________

5. In a right angled triangle, if one of the two angles other than right angle is 45°, then what is the name of such a triangle, why? ___________

6. Check whether a triangle XYZ with XY = 3 cm, YZ = 5 cm and XZ = 6 cm can be constructed or not? Explain. ___________

7. Check whether a triangle CAT with CA = 3 cm, AT = 5 cm and CT = 4 cm can be constructed or not? Explain. ___________

8. Check whether a triangle DTP with DT = 6.4 cm, TP = 10 cm and DP = 3.6 can be constructed or not? Explain. ___________

9. Check whether a triangle MAT with MA = 5 cm, $\angle M = 80°$ and $\angle A = 100°$ can be constructed or not? Explain. ___________

10. Check whether a triangle RAT with RA = 4.7 cm, $\angle A = 80°$ and $\angle T = 90°$ can be constructed or not? Explain. ___________

Mensuration

Chapters Covered

20. Perimeter and Area

Why this Theme Matters

Perimeter and Area relate to the measurement of two-dimensional space.

The areas of two-dimensional shapes are determined in many real life situations, such as

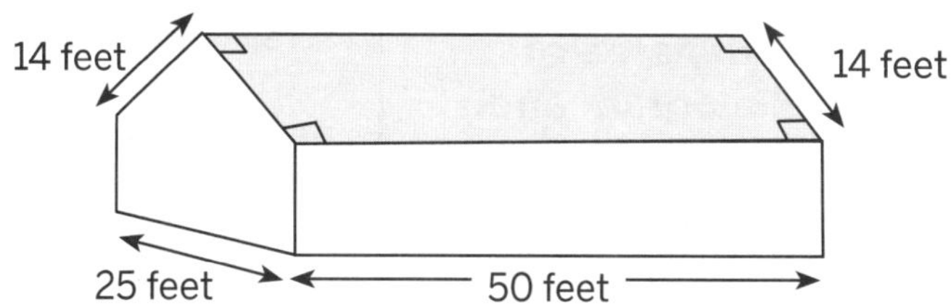

- Carpeting a floor
- Painting a room
- Planting a garden
- Establishing and maintaining a lawn
- Installing concrete and pavement
- Measuring land for farming or building construction.

Similarly, surface area of three-dimensional objects such as cubes and cuboids is useful in situations like:

- Finding the measurement of a cardboard needed to make boxes
- Finding the paper required to wrap gift boxes

THEME 5

Perimeter and Area

20

What I shall learn

- To recall how to calculate the area and perimeter of a square and a rectangle
- To find the area of a parallelogram and triangle
- To find the circumference and the area of circles
- To understand the concepts of surface area
- To find the surface area of cubes and cuboids

Let's Get Started

- If you want to decorate your school's notice board with a beautiful ribbon border, how will you calculate the exact length of the ribbon required?
- If a farmer wants to grow four types of plants in his field giving equal space to all types, how can he do that?
- How will your mother buy a carpet that will exactly fit the hall of your house?

For such situations, the concept of perimeter and area is used that we have learned in the previous classes. We have also learned how to calculate the perimeter and area of a square, rectangle and triangle.

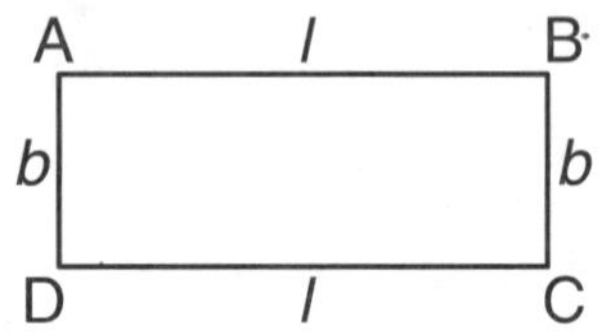

Perimeter of a rectangle ABCD = $2(l + b)$

Area of a rectangle ABCD $= l \times b$

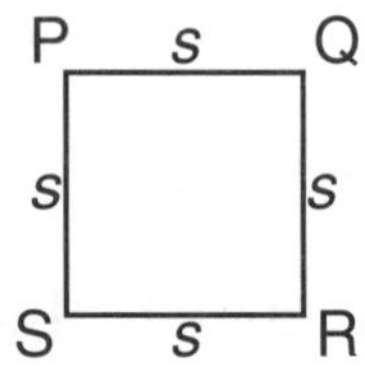

Perimeter of a square PQRS = $4s$

Area of a square PQRS = s^2

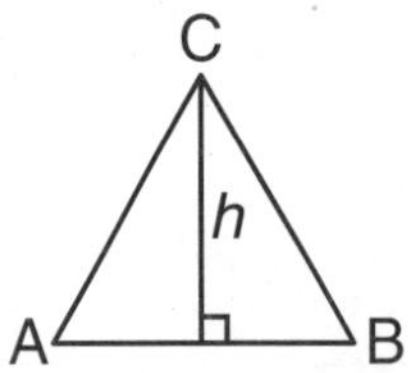

Perimeter of a triangle ABC = AB + BC + CA

Area of a triangle ABC $= \frac{1}{2} \times \text{Base} \times \text{Height} = \frac{1}{2}bh$

(where h is the height of ΔABC)

Exercise 20.1

1. The area of a rectangular park is 240 m^2 and its breadth is 15 m. What is the perimeter of the park?
2. Prema has a square-shaped garden whose side is 13 ft. What is the cost of fencing her garden at the rate of ₹100 per foot?
3. Find the area of the shaded region in the figure given here.

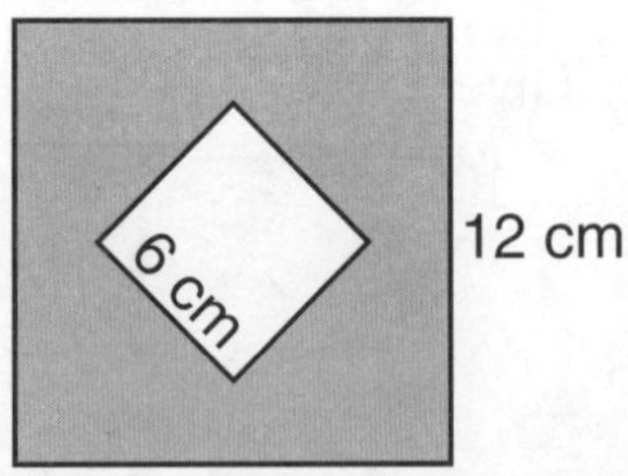

❹ The figure shown here is made up of 11 identical rectangles. The area of each rectangle is 22.5 cm^2. The length of each rectangle is 7.5 cm. What is the perimeter of the figure?

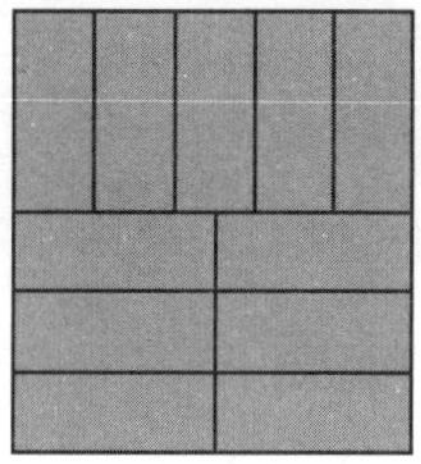

❺ Find the base and height of a triangular field if its height is $\frac{3}{2}$ of its base and the area of the field is 1200 cm^2.

Perimeter of Plane Figures

The perimeters of some plane figures are given below.

Shape	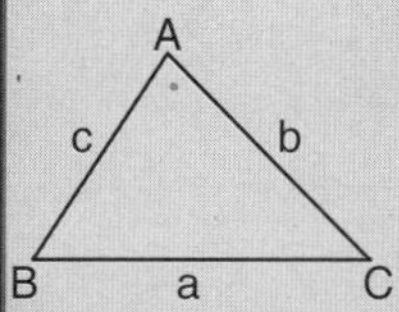	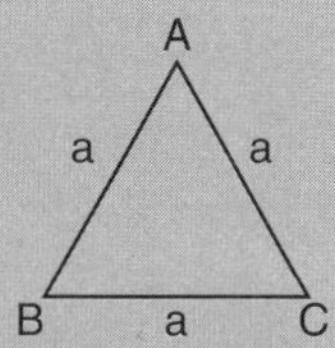	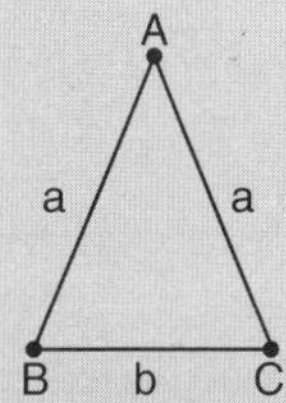	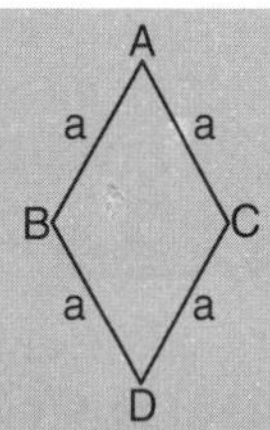	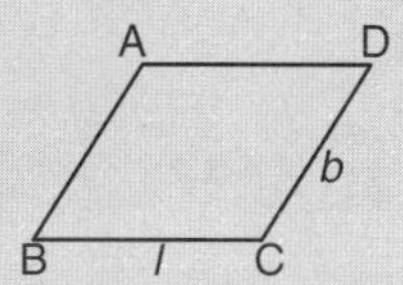
Name of the shape	Scalene triangle	Equilateral triangle	Isosceles triangle	Rhombus	Parallelogram
Perimeter	$a + b + c$	$a + a + a = 3a$	$a + a + b$ $= 2a + b$	$a + a + a + a$ $= 4a$	$l + b + l + b$ $= 2l + 2b = 2(l + b)$

Example 1: Find the third side of an isosceles triangle if its perimeter is 72 cm and each equal side is 22 cm.

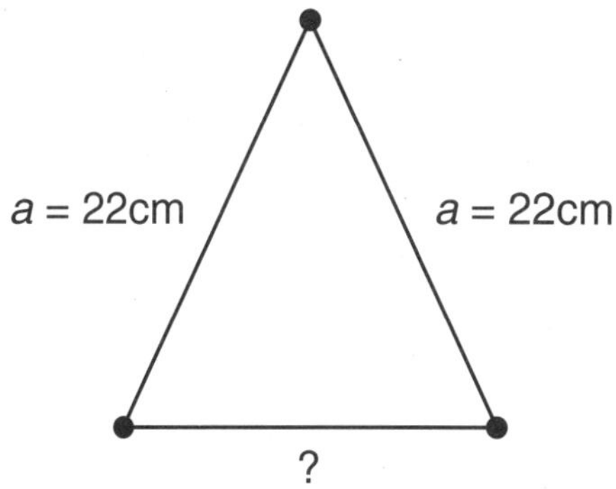

Given: Perimeter of the triangle = 72 cm

Each equal side (a) of the triangle = 22 cm

Perimeter of an isosceles triangle = $2a + b$

$\therefore 2a + b = 72 \Rightarrow 2 \times 22 + b = 72$

$44 + b = 72 \Rightarrow b = 72 - 44 = 28$ cm

Therefore, the third side of the isosceles triangle is 28 cm.

Example 2: The sides of a scalene triangle are in the ratio 2 : 3 : 5. If the perimeter of the triangle is 350 m^2, find the lengths of all the sides.

The sides of a scalene triangle are in the ratio 2 : 3 : 5.

Let the three sides of the triangle be $2x$, $3x$ and $5x$.

Perimeter of the triangle = $2x + 3x + 5x = 10x$

Given: Perimeter of the triangle = 350 m^2

$\therefore 10x = 350$

$x = \frac{350}{10} = 35$

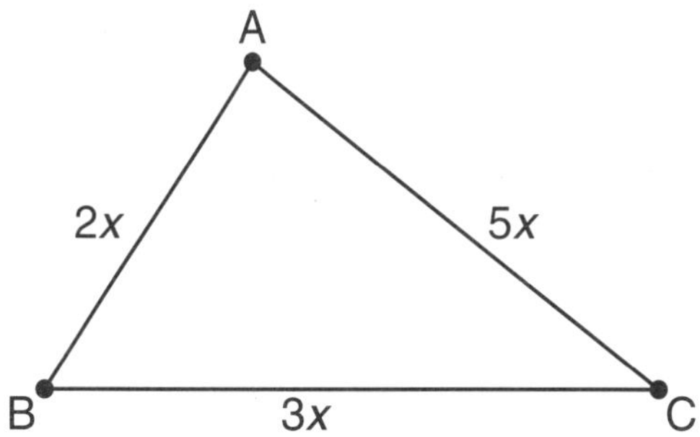

Sides of the triangle:

Length of side AB = $2x = 2 \times 35 = 70$ m

Length of side BC = $3x = 3 \times 35 = 105$ m

Length of side AC = $5x = 5 \times 35 = 175$ m

Example 3: Find the perimeter of the rectangle ABCD in the figure given below.

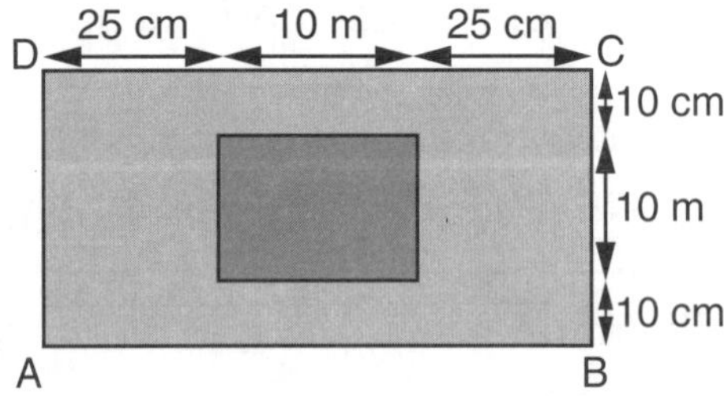

Length of the rectangle (l) = 25 cm + 10 m + 25 cm
= 25 cm + 1000 cm + 25 cm
= 1050 cm (since 1 m = 100 cm)

Breadth of the rectangle (b) = 10 cm + 10 m + 10 cm
= 10 cm + 1000 cm + 10 cm
= 1020 cm

Perimeter of the rectangle = $2(l + b) = 2(1050 + 1020) = 2(2070) = 4140$ cm

Exercise 20.2

1 Find the perimeter of the following figures.

a.
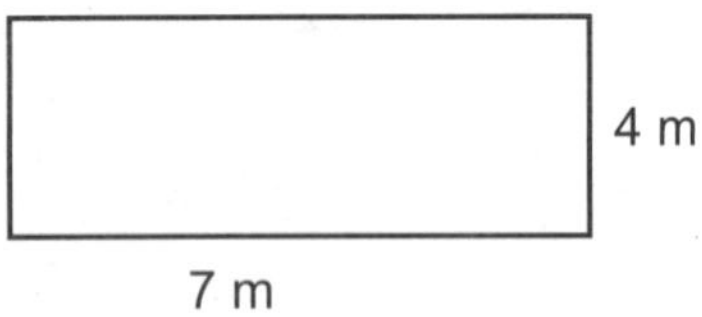

b.
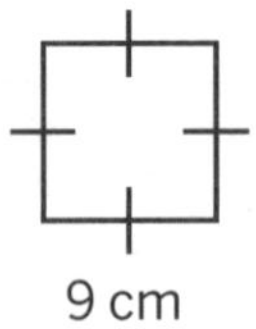

c.
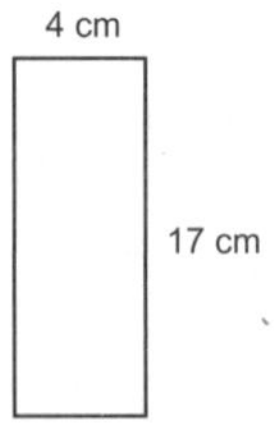

d.
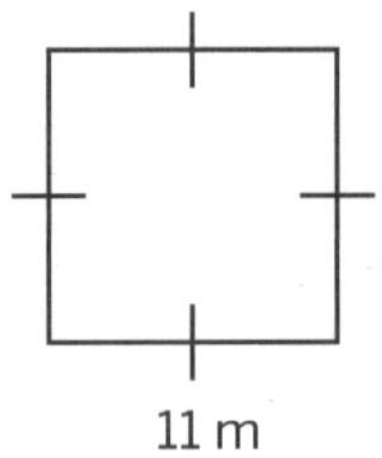

2 Find the perimeter of each of the following triangles.

a.
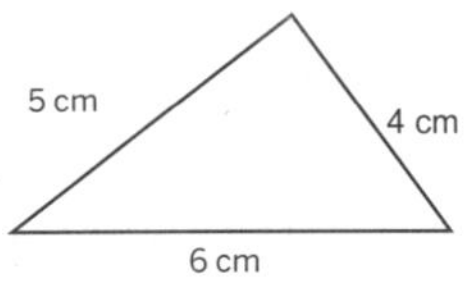

b.
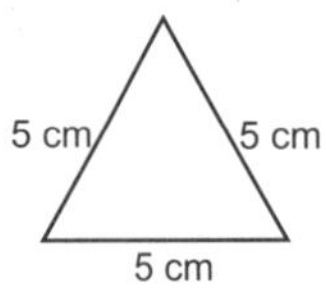

c.

3 Find the perimeters of the following.

a. Parallelogram whose length is 15 cm and breadth is 6 cm

b. Rhombus whose length is 7 cm

4 Find the length of the missing sides of the following figures.

a. Perimeter = 85 cm

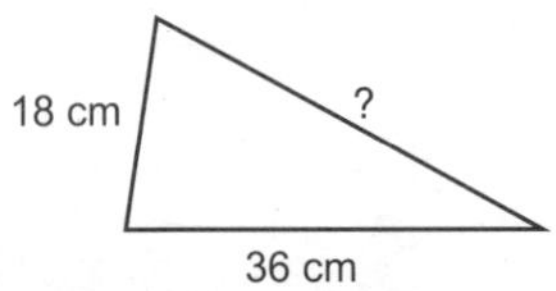

b. Perimeter = 76 cm

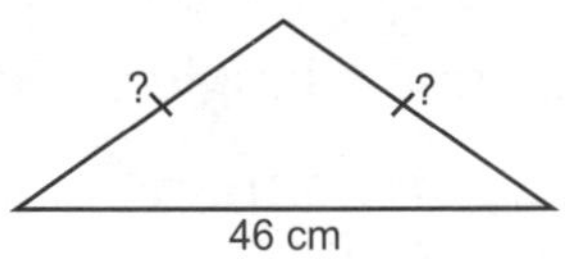

5 Julie has built a kennel whose base is in the shape of a rectangle of dimensions 10 m by 4 m. She wants to put a fence around it. Find the amount of fencing required in metres.

6 Vivek goes for walking to a nearby park which is in the shape of a square of length 600 m. Find the distance covered by him in 2 rounds. Write the answer in km.

7. What is the length of each side (in cm) of an equilateral triangle whose perimeter is 17.28 m.
8. The front surface of a parallelogram whose length and breadth are 14 m and 7 m respectively is given. Find its perimeter.

Area of Plane Figures

In the previous classes, we have learned that **area** is the amount of surface enclosed within a closed shape and the units of area are square units.

Units of Area

If a square has sides of 1 m, then its area is $1 \text{ m} \times 1 \text{ m} = 1 \text{ m}^2$ (square metre).

Square metre is the basic unit of area in the metric system. All other units of area are derived from square metre. (Note: 1 metre square means a square of side of 1 m).

The following table gives the inter-conversion of different units of area.

Unit of area (denoted as)	Unit multiplied two times is square units	Conversion to next bigger unit
Square millimetre (mm^2)	$1 \text{ mm} \times 1 \text{ mm} = 1 \text{ mm}^2$	$1 \text{ mm}^2 \times 100 = 1 \text{ cm}^2$
Square centimetre (cm^2)	$1 \text{ cm} \times 1 \text{ cm} = 1 \text{ cm}^2$	$1 \text{ cm}^2 \times 100 = 1 \text{ dm}^2$
Square decimetre (dm^2)	$1 \text{ dm} \times 1 \text{ dm} = 1 \text{ dm}^2$	$1 \text{ dm}^2 \times 100 = 1 \text{ m}^2$
Square metre (m^2)	$1 \text{ m} \times 1 \text{ m} = 1 \text{ m}^2$	$1 \text{ m}^2 \times 100 = 1 \text{ dam}^2$
Square decametre (dam^2)	$1 \text{ dam} \times 1 \text{ dam} = 1 \text{ dam}^2$	$1 \text{ dam}^2 \times 100 = 1 \text{ hm}^2$
Square hectometre (hm^2)	$1 \text{ hm} \times 1 \text{ hm} = 1 \text{ hm}^2$	$1 \text{ hm}^2 \times 100 = 1 \text{ km}^2$
Square kilometre (km^2)	$1 \text{ km} \times 1 \text{ km} = 1 \text{ km}^2$	

Example 4: Convert 13.5 km^2 into m^2.

We know that 1 km = 1000 m

$\therefore 13.5 \text{ km}^2 = 13.5 \times (1000 \text{ m})^2 = 13.5 \times 10^6 \text{ m}^2 = 135 \times 10^5 \text{ m}^2$

Note

Square hectometre (hm^2) is also known as **hectare** (ha). It is used to measure the area of a land.
1 hectare (ha) = 100 are^2 = 10^4 m^2 **are** (read as 'air') is also a unit of measuring area.
1 are (a) = 1 dam^2 = 100 m^2
Another unit of land area is **acre** (read as 'a-ker').
1 acre = 4046.86 m^2.
Can you find some other units of area?

Activity 1

Draw a rectangle on a sheet of paper.

Draw one of its diagonals.

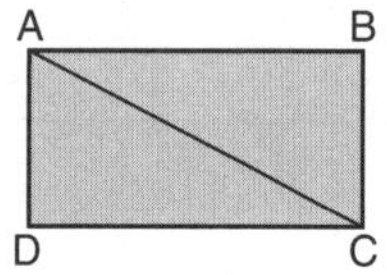

Cut the two triangles formed.

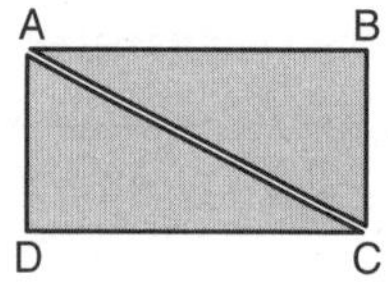

Overlap the triangles on each other.

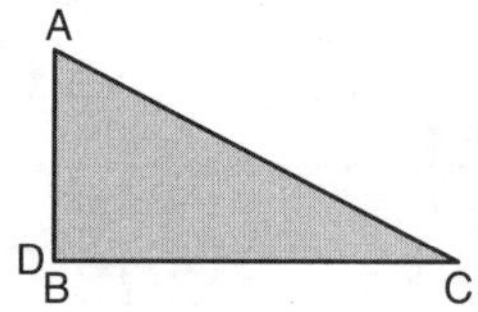

You can observe that the two triangles are congruent and hence, they have equal area.

Area of the rectangle ABCD = Area of the triangle ADC + Area of the triangle ABC

= Area of triangle ADC + Area of triangle ADC (Since areas of both the triangles are equal.)

Area of the rectangle ABCD = 2 (Area of triangle ADC)

$\therefore$ Area of the triangle ADC $= \frac{1}{2} \times$ Area of rectangle ABCD $= \frac{1}{2} \times$ length $\times$ breadth

Activity 2

Draw a triangle on a sheet of paper.

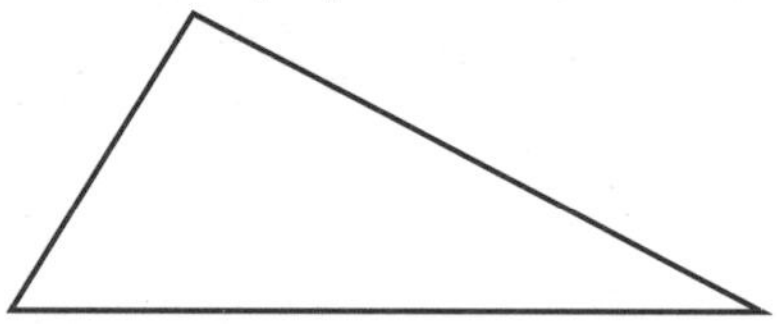

Take a patty paper and trace the triangle that is drawn.

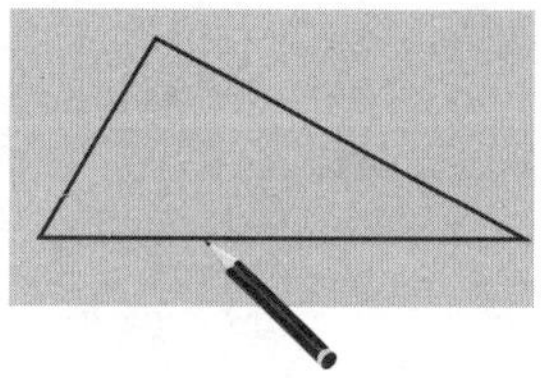

Rotate the triangle that is traced and form a parallelogram.

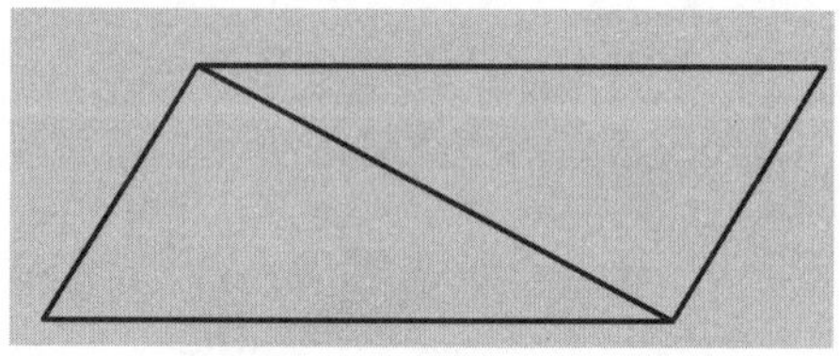

Since the triangles are congruent, their areas are equal.

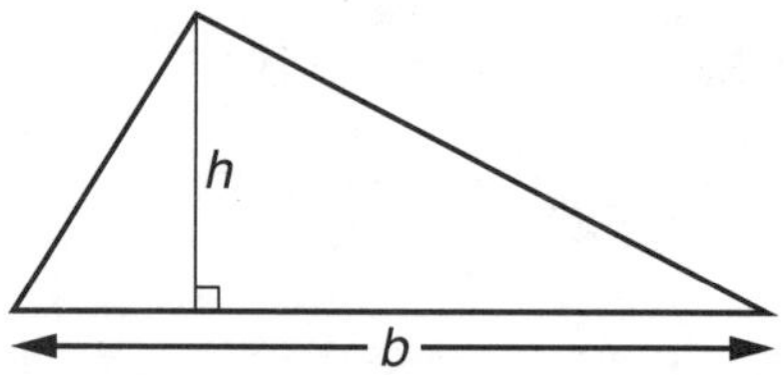

Area of the parallelogram = 2(Area of the triangle)

base × height = 2(Area of the triangle)

$\therefore$ Area of the triangle $= \frac{1}{2} \times$ base $\times$ height $= \frac{1}{2}bh$

Area of a Rectangle and a Square

Area of a rectangle = (Length × breadth) sq. units

Area of a square = Side × side = (side)^2 sq. units

Area of a Right-angled Triangle

Area of ΔABC = $(\frac{1}{2}\ l \times b)$ sq. units

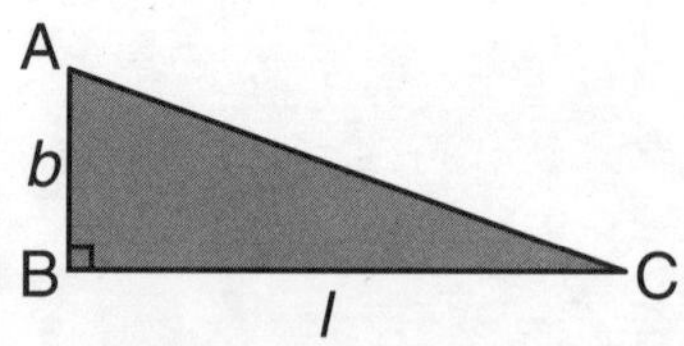

For a right-angled triangle, length is called the **base** and breadth is called the **altitude** or **height**.

Area of a right-angled triangle is equal to half the product of base (b) and altitude (h).

Area of $\Delta ABC = (\frac{1}{2} \times b \times h = \frac{1}{2} \times BC \times AB)$ sq. units

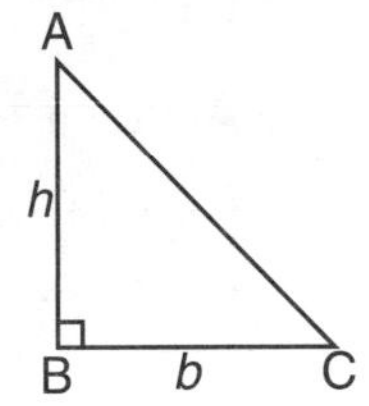

Area of a Right Isosceles Triangle

Right isosceles triangle is a right-angled triangle with two equal sides.

In the adjacent triangle, AB and BC are equal.

Here, BC is the base and AB is the height. Let BC = AB = a cm

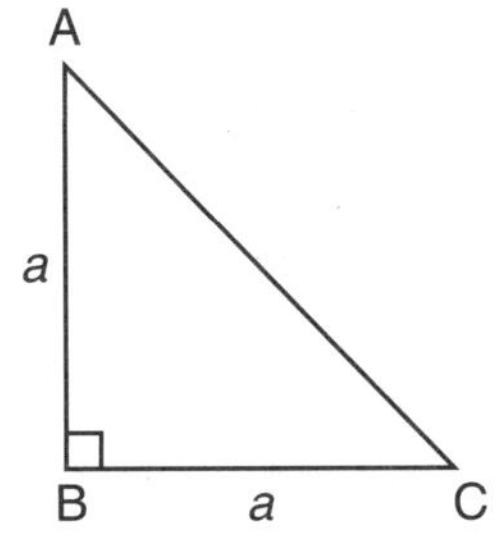

$$\text{Area of triangle ABC} = \frac{1}{2}(BC \times AB)$$

$$= \frac{1}{2}(a \times a)$$

$$= \frac{1}{2}a^2$$, where a is the length of one of the equal sides.

Example 5: A garden is in the shape of an isosceles triangle whose equal sides are 17 m each and the third side is 16 m. The height of the triangle corresponding to the non-equal side is 15 m. Find the area and the perimeter of the garden.

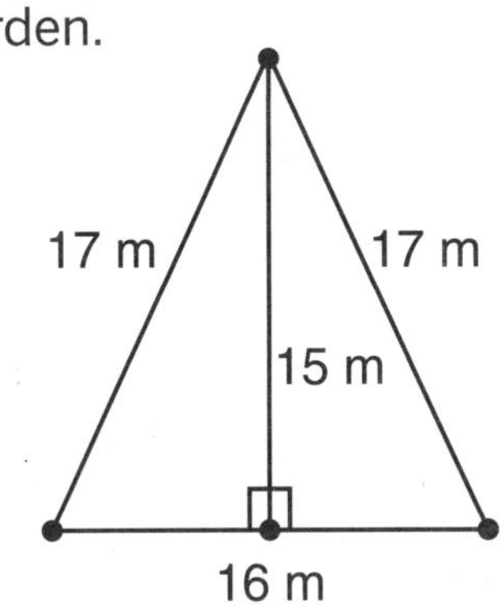

Perimeter of the garden = 17 m + 17 m + 16 m = 50 m

Height corresponding to the non-equal side is given as 15 m.

Therefore, the base is 16 m (as shown in the figure).

$$\text{Area of the triangular garden} = \frac{1}{2} \times \text{base} \times \text{corresponding height}$$

$$= \frac{1}{2} \times 16 \times 15 = 8 \times 15 = 120 \text{ m}^2$$

Example 6: The base of a triangle is 4 times the height and its area is 128 sq. ft. Find the height and base of the triangle.

Let the height of the triangle be h ft. Then, its base is $4h$ ft.

$$\text{Area of the triangle} = \frac{1}{2} \times \text{base} \times \text{height} \Rightarrow 128 = \frac{1}{2} \times 4h \times h$$

$$256 = 4h^2 \Rightarrow h^2 = 64 \Rightarrow h = \sqrt{64} = 8 \text{ ft}$$

Height of the triangle (h) = 8 ft   Base of the triangle = $4h = 4 \times 8 = 32$ ft

Example 7: An isosceles triangle is inscribed in a square of length 23 cm as shown in the figure. Find the area of the shaded portion.

The area of the shaded portion is obtained by subtracting the area of the inscribed triangle from the area of the square.

Area of the square ABCD = 23 cm × 23 cm = 529 cm^2

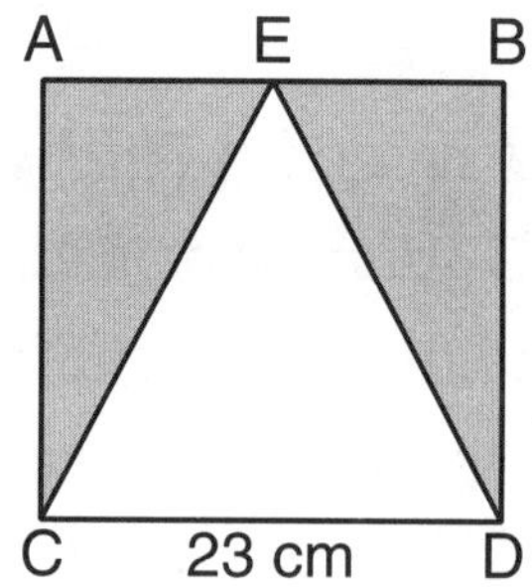

From the figure, we can see that the height of ΔCED is the same as the length of the square which is 23 cm.

Area of the $\Delta CED = \frac{1}{2} \times$ base × height $= \frac{1}{2} \times 23 \times 23 = 264.5\ cm^2$

∴ Area of the shaded portion = Area of the square – Area of the inscribed triangle

$= 529\ cm^2 - 264.5\ cm^2 = 264.5\ cm^2$

Area of Parallelogram

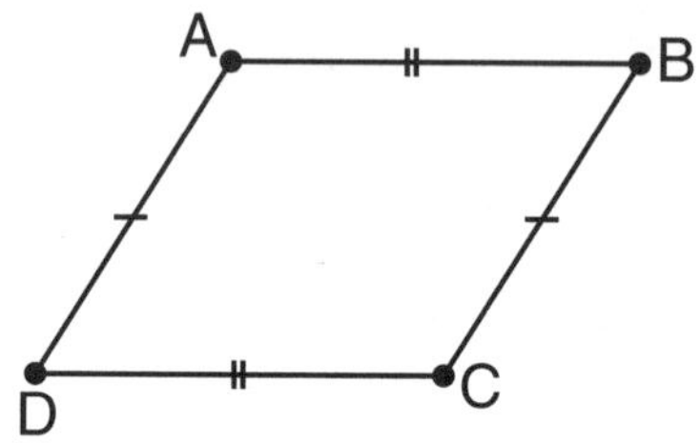

Parallelogram is a quadrilateral whose opposite sides are parallel and equal in length.

AB || DC and AD || BC

AB = DC and AD = BC

Area of a parallelogram = base × height = $b \times h$, where b is the base and h is the corresponding height of the parallelogram.

Activity 3

Take a grid paper and draw a parallelogram on it.

Draw the height of the parallelogram as shown here.

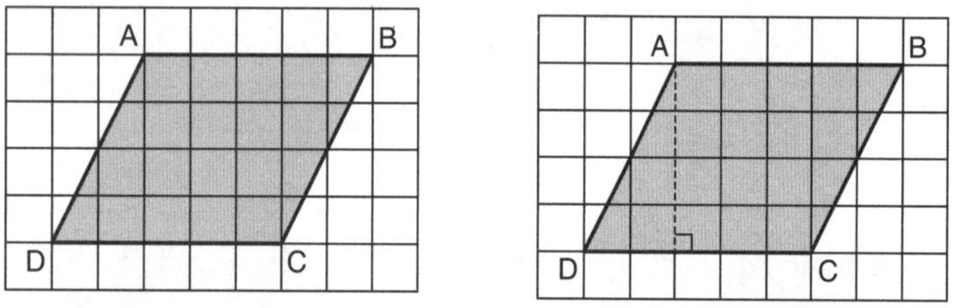

Cut the parallelogram into two pieces along its height.

Translate the triangle to the other side of the parallelogram to form a rectangle.

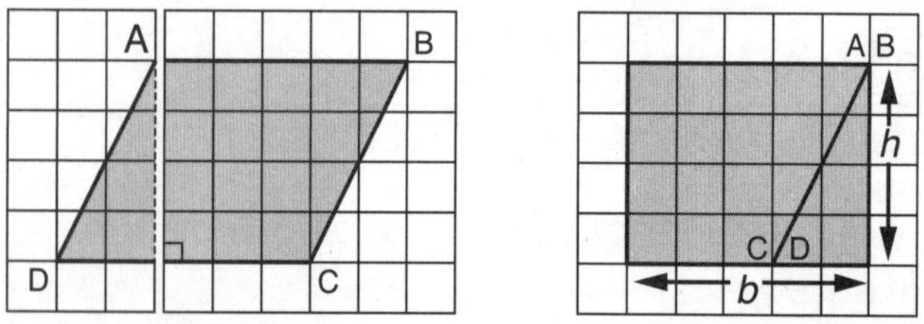

The parallelogram is converted into a rectangle whose length is b units and breadth is h units.

∴ **The area of the parallelogram = Area of the rectangle = length × breadth = $b \times h$**, where b is the base and h is the corresponding height of the parallelogram.

Example 8: Find the area of a parallelogram whose height is 9 cm and base is 7 cm.

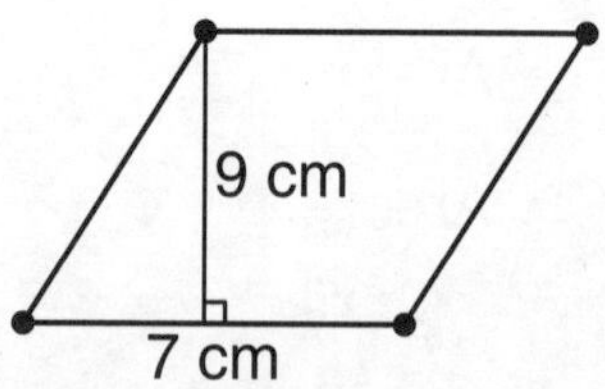

Area of the parallelogram = base × height

$= 7\ cm \times 9\ cm = 63\ cm^2$

Example 9: The base of a parallelogram is 7 in. and its area is 98 in^2. Find the height of the parallelogram.

Area of the parallelogram = base × height $\Rightarrow 98 = 7 \times h \Rightarrow h = \frac{98}{7} = 14$.

Thus, the height of the parallelogram is 14 in.

Example 10: ABCD is a parallelogram of area 2200 cm^2. AF and DE are the heights of the parallelogram corresponding to the sides CD and AC respectively. The adjacent sides of the parallelogram are 20 cm and 11 cm. Find the heights of the parallelogram.

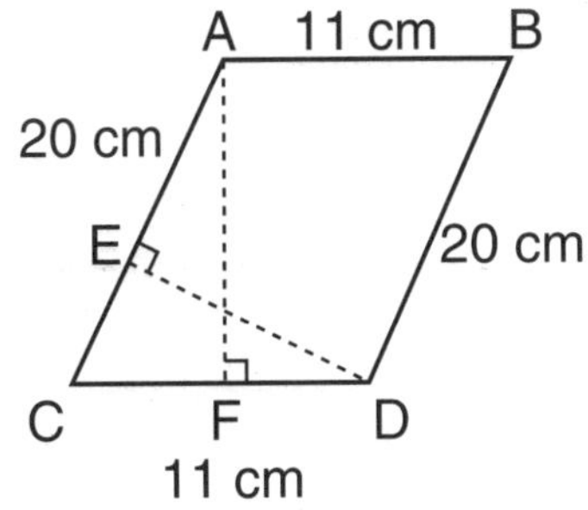

Area of the parallelogram = base × corresponding height

$$\Rightarrow 2200 = CD \times AF$$

$$\Rightarrow 2200 = 11 \times AF \Rightarrow AF = \frac{2200}{11} = 200 \text{cm}$$

Area of the parallelogram = base × corresponding height

$$\Rightarrow 2200 = AC \times DE$$

$$\Rightarrow 2200 = 20 \times DE \Rightarrow DE = \frac{2200}{20} = 110 \text{ cm}$$

Thus, the heights of the parallelogram corresponding to the bases CD and AC are 200 cm and 110 cm respectively.

Think and Answer

a.

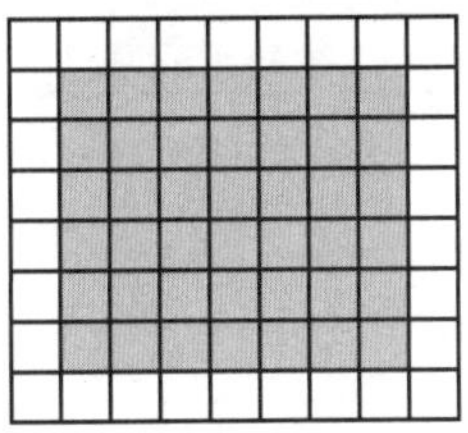

b.

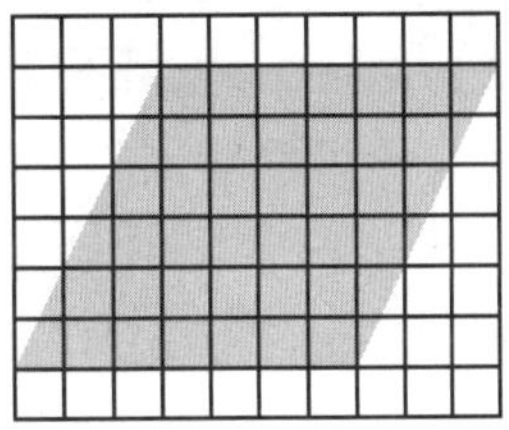

In the above figures A and B, which shaded portion has the bigger area?

Formulae to Remember

- Area of a square = a^2, where a is the length of the side
- Area of a rectangle = $l \times b$, where l is the length and b is the breadth
- Area of a triangle = $\frac{1}{2} \times$ base × height
- Area of a right isosceles triangle = $\frac{1}{2}(a)^2$, where a is the length of one of the equal sides
- Area of a parallelogram = $b \times h$, where b is the base and h is the height

Example 11: Find the area of the shaded portion in the given figure.

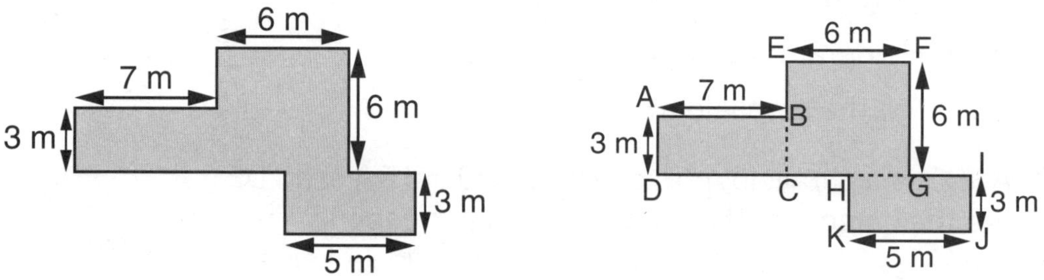

First, divide the given figure into suitable plane figures by drawing the dotted lines as shown below.

Observe that the whole figure is divided into rectangles ABCD, HIJK and square CEFG.

∴ Area of the shaded figure

= Area of rectangle ABCD + Area of rectangle HIJK + Area of square CEFG

$= (3 \times 7) + (5 \times 3) + (6 \times 6)$

$= 21 + 15 + 36 = 72\ m^2$

Example 12: A rectangular garden with length 85 m and breadth 60 m has two crossroads. One crossroad is 4 m wide and is parallel to the length and other crossroad is 3.5 m wide and is parallel to the breadth of the garden. Find the cost of constructing these crossroads at ₹17 per sq. m.

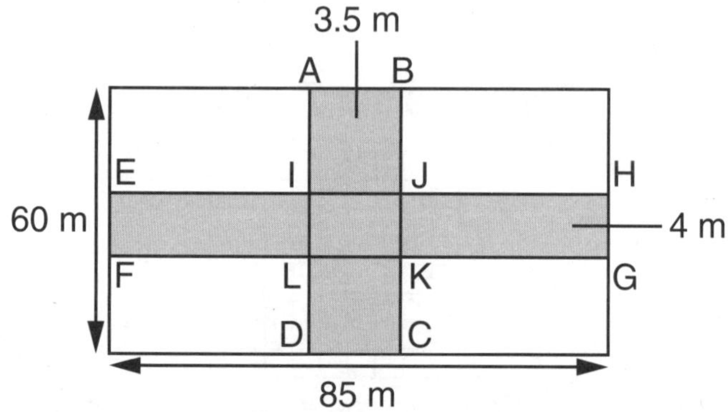

First, draw the garden as per the given problem.

Let ABCD be the crossroad that is parallel to the breadth of the garden and EFGH be the crossroad that is parallel to the length of the garden. Let IJKL be the common area of these crossroads.

Area of crossroad ABCD:

Length of ABCD = 60 m

Breadth of ABCD = 3.5 m

Area of crossroad ABCD = 60×3.5 = 210 sq. m

Area of crossroad EFGH:

Length of EFGH = 85 m Breadth of EFGH = 4 m

Area of crossroad ABCD = 85×4 = 340 sq. m

Area of the common area IJKL:

Length of IJKL = 4 m Breadth of IJKL = 3.5 m

Area of IJKL = 4×3.5 = 14 sq. m

Area of crossroads = Area of ABCD + Area of EFGH – Area of IJKL

= 210 + 340 – 14 = 550 – 14 = 536 sq. m

Cost of constructing these roads = 536×17 = ₹9112

Note

The area of IJKL is already included in the area of ABCD and the area of EFGH both. Hence, when we add the areas of ABCD and EFGH, the area of IJKL is getting added twice. Therefore, we subtract the area of IJKL once from the sum of the areas of ABCD and EFGH to get the correct area of the crossroads.

Exercise 20.3

1 **Find the areas of the parallelograms whose base and height are as given below.**

a. Base = 25 ft, height = 16.25 ft   b. Base = 20 cm, height = 0.75 m

2 The perimeter of a rectangular garden is 326 sq. ft and its length is 101 ft. Find the breadth of the garden.

3 The cost of fencing a square field is ₹252 at ₹4.50 per sq. m. Find the length of the field and its area.

4 The cost of flooring a rectangular hall is ₹3500 at ₹3.50 per sq. m. The length of the hall is 40 m. Find the breadth of the hall and the area of the hall.

5 The perimeter of a rectangle is equal to the perimeter of a square whose area is 625 sq. m. If the length of the rectangle is 32 m, find its breadth and area.

6 Find the area of the shaded region of the figure given below.

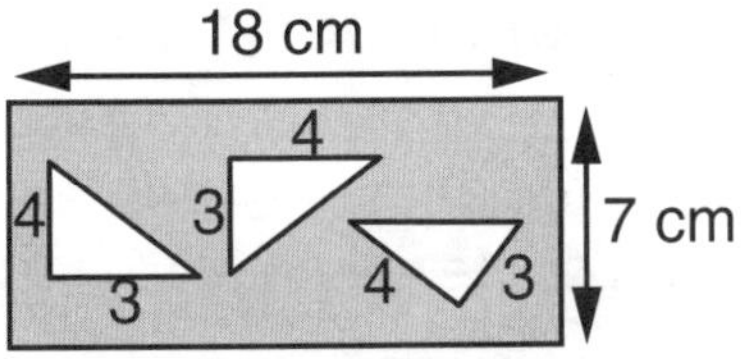

7 The area of the triangle ABC in the figure given below is 52.5 cm^2. Find the area of the triangle DBC.

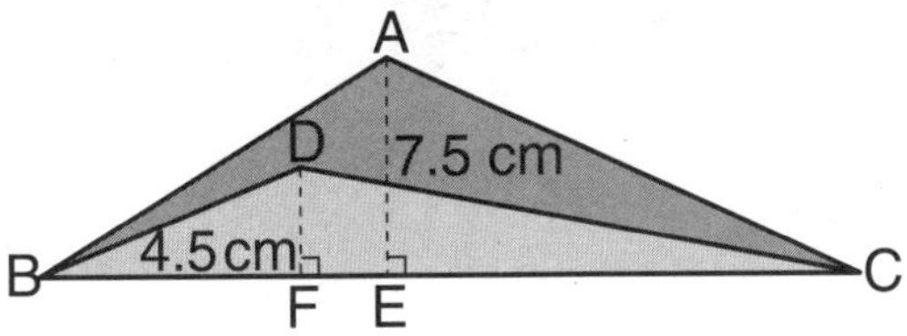

8 **Find the area of the shaded portions in the following figures.**

a.

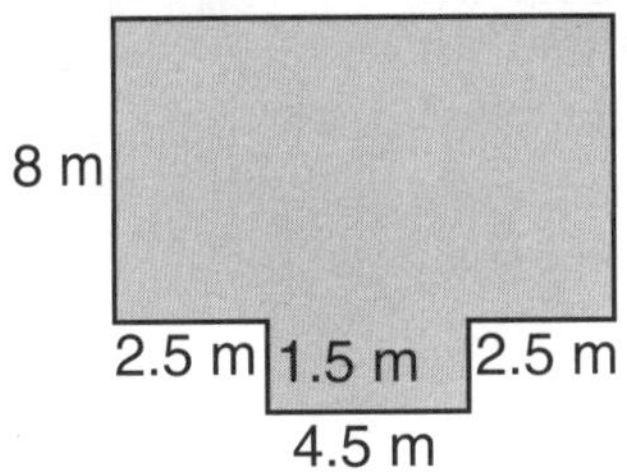

b.

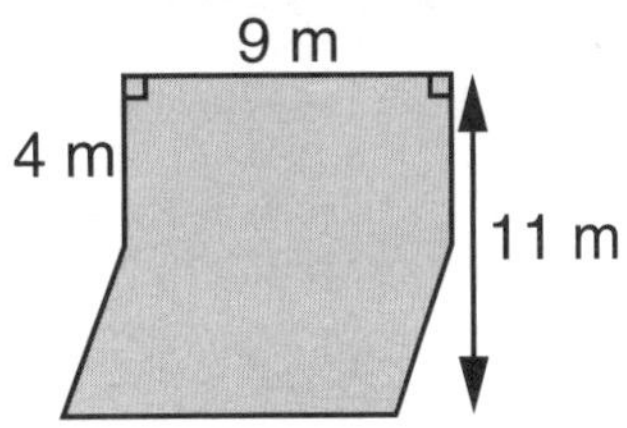

c.

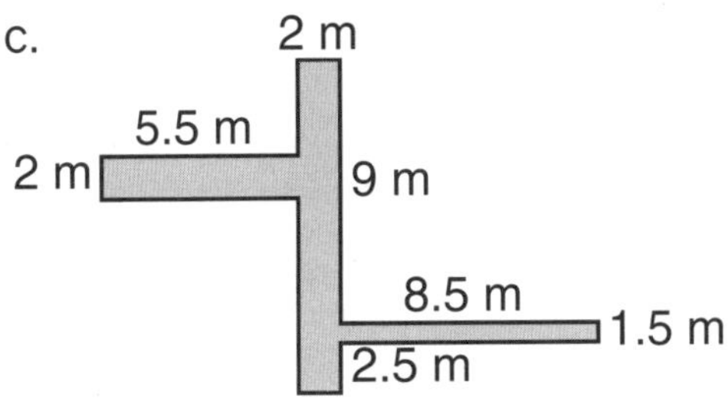

d.

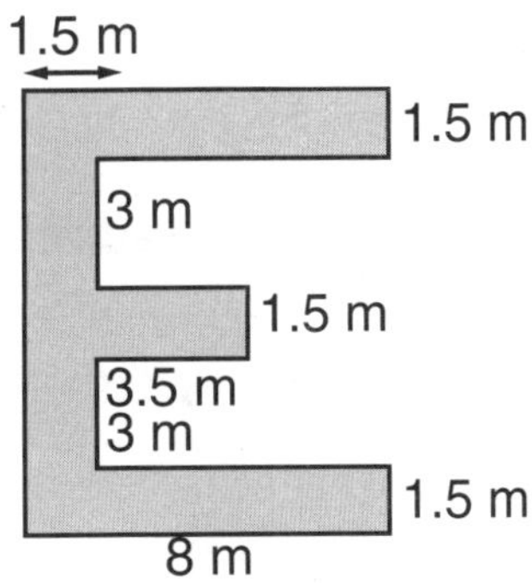

e.

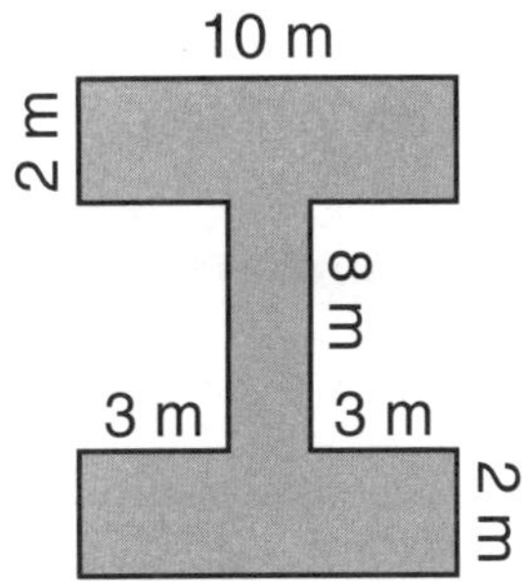

9 One side of a parallelogram is 2.5 times its consecutive adjacent side. If the perimeter of the parallelogram is 70 m, find its area and the measures of all its sides.

10 The area of a right-angled triangle is 84 sq. cm. If the base is 24 cm and the hypotenuse is 25 cm, find its perimeter.

Circles

Have you ever played with bicycle tyres by rolling them on the streets? Do you know how to find the distance covered by the tyre in one rotation? Let us learn how to find the distance covered by the circular wheels.

We know that perimeter is the distance along the boundary of any object or shape. The perimeter of a circular object is known as its **circumference**. Therefore, the circumference of a circle is the distance around a circle.

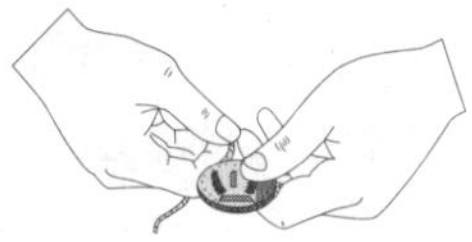

Activity 4: Take a few circular objects like coin, circular plate, bangle, CD, etc. Take a string and wrap it along its boundary and measure its length using a ruler.

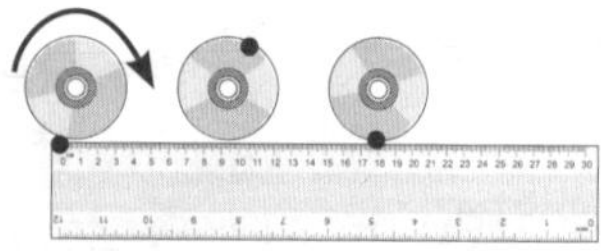

Activity 5: Mark a point on a circular object, roll it for one complete rotation on a ruler and mark its final position. The distance from the initial position to the final position gives the circumference of the circle.

Relation Between the Circumference and the Diameter of a Circle

Activity 6: Copy the following table in your notebook. Draw five circles of different radii. Measure their radii and the circumference using a string and fill the table. Observe the ratio of circumference to the diameter of each circle.

Circle	Diameter (2 × Radius) cm	Circumference (cm)	$\frac{\text{Circumference}}{\text{Diameter}}$
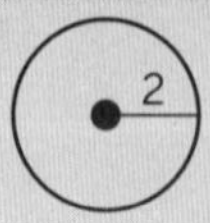	4	12.57	$\frac{12.57}{4} = 3.1428$

You can observe that in each case, **the ratio of circumference to the diameter of the circle is constant**. This constant is denoted by the Greek letter 'π', which is pronounced as 'pie'. Its approximate value is 3.14159....... This is an irrational number.

> **Note**: For calculation purposes, the value of π is taken approximately as $\frac{22}{7}$.

$$\frac{\text{Circumference}}{\text{Diameter}} = \pi \text{ (constant)}$$

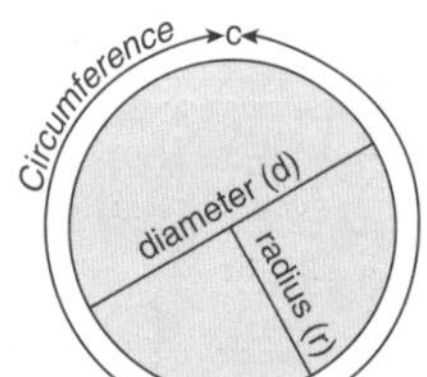

$\Rightarrow$ Circumference = π × Diameter $\Rightarrow$ Circumference

$= \pi \times 2r$ (Diameter = 2 x radius)

$\Rightarrow$ **Circumference = $2\pi r$**, where r is the radius of the circle.

Do You Know?

- Around 250 BC, the Greek mathematician Archimedes devised an algorithm to calculate the value of π.
- 'Pi Day' is celebrated on March 14, which resembles 3.14. The great scientist Albert Einstein was born on Pi Day, that is, on 14 March 1879.
- 'Pi Day' is also celebrated on 22 July.
- Pi has been calculated to over one trillion digits beyond its decimal point.

Solved Examples

Example 13: Find the circumference of a circle whose (a) radius is 5 cm (b) diameter is 15 cm.

(Take value of π as 3.14.)

(a) Circumference of the circle $= 2\pi r = 2 \times 3.14 \times 5$

$= 31.4$ cm

(b) Circumference of the circle $= 2\pi r = \pi(2r) = \pi d$

$= 3.14 \times 15 = 47.1$ cm

> If radius is known, then use $C = 2\pi r$.
> If diameter is known, then you may use $C = \pi d$.

Example 14 Find the number of rotations made by a circular wheel of radius 42 cm to cover a distance of 1056 cm? (Take value of π as $\frac{22}{7}$.)

Let the number of rotations made by the wheel be k. The total distance covered by the wheel is obtained by number of rotations × circumference of the wheel.

$\therefore k \times 2\pi r = 1056 \Rightarrow k \times 2 \times \frac{22}{\cancel{7}_1} \times \cancel{42}^6 = 1056 \Rightarrow k = \frac{1056}{22 \times 12} = \frac{1056}{264} = 4$

Therefore, the number of rotations made by the wheel is 4.

Example 15: Two semi-circles of diameter 7 cm are combined and made into the figure shown here. Find the perimeter of the figure.

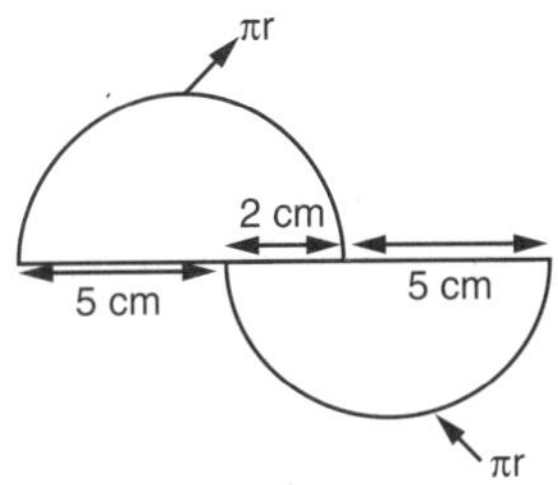

The perimeter of the figure is given by:

> $2\pi r$ = Circumference of a circle
> Hence, $\frac{1}{2} \times 2\pi r = \pi r$ = circumference of a semi-circle.

$\pi r + 5 + \pi r + 5$

$= 2\pi r + 10$

$= \pi d + 10$

$= \frac{22}{\cancel{7}_1} \times \cancel{7}^1 + 10 = 22 + 10 = 32$

$\therefore$ The perimeter of the figure is 32 cm.

Exercise 20.4

1. **Find the circumference of the circles whose radii are given below.**

   a. 12 m b. 19.7 cm c. 22.5 m d. 46.6 cm

2. **Find the circumference of the circles whose diameters are given below.**

   a. 36 cm b. 50 mm c. 102 cm d. 16 m

3. **Find the diameter of the circles whose circumferences are given below.**

   a. 35.8 m b. 101.7 cm c. 125.6 mm d. 37.7 m

4. Find the distance covered in 10 rotations by the front wheel of the road roller whose diameter is 4 m.

5. The ratio of the radii of two circles is 5 : 8. What will be the ratio of their circumferences?

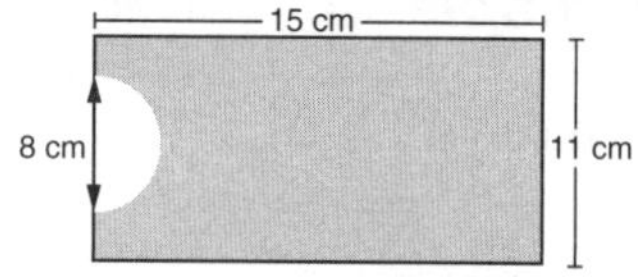

6. A semi-circular part was removed from a rectangular field as shown in the figure. What is the new perimeter of the field?

7. **Find the area of the circles whose radii are given below.**

a. 21 m b. 32 mm c. 49 cm d. 63 m

8. **Find the area of the circles whose diameters are given below.**

a. 28 m b. 40 cm c. 56 mm d. 30 cm

9. **Find the diameters of the circles whose areas are given below.** (Round off the decimals to the nearest integers.)

a. 706.5 m^2 b. 254.34 cm^2 c. 379.94 mm^2 d. 3140 m^2

10. If 1 kg of fertilizer covers an area of half square metre, find the amount of fertilizer required by a farmer for his circular field whose radius is 14 m.

11. Find the total area of Fig. 1 shown alongside.

12. If the area of the shaded region given in Fig. 2 is 39.47 cm^2, find the radius of the circle.

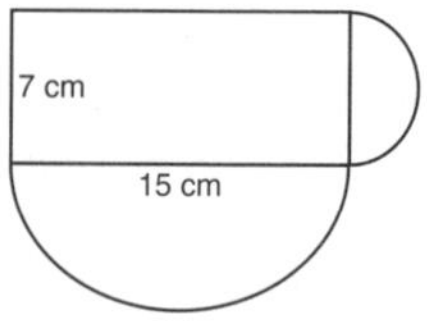

Fig. 1

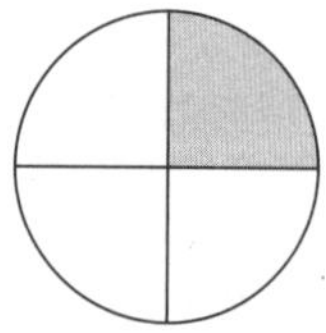

Fig. 2

Area of a Circle

A pizza restaurant has given the following advertisement.

Which deal is better, buying one pizza or two pizzas? In order to answer this question, you need to know how to find the area of the circle.

Let us find out through an activity.

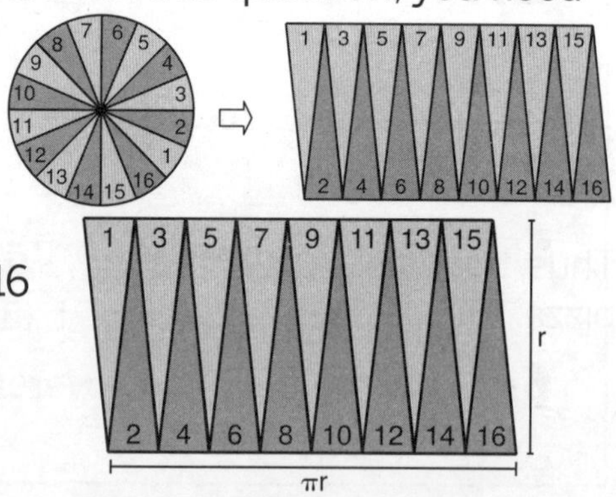

Activity 7: Take a cardboard sheet and cut circles of different radii. Take one circle and fold it such that the circle is divided into 16 congruent parts and colour them. Cut all the 16 sectors and arrange them on the chart as shown.

Which shape is formed after arranging all the parts? What are its base and height?

You can observe that the figure formed after arranging all the parts is approximately a parallelogram whose base is half of the circumference of the circle (πr) and height is the radius of the circle (r).

$\therefore$ Area of the circle = Area of the parallelogram

$$= \text{base} \times \text{height} = \pi r \times r$$
$$= \pi r^2$$

Area of the circle (A) = πr^2

Note: If the number of parts that the circle is divided into increases, then the figure formed after rearranging the sectors will be nearly a rectangle.

Solved Examples

Example 16: Find the area of the circle of diameter 28 cm.

$$\text{Radius of the circle} = \frac{\text{diameter}}{2}$$
$$= \frac{28}{2} = 14 \text{ cm}$$

$$\therefore \text{ Area of the circle (A)} = \pi r^2 = \frac{22}{7} \times 14 \times 14$$
$$= 616 \text{ cm}^2$$

Example 17: Find the diameter of the circle whose area is 1964.5 m^2.

$A = \pi r^2$

$$1964.5 = \frac{22}{7} \times r^2 \Rightarrow r^2 = \frac{7}{22} \times 1964.5 = 625$$

$r^2 = 625 = 25 \times 25 \Rightarrow r = 25$ m

$\therefore$ The diameter of the circle = $2r = 2 \times 25 = 50$ m

Example 18: Solve the problem on pizzas: For the same price, would it be better to buy two 10″ pizzas or one 16″ pizza?

To find out which is better, let us first find the areas of pizzas in both the cases.

Area of one 10″ pizza $= \frac{22}{7} \times 5 \times 5 = 78.57 \text{ in}^2$

[Radius of 10″ pizza $= \frac{10}{2} = 5''$]

10″ pizza means diameter of the pizza is 10″.

$\therefore$ Area of two 10″ pizzas = $2 \times 78.57 = 157.14 \text{ in}^2$

Area of one 16″ pizza $= \frac{22}{7} \times 8 \times 8 = 201.14 \text{ in}^2$

Thus, the area of one 16″ pizza is more than area of two 10″ pizzas. Hence, it is better to buy one 16″ pizza.

Representing 3-D in 2-D

2D shapes are plane shapes, which can only be measured in two dimensions, length and breadth.

Most of the things we see around us have length, breadth as well as height or depth. Such things have 3D shapes.

Pencil box

Book

Solid figures have faces, edges and vertices.

- Face is the flat surface of a solid shape/figure.
- Edge is the line formed by the intersection of two faces.
- Vertex is the intersection of two edges.

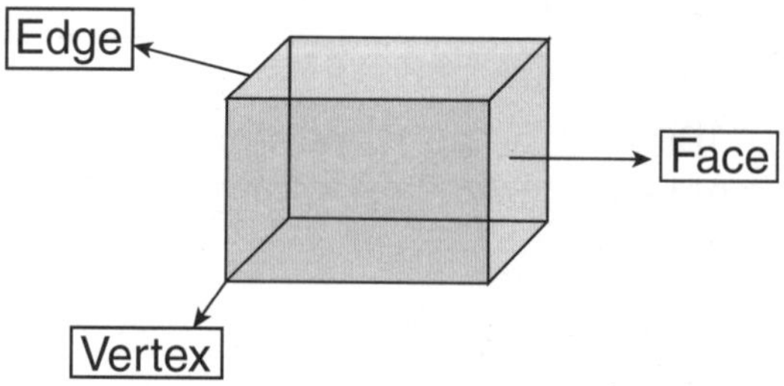

Cube

You must have played many games like ludo using a dice. A dice has 6 equal or congruent sides or faces.

Such a solid in which all 6 faces are squares is known as a **cube**. Thus, a cube is a solid 3D object with 6 equal square faces.

If any of the faces is considered as the base, the remaining faces that meet the base are known as the lateral faces.

A cube has 8 vertices, 6 faces and 12 edges.

In the given cube:

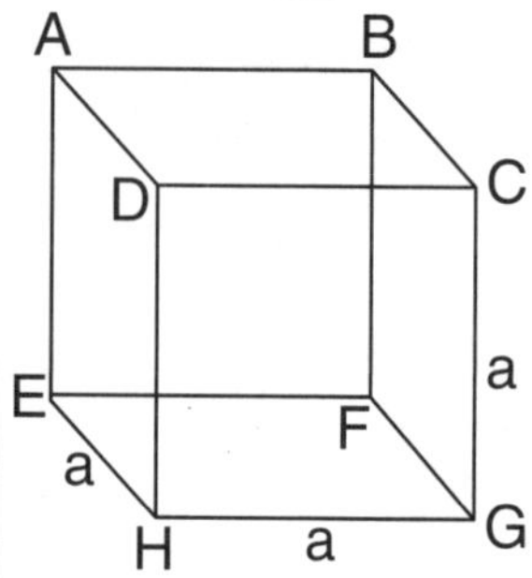

Vertices	A, B, C, D, E, F, G and H
Faces	ABCD, DCGH, ADHE, BCGF, AEFB and EFGH
Lateral faces (if EFGH is considered as the base)	AEFB, ADHE, BCGF and DCGH
Edges	AB, AD, AE, BC, BF, CD, CG, DH, EF, EH, FG and GH

Dimensions of a Cube

Let the length of the side of a cube be a units.

Since the cube has 6 square faces, its surface area will be the sum of the areas of the 6 faces.

Area of any face of a cube = Area of the square with side length a = a^2 sq. units

Lateral surface area of a cube is the sum of the areas of the four faces meeting the base.

Lateral surface area of a cube = Area of lateral faces
= Area of AEFB + Area of ADHE + Area of BCGF + Area of DCGH
= $a^2 + a^2 + a^2 + a^2 = 4a^2$ sq. units

Total surface area of a cube = Lateral surface area + Area of the top + Area of the base
= $4a^2$ + Area of ABCD + Area of EFGH sq. units
= $4a^2 + a^2 + a^2 = 6a^2$ sq. units

Example 19: Find the lateral and the total surface areas of a cube if the length of one side is 7 cm.

Length of one side of the cube (a) = 7 cm

Lateral surface area of the cube = $4a^2 = 4 \times 7 \times 7 = 196$ sq. cm

Total surface area of cube = $6a^2 = 6 \times 7 \times 7 = 294$ sq. cm

Remember

For a cube of side a:

Area of one face = a^2

Lateral surface area $4a^2$

Total surface area = $6a^2$

Cuboid

A **cuboid** is a solid 3D object with 6 rectangular faces. If any one of the faces is considered as the base, the remaining faces that meet the base are known as the lateral faces.

A cuboid has 8 vertices, 6 rectangular faces and 12 edges.

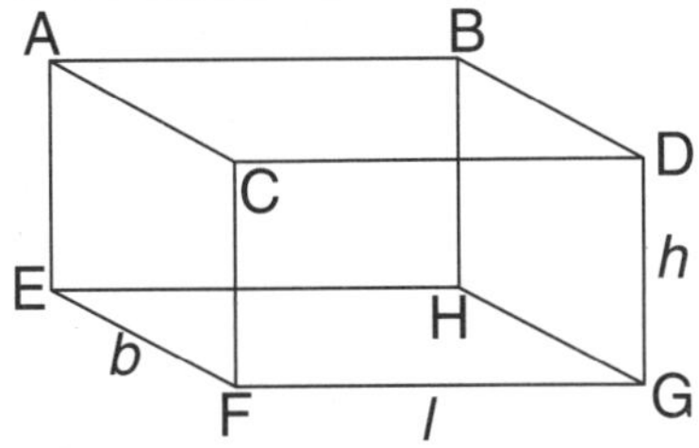

In the given cuboid:

Vertices	A, B, C, D, E, F, G and H
Faces	ABCD, AEFC, AEHB, CDGF, EFGH and BDGH
Lateral faces (If EFGH is considered as the base)	AEFC, AEHB, BDGH and CDGF
Edges	AB, AC, AE, BD, BH, CD, CF, DG, EF, EH, FG and GH

Dimensions of a Cuboid

Let the length of the cuboid be l, the breadth be b and the height be h.

Since the opposite sides of a cuboid are equal,

AB = CD = FG = EH = Length of each rectangular face = l units

AC = EF = BD = GH = Breadth of each rectangular face = b units

AE = CF = BH = DG = Height or depth of the cuboid = h units

Lateral surface area of the cuboid = Areas of the lateral faces

= Area of AEFC + Area of AEHB + Area of BDGH + Area of CDGF

$= b \times h + l \times h + b \times h + l \times h$

$= bh + lh + bh + lh = 2bh + 2lh$ sq. units

$= 2h(l + b)$ sq. units $= 2(l + b) \times h$

= Perimeter of the base $\times h$

Total surface area of the cuboid = Lateral Surface Area + Area of the top + Area of the base

$= 2h(l + b) + l \times b + l \times b$

$= 2lh + 2bh + 2lb$

$= 2(lb + bh + lh)$ sq. units

Example 20: Find the lateral and the total surface areas of a cuboid that is 12 m long, 10 m wide and 8 m high.

Length of the cuboid (l) = 12 m   Breadth of the cuboid (b) = 10 m

Height of the cuboid (h) = 8 m

Lateral surface area of the cuboid = 2h (l + b) = $2 \times 8\ (12 + 10) = 16 \times 22 = 352$ sq. m

Total surface area of the cuboid = 2 (lb + bh + lh) = $2\ (12 \times 10 + 10 \times 8 + 12 \times 8)$

$= 2\ (120 + 80 + 96)$

$= 2\ (296) = 592$ sq. m

Example 21: Priya needs to wrap a gift in a box for her friend. The dimensions of the box are given below.

- The top and bottom of the box are 7×4 cm.
- The sides are both 4×2 cm.
- The front and the back are 7×2 cm.

  How much wrapping paper would Priya need to wrap the box?

  [Hint: The wrapping paper will cover all the surfaces of the box.]

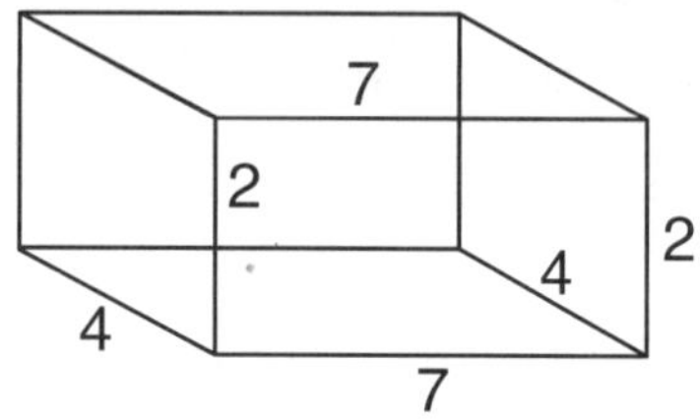

Let us draw the box of the given dimensions.

Length of the cuboid (l) = 7 cm

Breadth of the cuboid (b) = 4 cm

Height of the cuboid (h) = 2 cm

So, the wrapping paper needed to wrap the box will be total surface area of the cuboid.

Total surface area of the cuboid = 2 (lb + bh + lh) = $2\ (7 \times 4 + 4 \times 2 + 7 \times 2)$

$= 2(28 + 8 + 14) = 2(50) = 100$ sq. cm

Therefore, Priya would require 100 sq. cm of wrapping paper to wrap the box.

Exercise 20.5

1 **Find the lateral and the total surface areas of cubes with the given side lengths.**

a. 8 cm   b. 12.5 cm   c. 25 m   d. 16.5 m

2 **Find the lateral and the total surface areas of cuboids for each of the following dimensions.**

a. l = 6 cm, b = 3 cm, h = 2cm

b. l = 13.5 m, b = 10 m, h = 2.5 m

c. l = 4.5 cm, b = 3.5 cm, h = 1.5 cm

3 What is the lateral surface area of a box that is in the shape of a cuboid with base area 250 sq. m and total surface area 1750 sq. m?

4 How much material is required to wrap a cubical box of side 13.5 m?

❺ How much would it cost to paint an auditorium that is 15 m long, 12 m wide and 7 m high if the cost of painting 1 sq. m is ₹12.50?

❻ Neha needs to prepare a carton of 50 cm length, 35 cm breadth and 16 cm height. What will be the cost of the carton if the rate of 1 sq. cm is 10 paisa?

❼ Srishti decided to paint 4 walls of her room that is 15 m long, 6 m wide and 3 m high. Find the area of the four walls and the cost of painting at the rate of ₹50 per square metre.

Summary

1. Perimeter of a rectangle = 2 (length + breadth). Area of a rectangle = length × breadth
2. Perimeter of a square = (4 × side) units. Area of a square = (side × side)
3. Area of a triangle = $\frac{1}{2}$ × length × breadth square units
4. Area of right isosceles triangle = $\frac{1}{2}a^2$, where *a* is the length of one of the equal sides
5. Area of a parallelogram = base × height
6. Units of conversion:

Unit of length	Unit of area	Inter-relationships
Millimitre (mm)	mm^2	
Centimetre (cm)	cm^2	$1\ cm^2 = (10\ mm)^2 = 100\ m^2$
Decimetre (dm)	dm^2	$1\ dm^2 = (10\ cm)^2 = 100\ cm^2$
Metre (m)	m^2	$1\ m^2 = (100\ cm)^2 = 10{,}000\ cm^2$
Decametre (dam)	dam^2	$1\ dam^2 = (10\ m)^2 = 100\ m^2$
Hectometre (hm)	hm^2	$1\ hm^2 = (10\ dam)^2 = 100\ dam^2$
Kilimetre (km)	km^2	$1\ km^2 = (100\ m)^2 = 10{,}00{,}000\ m^2$

7. Circumference of circle (C) = $2\pi r$
8. Area of the circle (A) = πr^2
9. A cube is a solid 3D object with 8 vertices, 6 faces and 12 edges.

Cube (side *a* units)	
Lateral surface area	$4a^2$ sq. units
Total surface area	$6a^2$ sq. units

10. A cuboid is a solid 3D object with 8 vertices, 6 faces and 12 edges.

Cuboid (length *l*, breadth *b* and height *h*)	
Lateral surface area	2h (l + b) sq. units
Total surface area	2 (lb + bh + lh) sq. units

Revision Exercise

1. **Find the perimeter and the area of a rectangle having the following dimensions.**
   a. Length = 15 cm, breadth = 10 cm b. Length = 2.5 m, breadth = 140 cm

2. Find the area of a square whose perimeter is 160 cm.

3. Area of a rectangular hall is 506 sq. ft and its breadth is 11 ft. Find the perimeter of the hall.

4. The area of a square field is 81 hectare. Find the cost of fencing the field at the rate of ₹2.50 per sq. m.

5. Find the area of the shaded portion in the given figure.

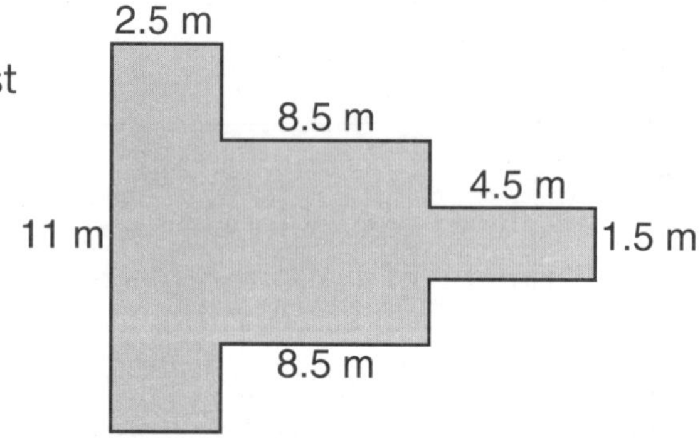

6. A rectangular garden is 120 m long and 75 m wide. It has two crossroads at right angles (exactly at the middle of the garden). One is 3 m wide parallel to the length of the garden and the other is 2.5 m wide parallel to the breadth of the garden. Find the cost of gravelling these crossroads at the cost of ₹15 per sq. m.

7. The figure below shows the dimensions of a rectangular field which measures 70 m by 35 m. There is a rectangular flowerbed at the centre of the field. Find the area which is not covered by the flowerbed.

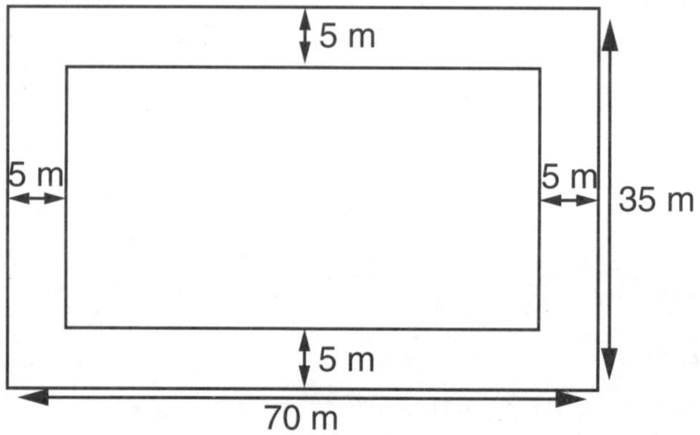

8. The length and breadth of a chart paper are 35 cm and 22 cm respectively. A strip of 6 cm width is cut out from it all around. Find the area of the remaining chart paper and also the area of the cut-out strip.

9. A rectangular farm has the dimensions 27 m by 22 m. A 3 m wide path is all around the farm. Find the area of the path and the money needed for tiling the path at ₹4.75 per sq. m.

10. An auditorium is 26 m long and 17.5 m wide. The event organizing committee decided to lay a carpet on the floor leaving a strip of 50 cm width from all the walls. Find the area of the carpet and the area of the strip uncovered.

11. Find the area and the perimeter of the shaded region in following figure.

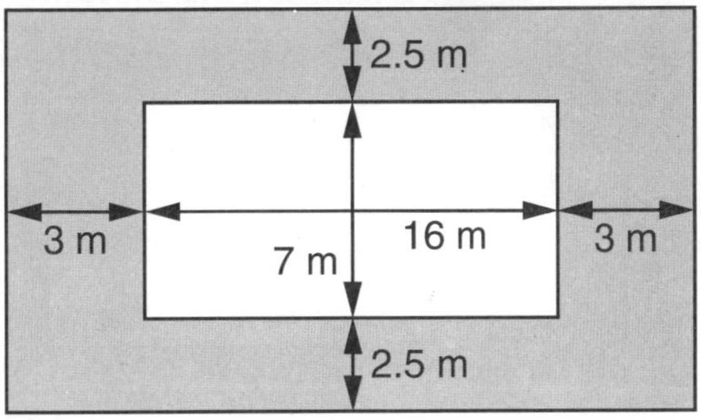

12. A boy rolls a wheel of diameter 21 cm on a straight path. Find the distance covered by the wheel after 45 revolutions.

13. Find the area of the shaded region in the given figure if the radii of the bigger and the smaller circles are 6 cm and 4 cm respectively.

14. Find the radius of the bigger circle if the area of a ring is 164π cm^2 and the area of the smaller circle is 61π cm^2.

15. A rectangular swimming pool has dimensions 45 m by 20 m. A concrete path 3.5 m wide is laid round it. Find the cost of laying the path at a rate of 25 per m^2.

16. Find the cost of the cardboard needed to prepare a box that is 32 cm by 26 cm by 12 cm if the rate is 60 paise per sq. cm.

17. Three cubes each of edge 7 cm are placed end to end. Find the volume and the surface area of the cuboid formed.

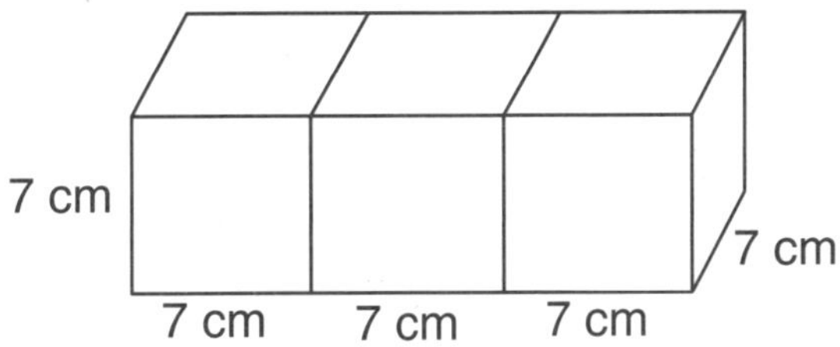

For the Curious Mind

A square lawn is surrounded by a path 3 m wide. If the area of the path is 144 sq. m, find the area of the lawn.

Theme Worksheet 5

1 Fill in the blanks.

a.

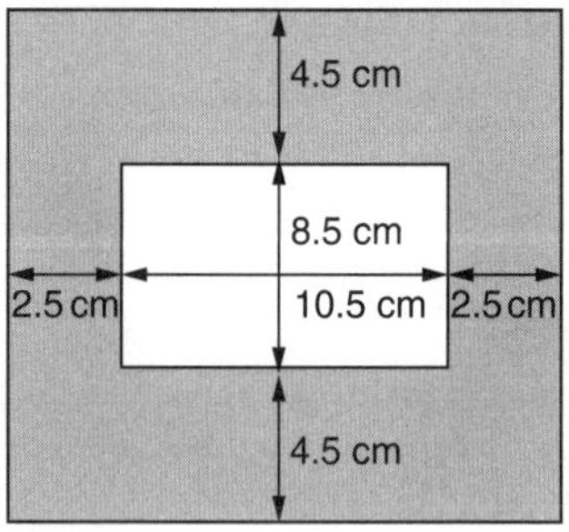

The area of the shaded region in the above figure = ___________

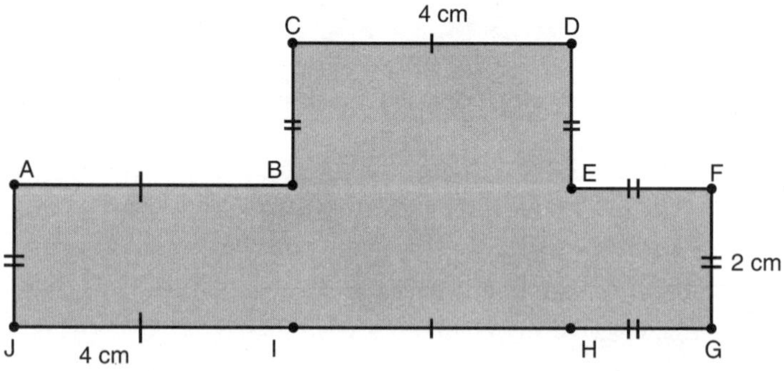

b. Perimeter of the figure above = ____________

c. Area of the figure above = ____________

d.

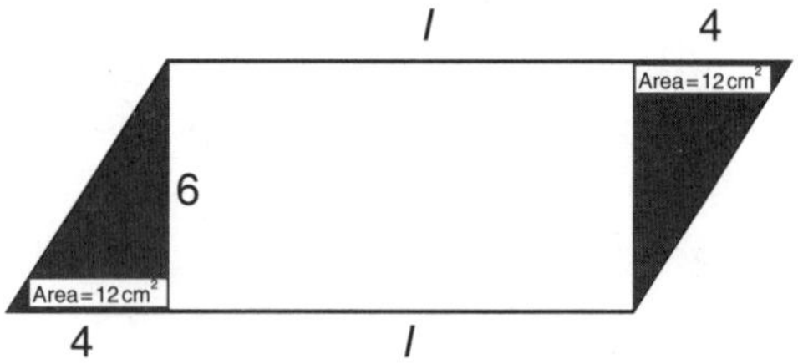

If area of the above parallelogram = 84 cm², then the value of l = ___________

e.

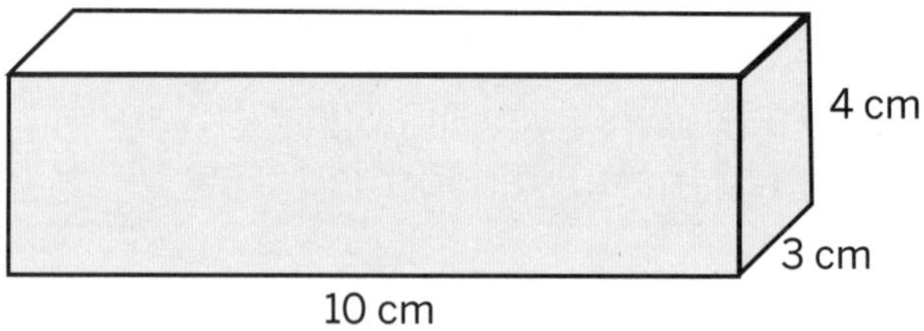

Lateral Surface area of the above figure = ___________

f.

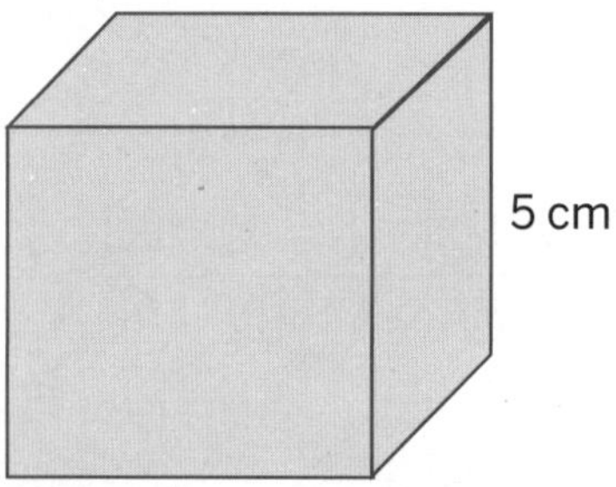

Total surface area of the above figure = ___________

Skill-based Worksheet - Solving Daily Life Problems

1. A company decides to use boxes for packing their products. It manufactures two different-sized boxes to check the feasibility. The first box measures 8 inches by 6.5 inches by 10.5 inches and the second box measures 9 inches by 5.5 inches by 11.5 inches. Which box requires more materials to make?
2. Chinmay wants to wrap a gift box. The top and bottom of the box are 12×10 cm, both the sides are 10×5 cm and the front and back are 12×5 cm. Find the measurement of the wrapping sheet needed by him?
3. A cobbler wants to make a cardboard box to pack the shoe. Find the measurement of the cardboard required to make a 12 by 8 by 6 inch box.
4. The length, width and height of the gymnasium are 50 ft, 30 ft, and 15 ft respectively. If the school children are painting the four walls and the ceiling of the gym, then find the area of the painted parts of the gymnasium.
5. The length, width and height of a living area are 10 ft, 15 ft and 12 ft respectively. After extending the length of the living area, its lateral surface area is 792 sq ft. Find the increased length of the living area.
6. The total surface area of a cubical box is 3750 cm^2. Find the measurement of each side.
7. A pit of length 180 m, width 70 m and depth 40 m is dug around a field. Find the total cost of laying the concrete inside the pit, if it costs 5 rupees per cubic metre.
8. Four cubes, each of side 6 cm, are placed adjacent to each other. Find the total surface area of the cuboid formed.

Mental Maths

Chapter 20 - Perimeter and Area

1. How many faces does a cube have?
2. How many edges does a cuboid have?
3. If the area of the faces of a cube is 9 sq units, what is its lateral surface area?
4. What is the formula used to find the total surface area of a cuboid?
5. The length, breadth and height of a box is 5, 4 and 3 units respectively. Find its lateral surface area.
6. The area of a rectangle is 24 sq units. Find the area of the right angled triangle formed by dividing the rectangle into 2 halves.
7. The base and height of a parallelogram is 6 and 11 units respectively. Find the area of the parallelogram.
8. If the perimeter of a square is 4s then what is the perimeter of an equilateral triangle?

Data Handling

Chapters Covered

21. Data handling

22. Probability

Why this Theme Matters

Probability

Probability is mainly used to predict something which has not happened. Most of the decisions taken in the modern world relies mostly on probability or simply termed as chance of happening.

The departments which mainly rely on probability are:

a. Weather forecast department – They predict weather conditions with the help of certain specific instruments and final outcome will be analyzed using probability.

b. Insurance department – Based on the past data, different policies are framed using the probability theory.

c. Defence department – They frame certain strategies using probability.

d. Sales department – Mainly automobile and electronics industry utilize reliability theory to reduce the probability of failure.

e. Traffic department – They use probability to control the flow of traffic through a highway system.

f. Telephone interchange/exchange department – They use probability theory to analyze the total number of phone calls received in an hour/day/month/year.

THEME 6

Data Handling

21

What I shall learn

- To find arithmetic mean, median and mode of a given set of numbers
- To construct and interpret bar graphs

Let's Get Started

Have you ever heard about the weather forecast? The future weather is predicted by using computer models by comparing previous weather with the current weather.

Such calculations are done using statistics. Today, we live in an age where information is of great importance. This information is presented in a systematic manner using statistics.

Arithmetic Mean

In statistics, the word 'average' means the number that measures the central tendency of the numerical data. **Arithmetic mean** is one of the averages. Arithmetic mean of a given set of observations is obtained by the following formula.

$$\text{Arithmetic mean} = \frac{\text{Sum of the observations}}{\text{Number of observations}}$$

In the above example, arithmetic mean $= \frac{219}{12} = 18.25$.

Median

In statistics, the middle term among the observations is known as the **median**. Once the raw data is written in an array, the $\left(\frac{n+1}{2}\right)^{\text{th}}$ term is its median for odd number of values, where n is the number of observations. For even number of observations, it is the sum of the two middle terms divided by 2.

Example 1: Find the median in the following observation.

Heights of the students of Class 8 (in feet): 5, 5.2, 5.5, 5.7, 5.3, 5.4, 5.8

Arranging the given information in ascending order to form an array, we get

5, 5.2, 5.3, 5.4, 5.5, 5.7, 5.8

Since the number of observations is odd, the median is $\left(\frac{7+1}{2}\right)^{th} = \left(\frac{8}{2}\right)^{th} = 4^{th}$ term, that is, 5.4.

Mode

Frequency is the number of times that an observation occurs in a data. The observation with the greatest frequency is known as the **mode** of the given data.

Example: The ages of 10 students are given below.

12.5, 12.1, 12.3, 12.4, 12.5, 12.3, 12.4, 12.3, 12.3, 12.4

We observe that the age of the maximum number of students is 12.3. Hence, 12.3 is the mode.

Range

The difference between the highest observation and the lowest observation of the given data is known as the **range** of that data.

Example 2: The highest temperatures recorded on some days in the month of January in North Karnataka are given below.

31°, 32°, 33°, 34°, 35°, 36°, 37°, 38°, 39°, 40°, 42°, 41°, 39°, 38°, 37°, 39°, 40°, 39°

Arranging them in ascending order, we get

31°, 32°, 33°, 34°, 35°, 36°, 37°, 37°, 38°, 38°, 39°, 39°, 39°, 39°, 40°, 40°, 41°, 42°

The observations range from 31° to 42°. Therefore, the range is 11°.

Exercise 21.1

1. The given data represents the number of people speaking English in 14 villages. Construct an array by arranging the given data in ascending order. Find the arithmetic mean, median and mode.

   2, 3, 5, 6, 8, 2, 0, 0, 3, 4, 5, 1, 1, 2

2. Given are the scores of Class 8 students in a cricket match. Find the arithmetic mean, median and mode.

   33, 45, 48, 32, 32

3. The following data represents the minimum temperature recorded in a city over 5 days in a month. Find the arithmetic mean, median and mode.

   24°, 30°, 22°, 20°, 24°

Bar Graphs

You know that **bar graph** is a pictorial representation of numerical data in the form of rectangles (or bars) of equal width and varying heights.

The rectangular bars can be drawn either vertically or horizontally, with equal spaces between them. The heights vary according to the value the rectangle represents.

Steps to draw a bar graph.

Step 1. Title, X-axis and Y-axis: On the graph paper, write the title of the graph. Draw a horizontal line OX and a vertical line OY. These lines are the X-axis and the Y-axis respectively.

Step 2. Labelling: Label the two axes according to the data given. Along the X-axis, mark points at equal intervals and write the names of the data that are to be plotted.

Step 3. Scale: Choose a suitable scale for the Y-axis and find the heights of the rectangular bars.

Choose an appropriate scale such that

- the graph occupies most of the page
- the divisions on the axis make it easy to plot the points accurately

Take 1 small division as 2, 5, 10, 25, 50, etc.

Step 4. Drawing: Draw rectangular bars of equal width and heights determined in Step 3. The bars should be centred on points marked on the X-axis. These bars represent the given data.

Example 3: The average marks in various subjects of Class 7 are shown below.

Subject	English	Hindi	Mathematics	Science	Social Studies
Average Marks	65	70	85	80	70

Represent this data on a bar graph.

You can draw the bar graph by following the steps given below.

Step 1. Title, X-axis and Y-axis: On the graph paper, write the title 'Bar graph showing average marks of all subjects of Class 7'. Draw a horizontal line OX and a vertical line OY. These lines are the X-axis and the Y-axis respectively.

Step 2. Labelling: Label 'Subjects' along the X-axis and 'Average marks' along the Y-axis. Along the X-axis, mark points at equal intervals and write the names of the subjects.

Step 3. Scale: Let the scale on the Y-axis be: 1 cm = 10 marks.

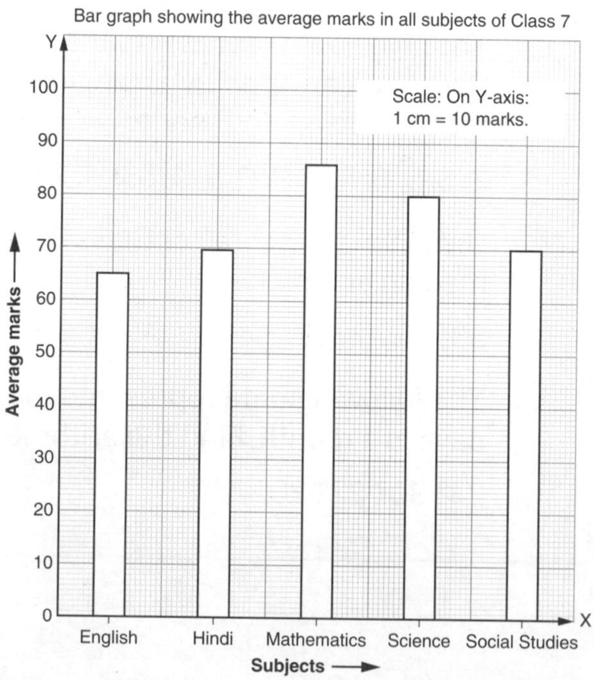

The heights of the various bars are: English = 65 small divisions = 65 marks, Hindi = 70 small divisions = 70 marks, Mathematics = 85 small divisions = 85 marks, Science = 80 small divisions = 80 marks, Social Studies = 70 small divisions = 70 marks.

Step 4. Draw rectangular bars of equal width and heights determined in Step 3 at the points marked in Step 2.

The completed bar graph is as shown above.

Drawing and Reading a Bar Graph

Example 4: Marks scored by some students in algebra test are given below.

Names	Hemant	Rishi	Sunita	Nisha	Abhi
Marks scored	70	68	74	85	60

Follow the same steps as followed in the previous examples. Draw bars of equal width and determine the heights for each student.

The completed bar graph is as shown below.

Bar graph showing the marks scored in algebra test

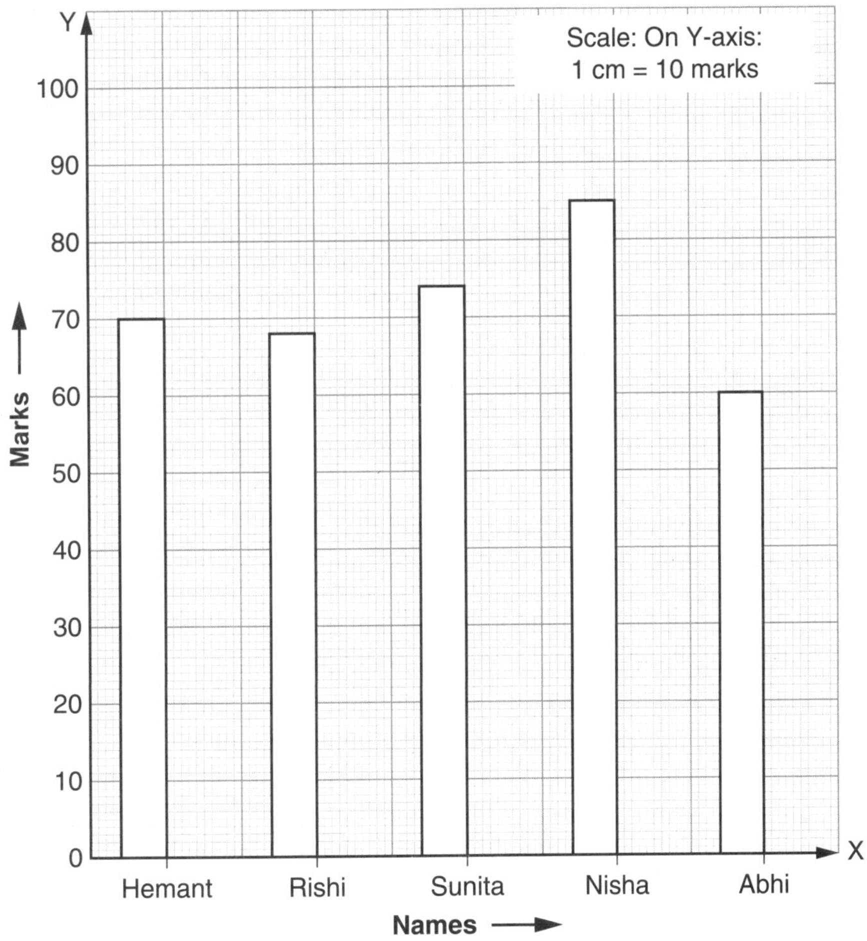

Rectangular Bars

These bars are of equal width and are drawn at equal intervals. This makes no impact on the information conveyed by the bar graph or in interpreting the bar graph.

This is done only to make the presentation look good.

Reading Bar Graphs

A bar graph uses rectangular bars to show comparison among different categories. You can draw conclusions from a bar graph. This is called **reading or interpreting the bar graph**.

Example 5: Given below is the bar graph showing the amount collected for donations by Section A of different classes.

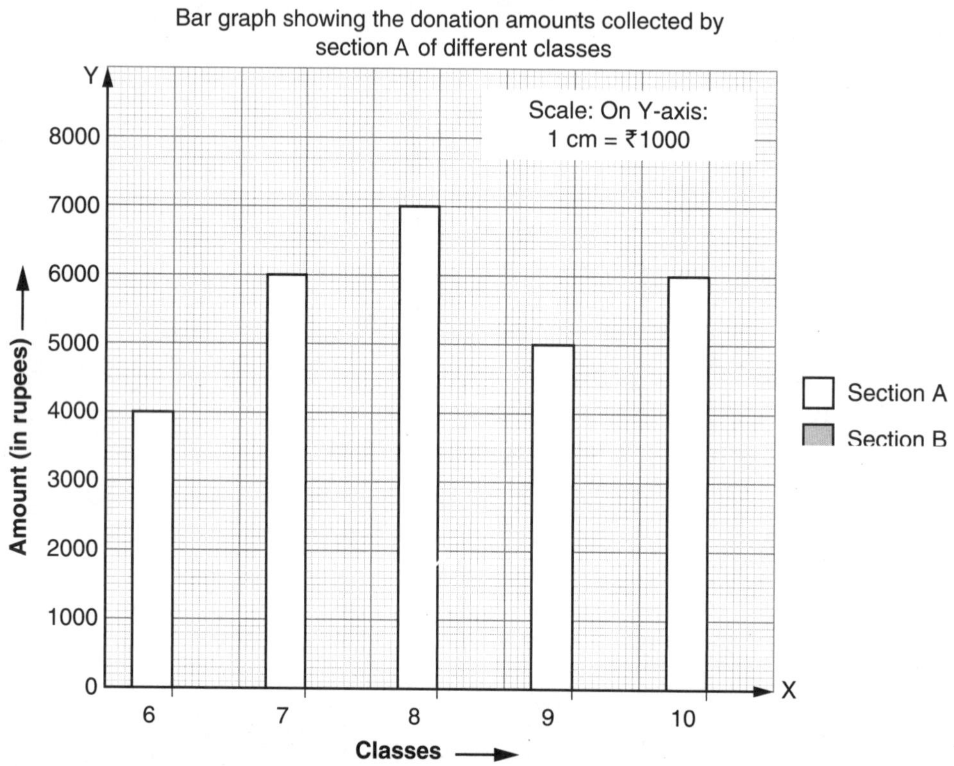

Read the bar graph and answer the following questions.

i. Which Class has collected more amount? How much?

ii. What is the difference in the amounts collected by Class 9 and Class 6?

iii. Are there any classes which collected the same amount? If yes, which classes and how much?

iv. Which class has collected the minimum amount? How much?

We have,

i. Class 8 has collected more amount. They collected ₹7000.

ii. The difference in the amounts = ₹5000 – ₹4000 = ₹1000

iii. Both Class 7 and Class 10 have collected ₹6000 each.

iv. Class 6 has collected the minimum amount, that is, ₹4,000.

Exercise 21.2

1. Given below is the data of outdoor games liked by 100 girls.

Games	Throwball	Volleyball	Basketball	Cricket
Girls	35	10	35	20

Represent the data using a bar graph.

2. Given below is the data on popular tourist destinations.

Cities	Agra	Mysore	Kashmir	Goa	Varanasi
Number of Tourists	20,000	30,000	35,000	40,000	25,000

Represent the data using a bar graph.

3. A school survey on students who play indoor games is given below.

Indoor Games	Carrom	Chess	Chinese Checkers	Ludo	Bowling
Number of Students	320	400	200	300	260

Represent the data using a bar graph.

4. The number of children who opted for various summer camps is given.

Camps	Sports	Swimming	Aerobics	Computers	Yoga & Meditation
Number of Students	700	800	500	850	500

Represent the data using a bar graph.

Summary

1. The mean for a given data is given by the following expression:

$$\text{Mean} = \frac{\text{Sum of the given observations}}{\text{Number of observations}}$$

Mean is also called average.

2. Median of data is the value of the middle observation when the given data is arranged in the ascending or the descending order.
3. Mode of data is the value of the observation that occurs most frequently.
4. The difference between the highest observation and the lowest observation of the given data is known as the range of that data.
5. A bar graph uses rectangular bars to show comparison among different categories.

Revision Exercise

1 The given data represents the goals scored by 15 kindergarten students in a football match. Construct a simple frequency distribution table and find the mean, median and mode for the following data.

2, 4, 1, 2, 5, 3, 4, 2, 1, 5, 6, 2, 2, 4, 6, 1, 2, 3, 5, 6

2 A survey was conducted to know which colours students like the most. The list of colours that students like are given below.

Pink	Red	Green	Yellow	Blue	Violet	Orange
300	200	100	150	150	150	100

Construct a bar graph to display the information.

3 **Fill in the blanks.**

a. Data in its original form is known as __________ data.

b. Data arranged in either increasing or decreasing order is known as __________.

c. The number of times an observation occurs in a data is known as __________.

d. __________ is a graphical representation of numerical data in the form of rectangles (or bars) of equal width drawn at equal spaces and having varying heights.

4 **Choose the correct options.**

a. Arithmetic mean is calculated using the formula

i. Arithmetic mean $= \dfrac{\text{Sum of the observations}}{\text{Number of observations}}$

ii. Arithmetic mean $= \dfrac{\text{Number of observations}}{\text{Sum of the observations}}$

iii. Arithmetic mean = Sum of observations – Number of observations

iv. Arithmetic mean = Sum of observations – Number of observations

b. If raw data is written in an array, the __________ term is its median for odd number of terms, where n is the number of observations.

i. $\left(\dfrac{n+3}{2}\right)^{th}$ ii. $\left(\dfrac{n+2}{2}\right)^{th}$ iii. $\left(\dfrac{n+1}{2}\right)^{th}$ iv. $(n+1)^{th}$

c. The observation with the greatest frequency is known as the __________ of the given data.

i. median ii. arithmetic mean iii. geometric mean iv. mode

d. For a given set of data, the value of mean, median and mode is __________.

i. always same ii. always different iii. sometimes equal iv. can't say

THEME 6

Probability 22

What I shall learn

- To learn about probability and related terms.

Probability

In our day-to-day interactions with friends and family members, we would have heard some sentences of the following type.

What do you think is the meaning of the word 'CHANCE'?

Dictionary Meaning: the possibility that something will happen

We generally use the term 'chance' in instances wherein we are not sure of things. It may happen or may not happen.

So, **probability** is basically determining the extent to which something may happen.

Consider some examples given below under each category.

Certain to Happen	Impossible	May or May Not Happen
Sun rising in the east.	A bird carrying an elephant.	It will rain in the month of August.
The month of April comes after the month of March.	An ant growing to a height of 5 metres.	Indian football team will qualify for the next Football World Cup.

Now, create at least three examples for each category.

Experimental Probability

Activity 1: Take a one rupee coin and observe both sides of the coin. Toss the coin and record the observation. Use tally marks to record your observation. Repeat this 9 more times and record your observation after every toss.

You will notice that there are only two possibilities, that is, either heads or tails.

Here, tossing a coin is known as **Experiment** and the two possibilities are known as **Outcomes**.

The set of all possible outcomes of an experiment is known as **sample space** of that experiment.

An experiment is said to be a **random experiment** if its outcomes cannot be predicted with certainty. The outcome of a random experiment is independent and it is not affected by the previous outcome.

Let us say you have the following data after performing the coin-tossing experiment for 10 times.

The sample space of this experiment is {Head, Tail}

Number of times heads appeared = 7 times

Number of times tails appeared = 3 times

Total number of times the experiment was repeated = 10

Heads	𝍸 ‖	7
Tails	|||	3

7 out of 10 times is the probability of heads appearing and 3 out of 10 is the probability of tails appearing. We can write this in fractional form as shown below.

Probability of heads = $\frac{7}{10}$ Probability of tails = $\frac{3}{10}$

In general, probability of an outcome = $\frac{\text{number of times the outcome occurs}}{\text{total number of times the experiment is repeated}}$

Probability can also be expressed in terms of percentage.

Probability of heads = $\frac{7}{10} \times 100\% = \frac{700}{10} = 70\%$

Probability of tails = $\frac{3}{10} \times 100\% = \frac{100}{10} = 30\%$

Notation: The capital letter 'P' is used to write the probability in short form. Also, the first letter of outcome is used in a bracket to write the probability. For example, the probability of the occurrence of heads can be written in the short form as **P(H)**. Similarly, the probability of tails can be written as **P(T)**.

Think: Do you think the probability of heads and tails will be the same if you repeat the experiment for 10 times?

Repeat the experiment and find the probabilities of heads and tails. You will notice that probability may or may not be the same.

Activity 2: Take a die with dots representing numbers from 1 to 6 on its faces. What are the possible outcomes in this experiment? Throw the die 15 times and record the observations each time.

Sample space for this experiment is {1,2,3,4,5,6}

1	2	3	4	5	6
‖	||||			|||	‖	|||

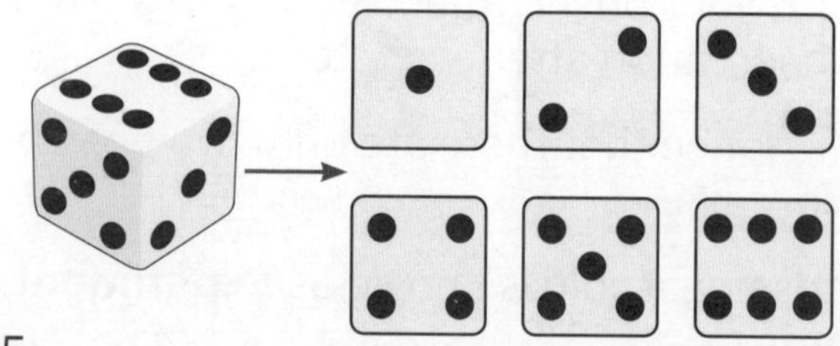

Total number of times experiment is repeated = 15

$$\text{Probability of outcome 1} = \frac{\text{Number of times the outcome occured}}{\text{Total number of times the experiment is repeated}} = \frac{2}{15}$$

$$\text{Probability of outcome 2} = \frac{\text{Number of times the outcome occured}}{\text{Total number of times the experiment is repeated}} = \frac{4}{15}$$

$$\text{Probability of outcome 3} = \frac{\text{Number of times the outcome occured}}{\text{Total number of times the experiment is repeated}} = \frac{1}{15}$$

$$\text{Probability of outcome 4} = \frac{\text{Number of times the outcome occured}}{\text{Total number of times the experiment is repeated}} = \frac{3}{15} = \frac{1}{5}$$

$$\text{Probability of outcome 5} = \frac{\text{Number of times the outcome occured}}{\text{Total number of times the experiment is repeated}} = \frac{2}{15}$$

$$\text{Probability of outcome 6} = \frac{\text{Number of times the outcome occured}}{\text{Total number of times the experiment is repeated}} = \frac{3}{15} = \frac{1}{5}$$

Notation: Probabilities can be written as P(1), P(2), P(3), P(4), P(5) and P(6).

Solved Examples

Example 1: A die numbered 1 to 6 is rolled 100 times and the results are recorded in a table. Find the probability of each outcome.

1	2	3	4	5	6
18	9	8	16	37	12

Total number of times the die rolled = 100

$\therefore P(1) = \frac{18}{100} = \frac{9}{50}$ $\quad P(2) = \frac{9}{100}$ $\quad P(3) = \frac{8}{100} = \frac{2}{25}$

$P(4) = \frac{16}{100} = \frac{4}{25}$ $\quad P(5) = \frac{37}{100}$ $\quad P(6) = \frac{12}{100} = \frac{3}{25}$

Example 2: A spinning wheel is divided into four equal parts, which are coloured with four different colours. The wheel is spun 20 times and the results are recorded in a table. Find the probabilities of each outcome.

The possible outcomes are blue, yellow, red and green. The wheel is spun 20 times.

Blue	Yellow	Red	Green
7	5	6	2

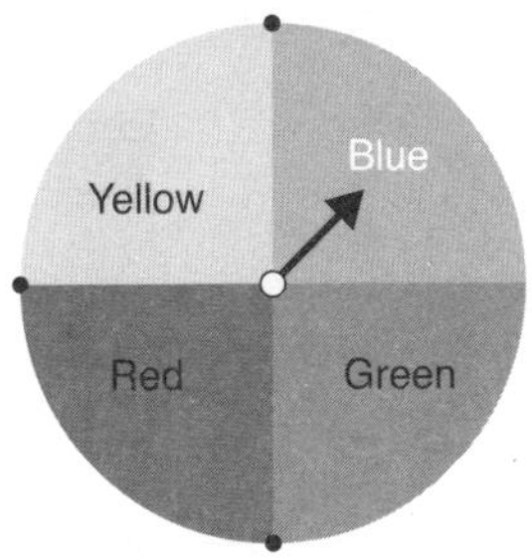

$\therefore P(B) = \frac{7}{20}$ $\quad P(Y) = \frac{5}{20} = \frac{1}{4}$ $\quad P(R) = \frac{6}{20} = \frac{3}{10}$ $\quad P(G) = \frac{2}{20} = \frac{1}{10}$

where B, Y, R and G refer to Blue, Yellow, Red and Green balls respectively.

Example 3: In a bag, there are three different coloured balls, that is, yellow, blue and red. A student is asked to pick a ball without looking into the bag. This was repeated 10 times and each time the result was recorded. Find the probability of each outcome.

Blue	Yellow	Red
4	5	1

Total number of times the experiment is repeated = 10

$\therefore P(B) = \frac{4}{10} = \frac{2}{5} \qquad P(Y) = \frac{5}{10} = \frac{1}{2} \qquad P(R) = \frac{1}{10}$

where B, Y, and R refer to Blue, Yellow and Red balls respectively.

Exercise 22.1

1 **Classify the following into three categories, that is, certain to happen, impossible and may or may not happen.**

a. Lightning will be observed on every Sunday of this year.
b. A coin shows heads after every toss.
c. As the side length of a square increases, its perimeter also increases.
d. Water flows from low-lying area to higher level without any external force.
e. A car without any fuel will travel 1000 km.
f. When a die numbered from 1 to 6 is rolled, it shall land with 9 on top.

2 **Write the sample space for the following random experiments.**

a. Tossing a coin
b. Rolling a die numbered 1 to 6
c. Spinning a wheel consisting of four parts colored as violet, red, white and yellow
d. Selecting an odd number between 1 to 20

3 A coin is tossed 500 times. Heads appeared 275 times and the rest of the times, tails appeared. Find the probability of heads and tails.

4 A die is rolled 200 times. Find the probabilities of each outcome using the information given in the table.

1	2	3	4	5	6
25	36	34	28	33	44

5 In a school of 400 students, a survey was conducted on their favourite subject. The results are given below. Find the probability for each subject.

Hindi	English	Maths	Science	Social Science
78	90	86	115	31

6 A spinning wheel shown below is spun 30 times and the results are recorded in a table. Find the probabilities of each outcome.

White	Green	Rose	Blue	Yellow	Red
7	10	6	2	4	1

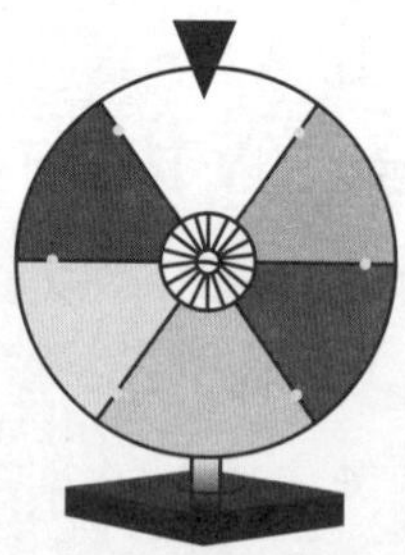

Revision Exercise

1. Classify the following into one of the following categories; 'certain to happen', 'impossible' and 'may or may not happen'.

a. A bike without any fuel and electric power can travel 500 km.

b. A coin shows tails after every 2 toss.

c. When a die numbered 1 to 6 is rolled, it lands with the number 0 on top.

d. Team A will win the football match today.

e. When a die numbered 1 to 6 is rolled, any of the numbers from 1 to 6 can appear on the top.

2. Choose the correct options.

a. A coin is tossed 30 times. Tails appeared 15 times and heads appeared the rest of the times. The probability of heads is

i. 25% ii. 50% iii. 30% iv. 60%

b. From a set of cards numbered 1 to 20, one card is randomly picked at a time. Find the probability that the card is a multiple of 5.

i. 40% ii. 20% iii. 50% iv. 60%

c. Each of the letters in the word 'HONEST' is written on separate cards. Then, they are kept face down on a table. If you pick a card at random, what is the probability that the letter written on it will be 'H'?

i. $\frac{1}{6}$ ii. $\frac{1}{3}$ iii. $\frac{1}{8}$ iv. $\frac{1}{10}$

d. When a die numbered 1 to 6 is rolled, the probability of getting an even number is

i. $\frac{3}{6}$ ii. $\frac{2}{6}$ iii. $\frac{1}{6}$ iv. $\frac{1}{6}$

e. The probability of picking a white marble from a bag of 20 marbles containing 4 white marbles is

i. $\frac{4}{20}$ ii. $\frac{1}{2}$ iii. $\frac{1}{5}$ iv. $\frac{2}{5}$

3. State whether the following statements are true (T) or false (F).

a. When a coin is tossed, the probability of getting a head is 5.

b. The probability of heads appearing 4 times if the coin is tossed for 10 times is 40%.

c. The probability of getting 1 if the die is thrown 5 times is 20%.

d. The probability of a card, numbered as 6, being picked if the pack of cards containing numbers from 1 to 10 is $\frac{1}{6}$.

e. The probability of picking a green ball out of 10 balls if there are 3 green balls is 30%.

Theme Worksheet 6

1. The number of tourists who visited different places in Mysore is given in the table below. Write the exact number of the tourists who visited the destinations, construct a bar graph and answer the following questions.

Tourist Places	Mysore Palace	Mysore Zoo	Jaganmohan Palace	Dasara Exhibition	KRS Dam
Number of tourists	Thrice as that of Jaganmohan Palace	Twice as that of Dasara Exhibition	Half as that of KRS Dam	Twice as that of KRS dam	200

a. Which tourist destination witnessed maximum number of tourists?

b. Which tourist destination witnessed minimum number of tourists?

c. Find the total number of tourists witnessed by all the tourist destinations.

2. A bag had 30 marbles. Find the probability of drawing different coloured marbles.

Colour of the marble	Number of marbles	Probability
White	3	
Yellow	5	
Pink	7	
Brown	8	
Green	7	

Skill-based Worksheet - Understanding and interpreting data

1. The table given below contains the area of 5 oceans in km^2 which is the approximated value when rounded off to ten crores and crore. Construct a bar graph.

Name of the ocean	Pacific ocean	Atlantic ocean	Indian ocean	Southern ocean	Arctic ocean
Area in km^2	17,00,00,000	9,00,00,000	7,00,00,000	2,00,00,000	2,00,00,000

2. The sales of different cars in a year are given. Find the mean, median and mode.

   15, 25, 21, 19, 23, 17, 24, 16, 22, 18, 20, 20

3. In an electronic showroom, 20 fridges were sold in a day out of 50. Find the probability of the fridges being sold and the probability of the fridges left unsold.

4. The weather forecast department recorded that it rained for 15 days in the month of April. Find the probability of the number of days it rained and the number of days it didn't rain.

Cross-curricular Worksheet- Integrating Art Education

The Taj Mahal is one of the wonders in the world. It is a white marble mausoleum located in Agra, India. It was built by the Mughal emperor Shah Jahan in memory of his wife, Mumtaz Mahal. The white marble has been inlaid with semi-precious stones including jade, crystal, lapis lazuli, amethyst and turquoise, forming intricate designs with in a technique known as pietra dura.

It incorporates the traditional design of Persian and Mughal architecture. The tomb is the main structure and the central focus of the entire complex. The spectacular feature is the marble double dome that surrounds the tomb with a broad padma kosa.

Its central dome is surrounded by four smaller domes; four slender towers, or minarets, stood at the corners.

Some of the features of the structure of Taj Mahal are given in the table. Construct a bar graph for the following.

Features of Structure of Taj Mahal	Central dome	Central inner dome	Tower	Building	Corner Minarets
Height in feet	213	81	133	186	137

Mental Maths

Chapter 21 - Data Handling

1. Find the mean of the following numbers: 6, 5, 5, 4, 3, 7.
2. Find the median of the following numbers: 45, 23, 25, 32, 21.
3. Find the mode of the following numbers: 23, 24, 15, 26, 27, 15, 12, 15.
4. Find the most appropriate scale to be chosen in a bar graph that represents the data given below:

   The number of students of different schools who attended science exhibition are 200, 300, 400, 500 and 600.
5. Find the most appropriate scale to be chosen in a bar graph that represents the data given below:

   The number of students who participated in different games are 10, 15, 35, 25 and 40.

Chapter 22 - Probability

1. Find the probability of the sale of 35 two-wheelers out of 50 two-wheelers.
2. Find the probability of purchase of 15 sarees out of 20 sarees.
3. Find the probability of damage of 12 glasses out of 50 glasses.
4. Find the probability of getting members for 4 insurance policies out of 20 insurance policies.
5. Find the probability of departure of 5 buses in an hour out of 10 buses.

Test 1

Chapters 1–5 **Maximum marks: 20**

1 Choose the correct options. **($5 \times 1 = 5$)**

a. The smallest fraction among $1\frac{2}{3}, 1\frac{4}{5}, \frac{2}{5}$, and $\frac{1}{3}$ is ____. [ ]

i. $\frac{1}{3}$ ii. $1\frac{2}{3}$ iii. $1\frac{4}{5}$ iv. $\frac{2}{5}$

b. $\frac{2}{6}$ x 36 is ______. [ ]

i. 72 ii. 6 iii. 8 iv. 12

c. $-84 \div 12 =$ _____ [ ]

i. 7 ii. −7 iii. 6 iv. −6

d. The value of $(7^5)^4$ is [ ]

i. 7^9 ii. 7^1 iii. 7^{20} iv. 7

e. $\frac{7}{8} \div \frac{8}{16}$ [ ]

i. $\frac{7}{16}$ ii. $\frac{1}{14}$ iii. $1\frac{1}{4}$ iv. $1\frac{3}{4}$

2 Fill in the blanks. **($5 \times 1 = 5$)**

a. The additive identity element is _____.

b. The product of a rational number and its reciprocal is _____.

c. Fractions with different numerators and denominators but having the same value are called ________ fractions.

d. a^m x a^n = _________

e. The number of distinct elements in a set is called _______ number.

3 Answer the following questions. **($2 \times 2 = 4$)**

a. Four students started walking from the same place. If their steps measure 24 cm, 32 cm, 15 cm and 36 cm respectively, at what distance will all four students step together?

b. Find the least number which should be multiplied with 3125 to get a perfect cube. What is this perfect cube? Find its cube root.

4 Answer the following questions. **($2 \times 3 = 6$)**

a. Find the value of $(2^5)^2 - \left(\frac{4^3 \times 27^4}{81 \times 36^3}\right)$

b. In a classroom of 30 students, $\frac{2}{3}$ of the students speak Telugu, of these $\frac{1}{5}$ also speak Kannada. Find the number of students who speak both Telugu and Kannada.

Test 2

Chapters 6–10 **Maximum marks: 20**

1 Choose the correct options. **($5 \times 1 = 5$)**

a. The simplest form of $5\frac{1}{2}:1\frac{3}{8}$ is ________. [ ]

i. 2 : 1 ii. 4 : 1 iii. 5 : 1 iv. 6 : 1

b. If the cost of 25 chocolates is ₹125, then the cost of 15 chocolates is ________. [ ]

i. ₹5 ii. ₹50 iii. ₹75 iv. ₹90

c. Profit is the difference between the cost price and the ________. [ ]

i. loss ii. selling price iii. profit iv. None of these

d. Rate of interest (R) in terms of simple interest (SI), time (T) and principal (P) is _____. [ ]

i. $\frac{P \times T}{100 \times I}$ ii. $\frac{100 \times T}{P \times I}$ iii. $\frac{I \times 100}{P \times T}$ iv. $\frac{I \times T}{100 \times P}$

e. Time taken (T) by a vehicle in terms of speed (S) and distance (D) is ________. [ ]

i. D + S ii. D × S iii. D ÷ S iv. S ÷ D

2 Write T for True and F for False. **($5 \times 1 = 5$)**

a. In a proportion, product of means = 2(product of extremes). [ ]

b. 0.003 is expressed as 0.03%. [ ]

c. If loss per cent and selling price (SP) are known, the cost price (CP) can be calculated as

$$CP = \frac{\{100\} \times SP}{100 - Loss\%}$$ [ ]

d. The simple interest on ₹1000 at 5% for 2 years is ₹500. [ ]

e. If an object travels equal distances in equal intervals of time, then the object has a uniform speed. [ ]

3 Answer the following questions briefly. **($2 \times 2 = 4$)**

a. Find the simple interest on ₹75,000 at $5\frac{1}{5}$% per annum for a year. Also find the amount.

b. A person sold two wireless routers for ₹3000 each, gaining 20% on one and losing 20% on the other. Find the gain percentage or loss percentage.

4 Answer the following questions. **($2 \times 3 = 6$)**

a. An amount of ₹462 is to be divided into three parts such that first one is $\frac{3}{5}$ of the second and the ratio between the second and the third parts is 7 : 2. Find the three parts.

b. A vehicle covers a certain distance in 52 minutes with a uniform speed of 60 km/h. How much time will it take to cover the same distance when its speed is decreased to 26 km/h?

Test 3

Chapters 11–12 **Maximum marks: 20**

1 Choose the correct options. **($5 \times 1 = 5$)**

a. An algebraic expression that contains two or more terms is called a _____. [ ]

i. monomial ii. trinomial iii. polynomial iv. binomial

b. The coefficient of x in the term $6x^3y^2$ is ________. [ ]

i. $x^2 + 4$ ii. $x^2 - 4$ iii. $6x^2y^2$ iv. $6x$

c. The degree of the polynomial $18x^2 - 2x^2y^2 + 6y^2$ is ________. [ ]

i. 2 ii. 6 iii. 4 iv. 8

d. $(6t - 5z) + (-3z + 2t)$ [ ]

i. $3t - 3z$ ii. $8t - 8z$ iii. $8t - 2z$ iv. 8

e. For $t = 1$ and $z = 1$, the value of expression $(6t - 5z) + (-3z + 2t) =$ ________ [ ]

i. 2 ii. 0 iii. -2 iv. -1

2 Write T for True and F for False. **($5 \times 1 = 5$)**

a. The degree of $4x^2y + 3xy^2 + 5xy + 7$ is 3. [ ]

b. $(18a - 2b) - (2b + 3a) = 21a - 4b$ [ ]

c. The number of letters in the English alphabet is a variable. [ ]

d. The solution set of $t < 4$, t belongs to N is $t = \{1, 2, 3, 4\}$ [ ]

e. $x + \frac{1}{x}$ is not a polynomial. [ ]

3 Answer the following questions briefly. **($2 \times 2 = 4$)**

a. i. What should be subtracted from $1 + m - m^2$ to get $2m + m^2$?

ii. What should be added to $a^2b^2 + 4ab + 12$ to get $4a^2b^2 - 3ab + 17$?

b. Solve the following linear equations.

i. $5x - 18 = -3$ ii. $\frac{7x}{12} = 21$

4 Answer the following questions. **($2 \times 3 = 6$)**

a. The sum of three consecutive multiples of 2 is 42. Find the multiples.

b. Find the solution set for the inequation, $-6 \leq 4x + 6 \leq 26$ where $x \in Z$.

Test 4

Chapters 13–15 **Maximum marks: 20**

1 Fill in the blanks. **($5 \times 1 = 5$)**

a. The complement of the 47° angle is ___________.

b. The line intersecting two or more lines at two distinct points is known as ___________.

c. If the exterior angle of a triangle is 105° and one of the interior opposite angles is 45° then the other two interior angles are ___________ and ___________.

d. A rectangle has ___________ lines of symmetry.

e. The angle of rotation in an equilateral triangle is ___________.

2 Write T for true and F for false. **($5 \times 1 = 5$)**

a. If the pair of supplementary angles is adjacent then they are known as linear pair. [ ]

b. If two lines in a plane are intersected by a transversal and the pair of interior angles is equal then the two lines are parallel. [ ]

c. If the interior angles of a triangle are in the ratio 1 : 1 : 2, then the triangle is an isosceles right-angled triangle. [ ]

d. Every polygon of *n* sides has *n* number of lines of symmetry. [ ]

e. A parallelogram has rotational symmetry of order 2. [ ]

3 Answer the following questions briefly. **($2 \times 2 = 4$)**

a. An angle is 30° less than twice its supplement. Find the measure of the angle.

b. If each base angle of an isosceles triangle is equal to twice its vertical angle, find the angles.

4 Answer the following questions. **($2 \times 3 = 6$)**

a. The width and height of a TV screen are 8 inches and 15 inches respectively. What is the screen size?

b. Draw a square and all its axes of symmetry and measure the angle between each pair of successive axes of symmetry? What do you observe?

Test 5

Chapters 16–19 **Maximum marks: 20**

1 Fill in the blanks. **($5 \times 1 = 5$)**

a. ____________ is a solid that contains 5 faces, 9 edges and 6 vertices.

b. If the actual distance from Shillong in Meghalaya to Mumbai is 2688 km and the distance on the map is 6 cm then the scale is ____________.

c. Two circles are congruent if they are having same ____________.

d. In the given figure, the $\Delta ARS \cong \Delta ATS$ by ____________.

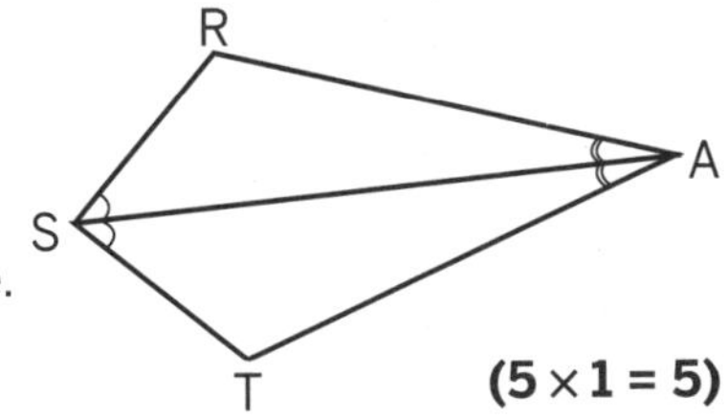

e. ____________ measurements are required to construct a unique triangle.

2 Write T for true and F for false. **($5 \times 1 = 5$)**

a. In isometric sketches, the measurements of the solids are not preserved. [ ]

b. The vertical cross-section of a cylinder is a rectangle. [ ]

c. Two regular polygons are said to be congruent if they have same side lengths. [ ]

d. If ΔABC and ΔDEF, If $AB = FD$, $A = F$ and $B = D$ then $\Delta ABC \cong \Delta DEF$. [ ]

e. A unique ΔXYZ with $XY = 3$ cm, $YZ = 5$ cm and $XZ = 6$ cm can be constructed. [ ]

3 Answer the following questions. **($2 \times 2 = 4$)**

a. Find the actual distance from Kanyakumari to Srinagar in Kashmir if the distance on the map is 7 cm and the scale used is 462 km for each cm.

b. Find the triangles which are congruent in the given figure and also write the congruency criteria.

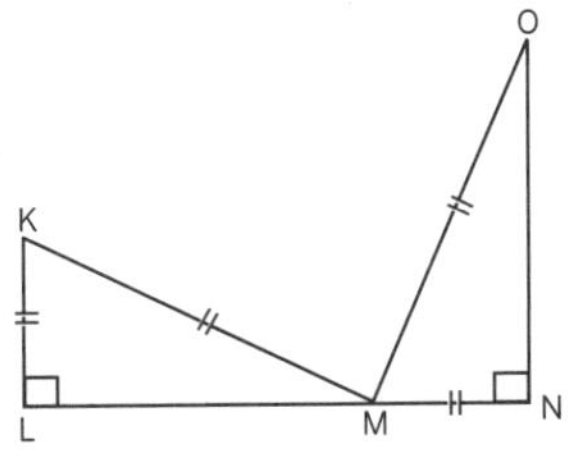

4 Answer the following questions. **($2 \times 3 = 6$)**

a. Draw the top, side and front view of the solid shown here.

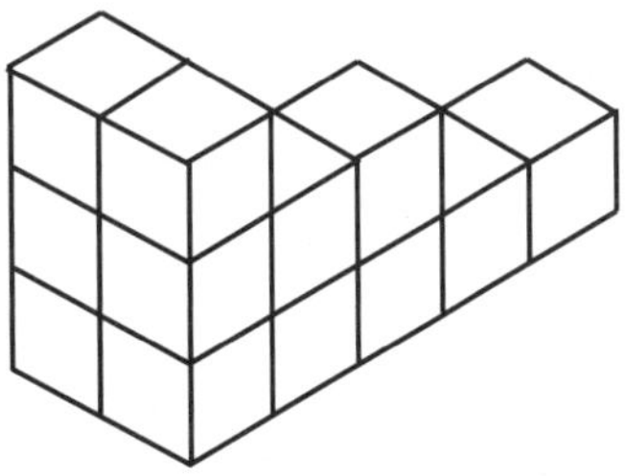

b. Construct ΔWIN with $WI = 6.4$ cm and $\angle W = \angle N = 40°$.

Test 6

Chapter 20 **Maximum marks: 25**

1 Fill in the blanks. **(5 × 1 = 5)**

a. The length of the boundary of a closed figure is called as ________.

b. If the total surface area of a cube is 486 sq. cm, then the length of its side is ________.

c. A parallelogram is a ________ whose opposite sides are parallel and equal in length.

d. The diameter of a circle is ________ times its radius.

e. The formula used to find the lateral surface area of a cuboid is ________.

2 Write T for true and F for false. **(5 × 1 = 5)**

a. The area and the perimeter of an equilateral triangle are always same.

b. The area of a parallelogram can be found by converting the same into a square.

c. The perimeter of a circular object is known as its circumference.

d. All the faces of a cuboid are always rectangles.

e. Cubes and cuboids have same number of faces, edges and vertices.

3 Find the missing measurement in the following figures. **(5 × 1 = 5)**

a. 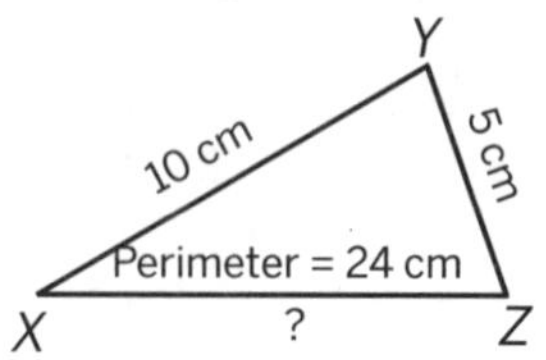

b. 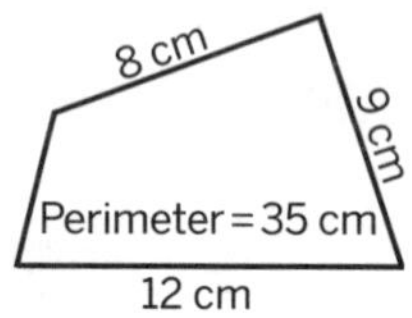

c. 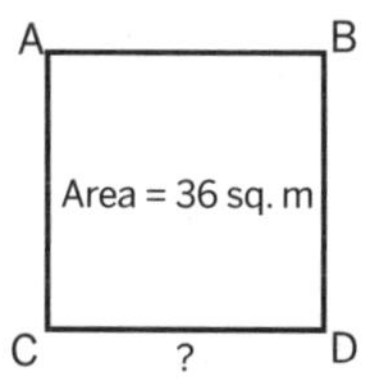

d. 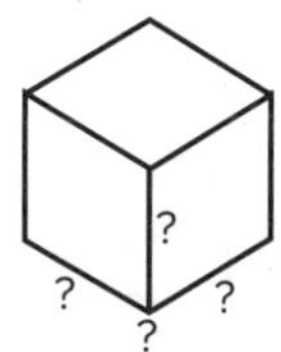

Lateral Surface Area = 100 sq. m

e. 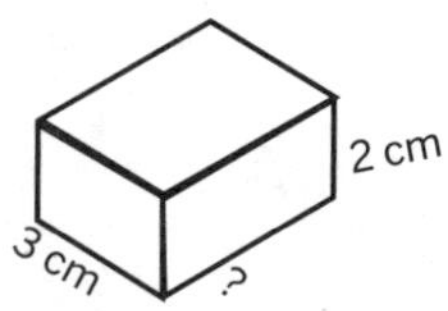

Total Surface Area = 52 sq. cm

4 Answer the following questions briefly. **(2 × 2 = 4)**

a. The area of a square field is 49 hectares. Find the cost of fencing the field if the cost of fencing is ₹3.50 per meter.

b. Find the radius and diameter of a disk, whose area is 616 cm^2.

5 Answer the following questions. **(2 × 3 = 6)**

a. Find the percentage increase in the total surface area of a cube if each of its sides is increased by 50%.

b. In a rectangular plot of dimension 100 ft × 60 ft, a triangular part of dimension 40 ft × 75 ft × 85 ft is utilized for garden, another rectangular part of dimension of 20 ft × 50 ft was used for parking and the rest is utilized for building. Find the area and perimeter of the garden, parking area and building.

Test 7

Chapters 21–22 **Maximum marks: 20**

1 Choose the correct options. **(5 × 1 = 5)**

a. The mean of the marks of 5 students scoring 12, 13, 20, 12, and 13 is ________.

i. 14 ii. 12 iii. 16 iv. 18

b. The median of the scores of 5 batsmen scoring 15, 20, 25, 30, and 35 is ________.

i. 30 ii. 25 iii. 15 iv. 20

c. The mode of the goals scored by the football players scoring 9, 8, 7, 6, and 6 is ________.

i. 9 ii. 8 iii. 7 iv. 6

d. The probability of getting the heads if the coin is tossed 15 times is

i. $\frac{2}{15}$ ii. $\frac{1}{15}$ iii. $\frac{2}{10}$ iv. $\frac{3}{15}$

e. The probability of getting the number 5 on top if the dice is thrown is

i. $\frac{1}{10}$ ii. $\frac{1}{15}$ iii. $\frac{1}{6}$ iv. $\frac{5}{6}$

2 Write T for True and F for False. **(5 × 1 = 5)**

a. The mean of the minimum temperature of a city recorded as 20.2, 20.3, 20.4, 20.5, and 20.6 is 20.3.

b. The median of the targets aimed by 5 people on a dart board scoring 3, 5, 4, 6, and 7 is 4.

c. The mode of the baskets reached by the basketball player scoring 4, 5, 2, 8, and 4 is 4.

d. The probability of a card drawn is numbered 4 from the cards numbering 1 to 10 is $\frac{4}{10}$.

e. The probability that it would rain today is termed as an event which may or may not happen.

3 Find the probability of drawing different coloured balls from a basket of 20 balls. **(1 × 4 = 4)**

Colour of the ball	Number of balls	Probability
a. White	4	
b. Red	5	
c. Green	3	
d. Yellow	8	

4 The table shows the number of students who would wish/like to go for a specific tourist destination in a class of 30. Construct a bar graph and answer the following questions. **(2 × 3 = 6)**

Tourist destinations	Goa	Ooty	Kerala	Delhi
Number of students	10	12	6	2

a. Which was the favourite tourist destination of the students?

b. How many students liked to visit Ooty compared to Goa?

Answers

Chapter – 1

Exercise 1.1

1. a. −51, −6, −3, −1, 0, 6, 8
   b. −633, −623, −263, 236, 266, 632
2. a. 1, 0, −1, −2, −5, −13, −113
   b. 517, 511, 157, −511, −517, −571
3. a. 0, 1, 2
   b. There is no integer between 6 and 7
   c. −5, −4, −3   d. −3, −4, −5, −6
4. a. 4   b. 7   c. 15   d. −4
5. a. −19   b. 11   c. −54   d. 148

Exercise 1.2

1. a. 18   b. −10   c. 4   d. −54   e. −28
   f. −162   g. 0   h. 1890   i. −480   j. 105

Exercise 1.3

1. a. −4   b. −2   c. 1   d. −2   e. −2   f. −31
   g. −9   h. 11   i. 68   j. −34   k. 6   l. −7

Exercise 1.4

1. a. 5; −9   b. −25   c. −12   d. −3; −15   e. −33   f. 0
   g. 1   h. 0
2. a. −120   b. 120   c. −295   d. 45
3. 1000   4. 15   5. 3

Exercise 1.5

2. a. not defined   b. 7   c. −2   d. 2

Exercise 1.6

1. ₹ 6120   2. 2 m   3. 110
4. 2650 ft below the sea level

Revision Exercise

1. a. True   b. True   c. True   d. False   e. False
2. i. e   ii. b   iii. d   iv. c   v. f
3. a. −4, −3, −2, −1, 0   b. −2, −1, 0, 1, 2
   c. −8, −7, −6, −5, −4, −3, −2
4. a. −868   b. −555   c. 10
5. a. 464   b. 1803   c. 7
6. a. −21659   b. − 1080   c. 0
7. a. −121   b. 216   c. 0   d. −1
8. 4°C
10. a. 0; Identity property   b. 1; Identity property
    c. 16; Identity property   d. 59; 25; Associative property
    e 12; Inverse element of −12   f. −65; Inverse element of 65
    g. −37; Commutative property   h. 112; Commutative property
11. a. True; Commutative property under addition
    b. True; Commutative property under multiplication
    c. False; Associative property is not satisfied under subtraction
    d. True; Associative property under multiplication
    e. False; Commutative property is not satisfied under subtraction
    f. False; Commutative property is not satisfied under division
12. a. 5   b. 15   13. ₹ 1200
14. a.

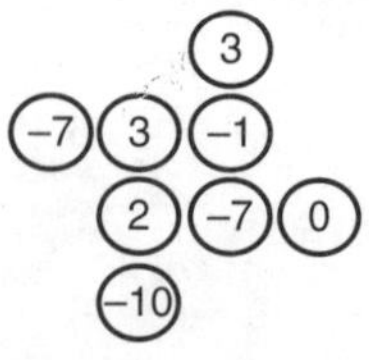

b.

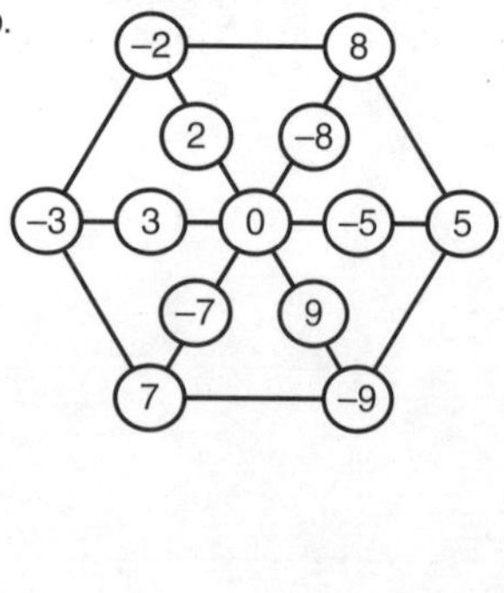

For the Curious Mind

18

Chapter – 2

Exercise 2.1

1.

Number	Numerator	Denominator
$\frac{1}{5}$	1	5
$\frac{-11}{13}$	−11	13
$\frac{-14}{-15}$	−14	−15
$\frac{7}{-8}$	7	−8
5	5	1

2. a. F   b. T   c. F   d. F   e. T
3. a. $\frac{-36}{2}$ b. $\frac{87}{3}$ c. $\frac{-202}{2}$ d. $\frac{630}{2}$ e. $\frac{-2468}{2}$
5. a. $\frac{29}{3}$ b. $\frac{35}{17}$ c. $\frac{5}{4}$ d. $\frac{4}{5}$
6. a. $\frac{35}{-56}$ b. $\frac{40}{-64}$ c. $\frac{50}{-80}$
7. a. 4   b. 14   c. 6   d. 42
8. a. $\frac{8}{18}, \frac{12}{27}, \frac{16}{36}, \frac{20}{45}$
   b. $\frac{-6}{10}, \frac{-12}{20}, \frac{-24}{40}, \frac{-48}{80}$
   c. $\frac{16}{-22}, \frac{32}{-44}, \frac{64}{-88}, \frac{24}{-33}$
   d. $\frac{14}{-18}, \frac{28}{-36}, \frac{56}{-72}, \frac{21}{-27}$
9. a. $\frac{-1}{7}$ b. $\frac{5}{4}$ c. $\frac{8}{7}$
   d. $\frac{-4}{5}$ e. $\frac{-3}{10}$ f. $\frac{4}{9}$
10. a. Yes   b. No   c. Yes
11. a. 500   b. 34

Exercise 2.2

1. a. >   b. >   c. <   d. >   e. <
2. a. $\frac{3}{7} < \frac{2}{3} < \frac{4}{5}$ b. $\frac{-11}{12} < \frac{-7}{10} < \frac{-13}{-30} < \frac{3}{5}$
   c. $\frac{-8}{3} < \frac{6}{-9} < \frac{4}{7} < \frac{2}{3}$ d. $\frac{5}{-2} < \frac{-5}{3} < \frac{-8}{9} < \frac{5}{-6}$
   e. $\frac{-2}{3} < \frac{-4}{9} < \frac{-5}{12} < \frac{-7}{18}$ f. $\frac{2}{3} < \frac{7}{2} < 4 < 9$
3. a. $\frac{-7}{-12} > \frac{4}{9} > \frac{-11}{24} > \frac{-4}{3}$ b. $\frac{3}{4} > \frac{-5}{-8} > \frac{3}{-16} > \frac{-13}{14}$

c. $\frac{4}{7} > \frac{2}{9} > \frac{-7}{8} > \frac{-13}{14}$ d. $\frac{-3}{-5} > \frac{17}{30} > \frac{-8}{15} > \frac{7}{-10}$

e. $\frac{-7}{-6} > \frac{-3}{-4} > \frac{1}{2} > \frac{2}{5}$

Exercise 2.3

1. $\frac{-9}{5}, \frac{-6}{5}, \frac{1}{5}, \frac{4}{5}, \frac{8}{5}$
2. The six rational numbers are $\frac{4}{11}, \frac{2}{11}, \frac{-2}{11}, \frac{-1}{11}, \frac{1}{11}$ and $\frac{6}{11}$
3. $\frac{1}{4}, \frac{1}{5}, \frac{1}{6}$
4. $\frac{11}{35}, \frac{12}{35}, \frac{13}{35}, \frac{14}{35}, \frac{15}{35}, \frac{16}{35}, \frac{17}{35}, \frac{18}{35}, \frac{19}{35}, \frac{20}{35}$

Exercise 2.4

1. a. $\frac{2}{3}$ b. $\frac{4}{17}$ c. $-1\frac{1}{5}$ d. $1\frac{11}{18}$ e. $-2\frac{7}{8}$
   f. $\frac{-5}{54}$
2. a. $1\frac{4}{9}$ b. $\frac{1}{12}$ c. $\frac{-5}{8}$ d. $\frac{3}{26}$ e. $\frac{29}{75}$
   f. $\frac{-37}{56}$
3. a. $\frac{35}{44}$ b. $\frac{-10}{99}$ c. $\frac{5}{6}$ d. $-2\frac{2}{15}$ e. 8
   f. $\frac{1}{8}$
4. a. -7 b. $\frac{32}{75}$ c. $\frac{-2}{21}$ d. $-1\frac{1}{15}$ e. $\frac{1}{8}$
   f. $-1\frac{1}{7}$

Exercise 2.5

1. a, c, d, f are terminating decimals and b, e are non-terminating decimals.
2. a. $\frac{7}{9}$ b. $\frac{89}{99}$ c. $\frac{567}{999}$ d. $\frac{219}{900}$
3. Distance travelled by A = 10/9 km, Distance travelled by B = 19/20 km, A travelled more distance
4. $18\frac{15}{16}$ Kg 5. 7 doses 6. $\frac{2}{15}$

Revision Exercise

1. a. $5 = \frac{10}{2}$ b. $-7 = \frac{-56}{8}$ c. $2.79 = \frac{279}{100}$
   d. $0.8 = \frac{8}{10} = \frac{4}{5}$
2. a. 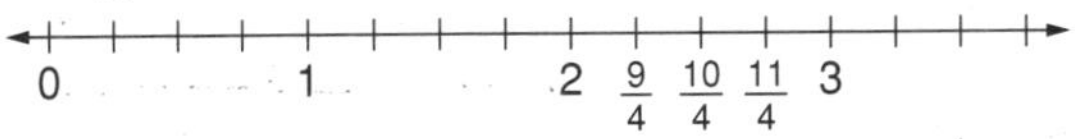

   b. 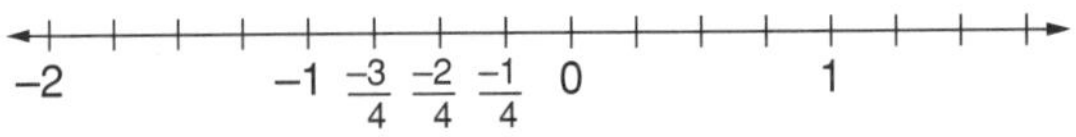

   c. 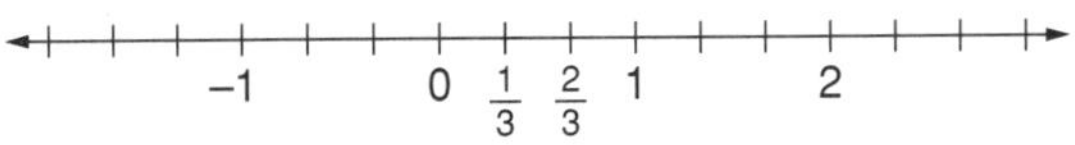

   d. 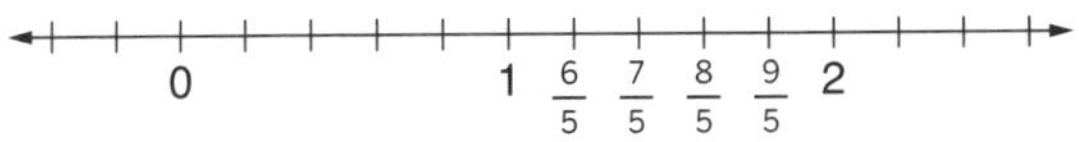

3. Positive rational numbers: $\frac{-4}{-5}, \frac{4}{5}, \frac{9}{13}$ and $\frac{-9}{-13}$
   Negative rational numbers: $\frac{4}{-5}, \frac{-9}{4}, \frac{-9}{13}$ and $\frac{9}{-13}$

4. a. infinitely many b. $\frac{-6}{14}$ c. −1 and 0
   d. 0 e. $\frac{15}{8}$ f. 1
5. a. T b. F c. T d. F e. F
   f. F
6. a. $\frac{-3}{4} = \frac{-6}{8} = \frac{-9}{12} = \frac{-12}{16}$ b. $\frac{7}{8} = \frac{14}{16} = \frac{21}{24} = \frac{70}{80}$
   c. $-\frac{1}{7} = -\frac{2}{14} = -\frac{10}{70} = -\frac{5}{35}$
7. a. $-\frac{24}{15} = -\frac{8}{5}$ b. $-\frac{24}{80} = -\frac{3}{10}$ c. $-\frac{105}{207} = -\frac{35}{69}$
8. a. $\frac{12}{25} > \left[\frac{-32}{52}\right]$ b. $\left[\frac{-17}{21}\right] < \left[\frac{-19}{26}\right]$
   c. $\left[\frac{-17}{21}\right] < \left[\frac{-1}{26}\right]$
9. a. $\frac{-67}{28}$ b. $\frac{-16}{13}$ c. $\frac{8}{21}$ d. $\frac{-46}{33}$ e. $\frac{-113}{56}$
10. a. $\frac{-21}{40}$ b. $\frac{1}{3}$ c. $\frac{-22}{117}$ d. $\frac{-32}{3}$
11. a. $\frac{4}{9}$ b. $\frac{12}{99}$ c. $\frac{777}{999}$ d. $\frac{119}{900}$
12. a. Place P is colder than Place Q.
    b. The difference in the height of the building and the tree = $7\frac{31}{35}$ feet
    c. The cost of $2\frac{1}{2}$ litre of petrol = ₹$184\frac{3}{8}$
    d. Raghu can distribute the cloth to 7 of his friends.
    e. $33\frac{1}{2}$

Chapter – 3

Exercise 3.1

1. a. 3 b. 4 c. 2 d. $10\frac{1}{2}$ e. $58\frac{4}{5}$
2. 9 3. ₹150 4. 8 hours

Exercise 3.2

1. a. $3\frac{4}{5}$ b. $1\frac{7}{48}$ c. $2\frac{5}{12}$ d. $7\frac{7}{12}$
2. a. $1\frac{6}{7}$ b. $\frac{1}{8}$ c. $\frac{5}{6}$ d. $3\frac{5}{8}$
3. a. 9 b. $9\frac{3}{5}$ c. $1\frac{1}{6}$ d. $\frac{153}{250}$
4. a. 81 b. $\frac{5}{48}$ c. 6 d. 2

Exercise 3.3

1. $47\frac{2}{5}$ kg sold and $53\frac{1}{10}$ kg left with the merchant.
2. ₹$550\frac{1}{4}$ 3. 6 4. 8
5. $11\frac{5}{8}$ kg 6. $2\frac{7}{12}$

Revision Exercise

1. a. 4 b. 25 c. 8 d. $\frac{1}{9}$
   e. $\frac{3}{1000}$ f. $\frac{51}{50}$ g. $\frac{1}{5}$ h. 1

2. $2\frac{3}{7}$ cm. 3. ₹334.80 4. $\frac{4}{9}$

5. ₹10165 pm. 6. $8\frac{3}{4}$ m. 7. 18 8. 6 cars

9. $7\frac{1}{3}$ 10. 31 students 11. 3

For the Curious Mind

1. The total number of passengers = 144 and Number of passengers in the upper deck =90
2. Total number of pages = 180. day 1 = 30 pages, day 2 = 40 pages, day 3 = 75 pages and left over = 35

Chapter – 4

Exercise 4.1

1. a. 1 b. 5^{21} c. 59049 d. 8
   e. 5^{27} f. 6^{10}
2. a. 3 b. 225 c. $(-2)^{49}$ d. $\left(\frac{9}{2}\right)^3$
   e. 1

Exercise 4.2

1. 9^8 tons 2. $2^9 \times 3^4$ 3. 10^7 words 4. 65 tonnes

Revision Exercise

1. a. $5^5 \times 2^6 \times 3^3$ b. 200 c. 32 d. 10^6
2. a. 192 b. $(3)^7$ c. 64
   d. $\left(\frac{4}{5}\right)^3$ e. 5
3. 10^4 sweets 4. 3 5. $2^{12} - 2^4$

For the Curious Mind

1. 4×10^8 m
2. 10^1 10^2 10^3 10^4 etc.

Chapter – 5

Exercise 5.1

1. a. Yes b. Yes c. No d. Yes e. No
2. a. A = {1, 2, 3, 4, 5, 6, 7, 8, 9, 10, 11, 12, 13, 14}
   b. B = {100, 102, 104, 106, 108, 110, 112, 114, 116, 118}
   c. C = {7, 14, 21, 28, 35, 42, 49, 56, 63, 70, 77, 84, 91, 98}
   d. D = {13, 39, 65, 91, 117}
   e. E = {B, h, r, t}
3. a. A = {x : x is a multiple of 5, $x < 35$}
   b. P = {x : x is a prime number, $x < 13$}
   c. S = {x : x is a letter in the word 'mathematics'}
   d. F = {x : x is a vowel in The English alphabet}
   e. N = {x : x is a month in a year from January to June}
4. a. n(A) = 8 b. n(B) = 7 c. n(C) = 1 d. n(D) = 2
   e. n(E) = 21 f. n(F) = 4

Exercise 5.2

1. Equivalent sets; b, c and d.
2. Equal sets; a, d and e.
3. Singleton sets; b and c
   Empty sets; a, d and e
4. Finite sets; a, c and e
   Infinite sets; b and d
5. a. --- iii. b. --- i. c. --- iv. d. --- vi.
   e. --- v. f. --- ii.

Exercise 5.3

1. Intersecting /Overlapping sets; b and c
   Disjoint sets; a, d and e
2. a. U = {a, b, c, d, e, f, g, h, i, j}
   b. U = {−1, −2, −3, −4, −5, −6, −7, −8, −9, −10}
   c. U = {2, 4, 6, 8, 10, 12, 14, 16, 18}
   d. U = {2, 3, 5, 7, 11, 13, 17, 19, 23, 31}
   e. U = {1, 2, 3, 4, 5, 8, 10, 15}

Revision Exercise

1. a. set R b. set P and set S
   c. set Q d. set P
2. a. Roster method b. Set-builder method
3. a. singleton set b. infinite set c. finite set
   d. empty set e. finite set f. infinite set
   g. singleton set h. empty set
4. a. U = {a, b, c, d, e, f, g, h, i, j, k, l, m, n, o, p, q, r, s, t, u, v, w, x, y, z}
   b. U = { 0, 1, 2, 3, 4, 5, 6, 7, 8, 9}

Theme Worksheet 1

1.

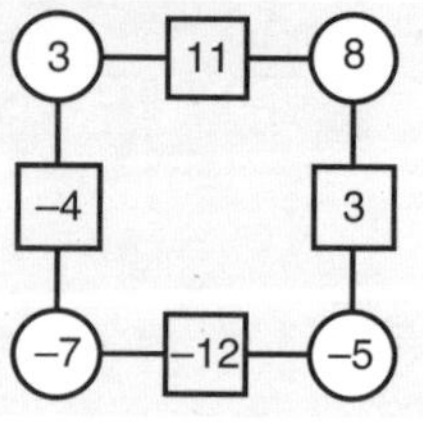

2.

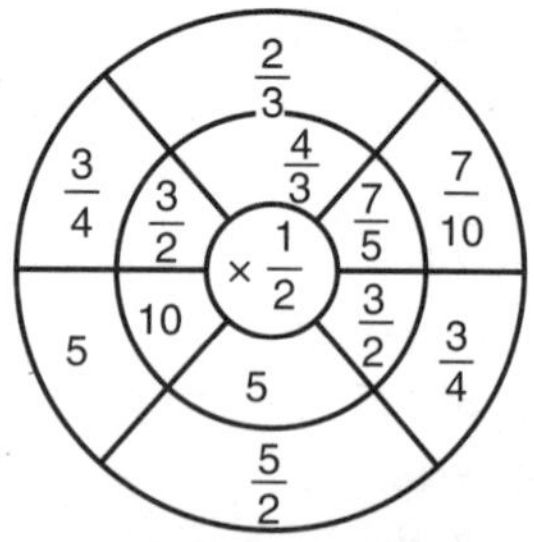

3.

5 + 3 = 8	3 + 5 = 8	Commutative property under addition
(9 + 3) + 5 = 17	9 + (3 + 5) = 17	Associative property under addition
2 (5 − 2) = 6	(2 × 5) − (2 × 2) = 6	Distributive law of multiplication over subtraction
12 × (3 × 5) = 180	12 × (3 × 5) = 180	Associative property under multiplication
52 × 1 = 52	1 × 52 = 52	Multiplicative identity of whole numbers

4. a. 5 b. 10
5. a. 2^{10} b. 17^{20}

Skill-based Worksheet

1. −2°C 2. 95.6°C 3. −95 m 4. ₹150 5. 2, 2, 12, 4
6. $\frac{1}{16}$ 7. 2^6 8. U = {1, 2, 3, 4, 5, 6, 7, 8, 9, 10}

Mental Maths

Chapter 1

1. 5000 2. −539 3. −500 4. −909 5. 211 6. −25

Chapter 2

1. $3\frac{3}{4}$ 2. 40 3. $1\frac{1}{4}$ 4. $\frac{1}{8}$ 5. 24 6. $1\frac{2}{3}$

Chapter 3

1. 9 2. $\frac{1}{9}$ 3. 1 4. 4 5. $\frac{1}{2}$ 6. $\frac{17}{169}$

Chapter 4

1. 3200 2. 81 3. 1 4. 25 5. 363
6. 1000

Chapter 5

1. S = {$\frac{1}{2}, \frac{1}{3}, \frac{1}{13}, \frac{1}{8}$} (any 4)
2. B = {violet, indigo, blue, green, yellow, orange, red}
3. G = {x I x is a primary colour}
4. 5
5. U = {10, 20, 30, 40, 50, 60, 70, 80, 90, 100}
6. U = {55, 64, 46, 37, 73, 28, 82, 19, 91, 20, 30, 40, 50}

Chapter – 6

Exercise 6.1

1. a. 1:1 b. 1:1 c. 3 : 2 d. 8:3
2. a. 11 : 15 b. 24 : 13 c. 12 : 7 d. 21 : 50
3. a. 8: 5 b. 1 : 7 c. 8 : 3 d. 8 : 3
4. a. 4 : 3 b. 3 : 5 c. 9 : 16 d. 51 : 28

6. a. 3:5 b. 5:2 c. 2:3

7. 20 8. 24 9. 6

Exercise 6.2

1. a. no b. yes c. no d. yes
2. a. 36 b. 125 c. 3 d. $2\frac{3}{4}$
3. 24 : 20 : 5 4. ₹3750; ₹3000; ₹4000
5. a. 22 b. 24 c. 10 d. 20
6. 32

Exercise 6.3

1. 3 things 2. 20 km 3. ₹10,000 4. 62 rotations
5. ₹420 6. 25 farmers

For the Curious Mind

1. 8 : 4 : 1 2. 2

Revision Exercise

1. a. Ratio b. *q* : *p* c. proportion d. *qr*
2. a. False b. True c. False d. True
3. a. 21 b. 9 c. 6 d. $5\frac{1}{3}$
4. One of the possible solutions is:
   a. 8, 7, 24, 21 b. 30, 45, 24, 36
   c. 13, 39, 11, 33 d. 5, 10, 8, 16
5. 1980000, 1080000
6. Veena is spending more than Leena
7. 10 : 24 : 21
8. 63 : 75 : 40
9. 90 cm, 153 cm, 72 cm
10. ₹210000, ₹262500, ₹315000
11. 275 cm; 165 cm
12. There is more sugar in the bottle A than in bottle B.
13. 21.71 kg., 35 books 14. 57 days

Chapter – 7

Exercise 7.1

1. a. $\frac{1}{50}$ b. $1\frac{3}{4}$ c. $\frac{17}{400}$ d. $\frac{1}{32}$
2. a. $8\frac{1}{3}$ % b. 58 % c. 510 % d. 625 %
3. a. 0.01 b. 0.75 c. 0.03125 d. 0.125
4. a. 21 % b. 2 % c. 120 % d. 12.5 %
5. a. 3:100 b. 12:25 c. 1 : 12 d. 3:40
6. a. 30 % b. $21\frac{2}{3}$ % c. 75 % d. 160 %

Exercise 7.2

1. a. 0.2 % b. 20 % c. 18 % d. 75 %
2. a. ₹12 b. 91 c. 4 d. 306 ml
3. a. 517 b. ₹281.25 c. ₹2800 d. 14 m
4. a. 43.75 b. ₹ 12500 c. ₹ 13.09 d. $12\frac{1}{2}$ kg
5. ₹153

Revision Exercise

1. a. $38\frac{8}{9}$ % b. 175 % c. 108 % d. 2.5 %
2. 4 3. $12\frac{1}{2}$ litres 4. ₹26,000 5. 300
6. ₹3000, ₹12,120, ₹20,880 7. $8\frac{1}{3}$ % 8. ₹46,930
9. ₹49500, 1%

For the Curious Mind

School A - 75% and School B - 80%.
School B has performed better.

Chapter – 8

Exercise 8.1

1. Profit – ₹22.50 2. Profit – ₹40 3. ₹7660
4. ₹913 5. i. ₹2 profit ii. ₹12 profit

Exercise 8.2

1. 24% profit 2. 5% loss 3. 15% profit 4. 25% loss

Exercise 8.3

1. a. ₹825 b. ₹546 c. ₹980 d. ₹460
2. ₹16800
3. ₹470000 if sold at loss of 6%. ₹530000 if sold at a profit of 6%

Revision Exercise

1. a. ₹100 b. ₹200 c. ₹310 d. ₹945
2. a. Profit – 20% b. Profit – 6.66%
   c. Loss – 8% d. Loss – 3%
3. a. True b. True c. False
4. a. Loss 20% b. ₹38150
   c. Profit 5% d. 150%

For the Curious Mind

1. Expected profit percentage = 20% and actual profit percentage = 12%

Chapter – 9

Exercise 9.1

1. a. ₹31.5 b. ₹312.75
2. a. ₹6500 b. ₹1875
3. a. 6% b. 3.5%
4. a. $2\frac{1}{3}$ years b. 2.5 years 5. ₹71,077

Revision Exercise

1. S.I = ₹2520; A= ₹16,520 2. $2\frac{1}{2}$ years
3. 10 % 4. $2\frac{1}{2}$ years 5. ₹9300 gain
6. ₹32,000 profit 7. 5%, 3 years
8. 3 years; 12 years 9. ₹12,000 gain

For the Curious Mind

₹21073.92, Not simple interest because the principal is changing every year

Chapter – 10

Exercise 10.1

1. 15 m/s 2. 20 km 3. 50 minutes 4. 180 km
5. 59.4 km/h 6. 29.17 km/h 7. 12.5 km 8. 20 km
9. 12 seconds; 48 seconds 10. 125 m; $8\frac{1}{3}$ m/s
11. 14 seconds 12. 11.25 seconds

Exercise 10.2

1. 400 m 2. 30 second; 10 second 3. 12 second
4. 80 m 5. 5 hours 6. 9.5 km/h
7. 91 km; 7 hours

Revision Exercise

1. 7.5 minutes 2. 60 km/h 3. 18 km/h
4. 7 km/h 5. 120 m/s
6. 3 hours; 24 km away from old town or 12 km away from new town
7. 6 hours 8. 1.5 km/h

Theme Worksheet 2

1. Unit 2. Division 3. Proportion
4. Unitary 5. Speed 6. Constant
7. Percentage 8. Loss
9. Overhead expenses 10. Simple Interest

Skill-based Worksheet

1. 24 2. 25,000 3. ₹1,15,000
4. Company B has a better offer. 5. ₹100
6. ₹50 7. ₹20,800 8. ₹12,960
9. 11 km/h 10. Length =150 m; Speed = 15 m/s

Mental Maths

Chapter 6

1. 3 : 7 is greater 2. Yes, they form a proportion
3. Yes , they are in proportion 4. ₹300 5. ₹180

Chapter 7

1. 550% 2. 20% 3. ₹300 4. ₹1,056 5. 100%

Chapter 8

1. Profit = ₹30 2. ₹900 3. 20% loss 4. 30% profit
5. ₹6,000

Chapter 9

1. ₹2,000 2. 2% 3. 10 years 4. ₹35,000
5. ₹12,250

Chapter 10

1. 100 km/h 2. 125 km/h 3. 216 km 4. 180 km
5. 8 h

Chapter – 11

Exercise 11.1

1.

Algebraic Expression	Terms	Factors
$36x^2y + 28xy + 10$	$36x^2y$	2, 2, 3, 3, x, x, y
	$28xy$	2, 2, 7, x, y
	10	2, 5
$2x^5 - 6x^3 + 28x^2 + x + 9$	$2x^5$	2, x, x, x, x, x
	$-6x^3$	−2, 3, x, x, x
	$28x^2$	2, 2, 7, x, x
	x	x
	9	3, 3
$5abc + 25a^2bc$	$5abc$	5, a, b, c
	$25a^2bc$	5, 5, a, a, b, c

2.

Algebraic Expression	Variable Term	Numerical Coefficient of Variable Term	Constant Term
$45x + 32y - 6$	$45x$	45	−6
	$32y$	32	
$3t^3 + 2t^2 + 10$	$3t^3$	3	10
	$2t^2$	2	
$\frac{h}{4} + 7h + 21$	$\frac{h}{4}$	$\frac{1}{4}$	21
	$7h$	7	

3. a. 4 b. 2 c. 6 d. 8 e. 5
4. a. 3 b. 3 c. 9
5. a. Like terms; Reason: All the terms have same variables raised to the same power.
   b. Unlike terms; Reason: The terms have different variables.
   c. Unlike terms; Reason: The terms have same variables but raised to the different powers.
   d. Like terms; Reason: All the terms have same variables raised to the same power.
6. a. Trinomial b. Monomial c. Binomial
   d. Trinomial e. Trinomial f. Polynomial

Exercise 11.2

a. Ravi's age = $x - 32$, where x represents the age of Ravi's father
b. Number of tigers = $y - 10$, where y represents number of lions
c. Rain fall in this year = x – 20% of x, where x represents rainfall of last year
d. Tom's age = $a - 4$, where a represent Steve's age
e. ₹300d
f. Amount of money for each employee = $\frac{1000}{x}$, where x represents the total number of employees

Exercise 11.3

1. a. $-11a + 10b$ b. $28h + 22g$
   c. $8p^3 - 3p^2 + p - 13$ d. $19a^2 - 4b^2 + 10ab$
2. a. $-36c + 19b$ b. 0
   c. $3k^2 + 16k - 15$ d. $12bc + 16ca - 10ab$
3. a. $14x^2 - 19y^2 + 45xy$ b. $-3x^2 - 31y^2 + 46xy$
   c. $47x^2 - 19y^2 - 12xy$ d. $-47x^2 + 19y^2 + 12xy$
4. $2a - 29b + 36c$ 5. $41x^8 - 28x^3 + 71x^2 + 19x - 147$
6. $16x + 4y + 24z$ 7. $19a - 3b + 8c$

Revision Exercise

1. a. False b. False c. True d. True e. False
   f. True g. False h. False i. False j. True
2. a. $27xyz + 12xy - 2z$ b. $-4x^2 + 34xy + y^2$
   c. $4pq + 19p^2q^2 + 5p - 8q$ d. $31a^2 + 11b^2 + 4c^2$
3. a. $95xy$ b. $8q^2 + 8q$
   c. $15h^2g^2 - 20h^2 + 13g^2$ d. $21k^2x - 4k^2y + 11k^2$
4. $3ab - 10bc + 8ca$ 5. a. $15 + 2(n - 1)$ b. $6z + 6$
6. a. – iv b. – iii c. – v d. – i e. – ii

For the Curious Mind

$7a^2b + 19c$

Chapter – 12

Exercise 12.1

1. $x = 3$ 2. $n = 6$ 3. $y = 7$ 4. $x = 12$
5. $a = -75$ 6. $x = 30$ 7. $c = \frac{25}{7}$ 8. $v = -\frac{3}{2}$

Exercise 12.2

1. The number is $\frac{5}{4}$ 2. The numbers are 4, 6 and 8
3. My age is 9 years 4. $x = 5$ years
5. 19 and 27 6. 36 and 42
7. The cost of a book = ₹110 and the cost of a pen = ₹60
8. The number is –5 9. 2 pants, 4 t-shirts
10. 20 km

Exercise 12.3

1. $x = \{5, 6, 7, 8, \ldots\}$ 2. $6 < x < 3$ 3. $-4 \le x \le 3$
4. $x = \{\ldots., -3, -2, -1, 0\}$ 5. $y = \{1, 2, 3, 4\}$ 6. $p = \{3, 4, 5\}$

Revision Exercise

1. a. one b. x
   c. an equation d. an inequation
   e. solution of the equation
2. a. $x = 20$ b. $x = 4$ c. $x = 6$
   d. $x = 5$ e. $x = -2$
3. a. $x > -1$ b. $x \ge \frac{7}{2}$ c. $2 \le x \ge 3$
   d. $-5 < x < 3$
4. a. The three consecutive odd numbers are 89, 91 and 93
   b. Number of 10-rupee coins = 15 and Number of 5-rupee coins = 10
   c. length = 10 cm and breadth = 8 cm d. 5 years

For the Curious Mind

Original Number = $90 - 9x$; Number after reversing the digits = $9x + 9$;

Original Number is 72.

Theme Worksheet 3

A	R	E	Y	O	U
1	$5x + 15$	Linear Equation	$-13x + 9y$	$2, 2, 3, y, z$	$\div 1$

S	L	E	E	P	I	N	G
5	Monomial	$t \geq 7$	Solution Set	9	-2	Domain	$12x$

Skill-based Worksheet

1. Akhil's age is 12 years and Nikhil's age is 7 years 2. 81
3. 65 4. 15 friends
5. Length = 21 units; Breadth = 9 units 6. 24 days 7. 250
8. ~1470 USD

Mental Maths

Chapter 11

1. 3, 5, k, k, k, x, x 2. $14bc^2$ 3. 16
4. 2 5. 0
6. $-2m^4x^2, 15m^4x^2, 5m^4x^2$ 7. monomial
8. $-10x^2$ 9. $8k^3 - 14b^2$ 10. $-20c^6 + 9c^3$

Chapter 12

1. 1 2. −16 3. 3 4. 12 5. 16
6. 20 7. 1 8. $x = \{1, 2\}$ 9. $x = \{6, 7, 8, ...\}$
10. $x = \{-5, -4, -3, -2, -1, 0, 1\}$

Chapter – 13

Exercise 13.1

1. 220° 2. obtuse angle – 150° and reflex angle – 210°
3. acute angle – 30° and reflex angle – 330°
4. i. 360° ii. 120° iii. 90° iv. 30°
5. 25° 6. 60° 7. 30° and 60°
8. 100° and 80° 9. 120° 10. 65°
11. 60° 12. 151.7°
13. a. 142°
 b. $\angle COR = \angle AOB = 60° \angle AOC = \angle BOR = 120°$
 c. $\angle POR = 30°, \angle ROS = 40°, \angle SOT = 50°$ and $\angle QOT = 60°$
 d. $\angle TSR = 60°, \angle TRS = 110°, \angle RTS = 10°$
 e. $\angle BOE = 50°, \angle DOC = 60°, \angle AOC = 120°$
 f. $\angle BOD = 100°, \angle EOB = 32.5°, \angle FOD = 47.5°, \angle EOC = 47.5°$ and $\angle FOA = 32.5°$

Exercise 13.2

1. a. $\angle PVU = 140°, \angle PVC = x = 40°, \angle UVQ = 40°, \angle AUV = 40°$ and $\angle BUV = 140°, \angle AUR = 140°$ and $\angle BUR = 40°$.
 b. $\angle ARU = 45°, \angle VCB = x = 135°, \angle VCR = 45°, \angle ARP = 135°$ and $\angle PRC = 45°, \angle QCR = 135°$ and $\angle BCQ = 45°$.
 c. $\angle EDC = 30°, \angle DCA = 30°$, and $\angle CAD = 110°$.
 d. $\angle BIE = 80°, \angle BIF = 100°, \angle EIC = 100°, \angle HEI = 80°$ and $\angle ICD = 100°, \angle GFI = 80°$ and $\angle ABI = 100°$.
 e. $\angle DGB = 100°, \angle CGB = 80°, \angle CGA = 100°, \angle AGD = 80°$ and $\angle FAG = 80°$.
 f. $\angle CDG = 20°, \angle ABC = 135°, \angle DEF = 45°$.
 g. $\angle IJM = 65°, \angle DJH = 65°, \angle MJH = 115°, \angle IJD = 115°$ and $\angle GIB = 115°, \angle GIL = 65°, \angle BIJ = 65°, \angle CMF = 60°, \angle CML = 120°, \angle FMJ = 120°, \angle ALM = 60°, \angle MLI = 120°, \angle ALE = 120°, \angle ELI = 60°$.
 h. $\angle ACD = 90°$.

Revision Exercise

1. a. Parallel b. Vertically opposite c. Right
 d. Complementary e. Arm, vertex
2. a. True b. True c. False d. False e. True
3. a. – v; b. – iv; c. – i ; d. –vi; e. – vii;
 f. – ii; g. – iii
4. 240° 5. 120°, 240° 6. 270°
7. 20°, 70° 8. 40°, 50° 10. 36°

For the Curious Mind

All supplementary angles need not be adjacent angles. But the sum of two angles in a linear pair is always 180° (supplementary).

Chapter – 14

Exercise 14.1

1. a. Yes b. Yes c. No d. Yes e. No f. Yes
2. a. Yes b. No c. Yes d. Yes
 e. No f. Yes g. Yes h. Yes
3. 50° 4. $\angle S = 50° \angle T = 50°$ 5. 48°, 60° and 72°
6. 60° and 40° 7. 50°, 50° and 80° 8. 30° and 60°
9. 90°, 45° and 45° 10. 60°, 60° and 60°
11. a. $\angle ACB = 3x° = 105°$ and $\angle CBA = x° = 35°$
 b. $\angle CBA = x° = 60°, \angle CAB = z° = 40°$ and $\angle ACB = 80°$
 c. $\angle ECD = x° = 20°$ d. $\angle ACB = x° = 50°$
 e. $y^0 = \angle BCD = 20°$ $\angle BDC = 80°, \angle BAD = x° = 40°$
 f. $\angle CDA = x° = 95°, \angle DCA = y° = 25°, \angle ECB = z° = 30°$
 g. $\angle FBG = x° = 115°, \angle ECF = y° = 110°$
12. 40°, 70°, 70° 13. 144°, 18°, 18° 14. 35°, 110°

Exercise 14.2

1. a. Yes; b. Yes; c. No
2. a. 12 cm; b. 26 cm; c. 14 cm; d. 82 cm
3. 15 km 4. 20 ft 5. 16 ft 6. $\sqrt{12}$ cm 7. 17 m

Revision Exercise

1. a. 180° b. 6 c. three
 d. hypotenuse e. obtuse angled
2. a. True b. False c. False d. False e. True
3. a. (iv) b. (ii) c. (i) d. (ii) e. (iii)
4. a. 30°, 60°, 90° b. 30°, 60° c. 70°, 70°.40°
 d. 15°, 75° e. 40°,40°, 100° f. 45°, 60°, 75°
 g. The possible combinations of the side lengths are (7 cm, 5 cm, 3 cm), (7 cm, 5 cm, 4 cm), (7 cm, 5 cm, 5 cm), (7 cm, 5 cm, 6 cm), (7 cm, 5 cm, 7 cm), (7 cm, 5 cm, 8 cm), (7 cm, 5 cm, 9 cm), (7 cm, 5 cm, 10 cm), (7 cm, 5 cm, 11 cm)
 h. i and ii i. 34 inches j. 250 km

For the Curious Mind

2. Equilateral triangle is always an equiangular triangle. Each angle of an equiangular triangle is 60°.
 $\angle ABC = \angle BCA = \angle CAB = 60°$
 $\angle BCE = \angle ABC + \angle CAB = 60° + 60° = 120°$. (The exterior angle of a triangle is equal to the sum of the interior opposite angle]
 $\angle BAD = \angle ABC + \angle ABC = 60° + 60° = 120°$. (The exterior angle of a triangle is equal to the sum of the interior opposite angle]
 $\therefore \angle BCE = \angle BAD$

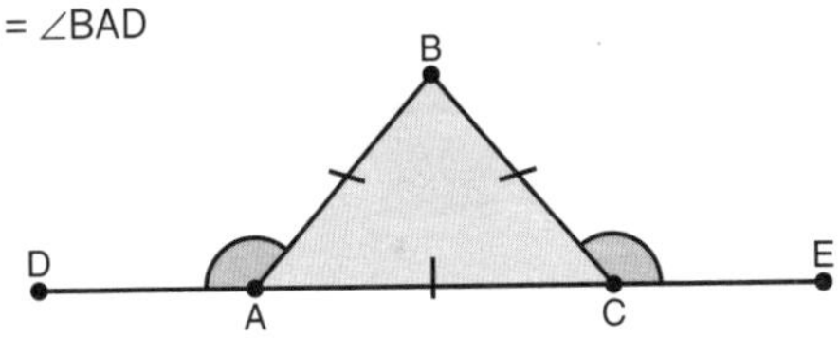

Chapter – 15

Exercise 15.1

1. a. 4, 4 b. 9 c. 12
2. a. 8 b. 8 c. regular octagon
4. a. 2 b. 6 c. 2
 d. 3 e. 6 f. 2

Exercise 15.2

1. a. 5, 36° b. 16, 225° c. 3, 120° d. 10, 18°
2. a. Order of rotation = 0 b. Order of rotation = 8
 c. Order of rotation = 3 d. Order of rotation = 4
3. A circle has all the three types of symmetries – Line and Rotational symmetry. It has infinite lines of symmetry and the order of rotation is also infinite
4. a. Rotational symmetry and Line symmetry
 b. Rotational symmetry and Line symmetry
 c. Rotational symmetry
 d. Line symmetry

Revision Exercise

1. a. False b. False c. True d. True e. True
2. a. n b. 5 c. $\frac{360°}{r}$ d. n; $\frac{360°}{n}$
3. Yes
4. a. Order of the rotational symmetry = 6
   b. Order of the rotational symmetry = 2
5. Yes, 7

Chapter – 16

Exercise 16.1

1. a 2. c 3. a
4. a. ii b. iv c. iii d. v e. i

Exercise 16.3

1. a. Circle, rectangle b. Circle, triangle
   c. Square, square d. Circle, circle
   e. Triangle, rectangle f. Square, triangle
2. a. Sphere
   b. Triangular prism, triangular pyramid
   c. Hexagonal prism, hexagonal pyramid
   d. Cube, cuboid
   e. Cuboid
3. Top view: Front and Side view:

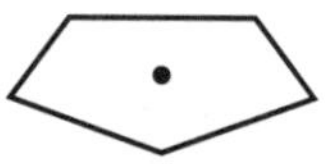

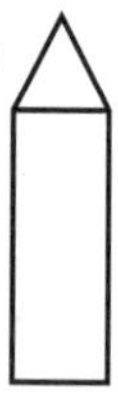

Revision Exercise

1. a. Cuboid b. Sphere c. Cuboid
   d. Cylinder e. Cylinder f. Cone
2. a. Pentagonal pyramid
   b. Hexagonal pyramid
   c. Hexagonal prism
   d. Pentagonal prism
   e. Triangular prism
   f. Square pyramid
3. Each vertex is shared by the three triangles.
5. The shape of the shadow is a rectangle
7. Top view Side view Front view

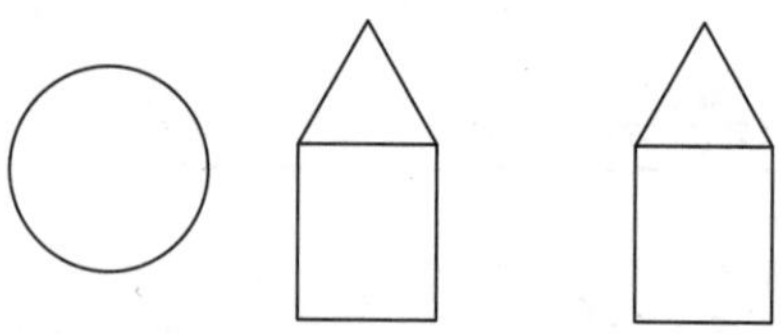

Observation: Top view and front view are the same
8. Pentagonal pyramid

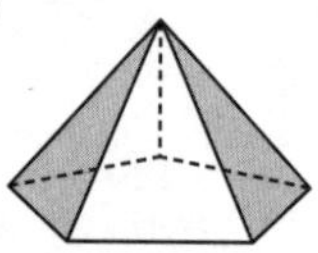

10. a. Square, Square, Square
    b. Rectangle, Rectangle, Rectangle
    c. Circle, Triangle, Triangle
    d. Circle, Rectangle, Rectangle
    e. Circle, Circle, Circle,

For the Curious Mind

1. a. 31 b. 27
2. One of the possible solids with the given views is shown here. Different solids are possible for the given views.

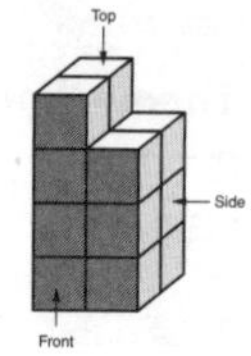

Chapter – 17

Revision Exercise

1. d.
2. a. Actual height = 2.85 m b. Actual length = 20 cm, Actual width = 15 cm
4. a. Maharashtra, Gujarat, Rajasthan, Uttar Pradesh, Chattisgarh
   b. 658 km, 602 km, 372 km, 570 km, 534 km c. Jaipur
5. 1 cm = 350 km

Chapter – 18

Exercise 18.1

1. a. A, C, D, E are congruent figures; F and G are congruent figures
   b. A ≅ C, B ≅ H, D ≅ G
5. AF ≅ RQ, FE ≅ MR, AE ≅ MQ, AB ≅ PQ, DE ≅ NM, DC ≅ NP and CB ≅ OP
   ∠AFE ≅ ∠QRM, ∠FAE ≅ ∠RQM, ∠FEA ≅ ∠RMQ, ∠ABC ≅ ∠QPO, ∠FDC ≅ ∠MNO and ∠BCD ≅ ∠PON
6. DR ≅ UV, RP ≅ VW and DP ≅ UW
   ∠DRP ≅ ∠UVW, ∠RDP ≅ ∠VUW and ∠RPD ≅ ∠VWU
8. Regular pentagon. They are congruent.
9. Yes, as the triangles are equilateral.

Exercise 18.2

1. a. AC = PR, AB = PQ, ∠BAC = ∠QPR
      ∴ Δ ABC ≅ Δ PQR {SAS congruence criterion}
   b. HE = ZX, EF = XY, ∠HEF = ∠ZXY
      ∴ Δ HEF ≅ Δ ZXY {SAS congruence criterion}
   c. GI = LT, ∠HGI = ∠SLT, ∠GIH = ∠LTS
      ∴ Δ HGI ≅ Δ SLT {ASA congruence criterion}
   d. KI = OM, IJ = MN, JK = NO
      ∴ Δ KIJ ≅ Δ OMN {SSS congruence criterion}
2. Yes 4. Δ KLM ≅ Δ MNO {RHS congruence criterion}

Revision Exercise

1. a. iii. b. iii. c. ii. d. ii.

For the Curious Mind

1. No.
2.

Size of squares	1 × 1	2 × 2	3 × 3	4 × 4	5 × 5	6 × 6	7 × 7	8 × 8	**Total**
Number of congruent squares	64	49	36	25	16	9	4	1	**204**

Chapter – 19

Exercise 19.1

2. Scalene triangle

Revision Exercise

3. Two congruent triangles can be constructed with the given sticks with the measurements 4 cm, 6 cm and 8 cm
4. No, it is not possible to construct a triangle.
6. a. (v) b. (iv)

Theme Worksheet 4

2.

Congruent triangles	Congruence relation	Congruence criteria
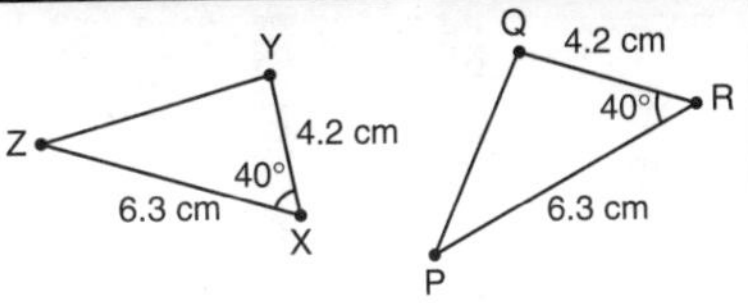	$\Delta XYZ \cong \Delta RQP$	SAS
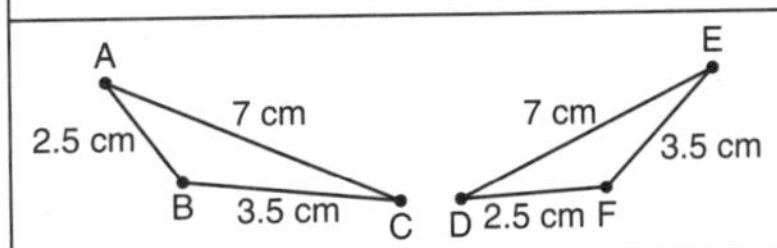	Δ ABC $\cong \Delta$DFE	SSS
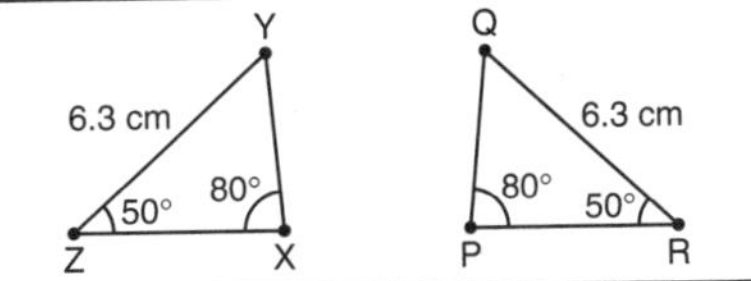	ΔDEF $\cong \Delta$IHG	ASA
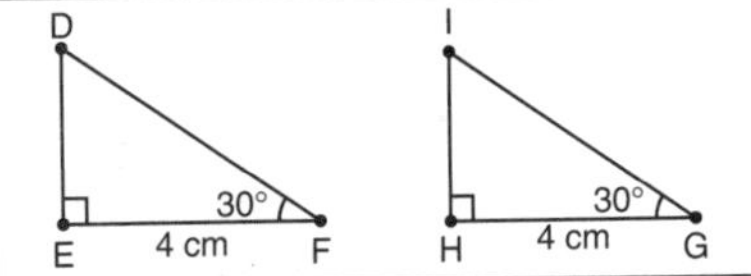	ΔDEF $\cong \Delta$IHG	ASA
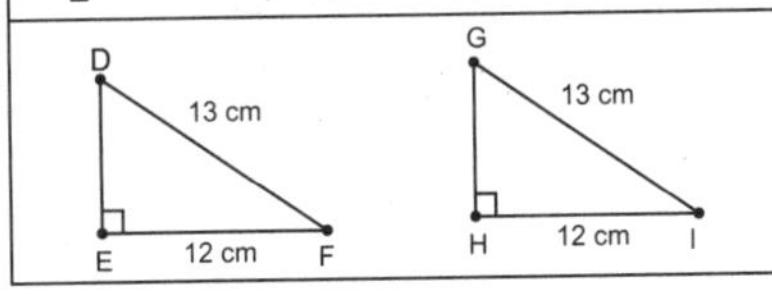	ΔDEF $\cong \Delta$GHI	R.H.S

Skill-based Worksheet

1. a. Hexagon b. Hexagon c. Pentagon
   d. Octagon e. Triangle
2. a. Cube b. Cylinder c. Cone
   d. Pyramid e. Sphere f. Cuboid
   g. Cylinder h. Cube i. Cuboid
   j. Cone k. Cylinder

Mental Maths

Chapter 13

1. a. 73° b. 67° c. 48° d. 35° e. 1°
2. a. 135° b. 96° c. 82° d. 65° e. 1°
3. 45° 4. 90° 5. transversal
6. 4 7. 2 8. 8 9. Parallel
10. 180°/supplementary

Chapter 14

1. 45°, 45°, 90° 2. 60°, 60°, 60°
3. hypotenuse 4. greater than the third side
5. less than two sides 6. perpendicular
7. isosceles right-angled triangle
8. scalene right-angled triangle 9. 34 m
10. acute-angled triangle

Chapter 15

1. Equilateral triangle 2. Square 3. 7
4. more than one 5. Octagon 6. 60°
7. rhombus and rectangle 8. 5
9. isosceles triangle 10. intersection point of two diagonals

Chapter 16

1. cube, sphere, tetrahedron 2. cube, cuboid
3. Prisms 4. Sphere 5. Cone
6. octagonal prism 7. hexagonal pyramid
8. Pyramids 9. cylinder
10. triangular pyramid /tetrahedron

Chapter 18

1. shape, size 2. congruent 3. Side length
4. 1.9 cm 5. Included angle 6. 6 cm
7. 6 8. ΔABC $\cong \Delta$PSR 9. Equal
10. Δ ABC $\cong \Delta$ BAD

Chapter 19

1. Three independent measurements are needed to construct a unique triangle.
2. Two independent measurements are needed to construct an isosceles triangle.
3. The measurement of one side is enough to construct an equilateral triangle.
4. Hypotenuse, because $c^2 = a^2 + b^2$
5. Isosceles triangle. If one angle in a right angled triangle is 45° then the other is also 45° by angle sum property.
6. Yes, since the sum of the lengths of any two sides is greater than the third side.
7. Yes, by SSS
8. No, since DT + DP = TP. That is, the given points are collinear points.
9. No, $\angle M + \angle A + \angle T \neq 180°$ 10. Yes, by AAS

Chapter – 20

Exercise 20.1

1. 62 m 2. ₹5200 3. 108 sq. cm
4. 63 cm 5. Base = 40 cm, Height = 60 cm

Exercise 20.2

1. a. 22 m b. 36 cm c. 42 cm d. 44 m
2. a. 15 cm b. 15 cm c. 120 mm
3. a. 42 cm b. 28 cm
4. a. 31 cm b. 15 cm each
5. 28 m 6. 4.8 km 7. 576 cm 8. 42 m

Exercise 20.3

1. a. 406.25 sq. ft b. 1500 sq. cm 2. 62 ft
3. Length = 14 m, Area = 196 sq. m
4. Breadth = 25 m, Area = 1000 sq. m
5. Breadth = 18 m, Area = 576 sq. m
6. 108 sq. cm 7. 31.5 sq. cm
8. Areas
   a. Fig(a) = 82.75 sq. m b. Fig (b) = 99 sq. m
   c. Fig (c) = 49.75 sq. m d. Fig (d) = 40.5 sq. m
   e. Fig (e) = 72 sq. m
9. Two adjacent sides are 25 m and 10 m respectively. Area = 250 sq. m
10. 56 cm

Exercise 20.4

1. a. 75.36 cm b. 123.77 cm c. 141.37 m
   d. 292.79 cm
2. a. 113.04 cm b. 157 mm c. 320.28 cm
   d. 50.24 m
3. a. 11.4 cm b. 32.38 cm c. 40 mm
   d. 12.006 m 4. 125.7 m 5. 5:8
6. 56.5 cm
7. a. 1386 m^2 b. 3215.36 mm^2 c. 7546 cm^2
   d. 12462.66 m^2
8. a. 616 m^2 b. 1256 cm^2 c. 2464 mm^2
   d. 706.5 cm^2
9. a. 30 m b. 18 cm c. 22 mm d. 63 m
10. 1232 kg 11. 212.6 cm^2
12. $\sqrt{50.23}$ = 7.08 cm

Exercise 20.5

1. a. LSA = 256 sq.cm; TSA = 384 sq.cm
   b. 625 sq.cm; 937.5 sq.cm
   c. 2500 sq.cm; 3750 sq.cm
   d. 1089 sq.cm; 1633.5 sq.cm
2. a. LSA = 36 sq.cm, TSA = 72 sq.cm
   b. 117.5 sq.cm ; 387.5 sq.cm
   c. 24 sq.cm; 55.5 sq.cm
3. LSA of tin = 1250 sq.cm 4. 1093.5 sq. m
5. ₹9225 6. ₹622 7. 126 sq.m; ₹6300

Revision Exercise

1. a. Perimeter = 50 cm, Area = 150 sq. cm
   b. Perimeter = 780 cm, Area = 35,000 sq. cm
2. 1600 sq. cm 3. Perimeter = 114 ft 4. ₹9000
5. 106.5 sq.m 6. ₹8100 7. 950 sq. m
8. Area of remaining chart paper = 230 sq. cm, Area of cutout strip = 540 sq. cm
9. Area = 330 sq. m, cost = ₹1567.50
10. Area of carpet = 412.5 sq. m, Area of the strip uncovered = 42.5 sq. m
11. Area = 1888 sq. m, Perimeter = 74 m
12. 2970 cm 13. 62.85 cm^2 14. $\sqrt{225}$ = 15 cm
15. ₹12,600 16. ₹1833.60
17. Surface area = 686 cm^2

For the Curious Mind

81 sq. m

Theme Worksheet 5

1. a. 182 cm^2 b. Perimeter = 28 cm c. Area = 28 cm^2
   d. l = 10 cm e. 104 cm^2 f. 150 cm^2

Skill-based Worksheet

1. First box requires 408.5 sq inches and the second box requires 432.5 sq inches; thus second box needs more materials.
2. 460 sq cm 3. 336 sq inch 4. 3900 sq ft
5. 8 ft 6. 25 cm 7. 163000 rupees
8. 648 sq cm

Mental Maths

Chapter 20

1. 6 2. 12 3. 36 sq units
4. 2 (lb + bh + lh) sq. units 5. 54 sq units
6. 12 sq units 7. 66 sq units 8. 3s

Chapter 21

Exercise 21.1

1. Ascending order – 0,0,1,1,2,2,2,3,3,4,5,5,6,8
   Mean = 3, Median = 2.5, Mode = 2
2. Ascending order - 32,32,33,45,48
   Mean = 38, Median = 33, Mode = 32
3. Ascending order – 20,22,24,24,30
   Mean = 24, Median = 24, Mode = 24

Exercise 21.2

1.

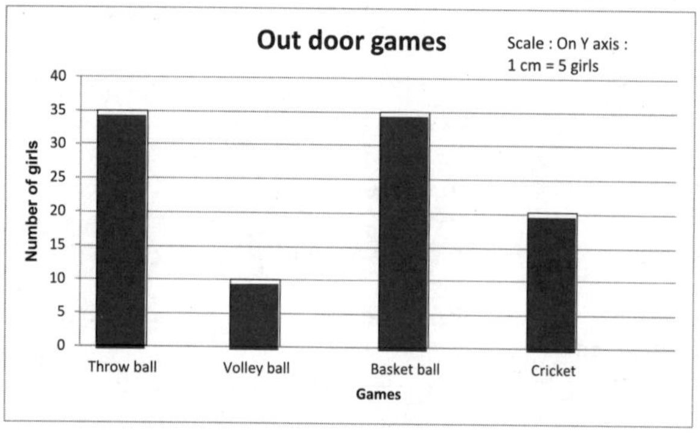

2.

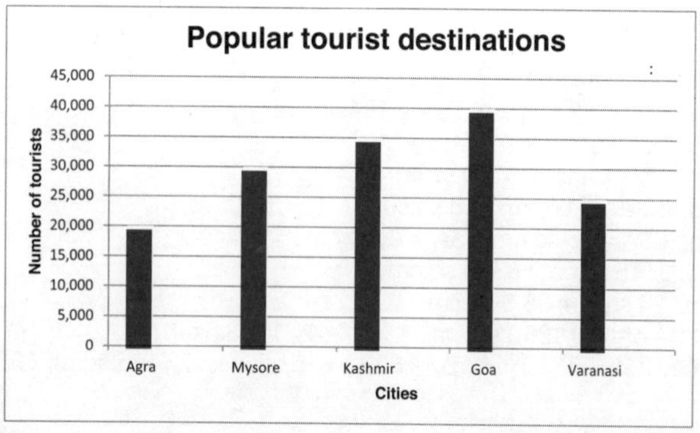

3.

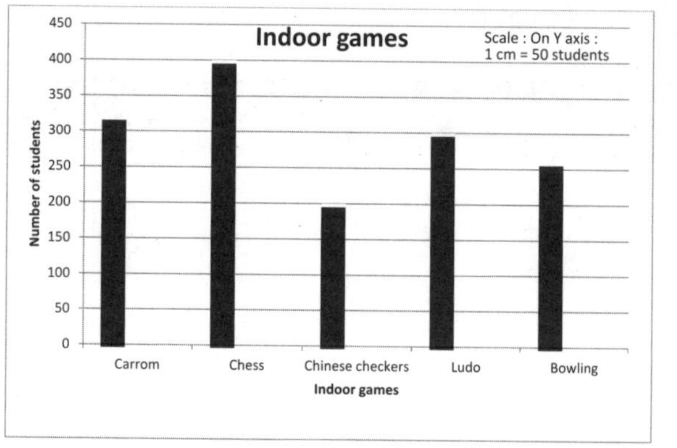

4.

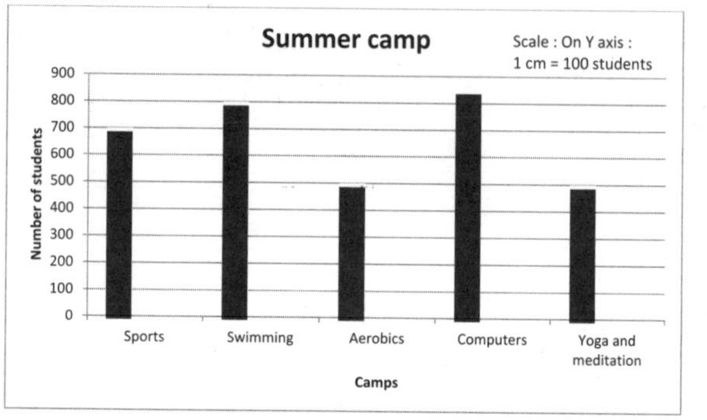

Revision Exercise

1. Ascending order – 1,1,2,2,2,2,2,3,4,4,4,5,5,6,6
   Mean = 3.27, Median = 3, Mode = 2

2.

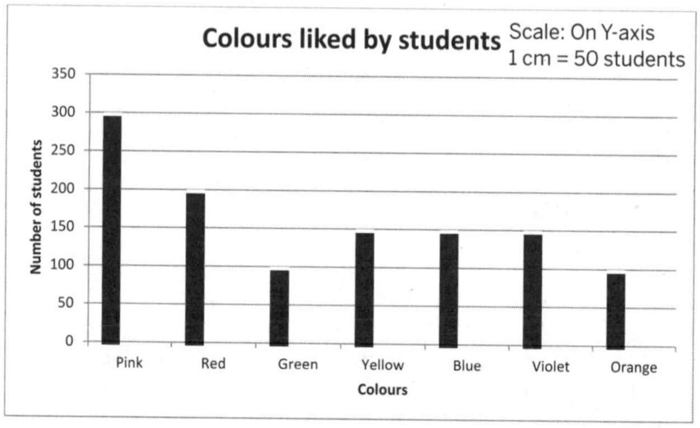

3. a. raw b. array c. frequency d. bar graph
4. a. i. Arithmetic mean = $\frac{\text{Sum of the observations}}{\text{Number of observations}}$
   b. iii. $\left(\frac{n+1}{2}\right)^{th}$ c. iv. mode
   d. iii. sometimes equal

Chapter – 22

Exercise 22.1

1. a. May or may not happen
   b. May or may not happen
   c. Certain to happen
   d. Impossible
   e. Impossible
   f. Impossible

2. a. {Head, Tail} b. {1, 2, 3, 4, 5, 6}
   c. {Violet, Red, White, Yellow}
   d. { 1, 3, 5, 7, 9, 11, 13, 15, 17, 19}

3. $P(H) = \frac{275}{500} = \frac{11}{20}$ $P(T) = \frac{225}{500} = \frac{9}{20}$

4. $P(1) = \frac{25}{200} = \frac{1}{8}$; $P(2) = \frac{36}{200} = \frac{9}{50}$; $P(3) = \frac{34}{200} = \frac{17}{100}$;

   $P(4) = \frac{28}{200} = \frac{7}{50}$; $P(5) = \frac{33}{200}$; $P(6) = \frac{44}{200} = \frac{11}{50}$

5. $P(H) = \frac{78}{400} = \frac{39}{200}$; $P(E) = \frac{90}{400} = \frac{9}{40}$;

   $P(M) = \frac{86}{400} = \frac{43}{200}$; $P(Sc) = \frac{115}{400} = \frac{23}{80}$; $P(So) = \frac{31}{400}$

6. $P(White) = \frac{7}{30}$ $P(Green) = \frac{10}{30} = \frac{1}{3}$ $P(Rose) = \frac{6}{30} = \frac{1}{6}$

   $P(Blue) = \frac{2}{30} = \frac{1}{15}$ $P(Yellow) = \frac{4}{30} = \frac{2}{15}$ $P(Red) = \frac{1}{30}$

Revision Exercise

1. a. Impossible b. May or May not happen
   c. Impossible d. May or may not happen
   e. Certain to happen
2. a. ii b. ii c. i d. i e. iii
3. a. F b. T c. T d. F e. T

Theme Worksheet 6

1.

Tourist Places	Mysore Palace	Mysore Zoo	Jaganmohan Palace	Dasara Exhibition	KRS Dam
Number of tourists	300	800	100	400	200

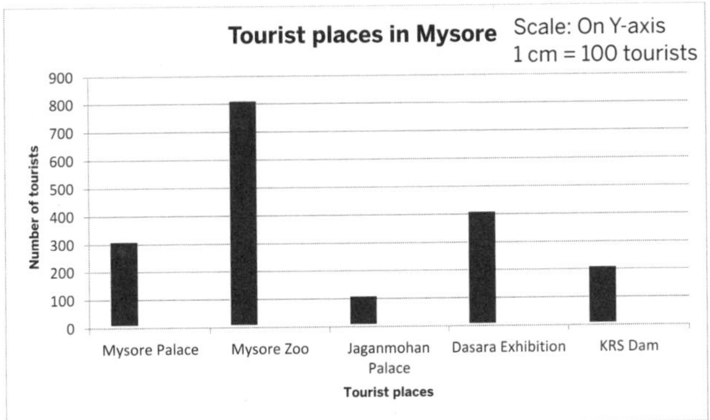

a. Mysore Zoo b. Jaganmohan Palace c. 1800

2.

Colour of the marble	Number of marbles	Probability
White	3	$\frac{3}{30} = \frac{1}{10}$
Yellow	5	$\frac{5}{30} = \frac{1}{6}$
Pink	7	$\frac{7}{30}$
Brown	8	$\frac{8}{30} = \frac{4}{15}$
Green	7	$\frac{7}{30}$

Skill-based Worksheet

1.

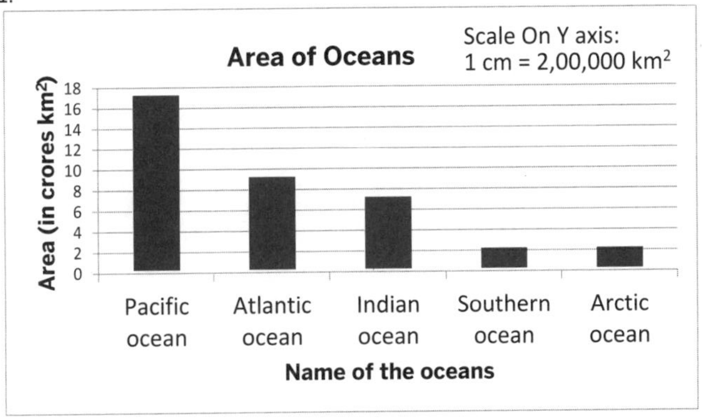

2. Ascending order = 15, 16, 17, 18, 19, 20, 20, 21, 22, 23, 24, 25
   Mean = 20, Median = 20, Mode = 20
3. The probability of the fridges being sold is 40% and the probability of the fridges left unsold is 60%.
4. The probability of the number of days it rained is 50% and the probability it didn't rain is 50%.

Mental Maths

Chapter 21

1. 5 2. 25 3. 15
4. On Y-axis, 1 cm = 100 students
5. On Y-axis, 1 cm = 5 students

Chapter 22

1. $\frac{35}{50}$ 2. $\frac{15}{20}$ 3. $\frac{12}{50}$ 4. $\frac{4}{20}$ 5. $\frac{5}{10}$

Test Paper 1

1. a. i b. iv c. ii d. iii e. iv
2. a. 0 b. 1 c. equivalent
   d. a^{m+n} e. cardinal
3. a. 1440 cm b. 5, 15625, 25
4. a. 1015 b. 4

Test Paper 2

1. a. ii b. iii c. ii d. iii e. iii
2. a. F b. F c. T d. F e. T
3. a. SI - ₹3900 and Amount - ₹78,900
   b. Loss percentage, 4%
4. a. ₹147, ₹245, ₹70 b. 120 minutes (2 hours)

Test Paper 3

1. a. iii b. iii c. iii d. ii e. ii
2. a. T b. F c. F d. F e. T
3. a. i. $1 - m - 2m^2$ ii. $3a^2b^2 - 7ab + 5$
   b. i. $x = 3$ ii. $x = 36$
4. a. 12, 14 and 16 b. {−3, −2, −1, 0, 1, 2, 3, 4, 5}

Test Paper 4

1. a. 43° b. transversal c. 60°, 75° d. 2 e. 120°
2. a. T b. F c. T d. F e. T
3. a. 110° b. 36°, 72°, 72°
4. a. 17 inches b. 45°, half of angle of rotation

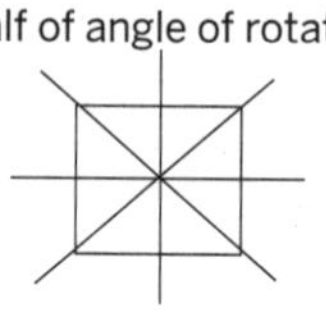

Test Paper 5

1. a. triangular prism b. 1 cm = 448 km c. radius
   d. ASA e. three
2. a. F b. T c. T d. F e. T
3. a. 3234 km b. ΔLKM ≅ ΔMNO by RHS criteria
4. a.

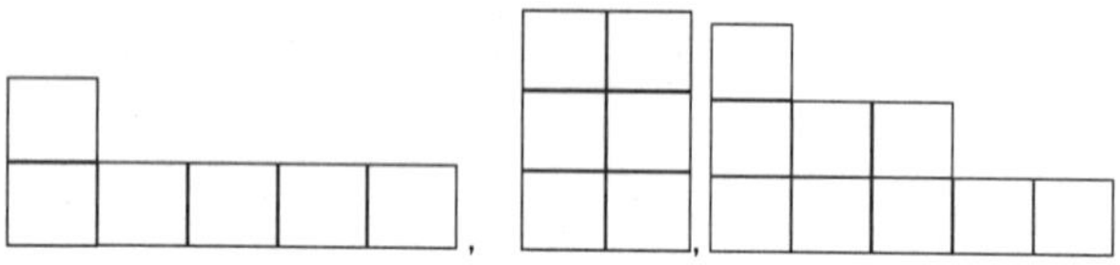

Test Paper 6

1. a. Perimeter b. 9 cm c. quadrilateral
   d. 2 e. $2h(l + b)$
2. a. F b. F c. T d. F e. T
3. a. 9 cm b. 6 cm c. 6 m d. 5 m e. 4 cm
4. a. 98 rupees b. R = 14 cm and D = 28 cm
5. a. 125%
   b. Perimeter of garden = 220 ft, Area of garden = 1500 sq ft
   Perimeter of parking area = 140 ft, Area of parking area = 1000 sq ft
   Perimeter of building = 290 ft, Area of building = 3500 sq ft

Test Paper 7

1. a. i b. ii c. iv d. ii e. iii
2. a. F b. F c. T d. F e. T
3. a. $\frac{4}{20}$ b. $\frac{5}{20}$ c. $\frac{3}{20}$ d. $\frac{8}{20}$
4.

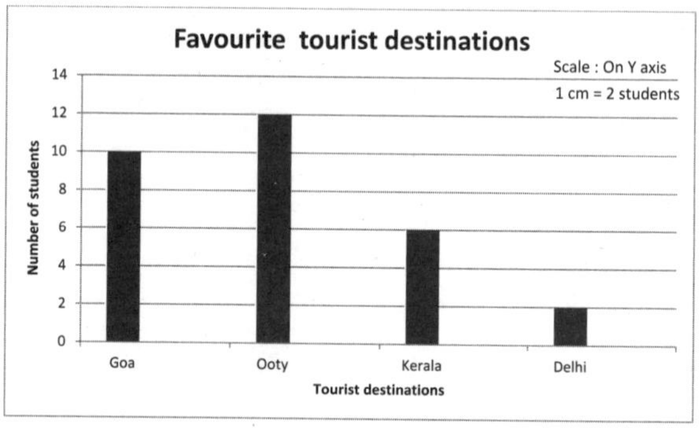

a. Ooty b. 2